Brokered Subjects

Brokered Subjects

*Sex, Trafficking, and the
Politics of Freedom*

ELIZABETH BERNSTEIN

The University of Chicago Press   Chicago and London

The University of Chicago Press, Chicago 60637
The University of Chicago Press, Ltd., London
© 2018 by The University of Chicago
Published 2018
Printed in the United States of America

27 26 25 24 23 22 21 20 19 18   1 2 3 4 5

ISBN-13: 978-0-226-57363-2 (cloth)
ISBN-13: 978-0-226-57377-9 (paper)
ISBN-13: 978-0-226-57380-9 (e-book)
DOI: https://doi.org/10.7208/chicago/9780226573809.001.0001

Library of Congress Cataloging-in-Publication Data

Names: Bernstein, Elizabeth, 1968– author.
Title: Brokered subjects : sex, trafficking, and the politics of freedom /
    Elizabeth Bernstein.
Description: Chicago ; London : The University of Chicago Press, 2018. |
    Includes bibliographical references and index.
Identifiers: LCCN 2018008599 | ISBN 9780226573632 (cloth : alk. paper) |
    ISBN 9780226573779 (pbk. : alk. paper) | ISBN 9780226573809 (e-book)
Subjects: LCSH: Human trafficking. | Prostitution. | Human trafficking—
    Prevention. | Human trafficking—Religious aspects—Christianity. |
    Human trafficking—Political aspects—United States. | Humanitarianism—
    United States. | Humanitarianism—Political aspects. | Feminist theory. |
    Feminism—Political aspects. | Neoliberalism—Social aspects.
Classification: LCC HQ281 .B584 2018 | DDC 306.3/62—dc23
LC record available at https://lccn.loc.gov/2018008599

♾ This paper meets the requirements of ANSI/NISO Z39.48-1992
(Permanence of Paper).

In loving memory of those who have passed

Contents

Acknowledgments

This book was born of a series of empirical and theoretical puzzles that developed at the tail end of a previous research project on sexual economies and globalization. I began researching sexual commerce in the early 1990s, before the notion of "sex trafficking" had come into political existence. This framework first emerged in Europe in the mid- to late 1980s, spurred by the collapse of the Soviet Union as well as accelerated cross-border migration streams from Southeast Asia. In the United States, public debates about how to best address the trafficking did not begin to take place until the late 1990s and the early 2000s, but they soon spread rapidly. What were the political implications of this new framework, and who were the social actors propelling it to ascendance? How did the new anti-trafficking discourse relate to broader trends in neoliberalism and to changing dynamics of race, class, sex, and gender? As I watched the migrant sex workers I had come to know grapple with their newfound status as "victims of trafficking," these were the questions that compelled me.

I was not alone in pursuing these inquiries. Many others in the community of scholar-activists that I pertained to shared my concerns. The genesis for this project was forged out of early conversations, conferences, and study groups with Carol Leigh, Penelope Saunders, Kerwin Kaye, Gayle Rubin, Carole Vance, Sealing Cheng, Laura Agustín, Svati Shah, and Denise Brennan, who have all gone on to produce significant works on the political complexities of the trafficking discourse and its effects on various sex-working communities. As my research took on a more coherent shape in the succeeding years, this core group expanded to include a number of other scholars and activists who were engaged in similar endeavors, including Ann Jordan, Juhu Thukral, Alice Miller, Janie Chuang, Janet Halley, Julia O'Connell Davidson, Kamala Kempadoo, Pardis Mahdavi, Prabha Kotiswaran, Gretchen Soderlund, Christine Jacobsen, Nicola Mai, Rutvica Andrijasevic, Melissa Ditmore, and Rhacel Parreñas. My former graduate students Elena Shih, Sine Plambech, and Jennifer Musto soon became prominent anti-trafficking researchers in their own right and important members of this still-expanding group. I am grateful for the input I have received from these intellectual fellow travelers, and I continue to rely upon their ongoing investigations in this area as important supplements to my own.

Other academic collaborations were also pivotal to the construction and elaboration of my scholarly approach to this material. The 2005 seminar "Sex, Secularism, and Other Religious Matters" at New York University's Center for Religion and Media provided a stimulating forum for generating some of my initial ideas about this project. During my 2011–2012 year in residence at the Institute for Advanced Study in Princeton, New Jersey, my research benefited from conversations with Didier Fassin, Joan Scott, Wendy Chun, Judith Surkis, Nancy Scheper-Hughes, Sherine Hamdy, and Karuna Mantena. The Barnard Center for Research on Women's transnational, interdisciplinary working group on Gender, Justice, and Neoliberal Transformations has been a vital venue for thinking about the case study of anti-trafficking policy in the context of broader political-economic transitions. At Barnard and Columbia, my colleagues Janet Jakobsen, Rebecca Jordan-Young, Jenna Freedman, Neferti Tadiar, Elizabeth Castelli, Laura Kay, Tina Campt, Debra Minkoff, Heather Hurwitz, Katherine Franke, Lila Abu-Lughod, Constance Nathanson, and Mark Nomadiou have provided multiple forms of support for my thinking and research. In addition, numerous scholars nationally and internationally have offered critical feedback on chapters of the manuscript as well as public presentations of this material. For their spirited engagement with key components of this project, I thank Éric Fassin, Janie Chuang, Kristin Luker, Gail Kligman, Lauren Berlant, Ann Orloff, Raka Ray, Randi Gressgård, Evren Savci, Linda Zerilli, Wendy Hesford, Kate Bedford, Roger Lancaster, Lisa Duggan, Ann Pellegrini, Lynn Chancer, Raewyn Connell, David Halperin, Mario Pecheny, Ana Amuchastegui, Cecilia Varela, and Adrian Favell.

Crucial to these acknowledgments are also the many people and organizations across several continents who generously shared their time and their perspectives with me, and who constitute the fundament of the ethnographic research for this project. I am extremely grateful to the various participants whose expertise and experiences I relied upon for this analysis, including those with whom I disagree. Although it is impossible for me to produce a comprehensive list here, I would like to highlight, in particular, the contributions of Liz Hilton and the other members of Empower Chiang Mai, the late Andrew Hunter from the Asia Pacific Network of Sex Workers, Penelope Saunders, Ann Jordan, Martina Vandenburg, Florrie Burke, Jennifer Butler, Shane Claiborne, Mark Lagon, Matt Friedman, and William Livermore.

I would also like to express my thanks to the various institutions that provided material and social support for this research: the Social Science Research Council, the American Association of University Women, the Mellon Foundation, the Institute for Advanced Study, the UN Research Institute for Social Development, the Institute for Social and Economic Research and Policy at Columbia University, and the Office of the Provost at Barnard College. This work would have been impossible to execute without the labors of several dedicated and talented research assistants, who combed through newspaper articles and published reports, tabulated statistics, and engaged in rigorous fact-checking of the manuscript, among other tasks. I would especially like to acknowledge Erin Ward and Ariane Rinehart, who provided indispensible and multifaceted research support during the final three years of this project, as well as the contributions of Shoshana Lauter, Jovonne Bickerstaff, Jennifer Nina, Pazia Miller, and Blaise Bayno-Krebs. I am most grateful to Doug Mitchell, Kyle Wagner, and Jenni Fry at the University of Chicago Press, who shepherded this book through the publication process with finesse and care.

Prior versions of chapters 4 and 5 appeared as Elizabeth Bernstein and Elena Shih, "The Erotics of Authenticity: Sex Trafficking and 'Reality Tourism' in Thailand," *Social Politics: International Studies in Gender, State, and Society* 21:3 (2014): 430–461, and "Redemptive Capitalism and Sexual Investability," in *Political Power and Social Theory* 30 (2016): 45–81. Portions of the arguments that I develop in this text appeared in an earlier form in my articles "Carceral Politics as Gender Justice: The 'Traffic in Women' and Neoliberal Circuits of Crime, Sex, and Rights," *Theory and Society* 41:3 (2012): 233–259; "Militarized Humanitarianism Meets Carceral Feminism: The Politics of Sex, Rights, and Freedom in Contemporary Anti-Trafficking Campaigns," *Signs: Journal of Women in Culture and Society* 36:1 (2010): 45–71, and "The Sexual Politics of the 'New Abolitionism,'" *Differences: Journal of Feminist Cultural Studies* 18:3 (2007): 128–151.

Finally, I would like to express my profound gratitude to the friends, family members, and confidantes who supported me in ways large and small as I pursued this research over the course of many years. The love and myriad forms of support provided by Kelly Moore, Patricia Clough,

Jackie Orr, Janet Jakobsen, Mark Padilla, Montserrat Guntín, Wendy Haft, Sealing Cheng, Ann Burlein, Rhys Williams, Dovar Chen, Jim and Gretchen Sandler, Christina Crosby, and Jan Bernstein-Chargin were critical to the completion of this book project (and to the maintenance of a sustainable life) in the face of some significant and unforeseen challenges. I am above all grateful to my life partner, Kerwin Kaye, who has contributed to the research and ideas that are reflected on every single page of this book. I am indebted to him for the analysis that follows, as I am for so many other matters of personal and political importance.

ONE

Tracing the "Traffic in Women"

It was just after midnight at the Can Do Bar in Chiang Mai, Thailand, and the mood was light and festive. On a dimly lit street not far from the city's main nightlife district, the bar that served as the local headquarters of Empower, the most prominent sex worker's rights organization in the country, was the only storefront still brimming with activity. As was typical for early August, the evening was hot and humid, and many of the women had taken to the outdoor patio while they awaited our arrival, drinking beers and chatting casually. Eager to hear the stories of our recent excursion with an organized "human trafficking tour" of the region, they welcomed us with keen interest, ice-cold drinks, and extra chairs. Within a few minutes, Elena and I were transported worlds away from the increasingly surreal travel experience that had occupied us during the previous seven days, a trip that had been co-organized by a coalition of evangelical Christian and secular NGOs from the United States. Exhausted by our hectic circuit though Bangkok, Chiang Rai, and Chiang Mai—as well as by the emotional strain of traveling with a "delegation" far removed from the needs of the populations that it claimed to represent—we felt relieved to have left the other North American tourists behind and to be there.[1]

Although the trip had been marketed to us as offering a stark glimpse into the realities of human trafficking, the main difficulties we faced were not due to the heartbreaking encounters with former sex slaves that the tour promised, but instead ensued from the frenetic pace of our travels, the poor coordination of our daily itineraries, a lack of clear communication on the part of the organizers, and the vague yet persistent feeling among many of us that, despite the humanitarian pedigree of the tour's two sponsoring NGOs, we were somehow being defrauded. Not only were we not introduced to any survivors of trafficking who could offer firsthand testimony of their experiences; many of the meetings with governmental officials and local NGOs that had been promised to us had been abbreviated, rescheduled for odd hours (when the most knowledgeable representatives could apparently not be present), or canceled. Even the "three star" hotels and meals that the NGOs advertised fell short, as we found ourselves crammed into the lowest level of accommodations in each of the cities we visited, and were frequently encouraged to participate in mass tourist staples like elephant rides and visits to handicraft markets in lieu of canceled meetings. When a few members of the group tried to find someone to complain to in order to remedy the situation, we soon discovered that it was impossible to clearly discern upon whom we should pin responsibility, as the sponsoring organizations had in fact subcontracted out the tour to a series of intermediaries—various layers of "consultants" who in fact knew little about the issue and were rarely in our company, as well as one amiable man from the hill tribes of the Northern region of the country who was placed in charge of all logistical considerations, and, we soon discovered, paid a pittance for his time and for actually organizing the tour.[2]

After hearing some of the stories from our difficult week of travel, Liz, a longtime Empower member, came over to join me and Elena, then a graduate student conducting research for her PhD who was my companion on this journey.[3] Liz turned toward me with a poker face and somberly declared, "In our work with women trafficked into the sex sector, we have encountered exactly three cases of women being trafficked that really concerned us in the last few years: yours, Elena's and one other woman who recently contacted us."[4] After pausing for dramatic effect, she redirected her gaze toward the half dozen or so other women who had gathered around our table to listen to the exchange, who collectively burst into laughter.

The phenomenon of "sex trafficking" is not typically the subject of joking revelry, but Liz's remark captured the fraughtness of the term from the perspective of many sex worker–activists, as well as their perception of visitors from the Global North who flood places like Thailand with the ambition to help. Elena and I had signed up for this trip in order to learn more about the nature of secular rights-based and evangelical Christian anti-trafficking collaborations, about the increasing commodification of humanitarian sentiment and social justice advocacy, and, most crucially, about the implications of both of these trends for the global politics of sex and gender. "You've been trafficked!" the women in the bar exclaimed when we told them the details of our journey, then set about calculating the proceeds that had likely been taken in by the NGOs that had sponsored our excursion, exploiting not only the local recipient communities but also the helping sensibilities of well-intentioned tourists.[5]

In fact, both Elena and I had already spent several years observing the diverse "helping projects" for sex workers that had sprung up around the globe, tracing the on-the-ground effects of contemporary anti-trafficking campaigns and their affiliated organizations. While I had been studying secular feminist and evangelical Christian activists' surprisingly close collaborations with the criminal justice system, Elena had been in Bangkok conducting research amid a group of students, expatriates, and full-time missionaries affiliated with an advocacy organization in Los Angeles, shadowing them as they did outreach at go-go bars in one of the city's principal entertainment districts.[6]

While enjoying the semblance of an evening breeze, Elena recounted to us how during these bar visits, anti-trafficking activists would offer the dancers alternative employment through their socially entrepreneurial business venture producing and selling jewelry made by "formerly trafficked women." Nearly all of the "victims" who accepted the offer were slightly older women (in their thirties and forties) who had previously chosen sex work as their highest-paying option but who, after accumulating some savings and finding themselves aging out of the prime markets in sex work, elected jewelry making instead. After accepting their new positions, the women soon discovered that their lives would be governed by some unwelcome regulations: they were officially prohibited from visiting their former colleagues in the red-light district, and their pay would be docked for being minutes late to their shifts, for missing daily prayer sessions, or for minor behavioral infractions. Many also complained about the uniforms that they were required to wear to work: shapeless black polo shirts with the organizational emblem embroidered on the chest, and the Thai word for "freedom" stitched boldly across the right arm.[7]

The women at the Can Do Bar listened with great interest as we told them these and other stories from our research, and were further intrigued when we showed them our pictures from the tour. Although many of our photographs provoked reactions of bemusement or dismay, it was the last photo we circulated that especially caught their attention. It was a night-time shot of the anti-trafficking tour participants walking through the Chiang Mai red-light district with knitted brows and worried faces, being led by a young, evangelical woman from the United States who ran a local NGO for sex-trafficked youth (one of a mere handful of anti-trafficking NGOs that our tour group was actually able to meet with). The sex workers' astonishment reached a pinnacle when they noticed that our photo had also captured a murky image of their friend Nong in the background, who had been standing in front of one of the massage parlors when the anti-trafficking advocates filed past. From the tourists' troubled expressions of pity and concern, it was clear that they regarded the sex worker who in front of them as the very epitome of the "sex trafficking victim" whom they had come so far to help. "But that's Nong—she is a worker, a mother, not a victim!" the women in the Can Do Bar exclaimed. What's more, they noted that Nong was an active Empower member who herself had been at the Can Do Bar earlier that evening. Just the week before, she had accompanied them to the annual sex workers' conference in Kolkata, India, where thousands of women, men, and transgender people from over forty countries and representing some five hundred different organizations had joined together to advocate on behalf of sex workers' rights.[8] A committed activist, Nong was hardly the pitiable victim whom the tourists or their young American colleague had imagined.

The apprehension exhibited by Empower's sex workers in their collision with current campaigns to combat "sex trafficking" provides the starting point for some of my central concerns in this book. Although the women we met with that evening had not had an easy time working in the sex trade (or, for that matter, in their lives preceding their employment in this sector), they resisted the increasingly prevalent terminology of "trafficking" as an apt description of their experiences.[9] Propelled by social circumstance rather than by brute force or organized crime, they were in many ways similar to the sex workers in other regions of the world whom I had worked closely with over the course of several decades. Even those who had begun sex work at young ages, or who had incurred debts to labor brokers, or who had experienced violence at the hands of customers or their employers overwhelmingly rejected this rubric and the implications of its associated lexicon of terms. Indeed, as both the anecdote here and an accumulating corpus of social scientific research have shown, the framework of "trafficking" (along with its attendant notions of sexual victimization and exploitation) has been far better suited to the goals of aid organizations and governments than it has been to the needs of sex workers. It is precisely the efficacy of this discourse for these and other constituencies that the subsequent chapters of the book seek to address.

Only recently have journalists provided the burgeoning "trafficking industrial complex" with a modicum of critical scrutiny, following revelations of falsified public accounts by one of the most high profile and celebrated of anti-trafficking activists, Cambodian "survivor-activist" Somaly Mam. A May 21, 2014 *Newsweek* cover story drew on years of research for the *Cambodia Daily* by investigative journalist Simon Marks and featured interviews with family members, neighbors, teachers, and hospital officials.[10] Marks not only called into question Mam's own backstory of sexual servitude (one she had carefully recounted in her best-selling autobiography[11]) but also debunked one of her foundation's most circulated stories of victim salvation. Among Mam's chief fund-raising vehicles was the story of Long Pross, presented as a young trafficking victim who had lost her eye to a brutal attack from the brothel owner. The *Newsweek* story revealed that the young girl had in fact suffered the injury after the surgical removal of a tumor, and that she had been placed at Mam's foundation at her parents' request because they were too poor to provide for her. After the release of the *Newsweek* exposé, not only was Mam herself forced to resign from her post as the Foundation's head, but her defenders were briefly spurred to consider the broader implications of her fictions.[12]

Over the past few years, there has also been a growing body of academic writing on particular communities of sex workers and the gaps and disjunctures between their experiences and those that have been asserted by the official trafficking discourse. In her study of migrant Filipina sex workers working in South Korea, for example, the anthropologist Sealing Cheng has found that their experiences "defy the binaries . . . of innocent Third World women vs. powerful First World men; well-intentioned nongovernmental organizations (NGOs) vs. evil-intentioned employers; the protection and shelter of rescuers vs. the danger of the clubs; and the risks of migration vs. the safety of home."[13] Taking issue with prevailing abolitionist accounts of the relations of force and coercion inherent in brothel-based prostitution in India, Svati Shah has likewise demonstrated through her careful ethnographic study of prostitution in Mumbai that sexual commerce "is not a totalizing context for everyone who sells sexual services," but rather one form of economic survival among many for rural migrants in the informal sector.[14] Writing about the situation of sex workers from the former Soviet states who have come to Norway, Christine Jacobsen and May-Len Skilbrei draw on extensive interview-based data to provide a sharp contrast between the women's own self-representations and the accounts of victimhood that prevail in international trafficking discourse. In particular, they note that prostitution, for their interviewees, is forced on them neither by cruel men nor by situations of dire economic hardship, but rather provides much coveted access to "consumption and leading lifestyles associated with 'modernity' and 'the West.' "[15]

Although the disparities between sex workers' experiences and the presumptions of contemporary anti-trafficking campaigns have been critically noted by various commentators, the significance of this disjuncture has yet to be adequately described. Why did narratives of sex trafficking suddenly reemerge after almost a century of slumber, resuscitating long-dormant accounts of the horrors of the "white slave" trade? How was the idea of a global "traffic in women" resurrected out of the framework of prostitution as a victimless crime, which prevailed in the 1960s and 1970s, and the gathering movement for sex workers' rights, which gained prominence over the following two decades? And what is it, precisely, that has enabled "trafficking" to travel so well—across secular and religious divides, across geographic borders, and across wildly variant activist constituencies? In law and policy and the mass media, on college campuses, in church pews and in corporate social responsibility campaigns, the "sex-trafficking victim" has become an iconic figure of our era, capacious enough to serve as the emblem for quite disparate imaginations of social suffering. In recent years, she has become a nearly ubiquitous symbol of gender inequality and exploited labor, of open borders and unbridled commodification, and of myriad forms of sexual violence.[16] While she has periodically shared the spotlight with a range of other iconic figures of sexual exploitation—from the burkha-clad Muslim woman to the presumptively white victims of sexual assault on college campuses and in elite workspaces—the image of the trafficking victim has been durable as well as malleable.[17] An initial aim of this book is thus to interrogate this image and to understand the work it does in the diverse sites of anti-trafficking activity that it has come to inhabit, even as it often fails to adequately capture what it purports to describe.

Like the various phenomena that are signaled by the term "trafficking" itself, the individuals and institutions that make up its associated "rescue industry" circulate through multiple layers of symbolic and material intermediaries.[18] As I describe in the pages that follow, these include local, state, and transnational governing institutions, secular feminist and faith-based activist campaigns, and a bevy of nonprofit as well as for-profit ventures that have recently emerged to "end sex trafficking" and

1.1   UNICEF anti-trafficking promotional campaign poster, on display in Midtown Manhattan.
       Photo: Elena Shih, 2013.

to help victims. As in other forms of neoliberal governance, these "bro-kers and translators" are rarely questioned in terms of the beneficence of their motives or the effects of their interventions.[19] Given the complex chains of brokerage and connectivity that characterize much of con-temporary political and economic life, a second aim of this book is to consider how and why certain kinds of social relations get singled out for moral and political redress, and the role that sex and gender play in forging these distinctions.

The final question that this study considers is suggested by both the opening anecdote of this chapter and the subtitle of this book. Like the sex workers in the Can Do Bar who listened in astonishment to our stories of activists' efforts on their behalf, we need to more closely interrogate the political implications of Western helping campaigns that are organized around women's carceral control, intimate refashioning, and purportedly redemptive labor. Looking beyond the specific contours of the case study at hand, this investigation should spur us to reexamine not only the kinds of social relations that are considered most exploitative—that is, those that, in prevailing versions of the anti-trafficking discourse, are deemed "tantamount to slavery"—but also to critically interrogate current imaginations of gendered progress and freedom.[20] At stake is the vision that is shared by contemporary activist campaigns to combat "sex trafficking," as well as an emergent and expanding set of mechanisms of global governance (often proceeding under the banners of "women's rights" and "empowerment") more generally.

A Genealogy of "Sex Trafficking"

I came to these queries via a particular ethnographic circuitry, one that, over the course of the past decades, had led me from the sociological study of sex work toward the study of the growing cadre of humanitarian projects that have emerged to reclassify all or certain forms of sexual labor as "trafficking" or "slavery," to press for laws that punish the individuals who are deemed responsible for this captivity, and to vigorously pursue sex workers' rescue. Before assuming this current research focus, I spent more than a decade investigating the highly diverse motives and experiences of women, men, and transgender people who engage in sexual labor in postindustrial cities. I had also spent many years as a participant-observer of sex workers' own organizing efforts to address some of the manifold injustices that affect sex workers locally and globally, including violence at the hands of police officers and customers, the absence of labor regulations in illicit as well as legal commercial sex sectors, and the threat of police apprehension and deportation that looms large over undocumented workers.[21]

While in the early and mid-1990s such struggles were increasingly pursued under the culturally and politically ascendant banner of "sex workers' rights," in more recent years this framework has been powerfully challenged by a bevy of anti-trafficking laws and policies that equate all prostitution with the crime of human trafficking and that rhetorically capture both of these activities under the new rubric of "modern slavery."[22] These laws have been pushed forward by a remarkably diverse array of social activists and policy makers—a coalition spanning from left to right and comprising secular feminists, evangelical Christians, human rights activists of diverse stripes, and a cadre of prominent celebrities and corporate officials. Despite renowned disagreements around the politics of sex and gender, these groups have come together to advocate for harsher criminal and economic penalties against traffickers, prostitutes' customers, and nations deemed to be taking insufficient steps to stem the flow of trafficked women.[23]

Many commentators have already noted the similarities between gathering attention to sex trafficking as "modern slavery" in the current moment and the infamous "white slavery" scare of the late nineteenth and early twentieth centuries.[24] While this earlier wave of concern engaged a similar coalition of "new abolitionist" feminists and evangelical Christians, prior to the Progressive Era the goal of eradicating prostitution had not seemed particularly urgent to either group (Christian leaders had previously been far more inclined to worry about adultery and fornication than about prostitution, whereas feminists had focused primarily on obtaining the vote).[25] By the beginning of the twentieth century, however, as tensions mounted over migration, urbanization, and the social changes being wrought by industrial capitalism, narratives of the traffic in women and girls for sexual slavery abounded. Such narratives drew upon the nation's legacy of race-based, chattel slavery as well as a resonance with biblical notions of "slavery to sin," conjuring scenarios of irrefutable moral horror: the widespread abduction of innocent women and girls who, en route to earn respectable livelihoods in metropolitan centers, were seduced, deceived, or forced into prostitution, typically by foreign-born men. Although empirical investigations would eventually reveal the white slavery narrative to be largely without factual basis—the evidence suggested that large numbers of women were not in fact forced into prostitution, other than by economic conditions—anti–white slave crusaders were nevertheless successful in spurring the passage of a series of "red-light abatement" acts, as well as the federal Mann-Elkins White Slave Traffic Act, which brought the nation's first era of wide-scale, commercialized prostitution to a close.[26]

At the international level, anti-trafficking committees worked together to incorporate anti-trafficking platforms into the League of Nations and then the United Nations by way of a succession of multinational anti-trafficking accords. Beginning in 1904, these accords sought to more stringently contain prostitution, both migrant and domestic, with each successive iteration. The 1904, 1910, and 1921 League of Nations accords would eventually give way to the 1940 United Nations Convention, which, without distinction between domestic and international trafficking, transformed brothel keeping and all procurement for prostitution into punishable offenses, regardless of the age or consent of the victims. As the historical sociologist Stephanie Limoncelli has observed, trafficking was in fact the first women's issue taken up in international accords, "well before other issues that were being advocated during the same period, including suffrage, education, and married women's citizenship."[27]

From the 2000s to today, the term "trafficking" has again been made synonymous in policy circles with not only forced but also voluntary prostitution, while an earlier wave of political struggles for both sex workers' and migrants' rights have been eclipsed.[28] According to observers both laudatory and critical, this displacement has been facilitated by the embrace of human rights discourses by abolitionist feminists, who have effectively neutralized domains of political struggle around questions of labor, migration, and sexual freedom via the reductionist tropes of "prostitution as gender violence" and "sexual slavery." Indeed, as one progressive human rights advocate who witnessed the early stages of the feminist trafficking debates has noted, by the time of the 1995 Beijing World Conference on Women, "trafficking as a labor issue had been successfully transformed into a sexual violence and a slavery issue."[29] In her much-heralded Beijing declaration that "human rights are women's rights, and women's rights are human rights," then First Lady Hillary Clinton made explicit reference to the political urgency of sex trafficking, declaring it "a violation of human rights when women and girls are sold into the slavery of prostitution for human greed." She went on to argue that "the kinds of reasons that are used to justify this practice should no longer be tolerated."[30] Indeed, from the perspective of abolitionist feminist anti-trafficking organizations, the shift to the human rights field was crucial to relocating a set of internecine political debates among feminists about the meaning of prostitution and pornography—the so-called "sex wars" of the 1980s and 1990s—to a humanitarian terrain in which the abolitionist constituency was more likely to prevail.[31] By reframing the harms of prostitution and trafficking as politically neutral questions of humanitarian concern about third-world women, rather than as issues that directly impacted the lives of Western feminists, anti-prostitution feminists were able to wage the same sexual battles virtually unopposed.

A simultaneous and similarly profound shift occurred during the same years within the US evangelical movement. If in the early 1990s most evangelicals had little to do with the human rights field, by the latter part of the decade a greater reliance upon NGOs by the United Nations, coupled with an awareness of the increasingly global spread of evangelical Christianity, would encourage many newly formed evangelical NGOs to enter the international political fray. Political scientists Doris Buss and Didi Herman have hailed 1994 as the year that evangelical Christians began to establish a more permanent presence at the United Nations.[32] They attribute this in part to the proliferation of UN-hosted conferences in the 1990s, which facilitated the expansion and further institutionalization of NGO involvement in international law and policy making. In combination with US evangelicals' growing interest in and organization around the issues of international religious freedom and Christian persecution, this would serve to propel new sets of religious actors into the trafficking debates and to become more prominent voices in the human rights field.[33]

Evangelical advocacy around human trafficking received another burst of energy during the administration of George W. Bush, who, in a noted embrace of evangelical framings of the issue, declared in a 2003 address to the UN General Assembly: "There's a special evil in the abuse and exploitation of the most innocent and vulnerable. The victims of the sex trade see little of life before they see the very worst of life—an underground of brutality and lonely fear. Those who create these victims and profit from their suffering must be severely punished. Those who patronize this industry debase themselves and deepen the misery of others, and governments that tolerate this trade are tolerating a form of slavery."[34] Significantly, Bush also expanded upon President Clinton's earlier Charitable Choice initiative to allow avowedly faith-based organizations to become eligible for federal funding. Since 2001, the year that President Bush established the Office of Faith-Based Initiatives, evangelical Christian groups have secured a growing proportion of federal monies for both international and domestic anti-trafficking work, as well as funds for the prevention of HIV/AIDS.[35] The rise of Christian NGOs on the global stage was thus enabled by the political ability of evangelical organizations to ensure their own funding alongside previously established secular groups. This was particularly important given a context of reliance on NGOs for the provision of social services, services for which the neoliberal state had itself relinquished responsibility.

The new focus on human trafficking featured historically old framings that linked "sexual slavery" together with voluntary prostitution, both migrant and domestic. For example, during his tenure in the US State Department's Office to Combat Trafficking in Persons from 2003 to 2006, the inaugural ambassador John Miller argued that the ongoing use of the term "sex worker" by certain NGOs, activists, and troublesome feminist academics served "to justify modern-day slavery, [and] to dignify the perpetrators and the industries who enslave."[36] In accordance with Miller's declaration, a spate of US anti-trafficking laws emerged to create an enforcement apparatus for Miller's view that all forms of sex work both within and beyond US borders should be regarded as the moral equivalent of slavery: stepping up criminal penalties for pimps and sexual clients, imposing financial sanctions on nations deemed to be taking insufficient steps to stem prostitution, and stipulating that NGOs that did not explicitly denounce prostitution as a violation of women's human rights were to be disqualified from federal funding. Miller's agenda not only remapped the field of fundable NGOs but also provided more general political support for the rapid proliferation of sexually and carcerally focused strands of anti-trafficking activism, both secular feminist and evangelical Christian in orientation.[37] Since 2001, the US Agency for International Development (USAID) has spent nearly $250 million on anti-trafficking programming internationally.[38]

A critical accompaniment and co-agent in state- and activist-led campaigns against sex trafficking has been the steady proliferation of media accounts, which have rehearsed similar stories of the abduction and sexual enslavement of women and girls whose poverty and desperation render them amenable to easy victimization in both first- and third-world cities. From critically acclaimed films like *The Whistleblower* to the box-office hit *Taken* to the Lifetime network's *Human Trafficking* television miniseries, a steady stream of old and new media—including movies, popular fiction, television shows, newspaper and magazine articles, blogs, websites, and online games and apps—has emerged to reinforce ideas of prostitution as sexual slavery, and ideas of heightened policing and low-wage labor as appropriate remedies.[39] Among the most influential in disseminating this point of view has been Nicholas Kristof, the Pulitzer Prize–winning journalist for the *New York Times*, whose weekly columns since 2004, best-selling book *Half the Sky* (which later became a two-part television special), and innovative online game have kept sex trafficking in the spotlight.[40] Most recently, a growing number of celebrity activists, including Angelina Jolie, Demi Moore, Ashton Kutcher, Mira Sorvino, and Jada Pinkett Smith, have also highlighted this issue through their allocation of financial resources, public service announcements, and testimony before US Congress and the United Nations.[41]

Although the story of prostitution's moral and political transformation from a "necessary evil" into "the Social Evil" of the late nineteenth century has been amply recounted by numerous scholars, the recent reinvigoration of this discourse has yet to be sufficiently explored. This book examines the constellation of factors that led to the (re)discovery of the "traffic in women" in the late 1990s, considering the ways in which burgeoning markets in sexual commerce have become intertwined with evolving feminist, evangelical, and political-economic interests. Beyond demonstrating the deleterious effects of this discourse on workers and migrants, this discussion provides an important window onto broader transformations of sexual politics, new paradigms of humanitarian intervention, and the subjective meanings and political techniques of late capitalism. One of my primary aims in this book is thus to demonstrate how the alliances that have been brokered among quite disparate sets of social actors have facilitated the global circulation and entrenchment of the trafficking discourse across a wide swath of cultural and political terrain.

In the chapters that follow, I argue that recent campaigns against the "traffic in women" have been spurred not simply by diffuse social anxieties around globalization, immigration, and the liberalization of sexual mores (as previous commentators have offered); they also are indicative of something more: a new politics of sex and gender that is directly brokered by the neoliberal state, is entrenched in right- as well as left-wing cultural spaces, and is expressed in both secular and religious idioms. It is for this reason, I suggest, that the explanatory trope of trafficking as but the latest in a series of recurrent "sex panics" is similarly inadequate for capturing the sociological and historical specificity of current discursive regimes. To the contrary, I argue that gathering attention to human trafficking demonstrates the extent to which questions of sexual politics have been vital to the ascendance of specifically neoliberal forms of governmentality—including phenomena as varied as carceral control, humanitarian endeavor, and new affective economies—even if these social technologies have not typically been imagined in these terms.

Definitional and Calculative Flux

Many sex workers' rights organizations have objected to the prevailing rubric of "sex trafficking," arguing that the term analytically separates trafficking for prostitution from circumstances of "human trafficking" more broadly, isolating sexuality as a special case. Yet as we will see in the chapters that follow, definitions of the latter are also ambiguous, and the term's patterns of usage remain no less ideologically driven, with matters of force, exploitation, and transport across borders often presumed but never specified. In his ethnography of anti-trafficking activism and the sex trade in Southeast Asia, the anthropologist Sverre Molland observes that the term "human trafficking" first appeared in the *New York Times* in 1976, in an article about the trafficking of persons out of East Germany. It resurfaced on two occasions some twenty years later, in reference to discussions preceding the 2000 UN Protocol on Trafficking in Persons, the policy instrument that has proved most influential in disseminating the trafficking discourse on a global scale. Usage of the term has increased steadily each year since that time, with the number of mentions in the newspaper reaching a total of 284 by 2012, and 1,972 as of December 2017.[42] Amid this rapid proliferation, the ambiguity of "human trafficking" as a signifier has been marked by both older vestiges of the term (in which residues of the nineteenth-century "white slave traffic" are ever present) and by successive political struggles at key institutional junctures (including the United Nations and the US State Department of State). Given that the very definitions of both "sex trafficking" and "human trafficking" have eluded clear consensus, efforts to try to quantify their prevalence, or to calculate numbers of victims, remain tenuous at best. What cannot be clearly defined or specified cannot be meaningfully counted.

For example, while the 2000 UN Protocol, the most frequently cited document on these matters, carefully enumerates the activities that constitute "trafficking" and "exploitation," it never precisely defines the term. According to article 3 of the UN Protocol:

"Trafficking in persons" shall mean the recruitment, transportation, transfer, harbouring or receipt of persons, by means of the threat or use of force or other forms of coercion, of abduction, of fraud, of deception, of the abuse of power or of a position of vulnerability or of the giving or receiving of payments or benefits to achieve the consent of a person having control over another person, for the purpose of exploitation. Exploitation shall include, at a minimum, the exploitation of the prostitution of others or other forms of sexual exploitation, forced labour or services, slavery or practices similar to slavery, servitude or the removal of organs.

What exactly is to be understood by the force, fraud, vulnerability, and exploitation that constitute the key elements of the crime of "trafficking" remains unclear. Most notably, the meaning of "the exploitation of the prostitution of others" is never stipulated, a phrase left deliberately ambiguous because of intractable arguments among activists about the nature of prostitution at the time the protocol was negotiated.[43] The awkward phrasing that resulted from these struggles allows for easy vacillation between understandings of exploitation as direct physical coercion and exploitation in the Marxist sense of mere economic benefit.

The US Trafficking Victims' Protection Act (TVPA) of 2000 is similarly vague in its definitions, and usage of the term has fluctuated across the TVPA's subsequent reauthorizations. According to section 103 of the original act, "sex trafficking" is defined as "the recruitment, harboring, transportation, provision, or obtaining of a person for the purpose of a commercial sex act" (here, the presence or absence of force is left unspecified), and "severe forms of trafficking in persons" are commercial sex acts that include an element of "force, fraud, or coercion," or those in which those who perform sexual labor are younger than eighteen years of age. Severe forms of trafficking in persons are also said to include "the recruitment, harboring, transportation, provision, or obtaining of a person for labor or services, through the use of force, fraud, or coercion for the purpose of subjection to involuntary servitude, peonage, debt bondage, or slavery." Although "trafficking" is explicitly equated with all forms of sexual commerce, the act later specifies that only "severe forms of trafficking" are subject to official state sanction. In successive renditions of the law, underage prostitution occurring within US borders (in which questions of consent are considered irrelevant) and certain nonsexual forms of labor have increasingly been marked as critical targets for state intervention, but the law's central definitional contradictions have never been resolved.[44]

Critical observers have also noted the dramatic ebbs, flows, and layers of imprecision that occur in official, activist, and media estimates of the prevalence of sex trafficking, both in the United States and transnationally. Writing as early as 2003, the sociologist and feminist scholar Wendy Chapkis observed that the US Trafficking Victims' Protection Act relied upon "slippery statistics and sliding definitions." She noted, in particular, the CIA's estimate that between forty-five thousand and fifty thousand women and children were trafficked into the United States each year, an estimate that was formulated using a broad and unspecified definition of trafficking to bolster the magnitude of the problem.[45] Although the United States' official estimate of the prevalence of transborder victims of trafficking has since been downgraded (to between fourteen thousand and seventeen thousand people per year), the CIA's initial figure is particularly noteworthy given that "50,000 trafficked women" was also the number that was circulated during turn-of-the-century debates around white slavery.[46] It is also remarkable given that, since 2000, the initial year of the law's passage, there have only been 6,384 T visas issued, 1,461 cases filed with the Department of Justice, and 896 convictions—for sex and labor trafficking combined.[47] In the city of New York, purportedly one of the central hubs of sex trafficking in the United States, since 2008 there have been only sixty-two convictions for the crime.[48]

Within the global arena, the circulation of numbers that highlight the prevalence of sex trafficking has been marked by similar degrees of imprecision. To take but a few examples: the anthropologists Thaddeus Gregory Blanchette and Ana Paula da Silva have shown that all currently circulating numerical estimates regarding the extent of sex trafficking in Brazil are based on a single and methodologically spurious report. They argue, in fact, that the report in question "has thus not so much *revealed* human trafficking in Brazil as actively *created* it."[49] Blanchette and da Silva raise various concerns about the study, ranging from the credentials of the research team that carried it out to the researchers' use of news stories as data to the inconsistent definitions of "trafficking in persons" that guide it (the authors use a definition that contradicts that of the UN Protocol, in which aiding the migration of prostitutes is taken to be analogous to trafficking even when the migration is voluntary and involves no human rights violations). Evidently, studies that consider all forms of migrant labor in the sex industry to be incidences of trafficking will produce much higher numbers than those that do not.

Similarly, as the researcher Thomas M. Steinfatt has demonstrated, the widely circulated data on sex trafficking in Cambodia—an alleged eighty thousand to one hundred thousand victims in the past decade—cannot be taken at face value. As with the case of Brazil, most of these numbers are in fact derived from one or two sources, with Steinfatt noting that none of the NGOs that issued these numerical estimates "studied or even sponsored an empirical study of the problem." Of the two primary sources that are most frequently cited, one does not even mention the figure of eighty thousand to one hundred thousand, and the second posits the same figure in reference to the total number of sex workers in Cambodia—not trafficked women and children. When Steinfatt and his own research team conducted ethnographic fieldwork to assess the actual extent of sex trafficking in the country, they estimated only 1,058 trafficked sex workers.[50]

Inflated estimations of the extent of sex trafficking have also flourished, in particular, around sporting events, as a careful investigation by the Global

Alliance against Traffic in Women (GAATW), a network of liberal-leaning, multisectoral anti-trafficking organizations, has revealed.[51] In their assessment, GAATW compared the numbers of anticipated sex trafficking cases at international sporting events to the actual numbers of sex-trafficking incidents that were reported, focusing on the 2006 and 2010 World Cup tournaments and the 2004 and 2010 Olympic Games. While forty thousand foreign women were expected to be trafficked to Germany for the 2006 World Cup and forty thousand to South Africa for the 2010 tournament, only five cases of sex trafficking were ultimately found to be linked to the former, and no cases of trafficking were linked to the latter.[52] Similarly, no instances of sex trafficking were identified at the 2004 or 2010 Olympics, and first-person reports suggest that business in fact declined for sex workers during the 2010 games. The authors of the report surmise that such consistent disparities reveal governments' symbolic, rather than substantive, commitments to eradicating sex trafficking.[53]

Finally, the symbolic efficacy of inflated statistical claims around sex trafficking has also been observed by the sociologist William McDonald, who has sought to "triangulate" official government estimates with the significantly lower numbers of prosecutions for trafficking crimes. He considers various explanations for the vast gulf between these two sets of figures, such as the difficulty of prosecuting cases, the obstacles to making connections with victims, a lack of police incentive to do so, and specifically in the United States, "the fragmentation of jurisdiction among local and federal law enforcement, immigration, and labor agencies." Yet even accounting for all of these factors, McDonald argues that the difference between the two sets of figures—and between empirical realities and political perception—is so vast that it can be understood only via its connection to "the potent image that continues to be used to frame the problem": the image of "the innocent, naïve decent girl seeking respectable work, who is deceived or forced into prostitution or sexual slavery."[54]

Panics and Politics

Among critical scholars of sex and gender, the most frequent explanation for the recent surge in attention to sex trafficking despite meager empirical evidence has been provided by the theory of "sex panics" (and its analytic predecessor, "moral panics"). In this view, the moral combustibility of sex inclines "panics" to arise periodically, often culminating in draconian and irrational criminalized regimes.[55] Arguing in this vein, many commentators have noted the similarities between the moral panic around sex trafficking in the current moment and that which surrounded white slavery in the late nineteenth and early twentieth centuries, which engaged a similar coalition of feminist activists and conservative Christians (a resonance I explore in greater detail in the following chapters). The central presence of evangelical Christians in both coalitions has led many secular observers to a kind of "aha!" moment in which any presumed complexity of the issue can henceforth be easily dismissed. On this reading, "puritanical" and sex-negative feminist activists have been duped into forging an alliance with sex-panicked Christians, who rally around trafficking as they have around other proxy issues (like abortion and gay marriage) in order to reassert a traditionalist sexual politics.[56]

The pivotal role played by evangelical Christians in fomenting and perpetuating the current anti-trafficking movement—in the United States and beyond—has certainly been well documented.[57] The heightened presence of evangelical Christians in disseminating particular visions of sexual freedom and human rights on a global scale, through transnational institutions like the United Nations, has also been aptly observed.[58] And it is incontrovertible that the United States has been dominated by a political coalition in which evangelical Protestants have played a major role since at least 1980, one that has led to a staunch conservatism in US policy on issues of both gender and sexuality. The most frequently cited examples of this conservatism include the US deployment of worldwide restrictions on women's reproductive freedoms, promotion of the male-headed nuclear family as the optimal model for social life, and the dismantling of government offices and programs that had been dedicated to ending gender discrimination in economic sectors.[59] As a result, it is easy to think that the pronounced presence of religious actors in the trafficking debates is in and of itself sufficient to account for the fierce antipathy to commercial sex that has shaped current political frameworks around the issue.[60]

Yet the case of trafficking simultaneously reveals that evangelical engagement with anti-trafficking politics has not diverged from the proclivity displayed by all significant political constituencies—including secular liberals, human rights activists, and bipartisan political officials—to remain tightly wedded to the imperatives of neoliberal globalization in forging effective policy remedies. While a focus on "sex panics" suggests a cycle of moral combustion that is destined to be endlessly repeated, this book argues that present-day attention to trafficking has emerged at the juncture of cultural and political formations that are not only entrenched and self-replicating, but also quite new. Significantly, contemporary evangelical anti-trafficking activists reveal a set of political commitments that both encompasses and transcends prior depictions of conservative Christians' sexual worldviews. The alliance that they have forged with secular feminists has occurred not only around a particular relational configuration of gender and sexuality (i.e., a commitment to an ideal of amatively coupled heterosexuality, one that cannot imagine a place for prostitution outside the scope of women's exploitation) but also by a shared commitment to neoliberal economic and cultural agendas. The pursuit of "women's human rights," in this shared vision, is imagined in terms of women's (legitimate) reinsertion into market economies and their protection by state apparatuses of criminal justice.

In the succinct words of one evangelical anti-trafficking activist who described to me her organization's successful transformation of Cambodia's Svay Pak (a district formerly known for child prostitution) into "a nice tourist town," "Our real goal is to bring people out of slavery into the free market." As described earlier, this view is also manifest via the practices that Elena Shih observed in both secular and evangelical Christian "rescue" projects in Thailand, as well as in the growing number of Christian humanitarian organizations globally that orient former prostitutes toward entry-level jobs in the service economy, teaching women to bake muffins for Starbucks or to prepare Western-style drinks and food. Evangelical as well as secular human rights groups have increasingly committed themselves to this approach, no longer framing the problem of human trafficking in terms of broader dynamics of globalization, gendered labor, and migration (the prevailing framework among many secular anti-trafficking NGOs in the 1990s), but rather as a humanitarian issue that the criminal justice system and global capitalists, working in tandem, can help combat.[61]

During her 2008 presentation at Columbia University, Somaly Mam, the aforementioned activist and self-declared trafficking survivor from Cambodia, was notably joined by a representative from the legal technology firm LexisNexis, who discussed the virtues of public-private partnerships as well as his company's aims to retrain former trafficking victims in hairstyling, seamstress work, and entry-level positions in manufacturing. In this regard, the company followed the lead of Nicholas Kristof, who as early as 2004 was avidly endorsing the construction of what he openly termed "sweatshops" in the developing world as an antidote to sex trafficking.[62] Before publication of the *Newsweek* exposé and her subsequent resignation, Mam had been heralded for her activism by a bevy of celebrities (ranging from Oprah Winfrey to Lauren Bush, as well as by CNN, *Time*, *Glamour*, and *Fortune* magazines), but harshly critiqued by sex workers' rights groups for coercing former prostitutes into "rehabilitation" programs in which they were retrained for assembly-line work, sewing, and weaving.[63] Whereas an earlier wave of anti-globalization activists had argued that the daily practices of capitalism created sweatshop conditions of labor that were unacceptable, "new internationalist" evangelicals, along with their secular champions, have come to identify such practices with the very definition of "freedom."

Sexual Politics and Neoliberal Freedoms

Of late, "neoliberalism" has become a rather fraught term within contemporary social analysis—not because of its sparseness as a signifier but because of its capacity to designate so many distinct processes and entities. For neo-Marxists, it is an agenda of upward economic redistribution, one that is characterized by structural adjustment policies and the relocation of industrial production to "developing" Global South markets. For Foucauldians, neoliberalism has been imagined as a cultural project, premised on marketized governmentalities that produce self-regulating good subjects. And for political sociologists, neoliberalism has often been conjured as a new mode of statecraft, with privatization, the shift from the welfare state to the carceral state, and the attendant rise of new governing institutions (including NGOs, churches, and corporate entities) as core features.[64]

Significantly, scholars of gender and sexuality have often sought to suture these divisions by emphasizing what Lisa Duggan has described as "the dense interrelations" among neoliberalism's economic and (gendered) cultural projects.[65] Writing about the World Bank in Ecuador in the 1990s, for example, Kate Bedford has suggested that the promotion of complementary love within sharing couples was a central part of the bank's push to embed markets in more sustainable ways.[66] In her ethnographic study of the Grameen Bank's heralded microcredit program in Bangladesh, Lamia Karim has similarly demonstrated how microlending programs relied on, and ultimately came to reinforce, preexisting gender inequities.[67] In a similar vein, various feminist and queer scholars have examined the intertwined economic, gendered, and sexual interests that coalesce in corporate campaigns around seemingly progressive causes such as LGBT rights and the fight against breast cancer, or in the neoliberal state's appropriation of formerly liberationist discourses (of feminism and queerness) in fomenting sexual nationalisms, carceral politics, and securitized borders.[68]

Contributing to this emerging body of scholarship, the analysis that follows further specifies the mechanisms by which contemporary sexual politics and neoliberal formations intersect. To this end, I trace points of intersection among anti-trafficking activists and policy makers on several key political fronts (engagements I have variously termed carceral feminism, militarized humanitarianism, and redemptive capitalism) and the distinctive social visions that undergird each of these modes of intervention. Together, these formations meld new techniques of governance with particular imaginations of gendered freedom while traversing traditionally understood distinctions between the progressive and the conservative, as well as between the civil, the economic, and the political. We shall also see that in each instance, sexual politics have a crucial role to play in conjoining affective commitments to liberation with contemporary techniques of power, and in dissolving the principles of division that previously separated these realms.

In sketching a genealogy of carceral feminism, I demonstrate the ways in which contemporary feminism—especially in its hegemonic, institutionalized guise—has increasingly served to facilitate, rather than to counter, the carcerally controlling arm of the neoliberal state. I use the term carceral feminism to designate a cultural and political formation in which previous generations' struggles for gender justice and sexual liberation are recast in terms of criminal justice (often via social actors and institutions that do not necessarily identify as feminist but have explicitly declared their allegiance to the empowerment of women and girls). From intimate partner violence to campus sexual assault, from sex trafficking to hate crimes to sexual harassment and rape, the carceral feminist agenda has increasingly supplanted other forms of feminist engagement in domestic and global policy circles.

The discussion of carceral feminism that I present is in no way intended to suggest that all existing feminisms—much less, feminists—are committed to a carceral agenda. Even within the mainstream of contemporary US feminism, for example, a liberationist vision still prevails around issues such as reproductive rights, the flagship issue of the liberal-left end of the political spectrum.[69] Around questions of sexual violence, however, including, but not limited to, the issue of human trafficking, a carceral agenda has indisputably prevailed. Through successive encodings of issues such as rape, sexual harassment, pornography, sexual violence, prostitution, and trafficking into federal and international criminal law,

I show how the goals of second-wave feminism have provided crucial ideological support for ushering in contemporary carceral transitions.[70] The burgeoning discourse of "women's human rights" has also served to recircuit feminist attention from the domestic spheres of home and nation to an expanding international stage, thereby asserting carceral versions of feminism on a global scale.

This intricate interweaving of feminism with punitive political agendas has, I argue, found a counterpart in the militarized humanitarian interventions (also frequently conducted under the banner of advocacy for "women's interests") that a growing number of state and nonstate actors have employed. While theorists such as Inderpal Grewal have previously used the term "military humanitarianism" to describe the state policy of using women's human rights to justify US military interventions in Afghanistan and elsewhere,[71] I suggest that the term "militarized humanitarianism" might also be applied in a more expansive sense, one that includes not only state-sanctioned military interventions in foreign nation-states but also nongovernmental actors' own application of carcerally oriented humanitarian strategies to the global stage.

If the encapsulation of social justice within criminal justice is one aspect of neoliberalism that has transformed the contemporary landscape of sexual politics, the ascendance of market-based agendas for gender freedoms through practices of social entrepreneurship, consumer humanitarianism, and "global corporate citizenship" is another.[72] Although US ambassador John Miller, the flamboyant Bush-era figure with ties to the religious right, is the public official most frequently associated with elevating the issue of human trafficking to a position of national prominence,[73] it was in fact his more subdued successor, Mark Lagon, who quietly and effectively sustained attention to it by brokering public-private partnerships among multinational corporations, NGOs, and the US Department of State. While many analysts of transnational feminism have trained their eye on the United Nations as the principle sphere of global feminist engagement,[74] the surge in advocacy of socially entrepreneurial actors around questions of women's human rights and new corporate commitments to "empowering women and girls" may prove to be equally consequential.

Accordingly, multinational corporations such as Google, the Body Shop, and Manpower Incorporated have come to play an increasingly prominent role as advocates within—rather than the targets of—anti-trafficking campaigns by providing funding, framing, and policy solutions to the perceived problems of sex trafficking. As these economic actors have assumed a more prominent role in reshaping the moral field, political articulations of sexual freedom and gender justice have been similarly transformed. Alongside emergent state-market hybrids like Humanity United and the Clinton Global Initiative ("dedicated to using market-based solutions to empower girls and women"), market-driven social justice movements have focused on issues such as women's leadership, women's role in corporate supply chains, and the trafficking and slavery of women and girls.[75]

The flourishing of this approach in the context of contemporary anti-trafficking campaigns is particularly interesting to consider given that in earlier stages of grassroots advocacy around this issue, multinational capital and corporations were imagined by many activists to be the enemies of gender justice, rather than its enablers. Within the contemporary anti-trafficking movement, as in other political arenas (including microfinance and development), the shift to market-based visions of freedom and justice has occurred among secular and faith-based constituencies alike. The faith-based counterpart to the rise of "global corporate citizenship" is the practice that evangelicals call "business as mission," in which the extension of the free enterprise system is figured as a gender-progressive quest. Deeply resonant with both socially liberal and conservative worldviews, I suggest that we might best term this new configuration *redemptive capitalism*—a capitalism that is understood by its proponents to be transforming not only of self but also of world, and, indeed, of capitalism itself in a postsocialist, post-welfare-state era.

The late twentieth and early twenty-first century's "traffic in women" has been accompanied by a global traffic in feminism, and by a circulation of newly emergent forms of sex and gender politics. Situated at the nexus of sex, religion, humanitarianism, and political economy, contemporary anti-trafficking campaigns provide a useful lens into the ongoing social transformations that are reshaping each of these domains. The politics surrounding trafficking also reveal the extent to which the neoliberal state has itself been reconfigured through a direct reliance upon corporations and NGOs, fostering new social actors and remapping activist terrains. Despite frequent progressive urgings to forge a "better" anti-trafficking policy (by shifting the focus of political attention from sex trafficking to labor trafficking, for example, or by enhancing the availability of social services for sex workers[76]), such proclamations do little to address a deeper set of issues that are also urgently at stake: the sexed and gendered contours of "freedom" and "justice," notions of citizenship and belonging, and the contemporary scope and limits of emancipatory discourses.

An Ethnography of a Discourse

Although there has been a steady stream of melodramatic and sensationalistic texts on sex trafficking by journalists and activists, and a number of more critical accounts of the contemporary trafficking discourse by scholars working within the tradition of cultural studies, this book aims instead to examine the discursive construction of "trafficking" ethnographically.[77] While existing critical treatments of the trafficking frame have primarily served to demonstrate its deficits, my project here is not only a critical but also an explanatory one, arguing empirically for the reasons behind the frame's (re)emergence, demonstrating the motives of the actors who have propelled it forward, and documenting broadly its embodied effects (both for those who work in the sex industry and for contemporary sex and gender politics more generally). The various academic volumes that have examined "sex trafficking" ethnographically have made crucial scholarly contributions—and in the pages that follow, I draw extensively on many of these case studies—but these investigations of specific communities of migrant sex workers make more narrowly delimited empirical and theoretical claims than this volume intends.[78] The pages that follow weave together multisited ethnography with multilayered social analysis, exploring the complex intersections of sexual commerce, neoliberal governance, and prevailing social practices of moral and political intervention. While my approach to this material is guided by prevailing theoretical and political questions around sex, gender, and political economy, it is given heft, depth, and specificity by my engagement with the empirical material that I have gathered.[79]

Taking as a departure point my previous ethnographic research with migrant and domestic sex workers and the social actors who aim to regulate their movements, I trace the ambitions of the diverse coalition of feminist activists, evangelical Christians, and corporate and state officials who have recently produced policy transformations on a scale unparalleled since the white slavery scare of the twentieth century. Drawing on in-depth interviews with anti-trafficking activists and political leaders as well as ethnographic research at policy meetings, in courthouses, and at "rescue projects" for women who have been designated victims of sex trafficking, I explore how contemporary campaigns against human trafficking have mobilized constituencies with divergent backgrounds and agendas, and the overlapping moral and political visions around which the alliance between these groups has been forged. Although my chief empirical focus concerns anti-trafficking campaigns originating in the United States during the years of the Bush and Obama presidencies (with the United States serving as a key engine of neo-imperial humanitarian intervention on this as well as other issues), I engage a wide array of secondary materials to trace their global extensions.[80] Because "trafficking" continues to proliferate and transform, there are no doubt many more empirical cases—emerging activist groups, laws and policies, media campaigns, and corporate initiatives—that could potentially serve to enhance the analysis presented here, but I believe that the range of cases considered is sufficient to build an argument which can be broadly construed. In the book's conclusion and afterword, I provide a brief examination of the continued twists and turns that anti-trafficking politics have taken since the time that the bulk of my empirical research was completed.

A theoretically driven *ethnography of a discourse*, my analysis is deliberately mobile and multisited, traveling with its empirical object across varied political and cultural domains. By "discourse," I mean to signal a constellation of words, materialities, and practices as they coalesce in historically and culturally situated ways, constructing the empirical object under consideration and the social locations in which it is manifest.[81] As the sociologist Mariana Valverde has written, "discourse," in this (non-idealist) sense refers not to language as separate from the "real world" but to organized sets of signifying practices that cross the boundary between "reality" and "language." Or, to paraphrase Judith Butler, it captures the inseparability of regulatory ideals and their worldly materializations.[82]

Discourse, on this reading, is neither totalizing nor uniform—it is, rather, "a domain of constraints."[83] While some commentators have cautioned against the "mechanistic and monolithic overtones" of the term and its presumed inability to capture the "micro-techniques through which specific interventions have been imposed, opposed, and fought over," my own case study highlights the extent to which contestation and fragmentation can be integral features.[84] For example (and as I elaborate upon in the coming chapters), although states, NGOs, faith-based constituencies, and some secular feminist activists have come to actively embrace the discourse of trafficking, its various deployments have been shifting and malleable, with the term variously signaling all forms of sexual labor or situations of violence and coercion only, as well as multiple and conflicting definitions of forced labor, child labor, and slavery in other industrial sectors. At the same time, Empower's sex workers, like sex workers from similar organizations around the globe, have organized to reject the discourse on both symbolic and practical grounds.[85] Despite this refusal and the discourse's failure to adequately "subjectify" most sex workers, their exposure to it on a daily basis via NGOs and police officers has rendered engagement with its terms to be obligatory.[86] One could say that the best evidence that a discourse has become politically and culturally hegemonic—as "sex trafficking" certainly has—resides in the compulsory repetitions and citations that it entails.[87]

What does it mean to study a discourse ethnographically? Unlike conventional ethnographies, I take the subject of this study to be socially constructed rather than naturally occurring, and cast the process of social construction itself as my chief object of inquiry.[88] As such, this volume represents a theoretical and methodological departure from the tradition of global and multisited ethnographies that denaturalize the presumed unity of cultures or the integrity of self-contained field sites but do not place the presumed self-evidence of the empirical phenomenon at hand under similar scrutiny.[89] Given the epistemological presuppositions I have outlined, my chosen field sites were, to the extent possible, generated by the institutional turns and swerves taken by the trafficking discourse itself over the years that I was engaged in this project, rather than being preselected at the outset of the research process (a "shadowing" of the discourse, so to speak).[90]

Between 2005 and 2012, I attended over a hundred anti-trafficking events (meetings, conferences, prayer gatherings, rallies, film screenings, and focus groups) with an ideologically diverse sample of secular rights-based and evangelical Christian anti-trafficking activists from the grassroots, governmental, and corporate sectors. The majority of these were held in metropolitan Washington, DC, or New York, but I also conducted interviews and attended events in Los Angeles, the San Francisco Bay Area, Boston, Denver, Philadelphia, and in other global cities, including London, Berlin, Copenhagen, Bergen, Barcelona, Hong Kong, Mexico City, and Buenos Aires. In addition to this, I conducted forty-eight in-depth, face-to-face interviews with prominent movement participants—politicians, members of activist groups, heads of NGOs, and corporate leaders. In the summers of 2007 and 2012, I made two brief research visits to Thailand to meet with local UN officials, anti-trafficking NGOs, and sex worker activists (the latter, as described above, in coordination with Elena Shih, who had been conducting doctoral research in Bangkok). I chose Thailand as a supplementary field site because of its role as an enduring focal point for global anti-trafficking interventions, because it could effectively supplement my prior research in the United States and Western Europe, and because of my existing field contacts in the region.

To the extent possible, I have sought to include the actual names of people, places, and organizations to preserve the historical and social specificity of my account. As Alexandra Murphy and Colin Jerolmack argue in a recent forum on the common practice of masking identities in ethnographic writing, "decisions about what and how to mask," though often deemed inconsequential, "are inherently theoretical choices" that may result in the omission of significant sociological data. They further note that many ethnographers report that interviewees themselves often request inclusion of their real names in published texts, which was also the case for many of the people I spoke with, as was their hope for a book in which recognizable place-names and organizations were included.[91] Despite my inclination to preserve as much specificity as possible, whenever research participants requested anonymity or if their preferences could not be established, I omitted or changed their names as well as any details that might identify them to other readers.

My ambition to provide an ethnography of a discourse may strike some sociologists as a bold and perhaps even heretical endeavor, but this approach is hardly unprecedented in recent ethnographic writing. For example, Shore and Wright's 1997 edited collection *Anthropology of Policy* considers questions such as how "policies construct their subjects as objects of power" and how "shifts in discourse are made authoritative." For Shore and Wright, this approach "offers a radical reconceptualization of 'the field'; not as a discrete local community or bounded geographical area, but as a social and political space articulated through relations of power and systems of governance."[92] Annelise Riles's ethnography of "the network," a fascinating, interdisciplinary study of women's nongovernmental organizations in Fiji, casts its object of analysis as "a set of informational practices," including attendance at meetings and conferences and the preparation of documents.[93] In her important study of global microfinance organizations, geographer Ananya Roy similarly makes the swerve from studying those living under conditions of poverty to "the poverty experts who produce knowledge about poverty and who set the agenda of poverty alleviation."[94] A classic exemplar of the discursive approach from within the field of anthropology is James Ferguson's *The Anti-Politics Machine*, which argues that "development" is best understood as the dominant interpretive grid "through which the impoverished regions of the world are known to us." In his study of development in Lesotho, Ferguson takes as his primary object of investigation not the people to be "developed" but the apparatus that does the developing.[95]

In like manner, in this book I am far more interested in the question of how "trafficking" is politically and culturally enacted than in recounting particular stories of trafficked women.[96] Although this chapter begins with the perspectives of sex workers in Chiang Mai (and in the chapters that follow, I return to some of the varied circumstances of people who engage in the performance and brokerage of sexual labor), my focus in these discussions is primarily around their encounters with the trafficking discourse and its alternately awkward and manipulable fit. By taking the discourse of trafficking, rather than the experience of "trafficking" itself, as my analytic object, I by no means wish to suggest that the violence that can occur within sexual labor is unimportant or that it is never a feature of sex workers' experiences. My point is rather that the political and cultural framework of trafficking highlights particular elements of the experience while deemphasizing others, and that it names and focuses our attention in particular ways—for example, through the lens of crime or gendered human rights abuses, as opposed to, say, structural violence.[97] As the opening anecdote of this introduction suggests, I will also argue that it pushes forward political remedies that are often a detriment to those it claims to help. It is for these reasons that it is crucial to understand the ways that the trafficking discourse functions as well as its genesis.

Finally, my methodological ambition to provide an ethnography of a discourse takes much inspiration from David Valentine's highly innovative "ethnography of a category." In his book *Imagining Transgender: the Ethnography of a Category*, Valentine describes this as the "critical ethnographic exploration of the origins, meanings, and consequences of the emergence and institutionalization" of distinct types of social categorization.[98] "Despite the collectivity and inclusivity implied by the term 'transgender,'" Valentine argues, "its employment in institutionalized contexts cannot account for the experiences of the most socially vulnerable gender-variant people."[99] Valentine's aim is not simply to document the inadequacies of "transgender" as empirical description; he is equally interested in tracing the production of the category's effects, "the complex social and political process" that he refers to as "imagining transgender."

What is common to all of the these approaches, as well as to my own, is an insistence that there is no "thing in itself" beyond its discursive construction, because the discourse produces the issue under consideration in the first place—shaping how the problem is defined, how it can be perceived, and the possible moral and political responses that can emerge. For example, is the "problem" of trafficking one of sex, of migration, of criminal networks, or of global social inequalities? Or, alternatively, is "the issue" one of gender, ethno-racial, and class exploitation within the context of sexual labor? This book seeks to explain how particular discursive formations arise and the kinds of solutions that get embraced, as well as the reasons that other possible interventions have often been foreclosed. In doing so, I aim not only to reconstrue the problem of "sex trafficking" as it is currently defined but also to better understand the politically complex laws, policies, and social actors that have together endeavored to stop it.

Plan of the Book

The "brokering" of subjects to which the title of this book refers thus takes place at several distinct levels that operate simultaneously—at the level of the sexually laboring subjects whose migration patterns and work are mediated by third parties; at the level of the activist campaigns initiated by the "helping subjects" who seek to ameliorate gendered suffering by curtailing sex workers' labor and cross-border movements; and at the level of global sexual politics, in which new political and economic formations and prevailing moral campaigns around sex work have become mutually reinforcing. These distinct yet simultaneous forms of brokerage—of sexual, helping, and political subjects—are the basis of the chapters that follow, and they constitute the central thematic components of this book.

Chapters 2 and 3 provide the backdrop for the discursive explosion of "trafficking" at the turn of the twenty-first century, tracing its sociological and political prehistory both in terms of the changing dynamics of sexual labor and vis-à-vis shifting paradigms of sexual regulation. How and why have commercial sexual transactions increasingly come to be understood as the global human rights violation of "sex trafficking" and through the lens of its close cultural correlate, "modern slavery"? What are the effects of these discourses on those who have been hailed by them as "human traffickers," and on the brokered sexual subjects that this framework purports to help? How has the issue been taken up, negotiated, and recirculated by diverse contingents of policy makers, NGOs, media channels, and secular and faith-based humanitarian campaigns? These two chapters provide an ethnographic analysis of the initial constituencies who resurrected the issue—secular feminist activists and conservative Christians—the key groups who would also inspire its travels through subsequent institutional, political, and cultural terrains. Basing my discussion upon oral histories with activists, documents from United Nations and US State Department meetings, and critical histories of the emergence and transformation of "women's human rights," I draw on both primary and secondary materials to provide a critical genealogy of the (re)ascendance of "trafficking." Chapter 4 further serves to illuminate the aims of secular feminist and evangelical Christian activists as they go about their work in the United States and Southeast Asia. These chapters also serve to introduce my central theoretical concepts—carceral feminism, militarized humanitarianism, and redemptive capitalism—and the pivotal role that they have come to play in contemporary sex and gender politics.

In Chapter 2, I focus in particular on the ways in which feminism, and sex and gender more generally, have become intricately interwoven with punitive agendas in contemporary US and global politics. Melding existing theoretical discussions with insights drawn from my own multisited ethnographic research (including first-person interviews with prominent activists, observations at key conferences and meetings, and an autoethnographic account of my role as expert witness in a federal sex-trafficking case) I elaborate on the ways that neoliberalism and the politics of sex and gender have intertwined to produce a politics oriented around carceral visions of gender justice and militarized humanitarian interventions on the global stage. In contemporary anti-trafficking campaigns, these goals have found expression in laws and policies that seek to severely punish sex traffickers and to "end demand" for prostitution on a global scale. Enforcement-wise, this has resulted in heightened police control over poor people of color who are involved in the peripheral corners of the global sexual economy, including pimps, clients, and sex workers alike.

For many secular critics of current anti-trafficking campaigns, the ideological commitments of evangelical Christian activists are usually presumed to be self-evident, and their political investment in this issue is assumed to be one and the same with the anti-pornography, anti-abortion, and anti–gay rights activism of decades past. In chapter 3, "Seek Justice™," I argue that although some avowedly Christian Right groups have indeed been active in the contemporary anti-trafficking crusade, they do not represent the majority of grassroots activity. Instead, a new group of young, highly educated, and relatively affluent evangelicals who often describe themselves as pertaining to the "justice generation" have pursued some of the most active and passionate campaigning around sexual slavery. In contrast to their Christian Right predecessors, the young evangelicals who have pioneered Christian interest in this issue not only embrace the languages of women's rights and social justice but have also taken deliberate steps to distinguish their work from the sexual politics of other conservative Christians. Ultimately, however, new evangelical efforts to "seek justice" (per one organization's patented slogan) remain beholden to an underlying carceral politics that serves to link them not just to those sectors of the contemporary feminist movement that have themselves veered rightward in recent decades but also to an entire right-wing spectrum of social and economic conservatives.

Chapter 4, "The Travels of Trafficking," draws on collaborative ethnographic research in Bangkok and Chang Mai (within the Bangkok and Chiang Mai red-light districts, at secular and faith-based "rescue projects," and as part of an anti-trafficking "reality tour" of Thailand jointly sponsored by US secular and faith-based organizations) to explore the surge in practices of social entrepreneurship, business as mission, and consumer humanitarianism that have arisen around "sex trafficking" in Southeast Asia. As a focus of current anti-trafficking activism and attention, and as a site where global campaigns against trafficking first emerged in the 1990s, Thailand is a key location for exploring how the discourse of trafficking has traveled globally between the Global South and the Global North, in multiple circuits and directions.[100] It is notable in this regard that international anti-trafficking campaigns peaked in Thailand at the same time that actual cases of human trafficking declined, and despite local activists' own assessment that the region had become so saturated with anti-trafficking NGOs that there were more organizations, both secular and faith-based, than there were trafficking victims.[101]

While secular and faith-based NGOs have increasingly relied on models of social entrepreneurship and business as mission to address sex trafficking, the issue has also become a key component of a growing number of corporate social responsibility campaigns, in which multinational corporations have furthered the pursuit of "market-based solutions" to contemporary social problems.[102] What are the implications of the rise of "global corporate citizenship" for transnational feminist advocacy and for social justice politics? How have neoliberalized and reconfigured institutions of global governance served to alter the terrain of sexual commerce and of the politics of sex and gender? Chapter 5 draws on in-depth interviews with and ethnographic observations of corporate actors from Google and Manpower Inc. to describe a brave new landscape of sexual politics that feminist social theorists have barely begun to consider.[103]

Ideological descendants of "compassionate conservatism," these interventions situate the morality of market exchange not in the supplementary private spheres of family, church, and charity but in the economic transaction itself as a key site of feeling and belonging. Via a suturing of the traditional gendered divides between public and private, paid and unpaid labor, and the family and the market, I demonstrate how women and sex are brought into this model of redemptive capitalism not as literal commodities for sale but as consumers and symbols, sources of affect, and key fonts of moral conviction. While resurgent alliances between feminists and evangelicals have been an ongoing preoccupation of critical scholarship on sex trafficking, equally pertinent to consider is both groups' current robust partnership with the economic agendas of a neoliberalized state apparatus. Could it be that the truly "strange bedfellows" alliance around sex trafficking is not the one between feminists and Christians that has preoccupied journalists and social researchers but rather that which binds together people of all religious varieties who have historically held very different ideas about the beneficence of markets, criminal justice, and the role of the state?

By way of a conclusion, chapter 6 places the example of "sex trafficking" in the context of other sexual-political issues to provide a more general assessment of the contemporary landscape of sex and gender politics. Although my analysis in this book focuses on recent mobilizations around the traffic in women, this issue is of course not alone in revealing the complex intertwining of gender and sexuality with state and metastate interests. The so-called headscarf debates in Western Europe as well as a succession of recent controversies around questions of sex, culture, and religion have also occurred squarely at this intersection, as have less publicized discussions around "gender mainstreaming" and the (hetero)sexual politics of development.[104] Situating the case of sex trafficking within a broader field of sexual and social politics allows us to further consider the power relations that undergird consensus-building humanitarian frames, frames that simultaneously produce visions of rightness, goodness, and justice, as well as criminal prohibitions.

Although the contemporary rubric of "fighting trafficking" has done little to protect most sex workers or others laboring under exploitative conditions, it has been highly effective as an ideological constellation that can travel widely and well, brokering alliances among otherwise disparate social groups—not despite but rather because of its ultimate incoherence as a discourse of social suffering. Given the efficacy and breadth of the travels of "trafficking," the more salient question may not be why and how such discursive regimes succeed but if and when they ever falter. I thus conclude this book by coming back full circle to where I started, with the alternative models of advocacy that are being embraced by sex workers at the Can Do Bar and its counterparts around the globe. Because history suggests that existing discursive formations of power can quickly unravel and reconfigure, I end by considering the potential for a different vision of sexual justice to emerge in what some have termed a "post-neoliberal" moment hastened by recent economic crises.[105] While gendered moral discourses have indeed been subsumable within broader geopolitical interests, they cannot be entirely contained. As in the previous century's white slavery panic, in which a decades-long feminist campaign against prostitution was eventually supplanted by medico-biological discourses focused on disease,[106] it is clear that new constellations of power can emerge to eclipse the urgency of "sex trafficking," freeing secular feminists, evangelical Christians, and others who advocate on behalf of a more just world to forge new political visions.

TWO

The Sexual Politics of Carceral Feminism

I've spent about 17 years working on this issue. Most of that time I was on the losing side, as those who supported "sex worker" rights won almost every political battle. . . . Those were the depressing years. . . . Now the truth about prostitution/ sex trafficking is emerging and agencies are responding as never before. I think more pimps and traffickers have been arrested in the last year than in the whole previous decade. DONNA HUGHES, ANTI-TRAFFICKING ACTIVIST AND ELEANOR M. AND OSCAR M. CARLSON ENDOWED CHAIR OF WOMEN'S STUDIES, UNIVERSITY OF RHODE ISLAND

Trafficking is like domestic violence. The only thing that prevents recurrence is fear of arrest. DORCHEN LEIDHOLDT, FEMINIST ACTIVIST FROM THE COALITION AGAINST THE TRAFFIC IN WOMEN, SPEAKING AT THE UN COMMISSION ON THE STATUS OF WOMEN

What do we want? A strong trafficking law! When do we want it? Now! CALL-AND-RESPONSE CRY AT NATIONAL ORGANIZATION FOR WOMEN RALLY IN SUP-PORT OF A NEW YORK STATE LAW INCREASING CRIMINAL PENALTIES AGAINST PROSTITUTES' CUSTOMERS[1]

For grassroots feminists of the second wave who were interested in critiquing mainstream economic and political institutions, it would have been a strange specter to imagine that a generation hence, pioneering figures such as Laura Lederer (author of the classic feminist volume *Take Back the Night*), Dorchen Leidholdt (a prominent advocate for victims of domestic violence), and Donna Hughes (Carlson Endowed Chair in Women's Studies at the University of Rhode Island) would find themselves on a bright July morning as the featured speakers at a panel sponsored by the Hudson Institute, a neoconservative Washington, DC, think tank, titled "The Profits of Pimping: Abolishing Sex Trafficking in the United States."[2] Sharing the stage with them were influential Hudson Institute fellows such as Michael Horowitz (a veteran of the Reagan administration and a prominent architect of the contemporary anti-trafficking movement); US ambassador Mark Lagon (a former aide to the five-term far-right Republican senator from North Carolina Jesse Helms, and then director of the Trafficking in Persons Office at the US Department of State), and Bonni Stachowiak (a professor of business administration at the evangelical Christian Vanguard University). As the all-white array of panelists spoke to the audience about the urgent need to root out inner-city street pimps and "pimp culture," to publicly stigmatize the male patrons of prostitutes, and to promote healthy families domestically and globally, the audience, composed of representatives from assorted right-wing organizations including the Heritage Foundation, the American Enterprise Institute, and Feminists for Life, erupted into frequent applause.

No less remarkable would be the testimony of organizations such as the secular feminist Coalition against Trafficking in Women (CATW) on behalf of the prosecution in an array of federal- and state-level trafficking cases, or of the left-right alliance comprising the Coalition to End Sexual Exploitation in the federal sex-trafficking case *United States v. Mujahid* (2010).[3] In *Mujahid*, an African American street pimp from Anchorage, Alaska, faced forty counts of human trafficking and a lifetime in prison for his violence-tinged relationships with the women concerned. Although punitive visions of gender justice have come to seem so right and natural as to be practically inevitable—particularly when questions of sexual violence are concerned—a revisiting of the recent history of feminist activism around such questions suggests that this has not always been the case. In a previous era of feminist activism, community interventions focused on educational and preventative measures, as well as attention to interlocking raced, classed, and gendered inequities, had been crucial grassroots strategies for combatting gender-based violence. Beginning with some of sex trafficking's key "predecessor" issues, however, especially heterosexual rape and domestic violence, complex and multidimensional feminist issues have increasingly been confined within the constrictive parameters of the criminal justice system. As such, wittingly or unwittingly, contemporary feminist activism around questions of sexual violence has become a crucial enabler of the late-capitalist carceral turn.

Of course, for those familiar with the evolution of what legal theorist Janet Halley has termed "governance feminism" (in which feminism "moves off the streets and into the state"[4]), as well as the historical precedent of the turn-of-the-century white slavery panic, the presence of prominent feminist activists at neoconservative think tanks and within federal courthouses might come across as less of a surprise. As we have seen, in addition to the echoes of white slavery, there are also important historical resonances between the current US anti-trafficking campaign and the Meese Commission anti-pornography hearings that took place during the 1980s, in which conservative Christians and secular feminists such as Catharine MacKinnon and Andrea Dworkin similarly joined forces for the sake of sexual reform. It has also been demonstrated that the feminist embrace of state-anchored sexual moralism is particularly apt to resurface during periods of right-wing ascendancy, like the Reagan years of the 1980s, when opportunities for more substantive political and economic change are elusive.[5] Indeed, a resurgent feminist-conservative alliance was also actively fostered by the George W. Bush White House—both rhetorically, as in the invasions of Afghanistan and Iraq, and through the cultivation of explicit political ties, as in the appointment of renowned feminist activist Laura Lederer as senior director for global projects on trafficking in persons at the US Department of State.[6] In addition to Lederer, other prominent feminists would go on to actively and publicly embrace Bush administration initiatives. Notably, in a February 2004 article in the *Washington Post* cowritten by iconic second-wave feminist Phyllis Chesler and women's studies professor cum anti-trafficking activist Donna Hughes, the authors provided a vigorous defense not only of the Bush administration's anti-trafficking policies but also of its military interventions in Afghanistan and Iraq, declaring that contemporary conservatives and faith-based organizations had become more reliable advocates of democracy and women's rights across the globe than the liberal left had ever been.[7]

The embrace of discourses of family values, democracy building, naming and shaming, and criminalization by a new crop of avowedly conservative feminists is certainly significant, with figures such as Sarah Palin and Ayaan Hirsi Ali constituting other prominent examples of the trend.[8] Yet important, too, is the extent to which feminists who identify as secular liberals and progressives have also found themselves in easy agreement with much of this agenda, and thus ready and eager participants in contemporary anti-trafficking campaigns. This partnership is crucial to consider because it points to a more thorough imbrication of mainstream feminist and neoliberal state interests than the oft-employed rubric of the "strange bedfellows" relationship between secular feminists and evangelical Christians implies.[9] While previous commentators have also pointed to a collusion between mainstream feminism and state agendas of border control in contemporary anti-trafficking campaigns (where feminist activism unwittingly supports the deportation of migrant sex workers under the guise of securing their protection), the ethnographic examples provided in the pages that follow provide an important elaboration of this insight, revealing the direct embrace of carceral politics and a securitized state apparatus to be increasingly hegemonic feminist remedies.[10]

This chapter assesses the ways in which feminism, and sex and gender more generally, have become intricately interwoven with punitive agendas in contemporary US and global politics. I discuss this through the rubric of carceral feminism, a term I first coined in 2007 and that has since been picked up, both laudably and critically, by a variety of activists and media commentators. It has been deployed to describe feminist responses to a growing range of contemporary issues—from domestic violence, sexual harassment, and rape to catcalling and "manspreading."[11] While commentators such as the *Nation's* Katha Pollitt have attempted to defend the kinds of feminist engagements that the term purports to criticize (arguing that johns should rightfully be arrested, even if sex workers should not be), this position sidesteps considerations of the broader sociohistorical context, in which formerly multidimensional political struggles have been increasingly recast in carceral terms. As the cultural theorist Roger Lancaster observed in his book *Sex Panic and the Punitive State*, since the 1960s, feminists and other liberals have steadily moved rightward on questions of punitiveness and criminal justice, particularly around issues of sex. In addition to the specifically feminist questions of sex trafficking, sexual harassment, and rape, the issues of child sexual abuse and hate crimes constitute other apt examples.[12]

Melding existing discussions of global trends with insights drawn from my own ethnographic research on the contemporary anti-trafficking movement in the United States—one of the most recent domains of feminist activism in which a crime frame has prevailed against competing models of social justice—in the sections that follow I elaborate on the ways that neoliberalism and the politics of sex and gender have intertwined to produce a carceral turn in advocacy movements that were previously organized around struggles for economic justice and personal liberation. Drawing on in-depth, face-to-face interviews with prominent anti-trafficking activists; ethnographic observations at state- and activist-sponsored policy meetings, conferences, and strategy sessions; and an autoethnographic exploration of my role as an expert witness for the defense in *United States v. Mujahid* (2010), this chapter also demonstrates how international human rights discourse has become a key vehicle both for the transnationalization of carceral politics and for folding back these policies into the domestic terrain in a benevolent, feminist guise.

In contemporary anti-trafficking campaigns, these trends have most recently found expression in laws and policies that seek to increase punitive measures against pimps and clients, to provide "helping" interventions for underage sex workers, and to "end demand" for prostitution on a global scale. Despite relatively small numbers of federal- and state-level trafficking cases and convictions, widespread feminist support for contemporary anti-trafficking policies has contributed to the multiplying islands of what Michel Foucault first described as the "carceral archipelago," comprising both formal and informal systems of control.[13] For sex workers and their associates, these include intensified regulation through border control and immigration restrictions; stepped-up enforcement of anti-prostitution, disorderly conduct, and public nuisance laws; and a growing array of mandatory "diversion" and "victim services" programs, which keep participants under state surveillance for longer and more intensive intervals.[14] Below, I begin to trace these connections through a discussion of existing accounts of neoliberal carcerality and its relationship to changing dynamics of race, class, sexuality, and gender.

Carceral Politics as Neoliberal Governance

When we govern through crime, we make crime and the forms of knowledge historically associated with it—criminal law, popular crime narrative, and criminology—available outside their limited original subject domains as powerful tools with which to interpret and frame all forms of social action as a problem of governance. JONATHAN SIMON, *GOVERNING THROUGH CRIME*

Sexist, racist, and xenophobic images and ideas have been mobilized in the media and by politicians to transform growing economic loss and dissatisfaction into calls for "law and order." Increasingly, social problems rooted in poverty and the racial wealth divide have been portrayed as issues of "crime," and increased policing and imprisonment have been framed as the solution. DEAN SPADE, *NORMAL LIFE*

In recent decades, diverse social analysts have sought to explain the rise of mass incarceration in the United States (and, to a lesser extent, Western Europe) since the 1970s, linking contemporary carceral strategies of social governance to the spread of neoliberal economic agendas, to late modern "cultures of control," to new modes of racial domination, and to the emergence of new political paradigms of "governing though crime."[15] In their groundbreaking 1992 article "The New Penology," law and society scholars Jonathan Simon and Malcolm Feeley first identified the series of interrelated shifts in penal ideology that began to transpire in the 1970s and 1980s, noting in particular the increased social reliance upon the imprisonment of entire populations deemed dangerous, as opposed to the apprehension and rehabilitation of particular individuals.[16] Since that time, successive waves of scholars have strived to understand the broader significance of mass incarceration as a strategy of social control in light of Foucault's earlier prediction that the modernist institution of the penitentiary would likely give way to more diffuse modes of governance.[17] Whatever explanations they have offered for the surprising arc that modes of punishment have taken, most theorists have tended to agree with Foucault's more general assertion that the study of penal policy is of paramount significance to an understanding of the organization of power more generally, and must therefore move from the margins to the center of contemporary social theory.

David Garland's 2001 volume *The Culture of Control: Crime and Social Order in Contemporary Society* still figures among the most influential works in this vein in its bold assertion that the pattern of social, economic, and cultural relations that emerged in America, Britain, and elsewhere during the last three decades of the twentieth century ushered in "a cluster of risks, insecurities, and control problems that have played a crucial role in shaping our changing response to crime."[18] Garland's widespanning discussion grants special attention to the professional middle classes, who have abandoned their prior allegiance to rehabilitative penal welfarism, noting that those who were formerly its staunchest advocates have done little to oppose the contemporary drift toward punitive policies. His analysis usefully points to the cultural underpinnings of punitive politics and a widening embrace of the carceral worldview, particularly among the affluent middle classes.

While seeking to explain a similar set of trends within contemporary culture and in emergent paradigms of criminal justice, Loïc Wacquant's *Punishing the Poor* makes a more pointed causal argument about the political roots of recent penal transformations. Specifically, he describes neoliberalism as a particular political-economic strategy in which the carceral state supplants previous regimes that were organized around the provision of material welfare. For Wacquant, neoliberalism does not represent a shrinking state apparatus as is often assumed, but rather a shift in the predominant form and functions of the state in which new penal policies are a core feature. Because neoliberal economic strategies redirect public monies away from the provision of goods and services, they in fact require an enhanced penal apparatus to contain newly disenfranchised populations. It is for this reason, Wacquant argues, that wherever neoliberalism reigns ascendant, carceral politics will too, an analysis that helps to explain the rise of carceral politics throughout much of Europe as well as in the United States.[19]

Whereas both Garland's and Wacquant's explanatory models highlight the relationship between neoliberal economic policies, the increased social disenfranchisement of the poor, and rising rates of incarceration, Jonathan Simon's theorization of contemporary crime policies highlights the impact of such policies on white, middle-class lives that are themselves increasingly sequestered within fortresslike gated communities and SUVs that resemble armored Humvees. Simon emphasizes the structural similarities that have emerged across boundaries of race, class, and ethnicity to justify carceral strategies of social control, whether that confinement occurs within the walls of one's own suburban home or through literal imprisonment. For Simon, it is the emergence of governing through crime as a political strategy that is of primary importance for social theorists to consider; the building of prisons, as well as the procurement of particular bodies to fill them, are but secondary and derivative phenomena. Challenging views of power that extend in clear, straightforward lines from the social center out to the periphery, Simon argues that new versions of liberal, middle-class freedom are secured not against but precisely *through* the domain of contemporary penal policy.[20]

Among the most provocative recent accounts of the rise of mass incarceration has been Michelle Alexander's *The New Jim Crow*, in which Alexander argues that US prisons are the emblem of a new racial caste system. For Alexander, this caste system is fueled by the American criminal justice apparatus, which constructs a predominantly black and brown undercaste that is legally denied rights. Alexander locates this caste system within the legacy of chattel slavery, Jim Crow laws, and the War on Drugs, arguing that mass incarceration must be seen as a contemporary counterpart to prior systems of racial control.[21] While admitting that her critique is most pertinent to the experiences of black men in the United States, and neglects many marginalized populations who are also affected by this caste system (and who may be "particularly vulnerable to the worst abuses and suffer in ways that are important and distinct") she calls upon other scholars to pick up this research where she has left off. [22]

Addressing precisely these gaps, a new wave of critical feminist scholarship has begun to trace a parallel history of incarceration and punishment, one that foregrounds the intersections of gender, race, and class in processes of penal transformation. These scholars have described the social implications of rapidly accelerating incarceration rates of female offenders as well as the control over women's lives and bodies that is increasingly exercised at a cultural level through a gendered and ubiquitous "fear of crime." Feminists of color, in particular, have focused their scholarly and activist work on the prison building, incarceration, and policing practices that have taken rise in the past three decades, including the disproportionate numbers of people of color who make up the prison population and the rapid increase in women's prisons and women prisoners. Women, they have pointed out—especially nonwhite women and women from the Global South—are the fastest-growing segment of the incarcerated population, typically for drug offenses. In the introduction to her volume *Global Lockdown*, scholar-activist Julia Sudbury notes that there was a 2,800% increase in incarcerated women between 1970 and 2001, coinciding with the implementation of neoliberal social and economic policies. A specific outcome of neoliberal globalization that she highlights is the criminalization of immigrants, demonstrating how neoliberalism has led to increased immigration of poor women from the Global South and, in turn, to their confinement within jails and prisons in the Northern Hemisphere.[23]

Perhaps most intriguingly, some feminist scholars have begun to explore the surprising ways that feminist activism itself—especially in its hegemonic, US guise—has often served to facilitate, rather than to counter, the carcerally controlling arm of the neoliberal state. Scholars of domestic violence and rape, for example, have traced the rise of carceral politics within second-wave feminism, describing the ways in which feminist campaigns against sexual violence have not only been coopted by—but in fact been integral ingredients in—the evolution of criminal justice as an apparatus of control. Aya Gruber and other critical legal scholars have argued that the raped-woman-as-crime-victim has emerged "as the idealized political subject of second-wave feminism," and that the feminist antiviolence movement, a movement that was previously oriented toward grassroots and social service remedies, has increasingly turned to the terrain of criminal justice to pursue its political goals.[24] In the United States, this shift is perhaps best emblematized by passage of the Violence against Women Act (VAWA) in 1994, which was celebrated upon its authorization as the long-awaited political recognition of violence against women. Yet since the law's passage, it has been sharply critiqued by a new generation of feminist scholars, who note that VAWA was in fact part of the Violent Crime Control and Law Enforcement Act of 1994, one of the largest crime bills in US history.[25]

In her most recent work, *Arrested Justice: Black Women, Violence, and America's Prison Nation*, the sociologist Beth Richie traces the history of the feminist antiviolence movement in the context of a growing prison industry, showing how the movement colluded with the increasingly punitive justice system at the expense of poor black women in the United States.[26] Recounting stories of violence exercised against poor and/or queer black women by police and through the criminal justice system (including sexual harassment and assault by police officers, false convictions, and ensuant imprisonment), Richie problematizes both the prison-industrial complex and the antiviolence movement's marriage to it. In this way, her consideration of race, class, gender, and sexuality with regard to experiences of violence allows for a concrete examination of the prison-industrial complex and the ways that it has resulted not in the provision of social stability and safety, but rather in increased violence for poor women of color.

Clearly, neoliberal cultural transformations, including the transformations in race, class, and gender relations that have occurred through and alongside transformations in political economy, are vital to understanding the heightened role of carceral politics within the United States and globally. But despite the robustness and importance of existing scholarly accounts, key questions remain about precisely why and how the aforementioned dynamics have come to pass. Why have carceral feminist frameworks gained prominence while welfarist and liberationist feminist visions have declined? How, concretely, do feminist versions of sexual and carceral politics get conjoined to drown out other social visions? To fill in the blanks that prior analyses have left vacant, it is necessary to delve more deeply into the intersections of neoliberalism, the carceral state, and the politics of sex and gender. To unravel these dilemmas, I turn to my own ethnographic research on contemporary campaigns against the "traffic in women"—one of the most prominent domains of feminist activism in which a crime frame has gained rapid ascendance, both within the United States and transnationally.

Carceral Feminism Confronts the "Traffic in Women"

On a cold and windy February afternoon, I approach the fifth in a series of lunchtime rallies on behalf of a new NY State law which would stiffen the potential criminal penalties against men who are convicted of patronizing a prostitute, from 90 days to a year in prison.[27] When I arrive at Foley Square, I encounter a group of fifty or so women (mostly White or Asian, and all conspicuously middle class as indicated by their stylish attire and educated patterns of speech) as well as a gathering pool of journalists and onlookers. Present too are several influential City and State-level political figures who have been invited by the organizers to speak.

Women from the rally's two sponsoring feminist organizations (NOW-NYC and Equality Now) as well as a smattering of other groups are gathered on the steps behind the speakers, holding up signs from their respective organizations and handing out press packets. Periodically, they coax the rest of the crowd to join together in a chant: "What do we want? A strong trafficking law! When do we want it? Now!" Or, "Elliot Spitzer, take the lead! A strong trafficking bill is what we need!"[28]

In their depictions of the sex industry, all of the speakers at the rally deploy the new antitrafficking buzzwords ("victim," "predator," "perpetrator," "exploiter") along with stock anecdotes of innocent women having their papers confiscated, being forced to sell their bodies, and being trapped or tricked. The narratives of women's victimization are coupled with an insistence upon the need to "focus on demand" and to aggressively pursue the perpetrators of sexual violence. Criminal law is rendered as a surprisingly powerful and effective deterrent to men's bad behavior: "We need to have laws that will make men think twice about entering the commercial sexual exploitation business," one passionate City Council member explains.

The final speaker at the event is Angela Lee from the New York Asian Women's Center. Fashionable and fortyish, dressed in a black leather jacket and fitted slacks, she makes no mention of the role played by global poverty in the dynamics of trafficking or prostitution, instead framing the issue in terms of the sexual integrity of families. "This is a family issue," she declares outright, "especially as Chinese New Year approaches and there are so many victims' families who won't be able to celebrate."[29] Lee goes on to link the dangers faced by trafficking victims to New York's State's lack of success thus far in imposing a law that would provide severe enough criminal penalties for traffickers and pimps. She concludes her speech with the emotional declaration that "We need to punish the traffickers and set the victims free!" FROM MY FIELD NOTES, NEW YORK CITY, FEBRUARY 2007

Although a decade of feminist research and activism has addressed the role of the neoliberal state in criminalizing the survival strategies of poor women, and of poor women of color in particular, the significance of feminism's own widening embrace of the neoliberal carceral state has only begun to come into focus. In recent years, the domain of transnational feminist activism in which the carceral turn has arguably become most apparent has been in gathering political and cultural attention to the "traffic in women." Until the mid-1990s, an incipient sex workers' rights movement had sought to decriminalize and to destigmatize women's sexual labor and to gain rights and protections for sex workers from within a labor frame, but since the early 2000s these efforts have been undercut by a bevy of new federal, state, and international laws that equate all prostitution with the crime of "human trafficking" and which impose harsh criminal penalties against traffickers and prostitutes' customers.

2.1 Poster for anti-trafficking campaign on the corner of Broadway and 113th Street, New York City. Cosponsored by the City of New York and the Somaly Mam Foundation. Photo: Ariane Rinehart, May 2014.

As the legal scholar Alice Miller has observed, in the late 1990s, this pivot first occurred within the context of transnational feminist organizing at the United Nations, an attention that brought with it "a focus on crime control methods and rescue, to the detriment of the promotion of the full range of rights needed by trafficked persons." According to Miller, the 2000 UN Protocol against Trafficking in Persons created international law "in the context of crime control—not human rights or labor protections."[30] The human rights lawyer Ann Jordan, who was herself present for the protocol negotiations has noted simply: "The Trafficking Protocol is not, unfortunately, a human rights instrument. The UN Crime Commission, which developed the Trafficking Protocol, is a law enforcement body, not a human rights body. Its Vienna location also physically isolates its members from the human rights bodies, which are located in Geneva and New York. For these reasons, the Trafficking Protocol is primarily a law enforcement instrument."[31] Other commentators have cautioned that the general focus on law enforcement rather than human rights in the protocol provides no guarantee that victims will be given more rights or more power to impact their situation. The UN anti-trafficking protocol, for example, mandates that states must take strong police action against traffickers, but it makes protections for victims a voluntary option.[32]

In the United States, the 2000 Trafficking Victims Protection Act (TVPA) that feminists lobbied for and supported was bundled together with a reauthorization of the Violence against Women Act, extending the latter's criminal justice approach toward gender violence to a new substantive domain. As in the UN Protocol, victim protection remains secondary to agendas of criminal punishment and prosecution. For example, while the TVPA offers victims participation in the Witness Protection Program and temporary visas enabling them to stay and work in the United States, these provisions are available only to a person who "is willing to assist in every reasonable way in the investigation and prosecution of severe forms of trafficking in persons." The TVPA thus added very little to the small modicum of rights that were already granted to irregular migrants (especially those willing to testify in criminal cases), and it must be seen against the backdrop of deportation that those victims deemed "uncooperative" must alternatively face.[33] Furthermore, as legal scholar Janie Chuang notes, the TVPA reaches beyond US borders to affect anti-trafficking policy abroad by establishing a sanctions regime authorizing the president to withdraw US (and certain multilateral) non-trade-related, nonhumanitarian financial assistance from countries deemed "not sufficiently compliant" with US government standards—a decision which, critics charge, is often entangled with other political concerns.[34]

Although some anti-trafficking activists continue to work toward the goal of decriminalizing and securing economic rights for sex workers, the overwhelming thrust of current feminist attention has been oriented toward widening—rather than curtailing—the sphere of criminal justice intervention in the sex industry. This is particularly remarkable given that sex worker activists have insisted that they are far more likely to experience violence at the hands of police officers and social service workers than they are from clients and pimps.[35] Recent state interventions on behalf of trafficking victims—including the passage of "safe harbor" laws for underage sex workers and the implementation of special prostitution and trafficking courts, which remand convicted prostitutes to mandatory social service programs—may appear on the surface to counter these trends, but in practice they serve to reinforce them. The stated aim of so-called "safe-harbor legislation" is to change how the criminal justice system treats minors in the sex industry. As such, safe-harbor laws understand minors in the sex trade to be de facto victims rather than criminals, and they depend on the implementation of programs that connect minors with services and resources (e.g., counseling, educational and vocational assessment, protective custody). This kind of service provision has often been facilitated through the creation of specialized prostitution and trafficking courts that combine assessments and court monitoring with the provision of social services.[36] Yet scholars and activists who have carefully observed these programs note that they extend the length and restrictive conditions of involuntary confinement and enhance existing mechanisms of coercion through mandatory drug testing and guilty pleas.[37] Others have pointed to the dissonance between the idea of sexually exploited youth and the experiences of the majority of underage sex workers who are independent, "defiant and oppositional to treatment," and who habitually run away from service providers.[38] Finally, Jennifer Musto points out that social services are offered to victims only insofar as "they are stabilized in being able to testify against their traffickers." In this way, they "provide a pathway to fulfilling the criminal justice goal of effectively prosecuting trafficker pimps and expanding the carceral state."[39]

As we have seen, although "trafficking" as defined in international protocols and in current federal law is capacious enough to encompass sweatshop labor, agricultural work, or unscrupulous labor practices on US military bases, it has been the far less common instances of sexually trafficked women and girls that have stimulated the most concern by feminist activists, the state, and the press.[40] Feminist anti-trafficking activists from mainstream and politically influential organizations such as Equality Now and the Coalition against Trafficking in Women have themselves acknowledged that a focus upon sexual violation rather than the structural conditions of exploited labor more generally—in addition to their strategic partnership on this issue with evangelical Christians—has been crucial to transforming trafficking into a legal framework with powerful material and symbolic effects. As one of the founding members of the prominent feminist anti-trafficking NGO Equality Now explained to me during an interview, framing the harms of prostitution and trafficking as politically neutral questions of humanitarian concern about third-world women, rather than as issues that directly affected the lives of Western feminists, was pivotal to waging the fight against commercial sexuality successfully. At events such as the February 2007 anti-trafficking rally that I attended at Foley Square in New York City, the political efficacy of conjoining the threat of sexual violence with calls for an expanded carceral state apparatus was apparent, with political leaders and feminist activists in strong agreement that human trafficking was primarily an issue of family values, sexual predation, and victimized women and children. At the rally, anti-trafficking activists located sexual menace squarely outside the home, despite a once hegemonic feminist contention that homes and families are the most dangerous places for women and children to be.

Various commentators who have critically assessed the rise of the anti-trafficking movement in the United States have attributed its ascendance to what they perceive to be the moralistic sexual politics of its two principal groups, "radical feminists" and conservative Christians.[41] They have argued that both groups harbor "archaic and violated visions of femininity and sexuality," a sexual ideology that is "pro-marriage" and "pro-family," and that they share an antipathy toward non-procreative sex.[42] Although ample critical attention has been devoted to the conservative legacy of feminist sexual politics that underpins contemporary anti-trafficking campaigns, most accounts have stopped short of looking at another sociologically significant linkage between the feminist and the evangelical Christian activist constituencies that have catapulted the "traffic in women" to its current position of political and cultural prominence—specifically, a carceral and far from historically inevitable paradigm of state engagement, both domestically and internationally. Left unaddressed by most commentators are the questions of why a vision of sexual politics that is premised upon a version of (feminist) family values should reign ascendant at this particular historical moment, as well as how these values might couple with broader sets of political and economic interests. Whereas theorists such as Garland, Wacquant, Simon, and Alexander astutely describe the rise of the carceral state but provide only a partial sketch of the dynamics of sex and gender that have facilitated its emergence, an equally significant deficit resides in analyses of sexual politics that fail to adequately consider feminist activists' newfound and often ubiquitous insistence on carceral versions of gender justice. In contemporary anti-trafficking campaigns, as in neoliberal governance more generally, the left and right ends of the political spectrum are joined together in a particular, dense knot of sexual and carceral values. A closer exploration of the role played by carceral feminism within one critical domain of neoliberal governance—specifically, the rapidly expanding criminal justice system—allows us to unravel this tangle of factors.

Sexual Labor and Brokered Justice

Consider several instances of sexual labor and its brokers: Tanya, a transgender woman from Stockholm, Sweden, who made the shift from public streetwalker to illicit "trafficker"—facilitating sexual commerce between Estonian women and Swedish men over the Internet—after the purchase of sexual services in Sweden was criminalized in 2000; Victor Virchenko, a Russian citizen and one of the earliest convicted sex traffickers in the United States, who arranged for the migration of fourteen women from rural Russia to work in urban strip clubs while providing them with crack cocaine (and thus, according to prosecutors, forcing their complicity); and Sabil Mujahid, an African American street pimp from Anchorage, Alaska, who faced forty counts of sex trafficking and a lifetime in prison for a crime that, ten years prior, would have earned him mere months or even weeks in jail, despite the strong evidence of domestic violence in his relationships with the women concerned.[43] While varying greatly in terms of the dynamics of force, fraud, and coercion that characterized each of their activities, all three were adjudicated under new carcerally oriented anti-trafficking frameworks, with ample feminist support.

Notably, none of the cases referenced here adheres precisely to the prototype of benign, affective kinship-based domestic units that the anthropologist Anthony Marcus and his colleagues have argued is most prevalent amongst street-based sex workers who rely on "market facilitators," based upon their methodologically rigorous study of street-based sexual labor in and around New York City. The first two cases, in fact, pertained more closely to the second-most prevalent category that Marcus and his coauthors identified, that of "relationships of opportunity . . . involving payment for services rather than long term management."[44] Mujahid, meanwhile, was clearly involved in an affective kinship unit with the women who worked for him, but he was also demonstrably violent in his relations with them. So violent, in fact, that involvement in his case was not something I would have ever deliberately sought out.

Although Mujahid's case is in many ways exemplary of the new trend to prosecute street pimps as traffickers, I got to know about Mujahid's story in a rather serendipitous manner, after being contacted by his lawyers to serve as an expert witness at his trial.[45] When I first spoke with the federal defense attorneys who were working on the case, I learned not only that Mujahid was being charged by prosecutors with forty counts of sex trafficking but also that he had a proven history of violence (he had been convicted of four counts of sexual assault of other inmates, crimes which occurred while he was in jail awaiting trial). The case he was currently being tried for revolved around accusations of brutal violence toward the women he lived with and employed, including forced sexual encounters and beatings severe enough to break noses and rib cages. Upon learning of these details, it is no understatement to say that I had a great deal of trepidation about getting further involved. If there were ever an instance that would seem to merit and even justify feminist engagement with the carceral state apparatus, surely this was it.[46]

But as I talked to his lawyers more, I came to understand that it was precisely these difficulties that made the case important to engage with—both for my own research and in terms of its broader ethical and political implications. As scholars and activists dedicated to the cause of prison abolition have often observed, an inevitable question that they must confront in their work is "What to do with the dangerous few?"[47] Moreover, in her incisive analysis of the continued buildup of the US carceral state, political scientist Marie Gottschalk has argued that persistent attention to the plight of nonviolent, nonserious, and nonsexual offenders discounts the fact that it is primarily long sentences bestowed upon violent offenders (rather than the imprisonment of petty criminals) that explains the rise of mass incarceration in the United States.[48] While thinking through the possibilities for my own participation in Mujahid's case, yet another source of inspiration was Sister Helen Prejean's carefully considered activism around the imposition of the death penalty. She has notably maintained that "the deepest moral question about the death penalty is not what to do about the innocent people; we know we shouldn't be executing innocent people. But what about when people *are* guilty? . . . That's where the deepest moral question of the death penalty comes."[49]

During our initial conversations, Mujahid's lawyers explained to me that my role in the case would consist of providing a critical assessment of the testimony provided by the expert witness on the prosecution side, Dr. Sharon Cooper, who would be arguing that the women concerned had clearly been forced into prostitution (i.e., "trafficked") despite the absence of any concrete evidence that demonstrated this coercion. Cooper, a pediatrician, had already written a lengthy report based on her interviews with the victims, which alleged that one can infer experiences of human trafficking and prostitution (the categories are used interchangeably, in her account) from certain psychological and physical symptoms, even when the women concerned do not describe their own experiences in these terms.[50] And so I agreed to review all documents and testimony in the case that were associated with proving "force," "fraud," and "coercion" into prostitution and to give them my honest assessment—a highly complex undertaking, as we have seen, since these terms are nowhere defined precisely in federal law.

The case files certainly did not make for easy or pleasant reading. I learned, for example, that most if not all of Mujahid's purported victims had not only grown up in circumstances of extreme poverty, homelessness, and familial instability but also had been subjected to a great deal of violence throughout the course of their young lives. Experiences of child sexual abuse at the hands of stepfathers and brothers were mentioned frequently, as were multiple instances of brutal stranger rape. Yet in her evaluation of the young women, Cooper attributed their current mental health problems and substance abuse issues directly to their participation in prostitution and to their experiences with Mujahid, arguing simply that their medical histories and current behaviors were "consistent with sexual exploitation through prostitution." In addition to failing to attend to a broader context of social harm in accounting for the women's current patterns of suffering, Cooper also consistently conflated the harms of intimate partner violence with the harms of prostitution. Throughout her report, she blurred the violence that occurred around Mujahid's sexual relationships with the women into her assumption that this violence was what propelled the women to enter into prostitution in the first place. Although she provided multiple examples of women who were victimized by intimate partner violence, she offered no evidence that these women had been forced to work in prostitution against their will. Indeed, her interviews with the victims instead revealed that the women often chose to work in prostitution as a money-making strategy, and some directly reported appreciating the revenues that they accumulated from this work.

Given that the first-person accounts suggested that the women typically entered into prostitution of their own accord, and that the violence they experienced at the hands of Mujahid primarily concerned other aspects of their relationships with him, it is not surprising that the prosecution deemed it necessary to provide an "expert" like Cooper to assert that force was at play even when it wasn't empirically demonstrated. The prosecution's argument was also helped along by their lay-anthropological, and frankly racist, reading of what they frequently termed "the subculture of pimping," and of pimp-prostitute relationships more generally. For Mujahid's prosecution was also a cultural one, with explicit appeals to lexicon, clothes, and patterns of family formation as indications of culpability. Indeed, during cross-examination at a Daubert hearing for a related case, Cooper described her particular expertise as deriving from two distinct domains: "the medical conditions of prostitution" and "the subculture of pimping." In her testimony, Cooper, herself African American, argued that

in the subculture, there's an absolute lexicon used in prostitution and most people would have no knowledge of what you are talking about . . . an example of that would be the stable. The term stable refers to the group of women who are working for a pimp . . . Another is wife-in-laws. The term wife-in-laws refers to all of the women who are working for one pimp. They are all wife-in-laws to the pimp daddy. . . . This if you will misconstruction of family terminology is another part that lures and grooms girls and women into believing they are actually in a family.[51]

Cooper's predetermined interpretation of the sex workers' relationship with Mujahid served to pathologize subcultural terminologies while ignoring the prevalence of domestic violence within culturally mainstream renditions of intimacy, and within hegemonic family forms.[52]

A similar emphasis on culture-as-culpability was demonstrated at two anti-trafficking trainings for police officers that I observed, one in Las Vegas, Nevada, in 2006, and one in New York City in 2007. At both events, as in Cooper's Daubert hearing, a great deal of time and attention were dedicated to presenting and translating terms that were deemed to be incriminating but were presumed to be opaque to white listeners (terms such as "daddy," "stable," and "bottom bitch"). Although the trainings were sponsored by two different organizations (the Law Enforcement Instructors' Alliance in Las Vegas and the NYPD in New York), in both instances this curious translation exercise was accompanied by a series of clichéd images of pimps taken straight out of 1970s mass media (complete with fur jackets, big hats, and bell-bottom jeans). These images were exhibited during well-attended plenary sessions, projected via PowerPoint onto enormous viewing screens.

This insistence on culturally legitimate versus illegitimate modes of family formation was also present during the proceedings of *People v. Vincent George, Jr., Vincent George, Sr., and Grip Entertainment*, a New York City case that was tried in 2013 and received a fair share of attention in the popular press.[53] As in the Mujahid case, *People v. George* represented a mélange of the different "ideal types" of market facilitation that Marcus and his colleagues have presented—blending elements of professional pimping and alternative kinship alongside contested degrees of force, fraud, and coercion. And as in the Mujahid case, mainstream feminist responses to the case revealed how normative understandings of the former indelibly shaped estimations of the latter. "The women have been sexually exploited and stripped of their self-worth," argued Norma Ramos, executive director of the Coalition against Trafficking in Women, to the press. She further observed that the tattoos the women had on their bodies were a common feature among sex-trafficking victims: "They're branding their women. . . . They're treating them like cattle."[54]

This conflict over the culturally constitutive components of "trafficking" came to a head when two of the women who worked for the Georges not only declined to testify against them but instead chose to testify on behalf of the defense. During the court proceedings, five of the women were photographed outside the courthouse dressed in homemade T-shirts, covered in pleas like "Free Vincent George Jr. & Sr.," "Not Guilty," and "We R A Family." While previously cases of sex trafficking would not have proceeded if the women concerned declined to testify, this case represented a shift in approach to combatting trafficking as a result of New York State's anti-trafficking law, which had passed in 2007. The law expanded the crime of "trafficking" to include coercion via drug use, material false statements, withholding or destroying government identification papers, requiring a payment of debt, and using either physical or verbal threats to compel a person into a pattern of behavior. Submitting wiretapped phone calls to the court, the prosecution built its case upon the latter definition of trafficking, arguing further that the women had no financial freedom from George Jr. or George Sr., since they had no bank accounts or property in their own names. Yet the women themselves dismissed these accusations, maintaining that they were well taken care of by the Georges and treated to a high standard of living, including nice cars and vacations. They described their relation-

2.2   Sex workers who worked for Vincent George Jr. and Sr., protesting at their trial, July 2012. New York City, New York. Photo: Getty Images.

ship to one another as that of "wives-in-law," and the collective that they were a part of as akin to a family.[55]

Neoliberalism's (Feminist) Family Values

In the 1970s our feminist goal was "liberation": liberation from discrimination at work, liberation from sexual constraints, liberation from forced sex, forced pregnancy and forced domestic service. . . . We were determined to occupy our cities, our jobs, our homes, our lives in courageous defiance of punitive—or protective—curfews and controls. We knew our movement was transgressive and, thus, dangerous, but we had no illusion about the sanctity or security of home. GAIL PHETERSON, "TRACING A RADICAL FEMINIST VISION FROM THE 1970S TO THE PRESENT" (2008)

The new liberal centrism of the 1990s converged with 1980s conservatism in advocating a leaner, meaner government (fewer social services, more "law and order"), a state-supported but "privatized" economy, an invigorated and socially responsible civil society, and a moralized family with gendered marriage at its center. LISA DUGGAN, THE TWILIGHT OF EQUALITY? NEOLIBERALISM, CULTURAL POLITICS, AND THE ATTACK ON DEMOCRACY

As Gail Pheterson and others who have tracked the changing contours of feminist political interventions have observed, a previously hegemonic feminist critique of normative, heterosexual family life receded at precisely the same time that its complicity with a broader embrace of carceral politics escalated, as demonstrated by a drift toward punitive, or "protective," curfews and controls. Although this latter shift might be explained simply in terms of the "new middle-class punitiveness" that criminologists such as David Garland have described, the mainstream feminist focus on forms of sexual violence that exceed the bounds of amatively coupled, heterosexual marriage is also a powerful demonstration of the co-constitution of neoliberal sexual and economic agendas. Notably, carceral feminists have turned their attention not only to the pimp-prostitution relationship as an especially troubling site of sexual violence, but have also placed special emphasis upon the presumed violence that transpires between female prostitutes and their male clients. What the Mujahid and Georges cases have in common with a recent spate of anti-client activism are the threats that such figures are imagined to represent to mainstream heterosexual relationships and to women's place within them—a power that the global sex industry is understood to erode.

"Seeing prostitutes shapes men's view of what sex is, who women are, and how they should be treated," remarked one white, middle-class activist at a popular anti-trafficking event that was sponsored by the feminist anti-trafficking NGO, the Coalition Against Trafficking in Women (CATW). "The idea that you can contain the value system of prostitution, and it will only affect *those* women, or those women in that country, and that it won't spill over into society as a whole . . . is an illusion," suggested another. As the British cultural theorist Jo Doezema has argued in regard to Western feminists' "'wounded attachment' to the third world prostitute," "the 'injured body' of the 'third world trafficking victim' in international feminist debates around trafficking in women serves as a powerful metaphor for advancing certain feminist interests, which cannot be assumed to be those of third world sex workers themselves."[56]

The link between global sex trafficking and the gendered power relations of heterosexual domesticity is also made explicit in a recent collection of essays, *Pornography: Driving the Demand in International Sex Trafficking*, published by a feminist anti-trafficking NGO. In one essay, the activist Chyng Sun emphasizes the damage that commercialized sex does to private-sphere, heterosexual relationships when it serves as the new standard for how all women "should look, sound, and behave." In a previous feminist collection, *Not for Sale*, the author Kirsten Anderberg issues a condemnation of the global sex industry after describing how watching pornographic videos with her male lover led to debilitating body issues and to plummeting self-esteem.[57] In the same way that a set of material and symbolic interests in heterosexual marriage undergirded the sexually "puritanical" nineteenth-century feminist battles against white slavery, abortion rights, and even birth control,[58] so too do contemporary feminist activists harbor a set of investments in "family values" and home that are decipherable in terms of the global interconnections of late-capitalist consumer culture. While contemporary discussions of the impact of the sex industry on normative heterosexual relations have ample historical precedent, the expanding scope and reach of sexual commerce under conditions of globalization, or what one influential anti-trafficking activist has termed "the prostitution of sexuality,"[59] have served to rapidly accelerate some feminists' concerns.

For contemporary anti-trafficking activists, a key ambition is to make the institution of heterosexual marriage more egalitarian and more secure by restoring an amative sexual ethic to sexual relations. Although anti-trafficking activists come from both heteronormative, liberal-feminist lineages and more "radical" lesbian-feminist traditions (as illustrated, for example, by the alliance between the National Organization for Women–NYC (NOW-NYC) and Equality Now at the 2007 rally), what binds the two groups to one another, as well as to their evangelical Christian counterparts, is their shared commitment to a relational, as opposed to recreational, sexual ethic.[60] More pivotal than the heterosexual versus lesbian-feminist divide of generations past,[61] the conviction that sexuality should be kept within the confines of the pair-bonded, romantic couple serves to cement a political alliance between ideologically disparate constituencies. As one feminist activist explained to me in recounting the initial forging of the alliance between the divergent groups that constitute the anti-trafficking coalition: "A whole consortium from the farthest left to the farthest right was in favor of making all prostitution trafficking. . . . What was really interesting is the coalition of people . . . a coalition that included Salvation Army and the lesbian-feminist Equality Now, and CATW up in New York and Michael Horowitz who's very conservative. . . . That's new politics. I had never before seen a group like that."[62]

From the perspective of various secular feminist and conservative Christian anti-trafficking activists whom I interviewed, the sexual revolutions of the 1960s and 1970s notably served to alter the balance of gendered power by creating extrafamilial sexual temptations for men. The influential anti-trafficking activist Donna Hughes has thus attributed the existence of human trafficking not only to prostitution, but also to the advent of a culturally liberal and permissive attitude toward sex that generates men's demand for sexual services.[63] Another anti-trafficking activist whom I interviewed about her engagement in the issue similarly sketched her perception of feminists' sexual dilemma in broad strokes, explaining that "through TV commercials, through billboards, through marketing, the sexuality continuously keeps increasing where there is no . . . protection anymore over our physical bodies, there are no more parameters, everything is acceptable." A third feminist commentator who is active in contemporary anti-trafficking debates has expressly attributed the "traffic in women" to the mainstreaming of prostitution, pornography, and sexually explicit mass media.[64] These activists are not mistaken in their identification of a new consumer-driven paradigm of sexuality that has co-emerged with other late-capitalist cultural transformations and that might best be defined as recreational, rather than relational, in its underlying ethic. What is ironic and surprising is the extent to which feminist anti-trafficking activists have embraced a pro-familial strategy for battling this trend, one that is itself intricately interwoven with neoliberal commitments to capitalism and criminalization.

Rather than regarding the heterosexual nuclear family as another institution of male domination to be abolished (and itself a key incarnation of the "traffic in women"[65]) contemporary anti-trafficking discourse situates the family as a privatized sphere of safety for women and children that the criminal justice system should be harnessed to protect. It was thus that one invited speaker at another CATW anti-trafficking event, a young woman who had previously worked in the sex industry and who described herself as a survivor of sex trafficking, attributed this experience to a combination of "no father figure" and an abundance of sexualized mass media. Conversely, she signaled that she had successfully overcome her ordeal by pointing out that she was now married and working full-time at "a good paying, real job." In contrast to an earlier moment in radical-feminist sexual politics, one that sought to link the sexual exploitation of prostitution to questions of violence against women more generally, including in the home,[66] in contemporary anti-trafficking campaigns it is specifically nonnormative (and racially as well as class-specific) forms of heterosexuality that have become the exclusive political targets.

This commitment to the home as safe haven undergirds what the feminist theorist Inderpal Grewal has described as the "gender of security" in the early twenty-first-century United States.[67] Grewal identifies a gender-specific emblem of the sequestered middle-class lives that theorists such as Jonathan Simon have also evoked—the figure of the "security mom" as one who seeks to harness the power of a securitized state apparatus to protect herself and her children. Akin to Grewal's analysis, ethnographic observations with feminist anti-trafficking activists reveal a specifically gendered set of investments in the neoliberal carceral state, one that is intricately interwoven with activists' own social locations as racially and class-privileged women. At the meetings with the anti-trafficking activists that I attended, the interlocking of multiple structures of privilege with a prosecutorial bent was manifest in various ways—from the professional settings of the conferences (e.g., the American Bar Association, the headquarters of the New York County Lawyers' Association, assorted white-shoe law firms) to the sets of interpersonal connections that activists drew on in their strategizing sessions. "Are there any women judges that are there for us?" asked one activist at the New York County Lawyers' Association meeting. "Are we on talking relations with the wife of the governor?" queried another. The professional upper-middle-class orientation of anti-trafficking activism that I observed in my research is also consistent with research on the class profiles of anti-prostitution activists in other national contexts and of contemporary transnational feminist activism more generally.[68] As members of the class fraction that is most likely to reap strong material and symbolic rewards from marriage, anti-trafficking activists are heavily invested in the maintenance and reproduction of this status and are ready to enlist the state apparatus on behalf of the gendered and sexual interests that are most pertinent to themselves: a version of "feminist family values" that is premised on liberal understandings of formal equality between women and men, and the safe containment of sexuality within the pair-bonded couple.[69] As with Grewal's analysis of the "security mom," these women utilize and promote the carceral state in order to securitize the sexual boundaries of home.

The feminist embrace of carceral politics and the articulation of these politics through normative ideals of gender, kinship, and sexuality was evident at the meetings of the anti-trafficking caucuses of NOW-NYC and the American Association of University Women (AAUW) that I attended between 2006 and 2008. At a November 2006 conference on violence against women that was cosponsored by the AAUW and other feminist organizations, several hundred professional women, predominantly white, spent the day discussing the necessity of abolishing prostitution for women's equality, while dozens of Black and Latina women dressed in catering uniforms circulated among them arranging tables and chairs and serving drinks. The keynote speaker was a lawyer from the feminist NGO Equality Now, who took the podium after being very graciously introduced as "a former prosecutor of sex crimes and a mother."

Visibly pregnant with a prominent diamond ring on her left finger, this well-coiffed and well-dressed lawyer reminded her audience of the important deterrent effects of criminal law and conveyed the horrors of human trafficking as follows:

I'd like to tell you the story of Christina, who . . . was a victim of human trafficking. She came here as a 19 or 20 year old woman in response to an ad for what she thought was a babysitting job, and when she arrived at JFK airport . . . she was then informed that the babysitting job wasn't available anymore. . . . Of course . . . she was forced to work in a brothel, and she describes that experience with the same words that any of us would use to describe it. She describes the sex of prostitution as disgusting, as degradation, and profoundly traumatic to her, and what I want to talk to you about is some of the lasting effects are for her, after she escaped the experience. She is infertile. She can never have children.

Nearly identical narratives were presented at the multiple anti-trafficking conferences that I attended throughout the course of my fieldwork, the only significant alteration being the victim's name.[70] Yet there is much to unpack in this exposition of the harms of trafficking through the presentation of "Christina's story," which in its sheer generality suggests that it is at least partially fictionalized and at best a strategically constructed composite case. Particularly notable are the moral and political legitimacy afforded to domestic care work as late-capitalist informal-sector employment,[71] the invocation of a single gendered (and uniformly negative) experience of "the sex of prostitution,"[72] and the construal of reproductive failure as the worst possible harm that could result for female victims. While individual elements of this narrative undoubtedly can and do happen to real individuals, as a representation of human trafficking the scenario described was far from the most empirically prevalent case. Even more curiously, files compiled by the US Department of Justice between 2004 and 2008 contained no trafficking cases which matched this description.[73] The lawyer's simultaneous commitments to the carceral state, the capitalist service sector, and the ideology of feminist family values perfectly paralleled the underlying neoliberal logic that united these realms, in which the social inequalities that globalization has wrought are legitimate so long as the sexual boundaries of middle-class family life can be maintained.

At a discussion focused on "ending demand" for sex trafficking at the Commission on the Status of Women meetings that I attended at the United Nations in March 2007, the link between sexual and carceral politics was once again revealed. At this meeting dedicated to problematizing men's "demand" for the services of sex workers, the panelists used the occasion to directly showcase how the carceral state could be effectively harnessed to achieve amatively coupled and sexually egalitarian nuclear families.[74] The opening speaker from the Coalition against Trafficking in Women explicitly hailed the five white, middle-class men in the room as exemplars of a new model of enlightened masculinity and urged the audience members "to bring their husbands, sons, and brothers" to future meetings. The model of prostitution and trafficking that the CATW panelists invoked bore little, if any, connection to structural or economic factors, rendering prostitution wholly attributable to the actions of bad men: husbands within the family who might appeal to the sexual services of women outside of it, or bad men outside the family (coded as nonwhite and foreign) who might entice women and girls within it to leave.[75] Although the CATW regards itself as a progressive feminist organization, members displayed no hesitation in their appeals to a punitive state apparatus. Nor did they demonstrate much awareness of the political-economic underpinnings, or limited historical scope, of the singular form of heterosexual familial intimacy that they advocated. As the panel chair repeatedly emphasized during her sharply condemnatory presentation about heterosexual men's purchase of sex: "The only thing that prevents recurrence is fear of arrest."

In my fieldwork with feminist activists, the utility of the carceral state for securitizing the middle-class family—and more specifically, for domesticating heterosexual men—was also manifest in frequent appeals to the case of Sweden as an exemplar of enlightened anti-trafficking policy. The criminalization of male sex purchasers, a policy model first implemented in Sweden in 1998, is often referred to by transnational feminist activists as the "Swedish Plan" to convey its feminist origins and impact, since Sweden is considered by many to be the most gender-egalitarian country in the world. It was thus that at a subsequent CATW panel that I attended called "Abolishing Sex Slavery: From Stockholm to Hunts Point," the Swedish policy of criminalizing the clients of sex workers was endorsed by speakers who not only applauded Sweden's reputation for gender equality but who explicitly referenced the Swedish welfare state's commitment to "promoting men to be home with their children at a young age." Left unremarked upon in the transnational dissemination of this carceral strategy is that Sweden itself embraced it only after its hallmark welfare state (which earned it its feminist reputation in the first place) had been seriously weakened in the 1990s.[76]

Elaborating on the mutual imbrication of "material" and "cultural" politics, feminist theorists of neoliberalism such as Lisa Duggan have pointed out the ways in which the ideology of "family values" becomes particularly critical when other possibilities for social relations are eclipsed. Marriage as an institution is "grounded in the privatization of social reproduction, along with the care of human dependency needs, through personal responsibility exercised in the family and in civil society—thus shifting costs from state agencies to individuals and households."[77] The demise of the welfare state and the ascendance of law-and-order politics, both premised on the promotion of "personal responsibility" and the condemnation of public disorder, are thus directly correlated not just as institutional alternatives to managing the racialized poor (as Wacquant has suggested) but also via "the dense interrelations" between neoliberalism's economic and (gendered) cultural projects. Specifically, Duggan argues that the rise of "family values" politics is necessary to fill in the caring gaps that the obliterated welfare state has left vacant. Building upon this analysis, we see that the neoliberal state can be harnessed to notions of "domesticating men" that operate simultaneously at two different levels: men, particularly poor and working-class men, are encouraged to do more care work within the home and to take on the burdens of social reproduction that arise when women themselves move into the sphere of paid work. At the same time, professional middle-class men are encouraged to constrain their commercial consumption in ways that are compatible with heterosexual domesticity and amative love.

Carceral Politics—Left, Right, and Center

The above examples highlight an important alliance between feminism and the carceral state, one that extends beyond recent feminist partnerships with the religious right wing. In her book tracing the coemergence of second-wave feminist attention to sexual violence and neoliberal agendas of incarceration, the political scientist Kristin Bumiller has similarly demonstrated the ways in which a myopic feminist focus upon the criminalization of rape and domestic violence during the 1990s contrasted with grassroots and early second-wave feminist concerns about women's social and economic empowerment.[78] Arguing that the neoliberal carceral imperative has had a devastating impact upon the ways that feminist engagement with sexual violence has been framed, Bumiller demonstrates that the reciprocal is also true: once feminism became fatally inflected by neoliberal strategies of social control, it could serve as an effective inspiration for broader campaigns for criminalization (such as the war on drugs). Bumiller observes that by the early 2000s, the neoliberal sexual violence agenda of feminism was increasingly being exported as part of American human rights policy, solidifying the carceral imperative within feminism domestically and spreading the paradigm of feminism-as-crime-control around the globe.

The evidence indeed suggests that contemporary anti-trafficking campaigns have been far more successful at criminalizing marginalized populations, enforcing border control, and measuring other countries' compliance with human rights standards based on the curtailment of prostitution than they have been at issuing any concrete benefits to victims. For example, Nandita Sharma—one of various scholars and activists who have argued that anti-trafficking measures have been complicit with anti-immigrant policies—has critically considered the impact of anti-trafficking politics on women who have migrated from China to Canada. Unlike their male counterparts, migrating women and children migrants were often labeled as "victims of trafficking" by Canadian feminists who hoped to garner sympathy and legal status for them. For the Canadian minister of immigration, however, this instead gave him a reason to confine the women in state-run detention facilities and jails.[79]

In like fashion, Sealing Cheng has highlighted the ways that Filipina migrant sex workers in South Korea have been constrained by the very forces that purportedly seek to protect them—specifically, the criminalization of sex work and migration for sex work, and the practices of NGOs and government organizations that seek to enforce these. Svati Shah has similarly shown how the exportation of US anti-trafficking politics to India has been to the latter's detriment, citing the 2005 ban against women dancing for tips in beer bars as an example. She explains that India's tier 2 position on the Department of State's annual *Trafficking in Persons Report* likely motivated the ban, so as to not move down to tier 3 and potentially lose all nonhumanitarian aid from the United States, India would have to show that the country was making significant efforts to comply with "the minimum standards for the elimination of trafficking."[80] Responding to related concerns, in 2008 Cambodia introduced anti-trafficking legislation ostensibly designed to suppress human trafficking and sexual exploitation. On the basis of observational research with female sex workers, Lisa Maher and her colleagues found that following the introduction of the law, there was an escalation in police crackdowns and brothel closures, with sex workers being displaced to streets and guesthouses, impacting their ability to negotiate safe sex and increasing their exposure to violence. Many sex workers and their children (alongside beggars, vendors, and other informal sector workers) were also arrested in the frequent street sweeps that accompanied passage of the new law.[81]

Finally, as the human rights lawyers Anne Gallagher and Elaine Pearson have observed, "in countries and regions around the world, including Bangladesh, Central and Eastern Europe, Cambodia, India, Israel, Malaysia, Nepal, the Russian Federation, Nigeria, Sri Lanka, Taiwan, and Thailand, it is common practice for victims of trafficking to be effectively imprisoned in government or private support facilities without being able to leave the shelter grounds beyond the occasional supervised excursion or trip to court." While they note that shelters differ in terms of size, location, required length of stay, services provided, and populations served, in many cases, they report, the facilities are in fact little more than jails.[82]

As these scholars have demonstrated, the failure of anti-trafficking campaigns to understand the complexities of the very phenomenon with which they purport to be concerned has resulted in more perilous journeys for economic migrants, more dangerous working conditions for sex workers, and heightened coercion and control of the very women and children that they seek to protect. These examples are more than mere "unintended consequences" of feminist anti-trafficking campaigns; rather, as Bumiller has argued, they have transpired as a result of feminists directly joining forces with a neoliberal project of social control. This is true both within the United States, where pimps of all varieties can now be given lifelong prison sentences as convicted "sex traffickers" and sex workers' clients are held criminally culpable for their actions,[83] as well as elsewhere around the globe, where the United States' tiered ranking of other countries has led to the tightening of borders internationally and to the passage of punitive anti-prostitution policies in numerous countries.

Most recently, with gathering feminist attention to so-called "domestic" forms of trafficking, in which the requirements of national and state border crossing are lifted, it has become clear that the shift from local forms of sexual violence to the international field back to a concern with policing US inner cities (this time under the guise of protecting women's human rights) has provided critical circuitry for the carceral feminist agenda. As described in chapter 1, the 2005 reauthorization of the US Trafficking Victim's Protection Act (TVPRA) established the crime of "domestic trafficking" on a moral and legal par with previous cross-border understandings of the crime.[84] According to a Department of Justice summation of 2,515 human trafficking investigations conducted between 2008 and 2010, of 389 confirmed incidents of trafficking, 85% were sex-trafficking cases, 83% of victims were US citizens, and 62% of confirmed sex trafficking suspects were African American (while 25% of

2.3   "Rescued" sex workers in lockdown in Phnom Penh, Cambodia. The 2008 mobile phone
      photo here, taken by a Cambodian human rights worker, captures the extent to which
      freedom and incarceration become literally equated in contemporary anti-trafficking
      campaigns, where women's freedom is obtained not just via the punishment of so-called
      "traffickers" but also through the incarceration of sex workers themselves. Photo: Asia
      Pacific Network of Sex Workers.

all suspects were Hispanic or Latino).[85] Adding empirical detail to these
statistics, US attorney Pamela Chen has noted that a full half of federal
trafficking cases currently concern underage women in inner-city street
prostitution.[86] Both domestically and globally, US anti-trafficking policies have thus facilitated a sharp reversal of the trend toward the increasing legitimacy of sexual labor and the recognition of sex workers' rights
that prevailed up until the late 1990s.[87]

A final example of the carceral feminist commitment to heteronormative family values, crime control, and the "rescue and restoration"
of victims (or what the religious studies scholar Janet Jakobsen has al-
literatively glossed as "marriage, militarism and markets") and the broad
social appeal of this agenda is powerfully illustrated by the 2008 documentary film *Very Young Girls*.[88] The film has been shown not only in diverse feminist venues but also on HBO, at the State Department, at various evangelical megachurches, and at the conservative Christian King's
College.[89] Under the rubric of portraying domestic trafficking, the film

2.4 Promotional poster for the film *Very Young Girls* (2007).

seeks to garner sympathy for young African American women who find themselves trapped in the street-level sexual economy. By framing the women as "very young girls" (in the promotional poster for the film, the seated protagonist depicted is so small that her feet dangle from the chair) and as the innocent victims of sexual abuse (a category that has historically been reserved for white and non-sex-working victims), the film can convincingly present its perspective as anti-racist and progressive.[90] Yet the young women's innocence in the film is achieved at the cost of completely demonizing the young African American men who profit from their earnings, and who, consistent with the classic tropes of carceral feminism, are presented as irredeemably criminal and subhuman. The film relentlessly strips away the humanity of young African American men in the street economy along with the complex tangle of factors beyond prostitution (including racism and poverty) that shape the girls' lives. At the November 2007 screening of the film that I attended at an elite law firm in New York, following the film some audience members called for the pimps not only to be locked away indefinitely but also to be physically assaulted. In *Very Young Girls*, as in carceral feminism more generally, a vision of social justice as criminal justice, and of punitive systems of control as the best motivational deterrents for men's bad behavior, serves as a crucial point of connection with state actors, evangelicals, and others who have embraced the anti-trafficking cause.

Conclusion: A Neoliberal Circuitry of Sex, Crime, and Rights

In the discussion above, I have sought to illustrate how the rise of a carceral feminist framework is connected to the collapse of a social welfare state in more ways than one—both as a new social strategy for regulating race and class others and as part of a neoliberal *gender* strategy that securitizes the family and lends moral primacy to marriage. Viewed as such, it becomes clear that as neoliberal economic policies extend their reach around the globe, they will serve to diffuse a new criminal justice-focused social agenda in tandem with a new political paradigm of gender and sexuality that is premised upon the (feminist) family value of amative, sexually egalitarian couples. This new paradigm has been disseminated through such disparate means as stepped-up laws and controls against sex offenders (including proposals for a new pan-European sex offender registry), the insertion of men into private-sphere caring labor via official World Bank development policy, and burgeoning international campaigns against the "traffic in women."[91] Indeed, one of the reasons that anti-trafficking campaigns have become such a galvanizing issue for feminists, evangelicals, and other activists is because the interlinked sexual, carceral, and economic commitments that constitute them can be harnessed to the now-hegemonic internationalist discourse of women's human rights. With "women's human rights" understood as pertaining exclusively to questions of sexual violence and to bodily integrity (but not to the gendered dimensions of broader social, economic, and cultural issues), the human rights model in its global manifestation has become a highly effective means of disseminating feminist carceral politics on a global scale.[92]

In this chapter, I have also sought to push forward arguments made by recent social analysts concerning the emergence of the carceral state and its relationship to more general patterns of cultural and political transformation. Building upon diverse accounts of the relationship between neoliberalism and the turn toward punitive modes of justice in contemporary social policy, I have highlighted the implicit gendered dimensions of this shift as well as its disparately raced and classed impact, melding theories of carcerality and punishment with insights drawn from my own empirical research on campaigns against sex trafficking. I have sought to show how an understanding of recent transformations within feminism, and within the politics of sex and gender more generally, is critical to the broad-sweeping analyses of the neoliberal carceral state that recent social theorists have formulated. Via successive encodings of issues such as rape, sexual harassment, pornography, sexual violence, prostitution, and trafficking into federal and international criminal law, mainstream feminists have provided crucial ideological support to the ushering in of contemporary carceral transitions.[93]

It is important to understand the underlying gendered and sexual dynamics that have inspired this shift in feminist emphasis and strategy. Many analysts of neoliberal carceral strategies (including Garland, Wacquant, Simon, and Alexander, among others) have failed to consider the gendered interests that underpin feminist advocacy on behalf of the neoliberal carceral state. My own ethnographic research in tandem with other feminist analyses of the sexual politics of neoliberalism helps to clarify this allegiance, demonstrating how the intersecting race, class, and gender locations of a prominent contingent of Western feminists has created deep political investments in the contemporary security state and in the middle-class family form.

Earlier in this chapter, I noted how Jonathan Simon usefully observed the ways in which the contemporary security state serves not only to police the poor but also to create middle-class understandings of securitized "freedom." Building on Simon's insight, we now see the important role that carceral feminism has played in advancing this very project. My research on the contemporary anti-trafficking movement helps illuminate precisely how and why feminists have reoriented their political aims toward carceral ends, situating ideological transitions in terms of the new political-economic horizons that feminists are confronting: contemporary feminist commitments to both "family values" and to a law-and-order agenda are facilitated by a neoliberal state apparatus in which poor as well as middle-class lives are increasingly governed through crime, and in which the privatized family is designated as the optimal institution for social support. Under such circumstances, the impetus to find noneconomic means to equalize the dynamics of sexual power in the family—such as governing through crime—becomes compelling to many feminist (and as we will see in the next chapter, evangelical Christian) social justice advocates. Rather than pursuing materially redistributive strategies, the versions of feminism that have survived and thrived are those that deploy the mutually reinforcing sexual and carceral strategies that a reconfigured neoliberal state is likely to support.

Most generally, this chapter has shown how attention to social actors' carceral commitments is pivotal to understanding the politics that have joined together "left" and "right," and feminists and evangelicals (as well as a disparate array of other social actors), on sexual issues, and vice versa. Via a close examination of anti-trafficking campaigns, we see how neoliberal sexual politics and carceral politics work together, and the cross-ideological alignments that have occurred around both sex and crime. As theorists of "strange bedfellows" political alliances have persuasively argued, in the present historical moment, sex is often the vehicle that joins left and right together around an agenda of criminal justice. My own analysis of contemporary anti-trafficking campaigns has demonstrated how the reciprocal is also true: criminal justice has often been the most effective vehicle for binding diverse parties together around historically and socially specific ideals of sex, gender, and the family. In this way, contemporary anti-trafficking campaigns can be viewed as an effective, feminist embodiment of neoliberalism's joint carceral and sexual projects, ushering in agendas of family values and crime control while asserting new understandings of gender justice and women's human rights. To fully understand the rise of the carceral state and its relationship to late-capitalist social transformations, we need a feminist analytics of neoliberalism that is cognizant of how mutually reinforcing sexual and carceral strategies have come to circulate together.

THREE

Seek Justice™

Seek justice, rescue the oppressed, defend the orphan, plead for the widow.
ISAIAH 1:17, FROM THE WEBSITE OF THE INTERNATIONAL JUSTICE MISSION

Trafficking is not a poverty issue. It's a law enforcement issue.
GARY HAUGEN, DIRECTOR AND CHIEF EXECUTIVE OFFICER OF THE INTERNATIONAL
JUSTICE MISSION[1]

We're seeking a business takeover—a freedom business takeover of the sex
business. KERRY HILTON, FREESET CORPORATION[2]

On Sunday, 18 February 2007, 5,800 Protestant churches
throughout the United States sang the song "Amazing Grace"
during their services, commemorating the two-hundredth
anniversary of the abolition of slavery in England. As the
congregants sang the lyrics of John Newton, the British
ship captain-turned-abolitionist, they were simultaneously
contributing to a growing political movement and to the
promotion of a just-released film. The film, *Amazing Grace*,
which focuses on the role of British parliamentarian William
Wilberforce's evangelical Christian faith in his dedication to
the nineteenth-century abolitionist cause, was produced in
explicit coordination with a campaign to combat "modern
day" forms of slavery, of which the organized Sunday sing-
along was a part.[3] "Slavery still exists," proclaimed the movie's Amazing Change campaign website, which directed web
browsers to "become modern-day abolitionists" through
prayer, donations to sponsored faith-based organizations,
and the purchase of Amazing Change T-shirts, buttons, and
caps. As Gary Haugen, founder of the International Justice

Mission (one of the campaign's four sponsored humanitarian organizations), sought to emphasize: "There are approximately twenty-seven million slaves in our world today—not metaphorical slaves, but actual slaves. That's more slaves in our world today than were extracted from Africa during four hundred years of the transatlantic slave trade."[4]

What does it mean to claim that there are twenty-seven million slaves worldwide, more than in the transatlantic slave trade? As Julia O'Connell Davidson has observed, current campaigns against modern-day slavery supplant "the theoretical, philosophical, and political problems" inherent in defining slavery via "the identification of its singular moral wrongness." Once the term "slavery" is "cut loose from its moorings in the New World institution of chattel slavery," she cautions, "it starts to billow out uncontrollably, stretching to include all manner of human rights violations."[5] Though the primary focus of O'Connell Davidson's analysis is secular anti-trafficking campaigns, her concerns are similarly apt when it comes to new evangelical discourse about the prevalence of modern-day slavery and sex trafficking in the contemporary world.

Exceeding even the ambitious statistical estimations produced by the US State Department, the figure of twenty-seven million is frequently invoked by the broad coalition of evangelical Christian activists and nongovernmental organizations that, since the late 1990s, have self-identified as "modern-day abolitionists" in their struggle to combat what they see as a diverse yet intertwined array of human rights abuses, one which potentially ranges from trafficking across borders to indentured labor in rock quarries to participation in some (or all) forms of commercial sexual activity. Although the trope of "modern-day slavery" and the numerical estimate of twenty-seven million derive from the work of Free the Slaves cofounder Kevin Bales, who has defined slavery as "the total control of one person by another for the purpose of economic exploitation," what the disparate abolitionist groups (or even Bales himself) mean by the term when they invoke it is by no means transparent.[6] How, for example, is "modern-day" slavery distinct from chattel slavery, wage slavery, or what was once known as white slavery? Of what, for the evangelical Christian activists and faith-based NGOs concerned, does the fight against modern-day slavery consist? Who is a slave? And how does the movement for slavery's (re)abolition relate to a contemporary evangelical worldview? Or to neoliberal cultural politics more generally?

My aim in this chapter is to further consider how it is that prostitution, something previously of concern only to local law enforcement and to relatively small numbers of committed feminists and sex worker–activists, would come to occupy the center of an ever-spiraling array of faith-based and secular activist agendas, human rights initiatives, and legal instruments. Building on my analysis of the emergence of carceral feminism in the previous chapter, my focus here rests on the less frequently examined (and usually presumed to be self-evident) ideological commitments of evangelical Christians. Evangelical advocacy on human trafficking achieved particular prominence after the Bush administration's expansion of the Charitable Choice initiative, which declared avowedly faith-based organizations to be eligible for federal funding. Since 2002, the year of its implementation, evangelical Christian groups have secured a growing proportion of federal monies for both international and domestic anti-trafficking work as well as funds for the prevention of HIV/AIDS.[7] Despite the displacement of formerly prominent religious right constituencies in debates over political issues such as gay marriage and abortion during the purportedly more secular presidency of Barack Obama, the fostering of evangelical activism around a broad array of social issues not only persisted but in fact accelerated.[8]

In this chapter, I consider the means by which evangelical activists successfully formed and perpetuated political alliances with secular feminists and state actors around a particular shared premise: that prostitution is a form of gendered social exchange that constitutes the antithesis of freedom. No doubt, the globalization, expansion, and diversification of sexual commerce in prior decades were relevant factors in fostering this consensus. Indeed, the first few sentences of the 2000 Trafficking Victims Protection Act stated explicitly that the explosion of the sex industry during the preceding years had been an important impetus for the law. Yet the position of cultural and political prominence that has been granted to prostitution in contemporary Christian narratives of slavery (and to the forced sexual labor of the "third-world prostitute," in particular) remains puzzling, given that the issue presumably exists at some remove from the lives of the overwhelmingly white and middle-class activists who embrace it as their cause. As we have seen, the portrayal of most or all prostitution as "slavery" is also curious in light of the actual working conditions of most sex workers. Given the distance of forced prostitution from activists' own lives and from the experiences of the majority of individuals who engage in sexual labor, it is necessary to summon other explanations in order to comprehend the significance of the campaigns to "free the slaves" that have spread through church pews, college campuses, and federal and state legislatures at the dawn of the twenty-first century.

In what follows, I draw upon my ethnographic and policy research with evangelical Christian activists to argue that the alliance that proved to be so efficacious in framing contemporary anti-trafficking politics was the product of two historically unique and intersecting trends: a rightward shift on the part of many mainstream feminists and other secular liberals away from a redistributive model of justice and toward a politics of incarceration, coincident with a leftward move on the part of many younger evangelicals away from the isolationist issues of abortion and gay marriage and toward a globally oriented social justice theology. Contemporary anti-trafficking politics have occurred squarely at this intersection, and, despite divergent political trajectories, both evangelical Christian and secular feminists have come to harbor similar understandings of freedom, justice, and foreign and domestic policy.

From White Slavery to "Modern-Day" Slavery

It is slavery, real slavery that we are fighting. The term "white slave" isn't a misnomer or a sensational term. . . . The words describe what they stand for. The white slave of Chicago is a slave as much as the Negro was before the Civil War, as the African is in the districts of the Congo, as much as any people are slaves who are owned, flesh and bone, body and soul, by another person, and who can be sold at any time and place and for any price at that person's will. That is what slavery is, and that is the condition of hundreds, yes, thousands of girls in Chicago at present. CLIFFORD ROE, "THE DANGERS OF A LARGE CITY; OR, THE SYSTEM OF THE UNDERWORLD EXPOSING THE WHITE SLAVE TRAFFIC"[9]

As we have seen in prior chapters, the sudden and dramatic refashioning of commercialized sex as "slavery" is not without historical precedent. At the turn of the twentieth century, for example, narratives of women's sexual enslavement abounded, drawing on both the nation's legacy of race-based, chattel slavery and a resonance with biblical notions of "slavery to sin." Thus, Clifford Roe, in his popular tract on white slavery from the era, also included the iconic image of "a White Christian woman behind bars, her hands clasped together as if in prayer, her eyes looking mournfully up to heaven."[10] Historians have also generally agreed that, in association with a rising tide of anti-immigrant sentiment, the late nineteenth- and early twentieth-century fight against white slavery served as a socially acceptable vehicle in which bourgeois women could channel their frustrations with the sexual double standard and an increasingly legitimate commercial sexual sphere. For both evangelical women and for secular feminists, the fight against white slavery served as a useful stepping-stone and surrogate for a host of additional causes, from social purity and moral reform to temperance and suffrage.[11]

As we have also seen, many of the tropes that animated the social uprisings around white slavery in the previous century have been recycled in campaigns against "modern-day slavery" in the current one, including those of violated femininity, shattered innocence, and the victimization of "womenandchildren."[12] Penelope Saunders thus notes that it is precisely such shared ideological constructions that have served to unite the diverse constituencies that comprise today's modern-day abolitionist cause.[13] Jacqueline Berman has posited that, for conservative Christians, stopping sexual slavery stands as a politically uncontroversial surrogate for an array of more familiar, right-wing concerns: advocacy around family values, the promotion of abstinence, and "the rescue of women from risky, post-1960s norms like work outside the home."[14] Similarly, Gretchen Soderlund has observed the dovetailing of right-wing efforts to curb prostitution and to curtail women's reproductive rights, arguing that current US anti-trafficking policy became "deeply intertwined with attempts by the Bush administration and its faith-based constituency to police nonprocreative sex on a global scale."[15]

The roster of prominent nongovernmental organizations that have catapulted the fight against sexual slavery to the top of their agendas would indeed seem to suggest that a sexual politics premised upon the reinstatement of traditional sex and gender roles underlies the attention that many conservative Christians have granted to the issue. Alongside established secular feminist constituencies such as the Coalition against Trafficking in Women, Equality Now, and the Feminist Majority stand such well-known Christian-right groups as Focus on the Family, the Family Research Council, and Concerned Women for America, an extraordinary left-right alliance that political scientist Allen Hertzke has gone so far as to describe as "the most significant human rights movement of our time."[16] My initial field research with conservative Christian anti-trafficking activists also seemed to bolster the conclusion that there is a traditionalist sexual and gender agenda at stake in fighting "modern-day slavery" that extends well beyond the issues of trafficking and prostitution. For example, at a Concerned Women for America anti-trafficking panel that I attended at the UN Beijing + 10 meetings in 2005, which occurred immediately after the group received a grant from the State Department to combat trafficking on the US-Mexico border, the presentation focused exclusively on the perils posed to women by abortion and premarital sex, with prostitution mentioned only once—and briefly—during the two-hour session. The chairwoman Janice Crouse responded to an audience member's question about the phenomenon of human trafficking not by discussing trafficking per se but by talking about the risks of promiscuity—and implicitly prostitution—faced by teenage girls at the mall. Observers of conservative Christian engagement in the abortion debates of the 1980s will also note the direct migration of language and slogans from earlier campaigns to curtail women's access to abortion, which similarly relied upon the metaphors of slavery, rescue, and abolition (as well as warfare and the Holocaust) to generate passion and commitment for their cause.[17]

The dovetailing of the anti-trafficking movement and of a traditionalist sexual and gender politics is further manifest in popular Christian Right publications such as *Focus on the Family*, *Today's Christian Woman*, and *World*, which have repeatedly featured lead articles on the "record numbers" of women being trafficked into commercial sexual slavery.[18] According to one such article, coerced abortions, family and sexual violence, biotechnology, human trafficking, and prostitution form the cluster of socially intertwined phenomena that place women's lives at greatest risk. Affirming the conclusions of scholars such as R. Marie Griffith, Linda Kintz, and Christian Smith who have described how evangelical women find "power in submission" to traditional gender roles and male headship, here it is modern sexual culture and technology that constitute the fundament of slavery, and traditional sex and gender roles that best encapsulate what it means for women to be "free."[19] As Berman has suggested, "In a globalizing world where women make decisions about illicit sexuality, capital, and movement in relation to prostitution, work, sex work, migrant sex work, and migration, these . . . groups have come to agree that it is the availability of these options that pose a danger to women, to 'our' culture, to 'our' communities."[20]

To read contemporary Christian campaigns against "modern-day slavery" as a reaction as much against "the modern" as against slavery is also consistent with an established body of sociological and journalistic work that argues that in late-capitalist America, individuals' experiences of economic disempowerment have often been compensated for with staunch commitments to traditional configurations of both gender and sexuality in the domestic sphere. Classic works such as Kristin Luker's *Abortion and the Politics of Motherhood*, Arlene Stein's *The Stranger Next Door*, and Thomas Frank's *What's the Matter with Kansas* have posited diverse ways in which the moral and sexual politics of conservative Christians can be read as class-based reactions to the hegemonic sexual cultures of elites.[21] For example, in her well-known study of pro-life and pro-choice activists in the abortion debates, Kristin Luker observed that the secular idea that personhood is social as opposed to God-given implies to conservative Christians that some individuals have a less compelling claim on scarce resources than others. This worldview is seen as particularly threatening by persons "who have reason to fear that they may be denied such access"

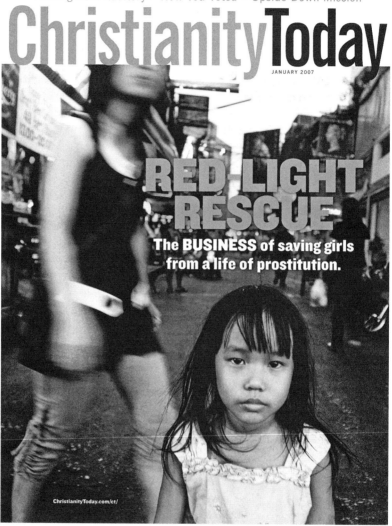

Reeling from Adultery • How You Voted • Upside-Down Mission

ChristianityToday

JANUARY 2007

RED-LIGHT RESCUE

The BUSINESS of saving girls from a life of prostitution.

ChristianityToday.com/ct/

3.1 (above) and 3.2 (right)   Representations of human trafficking in recent evangelical Christian media. Reprinted with permission.

to resources.[22] In her study of conservative Christian opposition to gay rights legislation, Arlene Stein similarly found that the debate over homosexuality could be decoded in class terms: "Attitudes towards homosexuality appeared to correlate with divisions between a declining working class that felt itself displaced and ignored, and a rising professional

Christianity Today
eSSENTIALS

The War on Women

*The world's worst holocaust,
and how Christians are saving
one girl at a time.*

· ·

MARIAN LIAUTAUD

Foreword by Mark Galli

3.3 A recent issue of *Christianity Today* celebrates evangelical advocacy around human trafficking. Reprinted with permission.

class [that] . . . tended to support abortion and gay rights."[23] And Thomas Frank has famously argued that "moral values" issues such as abortion and gay marriage in fact serve as an intricately managed spectacle to convince disenfranchised, working-class Americans to vote against their true economic interests. Correlating activists' ideological commitments with their material circumstances, these authors attribute evangelicals' conservative stances on matters of sexual politics to the spiritualized discontent of those whom the global economy has left behind.

New Abolitionists?

Yet as I delved further into my research, the relevance of this analysis seemed to fade in relation to the sexual politics of modern-day abolitionism, particularly as some of the most prominent anti-trafficking activists in question did not identify with the Christian right at all, but rather described themselves as Christian "moderates," and in some cases, even as Christian progressives.[24] Similarly, my interpretations of this movement began to shift when it became clearer to me that the most strident activism around sexual slavery had been fomented not by individuals who were especially disenfranchised, but by the emergent evangelical professional middle classes.[25] My ethnographic fieldwork with activists increasingly came to suggest the need for a more subtle and nuanced empirical rendering of evangelicals' sexual politics and class interests, one that would also complicate the relatively straightforward connection between moral politics and material circumstances that Luker, Stein, Frank, and others have posited.[26]

As I argue in this section, a new group of highly educated and relatively affluent evangelicals have pursued some of the most active and passionate campaigning around sexual slavery and human trafficking. These evangelicals embrace the languages of women's rights and social justice, and they have taken deliberate steps to distinguish their work from the sexual politics of other conservative Christians. Richard Cizik, the former vice president of the National Association of Evangelicals and a self-described evangelical moderate, has gone on record describing the efforts of his organization to reorient conservative Christians away from issues such as homosexuality and abortion, and toward more "common denominator" concerns such as global warming, prison reform, human trafficking, and HIV/AIDS. David Batstone, a former editor at the liberal evangelical *Sojourners* magazine and the author of *Not for Sale* (the official book of the Amazing Change new-abolitionist campaign), is also spearheading his own Not for Sale social movement, which aims to unite churches, universities, businesses, and individuals who take a pledge to fight slavery. And the officially nonpartisan International Justice Mission (IJM), the largest and most established Christian anti-trafficking organization in the United States, with upward of eighty full-time paid staff members and operations in fourteen countries, boasts the endorsements not only of Chuck Colson from the far-right Wilberforce Forum but also of noted "left" evangelicals such as Tony Campolo and Jim Wallis.[27] According to one IJM staff member whom I spoke with, the organization's staff members—who are required to endorse a Christian statement of faith as a condition for their employment and who spend the initial hours of each workday engaged in collective prayer—have even debated abandoning the term "evangelical" entirely because of its troubling associations with the right wing.[28]

The fact that contemporary campaigns against modern-day slavery have been vigorously embraced by Christian moderates and liberals does not, however, mean that they are linked to a sexual agenda that most sex workers' rights activists (or others with a critical feminist perspective) would likely find progressive. In the remainder of this chapter, I shall take a brief detour into several moments from my fieldwork that exemplify the sexual politics that a growing body of self-described moderate and liberal evangelicals bring to contemporary anti-trafficking campaigns. Consistent with the sexual politics of carceral feminism, new-abolitionist evangelicals adhere to a neoliberal (rather than a traditionalist) sexual agenda, one that locates social problems in deviant individuals rather than mainstream institutions, that seeks social remedies through criminal justice interventions rather than through a redistributive welfare state, and that advocates for the beneficence of the privileged rather than the empowerment of the oppressed. As such, this approach leaves intact the social structures that drive low-income women (and many men) into patterns of risky migration and exploitative informal-sector employment, including those relatively rare but very real situations that might rightly qualify as "trafficking" or "slavery." Finally, by examining more closely the dovetailing of contemporary secular feminist and evangelical Christian anti-trafficking efforts—which I describe, respectively, under the rubrics of carceral feminism and militarized humanitarianism—and both groups' pursuit of avowedly pro-business social remedies, I hope to reveal some of the neoliberal underpinnings, and political limitations, of both faith-based and secular variants of the modern-abolitionist cause.

"Our God of (Criminal) Justice": Militarizing Humanitarianism in New Evangelical Anti-Trafficking Campaigns

Citychurch [a pseudonym] is a Christian megachurch in Manhattan that I have attended occasionally since beginning this project, a church that several young evangelicals in the anti-trafficking movement have recommended to me highly.[29] Tonight I am at an event sponsored by the women's ministry, a discussion with faith-based movement leaders that is dedicated to the issue of sex trafficking. Our meeting takes place at the Church's midtown headquarters, where some hundred young women have gathered.

The session begins with a brief collective prayer led by a young white woman who addresses her entreaty to "Our God of Justice" as the congregants bow their heads solemnly. She beckons Him to allow His spirit to move tonight's speakers in sharing what He is doing "to bring about justice in the world." The panel moderator approaches the podium next: she is an exuberant young woman who describes how she has dedicated her life to helping the broken and the hurting. She explains that her own activism around trafficking was initially inspired by Maria's story, that of a virgin who left her hometown in Mexico only to find herself in a brothel. Although it remains unclear how she first learned about Maria, and the story itself is short on specifics, her eyes well up as she speaks to us, as do those of many other women who are gathered in the room.

The first panelist is a thin, white bespectacled woman in her mid-thirties who founded the group Restore, a New York organization for women coming out of sexual slavery. Recently, her organization has begun a collaboration with the New York Asian Women's Center, forging a Christian-secular alliance which works to the benefit of both groups: the fact that her own organization's funding comes from the Church means that they are not beholden to government guidelines (such as official certification) in order to identify victims. This allows them to work with people "they know have been trafficked" even if the women in question refuse to admit it. Members of the organization locate victims by stationing themselves in Queens and Manhattan community courts and approaching women who have pled guilty to prostitution charges after their brothels have been raided. She explains that "by them pleading guilty, they're court mandated to receive services from us which at least gives us some opportunity to gain their trust."

The next speaker, an Asian American man with a self-effacing but affable demeanor, discusses the trafficking situation between North Korea and China. He argues that the problem has been spurred on the supply side by the spiritual crisis that prevails in North Korea, and on the demand side by China's one child policy, the abandonment of girl children, and the consequent gender imbalance between women and men. The mission of his organization is to provide food and medical assistance to trafficking victims, in addition to sharing the gospel.

The last speaker is a young woman from the International Justice Mission, who begins her presentation by declaring her joy at being a part of "this global transformation of the Church." She applauds the new work that churches are doing to fight injustice, urging those in the audience to reconsider Psalm 10. "Listen to this description of an oppressor," she offers, before pausing briefly for dramatic effect: "He lies in wait near the villages. From ambush he murders the innocent. Watching in secret for his victims, he lies in wait like a lion in cover. He lies in wait to catch the helpless. He catches the helpless and drags them off in his net." FROM MY FIELD NOTES, MARCH 2009

Among many left-leaning secular critics of contemporary anti-trafficking campaigns, old stereotypes persist about the underlying cultural politics and broader social interests that have guided contemporary evangelical Christians toward this issue, a group that is frequently assumed to be one and the same with the anti-pornography, anti-abortion, and anti–gay rights activists of generations past. Although avowedly Christian right groups such as Concerned Women for America and the Salvation Army have also been active participants in the contemporary anti-trafficking crusade, my research in "justice-oriented" churches such as Citychurch, at prayer gatherings for trafficking victims, and at evangelical anti-trafficking conferences and film screenings suggests that such groups do not represent the preponderance of evangelical Christian grassroots activity.

Instead, a new group of young, highly educated, and relatively affluent evangelicals who often describe themselves as pertaining to the "justice generation" have pursued some of the most active and passionate campaigning around sexual slavery and human trafficking. Although many of these evangelicals remain opposed to the availability of both gay marriage and abortion, they do not grant these issues the same political priority as their more conservative peers. Instead, young evangelicals have argued that the best way to forge an effective politics is to move away from "hot-button" controversies around gender and sexuality and to focus upon issues of social justice and humanitarianism more broadly. It is for this reason that they have increasingly focused their attention and their activism upon what they understand to be uncontroversial and consensus-building issues such as global warming, human trafficking, and HIV/AIDS.

Despite these ambitions, we shall see that the new evangelical pursuit of social justice that has spawned the anti-trafficking movement remains wedded to a particular constellation of sexual and gender politics, one that, while sharing key points of continuity with their Christian right brethren, is, in equally important ways, quite distinct. At a basic level, new evangelicals' embrace of human trafficking as a focus of concern must be situated as a culturally modernizing project, rather than a traditionalizing one. Under the guise of moral condemnation and rescue, women in particular are granted new opportunities to participate in sexually explicit culture, international travel, and the previously forbidden corners of urban space. Moreover, contemporary evangelical anti-trafficking activists hew closely to a liberal-feminist vision of egalitarian heterosexual marriage and professional-sphere equality, one in which heterosexual prostitution, as for many middle-class secular liberals, represents the antithesis of both of these political aims.[30] And finally, although new evangelicals do care less about "culture wars" battles than they do about humanitarian issues and global social justice, their vision of social justice remains one that equates directly with criminal justice, and to the extent that economic issues are considered causal factors in human suffering, the solutions that they forge are imagined in neoliberal, consumer-friendly terms.[31] In this way, new evangelicals remain beholden to an underlying carceral politics that serves to link them not just to those sectors of the contemporary feminist movement that have themselves veered rightward in recent decades, but also (as with secular feminist anti-trafficking activists more generally) to the entire right-wing spectrum of criminal justice–oriented social and economic conservatives.

A stark example of the neoliberal criminal justice agenda that undergirds new evangelical humanitarian interventions is represented by the International Justice Mission, which has been at the forefront of the media-friendly militarized humanitarianism that has characterized the faith-based response to human trafficking since the late 1990s. Having risen to prominence through its spectacular rescues of women and children from South Asian brothels (often conducted in partnership with press outlets such as *Dateline*, CNN, and FOX News) the International Justice Mission has patented a "rescue and restore" model of activism, in which male employees of the organization go undercover as potential clients to investigate brothels around the globe, partnering with local law enforcement. Gary Haugen, IJM's founder and CEO, provides the justification for these techniques in his 2008 book *Just Courage*, arguing that the epic struggle of good versus evil necessitates the choice between "being safe and being brave."[32] Haugen's muscular vision of social justice activism explicitly identifies human trafficking as an issue that can redirect lives accustomed to suburban safety toward action and adventure ("We fret over what might happen to our stuff, our reputation, our standing. . . . All the things we value were never meant to be safeguarded. They were meant to be put at risk and spent"[33]).

IJM's operations have attracted some controversy—as, for example, in Cambodia, where "rescued" women used bedsheets to escape through the windows and climb to the ground in order to return to the brothels from which they had been "liberated," and also in India, where local sex workers threw rocks at their would-be liberators.[34] In Thailand, local activists were so offended by the organization's standard practice of breaking down brothel doors without regard to the age or willingness of the occupants that they collaborated to shut down its principal office in the Northern region of the country.[35] And yet the undercover and mass-media-oriented model of activism that IJM propounds has become the emulated standard for evangelical Christian and secular feminist organizations alike. The liberal feminist organization Equality Now, for example, has enlisted male volunteers to go undercover to find traffickers and to work with local law enforcement to bring them to trial, while the secular organization Polaris Project has enlisted student volunteers to conduct their own "field research"

3.4   Anti-rescue protests: Indian sex workers demand an end to forced rescues by Restore International, an organizational affiliate of IJM. Photo: Meena Seshu.

to assist the police.[36] Notably, IJM's tactics have been hailed by both the Bush administration and by secular humanitarians in the Obama administration such as Samantha Power.[37] As Power noted in her interview with Haugen for the liberal-leaning *New Yorker* magazine, "Haugen believes that the biggest problem on earth is not too little democracy, or too much poverty, or too few anti-retroviral AIDS medicines, but, rather, an absence of proper law enforcement."[38]

Through IJM's rescue missions, men are coaxed into participating in women's and other humanitarian issues by being granted the role of heroic crime fighters and saviors. As with some of its cultural predecessors from the Christian men's movement (such as groups like the Promise Keepers), the aim through these expeditions is to simultaneously shore up masculine identity and to provide "tender intimacy" with God.[39] As Jessica Johnson observed in her ethnographic study of a well-known evangelical megachurch in Seattle, "perverted sinners" can thus be transformed into responsible and productive "citizen-soldiers," creating a spiritual and affective milieu that accords with the goals of US empire. Unlike in other Christian men's groups, however, here it is not "headship" in the domestic enclave of the nuclear family that draws men in, or a militaristic role within the church itself, but rather the assumption of a leadership role in and against a problem that is global in scope and which requires transnational actors to combat.[40]

Haugen's perspective is also in line with that of secular liberal authors such as Nicholas Kristof and Siddharth Kara, who have similarly fashioned themselves as the rescuers and saviors of trafficked women. In 2004, journalist Nicholas Kristof recounted over three *New York Times* columns how he purchased the freedom of two prostitutes in Cambodia. He recalled how he posed as a client, purchased the time of two young Cambodian girls, and then paid their debts in order to release them from their brothel owners (only to find that one had returned to brothel work on her own accord several years later).[41] In 2009, Siddharth Kara, a former businessman turned anti-trafficking crusader, provided another example of this technique in his book *Sex Trafficking: Inside the Business of Modern Slavery*. In the book, Kara recalls his efforts to engage with the sex slaves he understood to heavily populate the Thai massage parlors of Los Angeles. He describes how he met Sunee this way, after purchasing a massage. When she offered him sex in addition to a traditional massage, he showed her his Free the Slaves membership card and offered to help her find a new job. While admitting that Sunee ultimately refused his help, Kara demonstrates scant understanding of the likely reasons for her reluctance, citing fear for her parent's safety, the need to send them money, and a distrust that the authorities would help her.[42] Neither author considers the possibility that "rescue" may be highly unpalatable to these young women given that they have already made what they consider to be their best choices within the context of a very limited set of economic options.

Rescue, Redemption, and Global Sexual Politics

I arrive late and breathless to a screening of the anti-trafficking film *Call and Response*, where I am struck by the crowd of several hundred that has spilled out onto the streets—the number of people is remarkable considering that this is an evangelical Christian human rights event in the heart of New York City, that it's 10 PM on a Tuesday night, and that the film has already been showing for several weeks. The young and fashionable attendees are brimming with excitement.

The film begins with sinister and grainy footage of young girls in Cambodian brothels, footage that the film leaves unattributed but which I recognize from a previous TV special. Following a clip of several school-aged children negotiating with a white Western client to exchange money for sex, the film cuts abruptly to performance footage of a Christian rock band whose members strum their guitars intently in urgent lament. This hip, fashionable version of Christianity merges so seamlessly with popular culture and with secular humanitarian impulses that the muted evangelical Christian perspective may not even be apparent to secular viewers.

The next segment of the film features a number of anti-trafficking "experts": the New York Times columnist Nicholas Kristof; the former US Ambassador to Monitor Trafficking in Persons, John Miller, as well as movie stars who have recently taken an interest in the issue like Ashley Judd and UN Goodwill Ambassador Julia Ormond. Even the philosophy professor and public intellectual Cornel West makes an incongruous appearance, discussing the history of race-based, chattel slavery in the US. The film cuts back and forth impressionistically between images of black bodies being whipped and close-ups of the faces of white Christian rock musicians whose eyes tear up when they recount the ravages of sexual slavery that they have heard about from others or in some cases witnessed. These scenes dissolve into footage of scantily clad women in the windows of geographically unspecified brothels until the camera finally settles upon a young Asian woman who declares to ominous sounding music and to audible gasps from the audience that she has slept with over 1,000 men. "I haven't been to school so I can't add it up," she offers meekly. This protagonist is the first of several to offer the audience a decontextualized and sensationalistic focus upon trafficking-as-rape and sacrificed virginity. Despite Kristof's insistence in the film that the exchange of sex for money per se is not what is most salient about trafficking, but rather the presence of force and brutality, here it is mundane prostitution scenarios from points around the globe—from Cambodia, India, and other places unnamed—that serve as the rallying cry for action. FROM MY FIELD NOTES, DECEMBER 2008

Of course, more than a bolstering of middle-class masculinity is at stake in the social activism and theological ideals that IJM has mobilized among conservative Christians, particularly since the majority of the organization's grassroots activists (as in anti-trafficking campaigns more generally) are middle-class young women. In contrast to Concerned Women for America's avowed embrace of sexual and gender traditionalism for Western women, IJM's members, like other new evangelicals, make frequent reference to the backward traditionalism of third-world cultures as one of the primary causes of sex trafficking, a framework that helps them to define and to reinforce their own perceived freedom and autonomy as Western women. In the promotional poster for *Call and Response*, the mouth of an unidentified brown-skinned girl is firmly taped shut, with the lineup of prominent Christian figures that cover the seal implying that it is up to them to speak on her behalf (in the film, creator Justin Dillon explicitly declares his intention to tell the story of girls who cannot tell their own stories themselves). Similarly, toward the film's conclusion, the actress Julia Ormond recalls an interaction in which she asked victims of sexual slavery what their most pressing need was, and the response that she reportedly received from the young women was "to tell my story."[43]

At the same time, new evangelical activism around sex trafficking also adheres closely to what Inderpal Grewal has identified as the contempo-

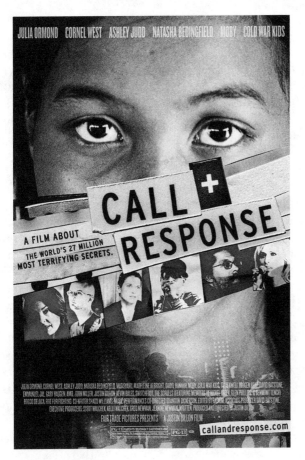

3.5   *Call and Response* poster, 2008.

rary feminist model of human rights activism, produced by subjects who imagine themselves as more ethical and free than their "sisters" in the developing world.[44] As Grewal and other postcolonial feminist scholars have repeatedly demonstrated, Western feminist concern for women in the third world works by way of a reassuring logic, in which the image of the oppressed "third-world woman" is produced and circulated in implicit contrast to Western feminist ideals of freedom and equality. As Chandra Mohanty has written, this image is situated "in contrast to the (implicit) self-representation of Western women as educated, as modern, as having control over their own bodies and sexualities, and the freedom to make their own decisions."[45] Similarly, in her discussion of recent feminist interventions in the Muslim world, Lila Abu-Lughod has remarked that proponents of "women's rights as humans rights" consistently posit Western culture as "the universal standard by which to measure societies," gauging this assessment on perceptions of gender equality in particular.[46] Through a consideration of the anti-trafficking activism of contemporary evangelical women, we see that it is not just secular feminists who bring missionary zeal to a normatively Western and secular women's rights agenda, but young missionaries, too, who share these secular feminist ambitions.

The embrace of the third-world trafficking victim as a modern cause thus offers young evangelical women a means to engage directly in a sex-saturated culture without becoming contaminated by it; it provides an opportunity to commune with third-world "bad girls" while remaining first-world "good girls." Whether by directly entering the third-world brothel or by viewing highly sexualized media portrayals, the issue of trafficking permits a sexualized frame to exist without threatening these women's own moral status or social position.[47] To listen to the repeated stories of bad men, big guns, and bolted chains that are deemed responsible for prostitutes' captivity is to participate in an experience that is viscerally stirring and that seems utterly life threatening and consequential—while never veering far from a seat of safety. One twenty-three-year-old evangelical anti-trafficking activist I encountered at the *Call and Response* screening bluntly reflected upon the Christian concern with trafficking in terms of the issue's "sexiness," noting that "*Nightline* does specials on it. . . . [I]t would be hard to do a *Nightline* special on abortion."[48]

Evangelical anti-trafficking efforts thus extend activist trends that have also become increasingly prevalent elsewhere, embodying a form of political engagement that is consumer- and media-friendly and saturated in the tropes and imagery of the sexual culture it overtly opposes. A recent photograph from a special issue of the magazine *Christianity Today* on sex trafficking titled "The Business of Rescue" makes this synergy quite clear. The image depicts a young female activist from a Christian human rights group who is ministering to a sex worker in a Thai brothel. What is particularly striking about the photograph is the evident rapport between the two women (as indicated by their relaxed postures and affectionate gestures) and both women's broad smiles. Although the magazine's evangelical readership would be likely to interpret the women's happy affect as evidence of Christ's love,[49] young missionaries' brothel visits are also situated within the contemporary practices of consumer humanitarianism, in which touristic adventures in exotic settings serve to create Westerners' good times.

3.6   Photograph of an evangelical "red light rescue" that originally appeared in *Christianity Today*, January 2007. The original caption reads "She's Got a Friend: Rachel Thiesen, right, a volunteer with Just Food Inc., with Apple, a prostitute and manager of a bar in Chiang Mai, Thailand. The bar girls look forward to the twice-weekly visits to speak to women who care about them." Jimi Allen Productions, reprinted with permission.

The smiling photograph from *Christianity Today* and the idea of a benignly humanitarian "business of rescue" forge a dramatic contrast with the skeptical reactions to Western helping campaigns that were expressed to me by the women at Chiang Mai's Can Do Bar, as described in chapter 1. They also diverge from the sex workers' accounts reported by sociologist Elena Shih, who has done ethnographic research with several different evangelical Christian rescue projects in Thailand and China. As noted earlier, she found that nearly all of the "victims" who were employed as jewelry makers by the projects were adult women who had previously chosen sex work as their highest-paying option but who, after accumulating some savings, elected to engage in evangelical Christian "prayer work" and jewelry making instead.[50] After signing on to the jewelry-making projects, they soon discovered that their lives would henceforth be micromanaged by their missionary-employers, that they would no longer be free to visit family and friends in the red-light districts, and that their pay would be docked for missing daily prayer sessions, for being minutes late to work, or for minor behavioral infractions. Many came to question whether their current lives really offered them more "freedom" than they had before.

The Place of Sex

Various observers have sought to account for the rise of the "new evangelical internationalism," attributing its ascension to broader dynamics of economic, political, and technological globalization, to the rising affluence of American congregations, and to the shifting "center of gravity" of evangelical Christianity.[51] At the same time, religious studies scholars such as Elizabeth Castelli and Melani McAlister have emphasized the shifting cultural and ideological dimensions of evangelical Christianity that have made global interventions both possible and desirable to participants. For example, Melani McAlister has strived to explain the growing global focus and influence of US evangelicals across myriad political issues, as well as the rise of an enabling cultural logic "that makes the world available" to them.[52] While evangelicals' focus has long concerned the suffering of specifically Christian bodies, it has more recently been transformed into a "globalized sense of Christian suffering" in which US Christians can enter into an "intimate public" with those in the global church of Christianity.[53] McAlister quotes Elizabeth Castelli in describing evangelical Christianity as a "critical theory of suffering," one that illuminates and offers global solidarity in suffering but also rationalizes it as part of God's divine plan.[54]

When sexual politics have been considered as an animating force in the globalization of evangelical Christianity, many authors have understood these to be crassly straightforward attempts to disseminate conservative Christian worldviews. For example, the authors of *Globalizing Family Values*, Doris Buss and Didi Herman, and of *Born Again: The Christian Right Globalized*, Jennifer Butler, have together described the growing influence of the Christian right in international politics through heightened participation in transnational institutions such as the United Nations. They have also considered the relatively rapid shift that has occurred in the political approach of the Christian right in recent decades—from opposing the global stage to making use of it to advance conservative Christian values. Regarding the traditional family "as the most basic unit of society," global activism around issues such as abortion and homosexuality (both are regarded as pernicious threats to "the family" as they understand it) figure prominently.[55] In addition, Buss, Herman, and Butler all note the ways that the Christian right has sought to counter the rise of reproductive rights in a variety of global contexts, including abortion, sex education, and population policy. Most notably, such commentators point out that, in countries like Uganda, evangelicals have brutally insisted upon the relevance of their abstinence-only stance to the global fight against HIV/AIDS.[56]

Arguing in a similar vein, theorists such as Jacqueline Berman and Yvonne Zimmerman have postulated that it is these self-same "family values" that have spurred contemporary Christian interest in the global fight against sex trafficking, where the latter is figured as a threat to marital sexuality rather than gender equality.[57] Yet as this chapter has cautioned, such analyses may serve to oversimplify the complex ways in which sex has come to animate evangelical activism on the global stage. In fact, one way to understand the place of sex in contemporary anti-trafficking campaigns is to consider the issue of sex trafficking alongside another humanitarian cause with evangelical support that rose and fell rapidly during a much more compressed span of time—the now-infamous case of *Kony 2012*.[58] Briefly considering these two issues side by side, one in which sex is foregrounded and another in which the sexual dimensions are absent or at least muted, can serve to more clearly reveal the place of sex—both symbolically and geopolitically—in contemporary modes of evangelical social engagement.

To review the basics of the Kony campaign, on March 5, 2012, an evangelical Christian nonprofit organization by the name of Invisible Children began a campaign against Joseph Kony, leader of the Lord's Resistance Army, with the launch of the video *Kony 2012*.[59] The goal of the video was to make Joseph Kony's legacy known by recounting the story of abducted children in northern Uganda who were forced to serve as child soldiers in the LRA. The video instantly became a viral Internet sensation, with thirty-two million views on YouTube by the following day and more than seventy million views over the course of the following weeks, making it the "fastest spreading online video ever produced."[60] At the outset, a number of prominent political figures and celebrities, including President Obama, expressed support for Invisible Children's campaign, helping to increase its popularity. Oprah, who hosted the creators on her television talk show to promote their social cause, also contributed to the video's viral success.[61]

Despite the accolades it received upon its debut, it was not long before the video campaign came under intense scrutiny by critics and the controversy of the campaign became a media frenzy in its own right. Detractors of the video put forth wide-ranging objections, claiming that it provided a misrepresentation and overly simplistic portrayal of a complex situation and, worse still, that it was reminiscent of long-standing colonial practices in Africa.[62] Concerns about the tactics and practicality of the campaign were also raised—specifically, questions about the expenditure of the millions of dollars it had raised through methods that even supporters of the campaign deemed dubious. Campaign methods such as encouraging viewers to share the *Kony 2012* video, to make a tax-deductible donation, and to purchase $10 *Kony 2012* bracelets and $30 *Kony 2012* "action kits" (which included the bracelet along with a T-shirt, stickers, buttons, and action guide) were acknowledged by many to be offensive and superficial. Over the course of several months, critics continued to take issue with the temporal specificity of the film's depictions, the failure of the video to acknowledge important geopolitical shifts in the region, and the skewed numerical estimates (such as the figure of thirty thousand child soldiers) that the video offered.[63] A much-circulated *Al Jazeera* video even documented the disappointment and anger of Ugandans in attendance at the first public screening of the video in the country.[64]

Perhaps the most prominent critic of *Kony 2012* was the Nigerian American author Teju Cole, who after watching the *Kony 2012* video responded with a seven-part response on Twitter decrying the "white savior industrial complex," which he called "Seven Thoughts on the Banality of Sentimentality."[65] The tweets provided a powerful critique of the paradigmatic salvational figure who "supports brutal policies in the morning, founds charities in the afternoon, and receives awards in the evening," and who regards the world as "nothing but a problem to be solved by enthusiasm." Rapidly retweeted and widely shared by readers, Cole's tweets soon sparked heated debate in the media about the "white-savior complex" at work in *Kony 2012*.[66] Nicholas Kristof, singled out by Cole, even responded in an interview by acknowledging that there might be something wrong about "the perception that Americans are going to ride in on a white horse and resolve it."[67] In the wake of the onslaught of negative media coverage and the ensuing personal troubles of the organization's founder, Jason Russell, by December 2014 Invisible Children had announced that its operations would soon be phased out.[68]

Considering the rapid rise and fall of *Kony 2012* alongside the scant public critiques that have been offered of campaigns to combat sex trafficking can help to further illuminate the role that sex plays in both evangelical and secular campaigns for global social justice. While *Kony 2012* skyrocketed to national attention but just as precipitously crashed, activist campaigns to combat sex trafficking have quietly endured, solidifying claims to their legitimacy and becoming more widely institutionalized with each passing year. Yet as global social justice campaigns, both *Kony 2012* and anti-trafficking share many important features, including similar bases of support among young evangelicals, broad-based humanitarian appeal, and substantial secular followings.

No doubt, the "sexiness" of sex trafficking is precisely what makes the issue feel so urgent and compelling to successive cohorts of young activists, including the young woman I interviewed at the *Call and Response* screening. Yet as feminists thinkers such as Patricia Clough and Svati Shah have observed, public representations of sex serve not only as an attractant but also as a powerful repellant, inviting gazes from a distance while simultaneously discouraging voyeurs from peering too deeply within.[69] The complex visceral entanglements that many feel with sexual issues (eloquently described by Shah as the "ick" factor) may discourage the close and careful attention that *Kony 2012*, by contrast, quickly generated, as well as the eviscerating critiques that followed from this scrutiny. While the frivolous premises and tactics of *Kony 2012* were rapidly dissected and mocked for lacking in political heft, the glossy veneer of "sex trafficking" is at once too attractive and too repellant to garner similar critical concern. Although sex adds to the public allure and marketability of trafficking as a political issue, it simultaneously inures it from deeper intellectual interrogation.

Justice, Incorporated

At the International Justice Mission's 4th annual Global Prayer Gathering, held in an affluent white suburb of Washington DC, I am greeted upon arrival by a row of well-scrubbed young women in chic haircuts and neat suits, the majority of whom appear to be in their mid-twenties. Behind the row of greeters, a lively group of women and men mingle, carrying sleek tote bags emblazoned with the IJM logo, SEEK JUSTICE™. Available for sale on the display table to the left of them are copies of prayer books by the German theologian Dietrich Bonhoeffer, who was hanged for his role in the Nazi resistance.[70] Along with a historical array of Christian anti-prostitution and anti-lynching activists, he is intended to serve as our moral exemplar for the weekend.[71]

Later in the evening, with the nearly 1,000 other Prayer Gathering attendees, I will migrate to the hotel banquet room for a plenary session, three course meal, praise music, and prayer. Compared to some other anti-trafficking groups, the definition of "slavery" that IJM imparts to us is relatively expansive: we hear not only about women trapped in brothels, but also about debt bondage in rice mills, cigarette factories, and brick kilns. The injustice of the latter is viscerally conveyed to us through a "live action" presentation, in which we pass heavily weighted buckets from hand to hand to symbolize the onerous burdens of the slaves. Seated next to me, a man hailing from a church in Madison, Wisconsin, offers the following perspective: "People in those countries just don't know how to treat women!" The next day, a PhD student in theology that I am lunching with expresses a variant of the same view: "It's time that white Western feminists took an interest in the rest of the world!"

In addition to organized "prayer outings" to the Lincoln Memorial and other Washington, DC, monuments, we will spend the weekend circulating through prayer rooms for IJM operations in different regions. In the Uganda room, we will learn about a young girl named Sara, and how difficult it is for people in her country to gain access to justice. In the Thailand room, we will visit four separate "prayer stations" and hear four different women's tragic stories, studying their photos and case documents and praying separately for each. In the Cambodia room, we will learn that not everyone who is rescued is initially grateful. According to the team leader, victims sometimes prefer the hell they know to that with which they are unfamiliar.

In a room called "Project Lantern," inspired by a recent Gates Foundation grant, the object of our prayers is less clear.[72] We're told that the project takes its name from the Underground Railroad, and is also a symbol of God's shining light. The room exists to honor an as yet uninitiated project: the creation of a law enforcement model to combat sex trafficking in the Philippines that will be replicable across countries and cultures. "What we thought that we might do here is paint lanterns with watercolors," explains the leader, "since creativity is the best way that we have to communicate with God." As she speaks her instructions, young women migrate to the table display of white paper lanterns on behalf of a project that has yet to be initiated, the specific aims of which are never discussed or acknowledged, solemnly painting and praying for victims of slavery that they know little about, and that in fact do not yet exist. **FROM MY FIELD NOTES, APRIL 2006**

While consumer-friendly and corporate-driven interventions have become a prevalent feature of many forms of social justice activism, they occupy an especially prominent place in contemporary evangelical anti-trafficking campaigns. As I describe in more detail in chapter 5, the Gates Foundation and a host of other private-sector actors have become increasingly prominent sponsors of anti-trafficking activism, a form of intervention that evangelical Christians have eagerly embraced and supported. This pro-market ideology is also manifest in consumer-activist campaigns, in which "new abolitionists" are frequently summoned to make purchases that will contribute to faith-based organizations (as in the ironically titled Not for Sale Freedom Store; see fig. 3.7) or by purchasing items that women who have purportedly been freed from sexual slavery have crafted. As such, they provide a global-evangelical twist on the phenomenon that recent cultural theorists have described as "commodity activism," in which social and political action are mobilized through consumer practices, via "brands, celebrities, and political virtue." In commodity activism, aspects of social and political life that would otherwise be seen as removed from the market economy are recast in economic terms, with "good consumers" and "good citizens" imagined as moral categories that are co-constitutive.[73]

From Max Weber onward, numerous observers have noted the convergence of capitalism and Christian values, but the specificity of evangelical engagement with neoliberal corporate and consumer cultures has only recently received critical attention.[74] In *To Serve God and Wal-Mart: The Making of Christian Free Enterprise*, historian Bethany Moreton explores the important role played by evangelicals in the rise of the Wal-Mart mega-corporation. She attributes the prodigious financial success of Wal-Mart in large part to Christian networking, arguing that evangelical workers, overseas missionaries, Christian business students, and Sunbelt entrepreneurs have engaged in a Christian service ethos that powers capitalism at home and abroad. Moreton notes that this marks a transformation in the traditional relationship between Christianity and commerce, with the former characterized "by stark prohibitions on profit, luxury, exploitation, sensual pleasure, even worldly work and ownership." Moreton argues that in the 1970s and 1980s, evangelicals would come to combine "religious efforts to regulate sex with an equally religious celebration of material comforts, self-expression, technological innovation, and secular success," which she refers to as "free enterprise as Christian service."[75]

For contemporary evangelicals, the capacity to travel to faraway lands and the purchase of consumer goods in the name of fighting trafficking thus serve a dual purpose in solidifying the distinction between "freedom" and "slavery." On the one hand, "freedom" resides in Western consumers' ability to purchase the trinkets and baubles that "trafficking victims" produce; on the other hand, it pertains to the practice that new evangelicals call "business as mission," in which former "slaves" are brought into "free" labor by producing commodities for Western consumers. The Business as Mission Global Think Tank (founded in 2011 "to champion the role of business in God's plan for the world") thus argues in its 2013 report that "freedom businesses are uniquely positioned to strike at the economically driven foundations of the sex trade. By combining the necessary components of economic productivity and holistic ministry, the staggering numbers of people caught in the trade can be reduced through the powerful response of freedom business."[76] Ultimately, "business as mission" can be seen as a global-capitalist refashioning of the nineteenth-century evangelical practice of rescuing women from prostitution by bringing them into domestic labor or teaching them to sew.[77]

At the same time, IJM's website, like that of the Amazing Change and Not for Sale campaigns with which it is affiliated, suggests that one can "become an abolitionist" simply by clicking an online button and donating money. To IJM's members, this is not a contradiction: at the IJM prayer gathering as well as at a subsequent IJM event that I attended, staff members insisted, "We can deploy our privilege for the sake of effecting positive changes in the world." Evangelical anti-trafficking efforts thus extend activist trends that are also increasingly prevalent elsewhere,

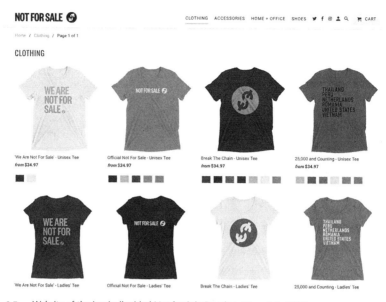

3.7   Website of the ironically titled Not for Sale Freedom Store, July 2017.

advocating a form of political engagement that is consumer- and media-friendly, saturated in the tropes and imagery of the very sexual culture which it aims to oppose.

Yet significantly, by defining "slavery" in a way that actually extends beyond prostitution, this new-internationalist class of evangelical anti-trafficking activists reveals a set of political commitments that both encompasses and transcends prior depictions of conservative Christians' sexual worldviews. In the *Christianity Today* cover story "The Business of Rescue" referred to earlier, the magazine profiles Christian humanitarian organizations that orient former prostitutes toward entry-level jobs in the service economy, teaching women to bake muffins for Starbucks and to prepare Western-style drinks and food. Other evangelical groups (including those affiliated with the Amazing Change and Not for Sale campaigns) as well as a growing number of liberal, secular groups have also hopped on board with this approach, no longer framing the problem of human trafficking in terms of broader dynamics of globalization, gendered labor, and migration, but rather as a humanitarian issue that global capitalists can help combat.

During an interview with Boreth Sun, a Cambodian anti-trafficking activist and frequent speaker at Not for Sale events, he explained to me that his ambition was to promote "a culture of entrepreneurship rather than a culture of dependency":

[This] means you make the decision of what you do, how you want to run your business. How do you link them with different places where they can get access to credit to borrow? If they don't know how, you should be capacity-building to give them the know-how. . . . They can make the decision to do something else and they can get the know-how to do something out of the traditional role where culture says, "Oh all the girls should do this and all the boys should do that." We want to create empowerment by letting them make the decision, give them the critical tools.

Whereas anti-globalization activists during the 1990s had argued that the daily practices of capitalism created sweatshop conditions of labor that were unacceptable, modern-day abolitionists such as Sun, as well as the *New York Times* Pulitzer Prize–winning journalist Nicholas Kristof, identify such practices with the very definition of freedom. According to Kristof, while it "shocks Americans to hear it, the central challenge in the poorest countries is not that sweatshops exploit too many people, but that they don't exploit enough."[78]

Conclusion

In this discussion, I have suggested that new evangelical sexual politics exhibit a neoliberal—rather than a traditionalist—sexual agenda, one in which social remedies are pursued through the expansion of criminal justice interventions and the global spread of consumer capitalism. Like the secular feminist anti-trafficking activists described previously, new evangelical anti-trafficking activists subscribe to a punitive approach toward social justice that leaves intact the social structures that incline low-income women and men to participate in risky migration strategies and the most exploitative kinds of informal-sector employment. Moreover, whereas the "old" evangelical sexual politics around issues such as abortion and gay marriage hinged upon an ideology of gender differences in the private sphere of the home, new evangelical politics are consistent with their secular feminist counterparts in their emphasis upon women's susceptibility to public and nonfamilial forms of sexual harm. In this way, contemporary evangelicals are able to simultaneously partake in late-capitalist consumer sex culture under the guise of condemning it (a dynamic of simultaneous participation and refusal that Wendy

Brown once famously identified as the "mirror of pornography"[79]) while also providing crucial bolstering for the neoliberal carceral politics that chapter 2 described.

Although sexual intersections are crucial to cementing the coalition between feminists and Christians that has given rise to the anti-trafficking movement, I have also sought to show in this chapter that they are not the only points of contact that are vital to understanding how this "strange bedfellows" coalition was enabled. Ultimately, new evangelical efforts to "seek justice" (as per IJM's patented slogan) must also be situated in terms of a series of broader political and cultural realignments that have occurred during a period in which the consumer and the carceral are increasingly seen as the preeminent vehicles of social justice. These shared political commitments—sexual, consumer, and carceral—serve not only to link contemporary feminists and evangelicals to one another but also to join both constituencies to a broad spectrum of secular and religious conservatives.

While there is a large body of critical feminist literature documenting the inseparability of Western feminist forays into the international human rights terrain from neocolonial state interests, this analysis points to the ways that neocolonial humanitarian interventions have also been used as a staging ground for the resolution of internecine Western feminist and evangelical Christian cultural conflicts. As the previous two chapters have shown, two different shifts in feminist and conservative Christian sexual politics have made the contemporary campaign against sex trafficking possible: the shift among many feminists from a focus on bad men inside the home to bad men outside the home, and that of a new generation of evangelical Christians from a focus on sexually improper women (as prior concerns with abortion suggest) to one on sexually dangerous men. What has also been revealed is a turning away of both groups from direct engagement with the gender politics of the family (which the gay marriage and abortion debates emblematized) toward a focus upon gender and sexual violence in the public sphere. It has been through these shifts that both groups have come to foster an alliance with neoliberal consumer politics and a militarized state apparatus that utilizes claims of a particular white, middle-class model of Western gender and sexual superiority in achieving its goals.

Although the cultural and political dynamics I have described here reached their fruition during the years of the Bush administration and religious right ascendance, what was in many ways a more secular, progressive era during the Obama presidency did not in fact portend a dramatic change of course.[80] With the change in administrations, many secular liberals initially celebrated the fact that US anti-trafficking policy would no longer be used as a proxy for religious right and "radical" feminist concerns about sex. Similarly, the appointment of former federal prosecutor Luis C. deBaca as US Ambassador to Monitor and Combat Trafficking in Persons (who had promised to train his prosecutorial eye upon labor trafficking as well as sex trafficking) was much heralded by the liberal wing of the anti-trafficking movement.[81] Yet as I have sought to demonstrate through my discussion, "liberals" and "conservatives" have tended to agree on the underlying carceral politics that have defined the issue of trafficking from the outset (with debates revolving around the narrow question of whether severe criminal penalties should extend beyond sex trafficking to other forms of trafficking as well). The hesitancy that a number of sex workers' rights organizations and human rights advocates initially voiced when the UN Protocol against Trafficking in Persons was first negotiated as a crime-control protocol has all but vanished from the realm of acceptable political discourse.[82] Notably, the neoliberal carceral strategies that I have described are also becoming common in countries where the religious right holds little influence but the welfare state is increasingly under siege.[83] At the same time, in many countries throughout the Global South, the anti-trafficking discourse has melded seamlessly into state-based agendas of securitization, and repressive police crackdowns on sex workers have become rampant.[84]

As other commentators have remarked upon, it is striking to behold the extent to which the politics of trafficking have traveled so seamlessly and effectively across national borders.[85] While the neo-imperialism of US and Eurocentric transnational governing instruments such as the Palermo Protocol are often and rightly identified as key culprits,[86] the "soft power" of evangelical Christian missions, transnational NGOs, global media campaigns, and short-term helping interventions by well-meaning Western activists also constitute an important part of the story. The following chapter thus returns us to the Bangkok and Chiang Mai red-light districts that I described in the opening of chapter 1, providing a window onto the global extensions of business as mission and consumer humanitarianism that have developed alongside state-based agendas of criminalization and border securitization in Southeast Asia. Via an ethnographic exploration of a "reality tour" of trafficking that I attended in Thailand sponsored by two US-based organizations, we will see how the travels of trafficking have become critical to the broader dissemination of neoliberal sexual politics. Indeed, the discourse of trafficking has provided fertile ground for the dissemination of carceral feminism, militarized humanitarianism, and contemporary modes of capitalist engagement.

FOUR

The Travels of Trafficking

WITH ELENA SHIH

Upon entering the international arrival terminal at Bangkok's Suvarnabhumi Airport, travelers must make their way through a barrage of placards and eager local guides holding signs for Thailand's largest hotels, resorts, and an array of private tour companies that operate in Southeast Asia's principal leisure hub. Arriving in the crowded and chaotic terminal on a sultry July afternoon, Elena and I struggled to locate the designated tour leader whose job it was to greet us. Wending our way through the numerous sturdy, professionally designed posters, we at last encountered a modest plain white sheet of paper with the words "Global Exchange" typed in black font. This small, unassuming sign was an easy one to miss for a tour whose boasts were ample: the "Thailand Delegation to End Human Trafficking and Modern Day Slavery" promised that participants would, over the course of seven days, "[confront] the realities of the global trade in human beings."[1]

During the summer of 2012, Elena Shih and I traveled to Thailand less with the hope of uncovering the phenomenon of trafficking itself than with the goal of understanding one of a growing number of "reality tours" that claimed to represent it. Our ethnographic ambition was to critically interrogate the "realities of the global traffic in human beings" that the tour endeavored to convey. What did commercially packaged reality tours reveal about the global politics of sex work and trafficking, as well as the dynamics of tourism and development in Thailand? How did claims to the expertise of transnational NGOs interact with local knowledge around trafficking, labor, and sexual commerce? And how did moral and political economies of authenticity circulate in the reality-tourist experience? These are the primary questions that our research in Thailand endeavored to address.

To situate this research sociologically, we had at our disposal our long-standing relationships with sex worker activists in the region, as well a number of fine ethnographic studies that had already been crafted.[2] Thailand has been a focal point of anti-trafficking activism and research since the late 1980s, when increasing numbers of Thai women from rural areas came to work in tourist meccas such as Patpong and Phuket, with many more migrating to pursue employment opportunities in Western Europe.[3] Commentators often date the emergence of widespread attention to the issue to 1984, when a fire in a Phuket brothel left workers unable to escape because they were found to be chained to their beds. The case sparked national and international attention and ignited debates among the nascent NGO community over appropriate responses to the burgeoning sex industry in Thailand.[4] Since that time, anti-trafficking NGOs in Thailand have burgeoned, ranging from the secular, rights-based Global Alliance against Trafficking in Women (GAATW) to the global evangelical organization International Justice Mission (IJM), to a steady stream of anti-trafficking "start-ups," both secular and Christian in orientation. Although many with in-depth knowledge of the situation confirm that the numbers of forced prostitution cases have decreased in recent years, this is not always reflected in accounts from NGOs and in news stories that rely on these organizations as sources for their claims. As one local activist explained to us, "There is a vested interest in keeping the numbers high so that groups can continue to raise money."[5]

The concerns of many researchers and activists have begun to shift, however, in tandem with changing patterns of migration, economic investment, and employment opportunities in the region. As Christina Arnold and Andrea Bertone first described in a 2002 study, "There has been a gradual decrease in the numbers of Thai women and girls in the sex trade, and an increase in the numbers of females from neighboring countries in the Mekong sub-region, as well as non-citizen, hill tribe girls from Northern Thailand."[6] Focusing upon the migration patterns of the later groups, researchers such as Sverre Molland have also been alert to the gaps between lived experience and official anti-trafficking discourse. For example, in his study of anti-trafficking policy and the sex trade in the Mekong region, Molland argues that prevailing discourse around trafficking tends to remove both traffickers and trafficked individuals from the social relationships that are key to understanding and combatting exploitation. He describes the many instances in which "victim" and "trafficker" identities are merged, or in which trafficking takes place based in localized, opportunistic ways, as opposed to the sophisticated and organized methods that are presupposed by most policymakers and activists. "Non-consensual recruitment takes place within social networks that are very much part of the life worlds of both alleged victims and traffickers," he observes. Molland describes sitting with his research assistant in the living room of Sutthida, a woman with many years of experience working in the sex industry who now runs a brothel out of her suburban home. It is the ordinariness of the scene, "not its uniqueness," that stands out to him: "What goes on inside the premises is not obvious for passers-by, yet it is not in any way concealed." While proximity to the Lao-Thai border facilitates the migration of willing sex workers, Sutthida and her familial colleagues do sometimes employ deceptive techniques of recruitment (i.e., "trafficking").[7]

The irony of endeavoring to write an ethnography of a reality tour of trafficking was not lost on us, given that we were well versed in the critiques of ethnographic writing's own realist pretensions.[8] Although it is not our intention to supplant one realist fallacy with another, it is our claim that ethnographic techniques—however partial, perspectival, and socially located they themselves are—can be useful in illuminating the representational strategies of this emerging commercial variant of humanitarian endeavor. We thus share Edward Bruner's conviction that the performance of culture that packaged touristic experiences represent is itself a significant cultural form meriting closer investigation—a form of "emergent culture," as Bruner writes.[9] We situate our exploration at the intersections of the expanding literatures on tourism and authenticity, as well as the critical literatures on sex trafficking and sex tourism, two terrains of scholarship that have infrequently been juxtaposed.[10] As such, we demonstrate how "trafficking" travels as both politics and industry, and the ways that the moral and political economies which undergird it are mutually reinforcing. While the circulations of this discourse are indeed global in scope, in this chapter we focus our discussion on the travels of trafficking between North America and Thailand.

Background and Methods

In the sections that follow, our primary ethnographic object is the commercially packaged reality tour of purported trafficking-related sites in Bangkok, Chiang Rai, and Chiang Mai that Elena and I jointly attended. Before embarking upon this trip, both of us had spent several years observing the diverse "helping projects" for sex workers that had sprung up around the globe, tracing the on-the-ground effects of contemporary anti-trafficking campaigns and their affiliated organizations. Although our discussion here takes the one-week reality tour as the chief domain of analysis, we also build upon the ample ethnographic research we have conducted in related settings—including amid Western volunteers affiliated with other anti-trafficking NGOs in Thailand, and at a variety of gatherings and events held by the tour's sponsoring NGOs in the United States. In particular, this chapter is informed by the many years of research that we have conducted among sex worker activists who have strived to address some of the manifold injustices that affect sex workers locally and globally, including those forms of violence and exploitation which have come to cluster under the banner of "sex trafficking."[11]

Initially, we learned of this reality tour through our long-standing familiarity with the tour's two sponsoring organizations, Global Exchange and Not for Sale. Although there are multiple organizations that offer similar kinds of tours of Thailand, as well as to other destinations in South and Southeast Asia, South and East Africa, and Latin America, we chose to attend this tour because of the sponsoring organizations' prominence in the social justice field, and because of Thailand's role as an enduring focal point for global anti-trafficking interventions. Before our departure, we obtained permission from the organizers to write about the reality tour provided that we attended as paying participants. The prohibitively high costs entailed by this arrangement unfortunately meant that we could not serve as participant-observers on more than one tour. The tour cost $1,200 per person, excluding airfare, making it in fact less expensive than similar tours offered by some of its NGO competitors. Other recent commercial offerings to Thailand have included the "See Human Trafficking Photography Expedition" and a tour focused on social entrepreneurship projects to combat human trafficking. In neighboring Cambodia, undergraduate students at the evangelical Christian Bryan College can participate in the Human Trafficking Study Tour, and business school students at the University of Southern California's Marshall School are given the opportunity to visit Phnom Penh as part of a special anti-trafficking tour for MBAs.[12]

Once we arrived in Bangkok, we met the other fifteen tourists who were embarking on the trip; they were primarily North American women ranging from twenty to seventy years of age and spanning a range of middle-class professions (teachers, students, and social workers, in particular, figured prominently). On the ground in Thailand, the tour was led by two male guides: one a Cambodian American expatriate living in Phnom Penh, and the other a freelance Thai tour guide based in Chiang Rai. In addition to participating in the daily itineraries that the guides assembled (which usually consisted of meetings with several NGOs as well as recreational activities and meals), and conducting in-depth interviews with the guides and the tour organizers, we also arranged supplemental trips on our own before, during, and after the tour to visit with activists and organizations that were not included in the official itinerary. These visits included meetings and interviews with members of the Global Alliance against Traffic in Women, the Asian Pacific Network of Sex Workers, and the Empower Foundation.

The tour that we attended has been co-organized since 2008 by the secular, progressive organization Global Exchange, in coordination with the evangelical Christian group Not for Sale. Not for Sale is a registered 501(c)(3) nonprofit and is not officially listed as a faith-based organization in the World Bank's Database of Faith-Based Organizations. However, on the basis of our research at numerous Not for Sale events and an evaluation of the organization's book and campaign materials (see, e.g., chapter 3), we deemed it to be a primarily evangelical Christian organization in terms of discourse and membership. Although it also strives to appeal to a broad secular audience, Not for Sale's primary source of outreach consists of evangelical churches globally and within the United States.

The fact of this partnership in and of itself offers a fascinating window into the two organizations' shared moral and political understandings of sex, commerce, and humanitarian endeavor. The organizations claim that these efforts extend the redemptive effects of humanitarian tourism beyond the parameters of a single visit, that short-term travel will lead to long-term advocacy, and they promise that tourists (who are termed "delegates" in the promotional literature for the trip) will obtain expertise that will embolden them to become anti-trafficking abolitionists once they return home. Not for Sale also offers participants the opportunity to complete a US-based training program, in which enrollees learn how to map cases of human trafficking by locating brothels and street prostitution in their own communities.[13]

Founded in 1988, Global Exchange is an international human rights NGO whose declared mission is to "promote social, economic and environmental justice" throughout the world.[14] During the US-led anti-sweatshop movement in the mid-1990s, Global Exchange contributed public relations resources through its activist network that resulted in sustained mainstream media coverage of exploitative labor practices in the global apparel industry. In the late 1980s, the organization introduced the idea of reality tours, driven by the principle that tourism could offer educational and activist opportunities to promote social justice. Global Exchange currently offers a wide variety of reality tours that are focused on social justice issues in many different destinations, and several tours are affiliated with the organization's social justice campaigns in the United States. For example, a tour to Nicaragua offers delegates the opportunity to "harvest social justice" through travel by planting and picking coffee with Central American farmers. Upon returning home, the organization stipulates in its materials that participants must demonstrate commitment to "working on a Fair Trade campaign in your own community."

Although a handful of the participants on the Thailand reality tour were drawn to the trip through Global Exchange, we discovered upon arrival that most participants had learned of the opportunity through the partner organization, Not for Sale. Founded in the mid-2000s, Not for Sale aims to engage the private and public sectors in order to foment social enterprises that "benefit enslaved and vulnerable communities." Like the avowedly Christian practice of business as mission, the commitment to social enterprise involves the blending of for-profit business development with public-interest goals. This model of business practice has existed since the 1960s, and the designation can apply to organizations whether they are registered nonprofits or private corporations.[15]

Not for Sale has made global campaigns against human trafficking accessible to a growing North American support base that comprises primarily young evangelical Christian women and students from the United States. In addition to the reality tour, its Freedom Worship program has registered more than 5,800 churches that pledge to devote a Sunday in February to pray for an end to human trafficking, while its annual Freedom Forum draws several thousand individual participants to the Not for Sale headquarters in Northern California for a weekend of talks, workshops, concerts, and art shows about human trafficking. As depicted in figure 3.7, its affiliated Not for Sale store offers an opportunity to "buy for freedom" by selling products—including jewelry, handbags, fair-trade coffee, and chocolate—that are marketed as made by victims of human trafficking. As Shih has argued elsewhere, these claims are made despite the fact that the conditions of employment in vocational training programs for sex workers are often characterized by protectionist policies that aim to discipline workers as a part of their rehabilitation. As noted by Shih, these workers frequently contest being labeled as "victims of human trafficking," asserting instead that their decision to do sex work was the best choice available to them amid a limited menu of low-wage options.[16]

Secular and Christian, progressive-left and center-liberal, it is notable—but we argue, not surprising—that these two organizations have joined forces to offer tours of sex trafficking in the Southeast Asian context. In the pages that follow, we demonstrate how reality tourism has emerged amid a growing number of alternatives to mass tourism that reflect the increasing commercialization of "humanitarian reason," a trend that is at once guided by and itself has important implications for the global politics of sex and gender.[17] We will show how anti-trafficking reality tours merge their commercial objectives with a political agenda that collapses sex work and disparate social ills, relying upon Thailand's touristic infrastructure and burgeoning NGO sector to confirm tourists' preexisting ideas of rampant sexual slavery in the region.

Reality Tourism and Its Precedents

Tourism is a backbone industry throughout Southeast Asia, for which Bangkok is the unrivaled tourist hub. Revered for its pristine beaches, well-preserved historical sites, diverse indigenous and ethnic minority communities, and relative political stability, Thailand has been an ideal destination for mass tourism from the West for decades. The hospitable tourist environment is supported by significant funding from the Thai government through the Thai Ministry of Tourism. Since the 1960s, Thai development strategies have been closely linked to international economic policies, and in 1975, based on the recommendations of the World Bank and International Monetary Fund, Thailand instituted a National Plan of Tourist Development that implemented a shift from agriculture-based development to tourism. Following the Asian financial crisis in 1997, the Thai government invested 1.5 billion baht (US$39.5 million) in the Amazing Thailand tourist campaign as a strategy for economic revitalization and as an effort to repay IMF loans incurred during the crisis.[18]

Given the tourist industry's prominence as an engine of financial growth in Thailand, the Thai government has been an avid supporter of all forms of touristic development. Its success as a tourist destination can be attributed to several structural factors, including the mammoth Suvarnabhumi Airport (which serves as a crossroads for air transport in the region), the availability of international-standard hotels, advanced in-country transportation networks, pervasive English-language signage, and relatively low rates of crime, war, and conflict. These factors have contributed to Thailand's prolific presence in international tourism: it is ranked third in international visitors by MasterCard's Global Destination Cities Index, after London and Paris, and *Travel and Leisure* has named it the number one travel destination in Asia for several years in a row.[19] Even in the wake of the May 2014 takeover of the Thai government by military forces, the annual number of tourists to the country has continued to mount.[20]

The reality tourism that we participated in thus has a curious political and economic genesis. Like the discourse of "trafficking" itself, it is a cultural form that emerged out of what were initially progressive, anticapitalist critiques. Critical responses to mass tourism in the region trace back as far as the 1960s, stemming from indigenous and NGO critiques of tourism for contributing to the decay of local resources.[21] Although the IMF and World Bank had advocated for mass tourism as a strategy of national development, critics argued that profits typically tended to benefit international tour operators, foreign investors, and large hotel chains, with financial gains rarely trickling down to local communities. Alternative forms of tourism soon emerged in an attempt to remedy some of these inequities by designating social justice, humanitarianism, and volunteerism as their foci.[22] Ecotourism, for example, emerged as a form of alternative tourism to leverage tourist resources into local communities, redistributing profits that are conventionally paid to corporate intermediaries while educating participants about local environmental challenges. Volunteer tourism is another emergent strategy of alternative tourism that arranges community development projects (typically short-term volunteer opportunities) for tourists who pay for travel, placement, housing, and organizational costs.[23] The growing popularity of slum tourism and disaster tourism in destinations across the world further illustrates the desire of tourists to witness the realities of social suffering and poverty through leisure-time travel.[24]

Yet critics of mass tourism, as well as of the emergent forms of travel that aim to replace it, note that all of these variants partake in asymmetrical relations of power and access between insiders and outsiders, and between natives and others. For instance, Juno Parreñas notes that the recent popularity of British volunteer tourism to wildlife rehabilitation centers in Borneo reproduces unequal relationships of power and risk across national identities and across species, creating what she describes as a "postcolonial economy of volunteer tourism."[25] Barbara Heron, in her study of Canadian aid workers' excursions to Africa, remarks on the extent to which, for white women from the Global North, "altruism becomes our passport to the South, and we think that is as it should be. . . . [D]evelopment appears thus as a means to a fuller life experience for bourgeois subjects."[26] Meanwhile, Wanda Vrasti has observed that the escalating interest in "global voluntourism" in the neoliberal age has fostered a highly profitable economy of prepackaged volunteer opportunities as "all-inclusive commodities." Such commodities include not only the operational costs of travel and volunteer placement but also the fulfillment of expectations around the presumed authenticity of the volunteer experience and the value of aid work to recipient communities. According to Vrasti, volunteer tourism may be less about the material impact of social change than about "exposing young adults to the adventure and authenticity they believe they are missing from modern capitalist life." Significantly, when volunteer tourists are confronted with the fact that they may not be able to effect substantive change during their brief volunteer tenure, they assuage feelings of disappointment by finding alternative meanings in the "authenticity" of their experiences. As Vrasti argues, participants find unique value in the tourist experience because it cultivates a worldly outlook and equips them with the social capital required of citizens, students, and potential employees in the global marketplace.[27]

The Global Exchange and Not for Sale anti-trafficking reality tour similarly reflects the changing nature of tourism and the intertwined socioeconomic, moral, and geopolitical tensions that it represents. It suggests a brave new world in which humanitarian interventions and market transactions are understood to be mutually reinforcing rather than contradictory (or even supplementary) modes of worldly engagement. Premised on an updated Protestant ethic which locates morality in the consumptive, rather than productive, moment of capitalist exchange, this model can also be distinguished from earlier market paradigms that situate sentiment and morality outside of it.[28] At the same time, and as we shall demonstrate here, anti-trafficking reality tours suggest an additional way in which these tensions can be simultaneously maintained and yet never made fully legible: through the morally charged circulations of gender and sexuality that structure the reality-tourist experience.

Sexual Imaginaries and Touristic Infrastructures

As the anthropologist Rosalind Morris has persuasively argued, "Few nations have been so thoroughly subject to Orientalist fantasies as Thailand. Famed for its exquisite women and the pleasures of commodified flesh, the Thailand of tourist propaganda and travelogues is a veritable bordello of the Western erotic imaginary."[29] It should thus not come as a surprise that among the four reality tours that Global Exchange was offering during the period of our research, the human trafficking tour in Thailand was its most popular destination.[30]

Although the sale of sexual services is currently illegal in Thailand, the Thai government does little to curb the existence of businesses that cater to sex tourists.[31] In fact, the government has historically supported sex tourism because of its military and economic positioning in the area. The US military presence during the Vietnam Wars, including both the stationing of American troops in Thailand and the flow of other foreign troops for "rest and recreation" (R&R), fostered one of the earliest infrastructures for tourist exchange and commercial sex tourism in the world.[32] At the urging of US Secretary of Defense Robert McNamara, the Thai government supported seven R&R facilities for foreign military servicemen stationed in Indochina. By 1969, over forty-nine thousand military personnel were based in Thailand full-time, and as many as seventy-one thousand military personnel frequently visited Thailand for R&R. Each military station was surrounded by a "pleasure belt" that offered diverse settings for intimate encounters, ranging from restaurants and bars to massage parlors and brothels.[33]

Despite the formal exit of US military troops from Southeast Asia in the early 1970s, commercial sex has remained central to the Thai tourist industry's expansion. Analysts of the Thai political economy note that this export-driven economy—planned and funded by the International Monetary Fund and World Bank loans—privileges exports, tourism, and corporate expansion, primarily in Bangkok.[34] Bangkok's rapidly developing economy, alongside Thailand's relative political stability compared with the neighboring countries of Cambodia, Myanmar, and Laos, has also generated significant undocumented migration from those regions.[35] Within Thailand, disparities in wealth between rural and urban regions have been exacerbated by this economic model and have led to successive phases of internal migration to Bangkok for a range of low-wage service-sector opportunities. Alongside other jobs such as waitressing, domestic work, and retail sales, sex work is just one of many forms of service-oriented employment for female labor migrants in Thailand. While the Thai sex industry mainly comprises female sex workers, large numbers of men and third-gender people also work in commercial sex establishments.[36]

The changing organization of sex work in Thailand is historically situated between the Thai government's robust support of tourism, public health concerns around HIV/AIDS, and ongoing legal restrictions pertaining to prostitution. In the late 1980s, rising rates of HIV infection among sex workers and injecting drug users caused public alarm about a potential HIV/AIDS epidemic. The Royal Thai Government responded with political commitment at both national and regional levels, launching the 100% Condom Programme in 1991, which demanded condom use in all commercial sex establishments. Public health organizations like the World Health Organization and UNAIDS joined Thai research universities to promote education and awareness about HIV transmission. The public alarm around HIV/AIDS led to increased legislative control over sex work.[37] Subsequently, for example, prostitution in Thailand was made illegal under the 1996 Prevention and Suppression of Prostitution Act, which penalized sex workers with a maximum thousand-baht fine or thirty days' imprisonment for prostitution offenses. The corresponding Entertainment Place Act, amended in 2003, required entertainment establishments—including karaoke bars, massage parlors, and go-go bars—to be formally registered. The formalization of registration under the Entertainment Place Act was intended to limit the employment of underage and undocumented workers, and to formalize employment in the entertainment sector, although only a third of entertainment venues have ever bothered to register.[38] Under these legal mechanisms, the majority of Thai sex workers are currently employed in public entertainment venues (including karaoke clubs, pool halls, massage parlors, and bars) and provide sexual services off-site.

While many popular accounts and much of the early scholarship discussed the archetypal relationship between Western male sex tourists and female Thai sex workers, commercial sex venues in Thailand in fact cater to a wide range of customers, including patrons from East Asia, the Middle East, Australia, Africa, North America, and Western Europe, as well as domestic Thai patrons. Like other service industries, these entertainment businesses cater to the preferences of the clients they wish to attract, including all-inclusive escort tours for Japanese clients, go-go bars for American and Australian tourists, niche hotels for Middle Eastern men, and a handful of bars that even forbid patronage by Thai men. Clients have been drawn to commercial sex in Thailand for a host of reasons, including the wide range of commercial sex establishments, relatively lenient legal restrictions against prostitution, and attraction to the stereotype of "beautiful, pliant, and docile Oriental women who offered more than paid sex."[39]

Writing about sex tourism in the contemporary Vietnamese context, the sociologist Kimberly Kay Hoang has described the ways in which

Western sex tourists have come to seek out not only sex but also "virtuous third world poverty" in their travels, where sex workers' poverty alongside Western clients' helping capacities are both deemed fundamental to the erotic encounter. Following the 2008 financial collapse in the West, she notes, both businessmen and backpackers looked toward burgeoning Asian industry for economic opportunities as well as for intimate relations. Sex workers serving these niches were able to glean the most profit by presenting themselves as both exotic (e.g., wearing makeup that made them look darker), and in desperate need of help (e.g., creating stories about family illness and destitution). In this way, Hoang argues, Vietnamese sex workers helped Western businessmen and Western budget travelers to "negotiate their personal sense of failed masculinity in the context of Western economic decline."[40]

In the following sections, we argue that Hoang's notion of virtuous third-world poverty is also useful for describing the melding of racialized eroticism and humanitarian sentiment that congeal in Southeast Asian sex tourist experiences more generally, including for the reality tourists that we encountered. The pursuit of eroticized virtue and abjection is not only a central pursuit of conventional sex tourists but also key to the ambitions of their successor cohort of alternative travelers. Preconditioned by anti-trafficking NGOs and popular representations of human trafficking, reality tourists interpret commercial sex as a deplorable symptom of third-world poverty and regard sex workers as victims-by-definition who lack meaningful voice and agency. The erotically charged images of anti-trafficking campaigns and the reality tourists' desires to save worthy victims ironically mirror the humanitarian impulses that inflect some forms of sex tourism—revealing a neocolonial formation that includes not only secular and evangelical activists but also those clients of sex workers who also endeavor to "help."

Anti-Trafficking Tourism as Humanitarian Endeavor

Previous chapters have pointed to the various ways in which moral agendas around sex work have become intricately interwoven with contemporary anti-trafficking campaigns. They have also described anti-trafficking activists' frequent equation of even adult and voluntary forms of prostitution with sex trafficking, and the tendency among activists (including when their focus is expanded to include forms of trafficking into other labor sectors) to single out sex trafficking as the most devastating case. As commentators such as legal scholar Jennifer Chacón have

4.1 Promotional photo for Global Exchange/Not for Sale Trafficking Reality Tour, from the organization's website, 2012.

noted, "trafficking" as defined in current federal law and in international protocols could conceivably encompass sweatshop labor, agricultural work, or even corporate crime, but it has been the far less common instances of sexually trafficked women and girls that have stimulated the most concern by evangelical Christians, prominent feminist activists, and the press.[41]

The tour operators on our trip frequently reproduced such assumptions and elisions, as did the promotional materials for the tour. For instance, the photo that advertised the Thailand tour in Global Exchange's promotional materials invokes the simultaneous moral and erotic allure of the enigmatic industry. It depicts an interracial couple embracing in a public balcony ensconced in bright red light. The blurry image, never explicit in its caption of what viewers are actually witnessing, suggests a clandestine peek into what is referred to in the accompanying text as a photographic representation of the global sex trade.

The photo foregrounds the red light district as evidence of the realities of human trafficking, despite the fact that brothel-style sex establishments such as the one depicted have all but disappeared from Thailand due to the aforementioned combination of changing local market economies, public health concerns around controlling HIV/AIDS, and recent legislation around prostitution.[42] Furthermore, the district that the photo is meant to portray would likely include a diverse range of beer bars, go-go bars, massage parlors, and karaoke bars, all distinct types of commercial establishments that employ sex workers to provide various forms of entertainment. Reality tourists are thus not encouraged to see the vast array of possible labor arrangements and power relations that encompass commercial sex work, or the particular political and economic factors that make the situation of the Thai sex industry unique.

Both the tour leaders and the participants on our reality tour shared the conviction that commercial sex and human trafficking cannot be easily distinguished, a fact that became clear during the initial round of group introductions. During our first dinner together, over a table of Thai tourist staples like pad thai and Singha beer, the tour leaders asked participants to introduce themselves and to briefly explain their interest in the anti-trafficking tour. Several of the young women named popular movies on both sex work and sex trafficking, like *Born into Brothels* and *Taken*, as their primary motivation for joining the tour.[43] As one master's degree student from a university in central California eagerly shared: "We watched *Born into Brothels* in one of my classes and that just opened the door for me." The deeply felt significance of this film was shared by a journalist from Atlanta, who echoed: "I am very passionate about ending human trafficking. *Born into Brothels* was also the film that really introduced me to the sex trade." Other participants attributed their interest in the issue to the 2004 Hollywood film *Taken*, which tells the story of an American teenager who is kidnapped on a vacation to Paris and nearly forced to become a sex worker before she is rescued. Reflecting on these films as a "wake-up call" as to just how pervasive global sex trafficking had become, another female tourist noted that movies like *Taken* alerted her to "the reality" of human trafficking.

The grounding of knowledge claims in sensationalist films about sex trafficking had thus shaped tourists' convictions and led them to broadly define all sex work as human trafficking before they had even left US soil. Consistent with the findings of other studies of humanitarian travel, the reality tour that travelers embarked on in Thailand did nothing to disabuse the tourists of their preexisting feelings and beliefs. In her study of Canadian aid workers, Barbara Heron emphasizes the important role played by Western media in the process of othering Global South nations, and the ways in which such accounts "normalize our centering of ourselves in relation to other people's needs."[44] In her ethnographic research on volunteer tourism in Guatemala and Ghana, Wanda Vrasti similarly found that tourists had established certain expectations of travel prior to departure, including levels of poverty that deem a tourist destination worthy of aid, and a gracious and welcoming recipient population in the host country.

In her research, Vrasti also discovered that volunteer tourists frequently expressed disappointment when their expectations failed to mesh with the realities they encountered on the ground: "Travelers repeatedly complained of 'not feeling needed,' either because local communities were not deemed 'poor enough' to require foreign assistance or because these programmes were not equipped to deliver humanitarian support."[45] Unlike development work or volunteer tourism which places tourists in communities with the purpose of fulfilling certain need-based projects (such as building homes, organizing libraries, teaching English, repairing dams), however, reality tourism steers clear of direct participant engagement with local populations, mediating tourists' contact with local communities through NGOs and tour guides. While volunteer tour organizers have limited control over how volunteers subjectively experience the tour, organizers of reality tours are better equipped to manage tourist experiences of "reality" through the explicit crafting of all aspects of the travel experience.

On our tour, one of the chief ways that tour organizers' shaping of reality was accomplished was through the allocation of time on the itinerary to particular NGOs, as well as through the omission of the perspectives of other organizations that might provide alternative views. For example, though most participants cited sexual exploitation as their principal interest in human trafficking, neither tour organizers nor participants on our tour deemed it important to visit sex workers' rights organizations or to speak directly with sex workers. When we asked the tour organizers why such opportunities were omitted, we were offered two different, and somewhat contradictory explanations. The first was that organizers were unaware of the existence of such organizations—a gap in knowledge that is noteworthy, given that Thailand is the base of several pioneering organizations that support sex workers' rights, including the Global Alliance against Traffic in Women, the Empower Foundation, and the Asia Pacific Network of Sex Workers.[46] The second explanation we were offered for the lack of sex worker perspectives was that the vulnerability of sex workers had already been sufficiently well documented. For the organizers as well as the attendees, sex workers had already been adequately spoken for—not by the pimps and *mamasans* who allegedly controlled them, but by the prevailing narratives in the mass media with which participants were already well acquainted, as well as by the advocacy campaigns of organizations such as Not for Sale.

The prevalent media narrative equating sex work, poverty, and human trafficking set the tone for the reality tour during our tour guide's brief introductory remarks on the issue. The guide posited a hypothetical scenario in which a young Thai woman from an impoverished rural area faces enormous financial pressure to provide for her family, and thus accepts a job as a sex worker in Bangkok. Our tour guide tried to encourage our group to understand how this could be considered a case of human trafficking even in light of the woman's choice to pursue sex work, posing the rhetorical question, "Do you *really* have a choice if you are living in poverty and have no other options?" The implicit framing of this hypothetical young woman's dilemma conditioned tourists to understand sex work as the worst of all possible occupational outcomes, as a grim inevitability rather than a socially constrained choice. Beyond the moral objection to selling sex and the narrow understandings of poverty and choice that our guide offered, no sustained explanation of the concrete connections between sex work and human trafficking was articulated at any point during the tour.

Throughout the trip, the tour guides' tactic of definitionally collapsing sex work, poverty, and human trafficking directly impacted how some reality tourists framed and made sense of Thai sex workers' experiences. By framing sex workers as choiceless victims, tourists were able to reiterate the narratives they had heard prior to arriving without any concern for how workers themselves spoke of their employment. The definitional ambiguity concerning the parameters of human trafficking—and the unclear links between human trafficking, sex work, and poverty—also allowed the predominantly white reality tourists to yearningly profile all the young Thai women they encountered as sex workers or as potential sex workers (and thus as victims of some kind), a humanitarian variant of the hypersexualized gaze that apprehends Asian femininities in cinema and beyond.[47]

This hopeful profiling of potential trafficking victims was consistent with the behavior of Western volunteers in anti-trafficking rescue projects in Bangkok, who frequent go-go bars and other commercial sex establishments on a weekly basis, hoping to recruit sex workers to participate in anti-trafficking rehabilitation projects. During participant observation on one such evening of outreach to several go-go bars in Bangkok, volunteers were instructed to buy drinks in order to make contact with "younger girls," who may appear "shy or awkward" dancing on stage. The director of the NGO explained that this profiling was helpful for identifying dancers who were new to sex work, and that shyness or discomfort would typically signal a victim in need of rescue. Despite the persistent search for young-looking and "innocent" women as ideal victims in need of rescue, it is in fact older sex workers who are the most likely to seek out alternative employment outside of sex work, particularly those for whom sex work becomes less lucrative with age. As one member of the Asia Pacific Network of Sex Workers explained to me during an interview, "What is really tragic is that there are hundreds of thousands of sex workers fifty-plus years of age who would give their eyeteeth for a bed. Instead, they end up on the street begging. But these are people that no one wants, and no one wants to fund. In Southeast Asia, the women's prisons are full of them."[48]

As previous analysts of sex tourism have also observed, being on vacation often provides tourists with opportunities to partake in certain liberties that they would never indulge in at home.[49] For instance, passing through a bar district where hostesses stood at the entrances to bars to greet and attract customers, one reality tourist pointed her finger in the direction of a young woman in a red sequined dress and gasped audibly, "Oh no, look at that poor thing . . . [I can't imagine] standing there every day, dressed like *that*, having to sell yourself." Unable to conceive of bar hostessing as a job with advantages as well as limitations, the tourist could not transcend her own horror at the thought of placing herself in this sex worker's shoes. This blend of repulsion and attraction was common to many of the reality tourists on our trip, even as the "realities" of sex trafficking remained as blurry as they appeared in the trip's promotional photo.

NGOs as Experts and Authenticators

Human trafficking's allegedly illicit and hidden nature—the very features that make it difficult to empirically assess—would seemingly make it an unlikely subject for a reality tour, in which the visible and sensorially apprehensible would presumably be paramount. As described in chapter 1, there are profound methodological challenges in attempting to estimate the prevalence of trafficking, obstacles that include safety for both the researcher and the research subjects, disparate definitions of human trafficking in different countries, and a lack of political will to provide transparency around the issue. Furthermore, trafficked persons themselves often do not embrace the vocabulary of trafficking, as the anthropologist Denise Brennan has highlighted in her review of the methodological challenges of studying trafficking. As Brennan writes,

"Even when trafficked persons enter emergency rooms, police stations, or call service providers, they usually do not describe themselves as trafficked, but rather seek help for other issues such as for immigration or domestic violence." Brennan quotes Nadra Qadeer, director of the Anti-Trafficking Program of the organization Safe Horizon in New York City, who observes: "People do not talk about trafficking ever. They talk about abuse, things like 'My boyfriend beat me.' "[50]

The methodological difficulties inherent in documenting cases of human trafficking ought to present a robust challenge to a "reality tour" that seeks to provide empirical evidence of its existence to consumers. Without access to the perspectives of trafficking victims themselves, reality tours must supplement participants' preexisting stereotypes and convictions with a reliance on the accounts of nongovernmental organizations. As our guides advocated, and as other scholars have noted, NGOs have served as brokers of knowledge for a slew of outsiders, including researchers, journalists, volunteers, and alternative tourists. The ethnographer Paige West observes that reliance on NGOs is also a strategy that has been employed by researchers seeking to gain insider knowledge without disrupting local realities.[51] Reality tourists may similarly assume that visiting NGOs is a reliable form of knowledge-producing activity that can provide them with access to the "back stage" of social interaction.[52]

The Mirror Art Foundation, a Thai NGO that focuses on the social and economic concerns of ethnic minority and stateless persons, was the focus of our group's visit to Chiang Rai, Thailand's northernmost city, which shares a border with Myanmar. Our delegation was housed for one evening at the Mirror Art Foundation's guesthouse, a social enterprise that supports the foundation's work by utilizing guesthouse profits to cover organizational costs. Additionally, handicraft items made by the organization's various recipient or beneficiary populations are sold in their expansive gift shop. The largest social enterprise profits the NGO receives are gleaned from the foundation's hill-tribe tours, which promise ethical and sustainable itineraries for traveling through Northern Thailand.[53] Since 2008, the Mirror Art Foundation has also dedicated time and resources toward a human trafficking project, claiming that "the extreme poverty of the region is fertile ground for those wishing to traffic women and children to wealthier areas of the country and the world."[54]

One day of our anti-trafficking reality tour was subcontracted to the Mirror Art Foundation, which agreed to provide us with an ecotour of the region, including an elephant ride, dinner, and participation in a dance performance in an ethnic minority village. Our group was driven down a bumpy, unpaved road located about twenty minutes from the nearest highway and deposited at the foot of a local Akha community. One of six indigenous hill-tribe populations in Thailand, the Akha are based in rural mountainous areas in the north, and many Akha persons continue to be without Thai citizenship and thus ineligible for land, services, or social protection under the law. Traditionally practitioners of subsistence farming, Akha communities now engage in cash cropping for sale, and increasingly participate in the tourist economy by hosting ecotours and producing ethnic handicrafts.[55]

As we disembarked from our van, half a dozen Akha women stood waiting at the entrance to the village, adorned in colorfully woven headpieces and dresses, and unveiling baskets full of handicraft items for sale. After completing their purchases, our group was ushered to sit in a giant circle of chairs where we were given the opportunity to direct questions to a person described as the village leader. Eager to have this opportunity, a social worker from Boston asked earnestly: "Have you had any cases of human trafficking here?" Through a translator provided by the Mirror Art Foundation, the Akha village leader told us he had never heard of the term "human trafficking," and after some clarification of the terminology, he told the group that this was not a key problem in the village. Disregarding his response, other reality tourists persisted with similar lines of questioning: "What about migration? Do people from this village leave to work?" The village leader once again said that this wasn't their primary problem.

As the discussion circle disbanded and we headed to a meal that had been prepared for us (described by tour guides as a "typical" Akha dinner of seasoned pork, stewed vegetables, and rice spread elaborately across a bed of banana leaves), tour participants huddled together and agreed that the village leader must have been lying. They easily dismissed the village leader's claim that in lieu of human trafficking, the more pressing issues of concern were securing Thai citizenship for ethnic hill-tribe populations and the aggressive infringement of land by corporations and the Thai government.[56] While they appreciated the Akha village's food, handicrafts, and costumes as an "authentic glimpse" into hill-tribe life, they quickly dismissed as fabricated the village leader's claim that his village was not particularly vulnerable to human trafficking. Just as Vrasti found in her study of volunteer tourism, the cultural authenticity of the tourist experience and the validity of insider claims were called into question only when they violated tourists' preexisting notions of social realities.[57] Significantly, the tourists ignored the most "authentic"

4.2   A startling proclamation for the reality tourists to an Akha village, as the village leader claims there is no human trafficking. Photo: Elena Shih.

voice they had heard so far—that of the Akha village leader himself—because it did not conform to the understandings of human trafficking that they already harbored, accounts that had been confirmed for them by the Mirror Art Foundation's "experts."

Selling Sex and Trafficking: Conflations and Contestations

In contrast to the Akha village leader who claimed that human trafficking was not as relevant as were concerns about citizenship and land rights—issues that were never otherwise addressed during the tour—the reality tour's insistence on the pernicious and pervasive nature of human trafficking was explicitly asserted during our visit to the Labor Rights Promotion Network in Bangkok, an organization that focuses on the labor rights of migrant workers in the Thai fishing industry. Founded in 2004, LRPN was one of the earliest advocates and service providers for victims of labor trafficking in deep-sea fishing and the shrimp-peeling industries.[58] Alongside the growth of global anti-trafficking campaigns, LRPN has received a significant amount of international attention for addressing the problems of severe labor exploitation in the Thai fishing industry. LRPN has also received a steady stream of funding to pursue research, advocacy, and direct interventions in human trafficking.

During our visit to the organization, we huddled around a large table in the organization's meeting room while LRPN's director of human trafficking programs described the basic parameters of three recent trafficking cases that they had worked on: a labor trafficking case, a case of trafficking for domestic servitude, and a case of sex trafficking. When describing the sex-trafficking case, LRPN pulled up photographs of a raid that they had conducted in collaboration with the Thai Department of Special Investigations, one of the government anti-trafficking agencies. The majority of photographs focused on the special team that had been assembled to deal with the case: a large group of first responders including cameramen, note takers, social workers, and police agents converging on a room where several sex workers lived. One grainy photo that briefly flashed on the screen depicted eight women sitting in a simple living room adorned with only heavily worn furniture. The presenter explained that the squalid living conditions in this home represented a clear indication of human trafficking. Aside from the brief and occluded glimpse into what appeared to be merely a room full of Asian women, the presenter never indicated to us why this case was considered a case of trafficking under current Thai law.[59]

Puzzled by the still-unspecified particulars of the alleged sex-trafficking case, we queried the LRPN representative further, hoping to get a better sense of how the organization identified trafficking cases and how they distinguished consensual from coerced forms of sexual labor. Frustrated by our persistent questioning, one reality tour participant shook her head grimly and whispered to her neighbor: "Why don't they believe that it's trafficking? Did you see the conditions they were living in?" Like the other tour participants, she was already schooled in the cinematic language of what the anthropologist Carole Vance has termed "melomentary," a cinematic genre in which "the horror of sex is amplified by the horror of poverty." In melomentaries, Vance notes, the camera visually attributes "residential crowding, lack of clean water, TB, poor hygiene, disease, and living on the street specifically to brothels, prostitution, and sex trafficking, rather than to the more general and widespread living conditions of impoverished people."[60] Fluent in the cinematic languages of melomentary that Vance describes, the tour participants required no proof of human trafficking beyond the photos of the dimly lit and crowded living conditions in a brothel located in one of the poorer sections of town.

In fact, we were soon to discover that the actual case turned out to be significantly more complicated than initially presented. When we interviewed the LRPN presenter on our own following the larger group meeting, we learned that the case concerned a group of migrant Laotian sex workers, many of whom, LRPN admitted, were working willingly. Given that they were undocumented, the police raid that was done in the name of combating human trafficking left the majority of workers facing deportation. Meanwhile, those workers who were under the age of eighteen were automatically classified as "victims of trafficking," because as minors, they legally did not have the right to choose to be sex workers. This latter group was taken to government shelters, where they would be held (with or without their consent, it was not clear) until the legal proceedings against their brothel owners were completed.

Through our own supplementary research with local sex worker organizations and activists, we would also later learn that many sex workers find such protectionist interventions to be even worse than jail or deportation because the "sentences" are indefinite, and because once they are deemed to be victims of trafficking, apprehended sex workers are subject to a number of gender-specific forms of discipline and control. The Empower Foundation has identified a number of common anti-trafficking practices which are justified by the state in the name of providing protection but are often experienced by sex workers as intrusive and discriminatory, including compulsory medical testing.[61] In Empower's report *Hit and Run: Sex Workers' Research on Anti-Trafficking in Thailand*, the authors note:

All women who are apprehended in raids routinely undergo mandatory medical tests with no information provided to them as to why the tests are required, and no genuine opportunity to refuse these testing procedures. There are no trained translators employed by hospitals where these tests are taken. Screening includes blood tests for infectious diseases, including HIV and internal vaginal examinations for sexually transmitted infections. Both exams are only enforceable under Thai National Security laws and/or if directly ordered by the court for specific purpose. In all other situations, mandatory testing is a serious breach of rights under the Thai Constitution. There is no clear process, procedure or evidence of whether women are informed of their results or not; when that might be; or if HIV treatment is ever offered.[62]

The Australian human rights lawyer Anne Gallagher further observes that "protection from further harm is one of the most commonly cited justifications for keeping trafficked persons in shelters against their will. Female victims of trafficking are widely considered to need this protection more than their male counterparts . . . It is not surprising that many shelters for trafficking victims in South East Asia are either modeled on, or have evolved from, institutions and arrangements originally designed to rehabilitate female sex workers."[63]

During our visit to the Can Do Bar in Chiang Mai, a sex worker–owned and –managed bar that is one of the Empower Foundation's projects, sex worker activists described how, in Thai government shelters, victims may wait up to two years to testify as witnesses against their "traffickers," and while awaiting trial, they are forbidden from seeing their families or leaving shelter premises. According to the Empower Foundation, undocumented migrant sex workers who are apprehended in "raid and rescue" operations are held in mandatory detention in police cells or women's shelters while receiving support or awaiting court hearings. Sex workers are held in detention when they are presumed to have been trafficked or when they are expected to act as witnesses in anti-trafficking prosecutions.[64] By keeping women captive, Gallagher further notes the extent to which "shelters can . . . serve the political and strategic interests of governments." She observes that in Thailand, "the major closed shelter is widely considered—and promoted—as strong evidence of the government's commitment to a victim-centered approach to ending trafficking." At the same time, "a captive and permanent victim population ensures that tours of the facility can be provided at short notice to important visitors including heads of state and donors."[65]

At the Can Do Bar, we also heard the stories of apprehended sex workers who had their mobile phones confiscated while in state custody. Although state officials claim that this is done to maintain the anonymity of shelter locations and to protect all residents from the possibility of being located by their traffickers, the consequence for apprehended sex workers is that they have no way of getting in touch with legal representatives or friends and family members (including their dependents and young children) for the duration of their stay. Required to surrender numerous personal freedoms as "victims of trafficking," many sex workers prefer swift deportation to lengthy periods of detention in shelters. Empower has even published a manual titled *I Came on My Own*, which explains human trafficking and prostitution laws so that sex workers are better equipped to understand the potential consequences of being identified as trafficking victims during police raids.[66]

Had the delegation accompanied us to the Can Do Bar to meet with local sex worker activists, it would likely have been an unwelcome surprise for them to hear from women who had ample experience working in the industry and who fundamentally understood exploitation and trafficking better than our purportedly expert guides. For instance, Malee Buyu, a self-described "35+"-year-old sex worker and staff member of Empower, who conducts outreach to other sex workers in seven languages and dialects, shared some of her experiences with us. Malee explained that she had endured years of exploitation in numerous low-wage jobs in Burma and later in Thailand after fleeing her country because of violent armed conflict and poverty. Eventually she had the opportunity to start to do sex work: "For years I had been exploited and abused," she explained. "All that time I had avoided 'selling my body' because I understood it to mean cutting off bits and literally selling my flesh. [Then] I discovered it simply meant sleeping with a man and getting paid for it! I had wasted a lot of time."[67]

The women in the bar also shared stories of exploitation with us—instances of violence that they had experienced at the hands of employers, of customers, and most especially at the hands of the police. Yet notably, the stories they recounted (many of which have also been transcribed and translated into English in the organization's pamphlet *Bad Girls Tales*) bore little in common with the stock renditions of what trafficking is typically understood to consist. One woman, for example, described having worked at a karaoke bar, expecting the three-thousand-baht monthly salary that the bar owner had agreed to pay her. Instead, she discovered that her pay would be docked by two thousand baht to pay for the uniforms she was required to wear, and other monies would be deducted for arbitrary infractions. A second woman of Akha background explained to us: "When you have no documents or proof of identity in practically any entertainment place you work, you will have the salary cut to pay the police on top of the normal protection fees taken out to pay them. Not only that but we also have our salary cut for uniform expense, getting to work late, and any other reason the boss can think of." A third woman described the police as "the absolute worst yet most unavoidable customers," after clarifying that she had had "dreadful experiences with police. . . . [T]hey have bled me dry and I'm powerless to do anything."[68]

As Jo Doezema, the sex workers' rights activist and researcher has eloquently argued, the mass appeal of "trafficking" as an issue of humanitarian concern is predicated upon the notion of the non-sex-working innocent victim: "If it is recognized that the majority of those in the sex industry who end up in debt-bondage or slavery-like conditions were *already* working as sex workers, it is impossible to avoid the conclusion that it is prostitutes whose human rights are being violated on a massive scale. Of course this is unpalatable to the international community: it is one thing to save innocent victims of forced prostitution, quite another to argue that prostitutes deserve rights. It is not only governments who prefer saving innocent women to giving rights to guilty ones."[69] The firsthand accounts that were shared with us by sex worker activists illustrate that the definition of human trafficking is still widely contested by a diverse array of stakeholders, including Thai law enforcement officials, local and international NGOs, individual village chiefs, sex workers, reality tour operators, and the tourists embarking upon "reality tours." What is certain, however, is that sex workers' perspectives—which often oppose the well-rehearsed narrative that all sex work is human trafficking—were ignored by our tour because these alternative narratives did not confirm the realities that tourists had paid to witness.

New Experts

As the culminating and most eagerly anticipated event of the trip, the director of Urban Light, a newly founded NGO dedicated to rehabilitating boys in the sex industry (although most of the young men they encounter are in fact in their early twenties), met with us to discuss her anti-trafficking work and to take us to one of Chiang Mai's principal bar districts.[70] The evening began over a late dinner in a local restaurant, in which the director of the organization chatted casually about her work and briefly introduced us to several of the young men who had recently completed the organization's employment training program. Designed to "enable preparation to live a life beyond the red-light district," their participation in this meeting was facilitated by the fact that they were currently employed in the restaurant's kitchen washing dishes, like many of the other clients of Urban Light.[71]

The director, a recent graduate of Pepperdine University, an evangelical Christian University in Southern California, shared her own experience of coming to Thailand on a previous reality tour where she had observed the "indignities of the slave trade" for the first time. Upon returning home to California, she felt compelled to leave her husband behind and to return to Chiang Mai to fight the scourge of human trafficking. She described to us how, armed with nothing but passion for the issue, she came to Thailand to found her organization for sex-trafficked boys. In so doing, her efforts were consistent with a recent trend in which evangelical Christian organizations have been more likely than secular groups to turn their attention to sex-trafficked boys as well as girls, in Thailand and beyond.[72]

The Urban Light director then led the group to Loi Kroh Road, one of the primary commercial sex districts in Chiang Mai, and one of the areas where she "came to understand the issue of trafficking" for the

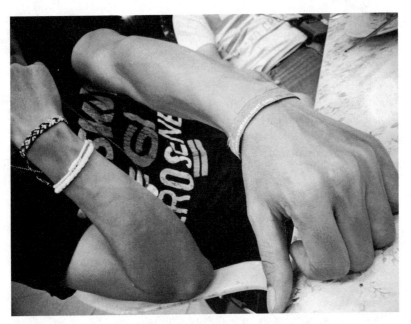

4.3   The braceleted wrist of a young man who has completed rehabilitative training with the
       Urban Light Project. The Urban Light bracelet he is wearing reads, "I wish the sex trade
       disappeared." Photo: Elena Shih.

first time. This statement was striking to us, given that the sex worker
activists we had met with at Empower suggested that Loi Kroh Road's
ample bar scene and foot traffic made it one of the safest places in the
city to work. Passing by a variety of bars where sex workers had positioned themselves outside to attract clients, the reality tourists marched
briskly down the street, avoiding eye contact presumably to indicate
their disapproval of the industry. Once we arrived at an intersection, the
director pointed out several bars that she referred to as "boy bars,"[73] and
she instructed the group that she would not be able to accompany us
inside the bars because this would draw too much attention to her and
compromise her ability to provide future assistance. Four group members also abstained from entering the bars, asserting that they did not
want to contribute to the industry that was supporting the sex trade, and
as an alternative, chose to shop for Thai silks and ethnic minority handicrafts in a nearby night market.[74]

    The following morning was the last day of our trip, and participants
were gathered in the lobby of the guesthouse to recount their experiences walking in Loi Kroh Road the night before:

Tourist 1: The boy-girls were talking to me.

Tourist 2: There were boy-girls?!

Tourist 1: Whoa you didn't see the boy-girls? They were boys who look like girls—got boob jobs.

Tourist 3: How was it talking to the transsexuals?

Tourist 1: Oh everything that we learned . . . nailed it! One boy told me: "I came down here and I paid off my parents and I don't have to work anymore and I'm freeeee," and you know just really charismatic, everything we learned, and another one also wasn't flamboyant but he was like rubbing up on this old man—sitting with this really nasty, crusty old man.

Group: Oh, so gross.

Tourist 1: He was trying to talk to me, he was saying that—he was using his hands— "I run from Burma boom, boom, boom, boom, boom. No mama, no papa and I have to beg, and now I'm here."

Tourist 3: Was that a she-man or just a boy?

Tourist 1: It was a boy.

Amid the narratives of sexual slavery that participants were intent on re-creating, they often missed the claims that came directly from the voices of the sex workers themselves. In the conversational extract recounted here, the first young man whom the tourists spoke with actually described his pride in being able to send money back home to his family; he explained that having repaid his parents for the cost of his initial transport, he was "free" and had chosen to work in the bar. For the reality tourists, however, the excitement that "everything we learned" was true overpowered the alternative realities that the subjects they encountered had actually expressed. As other theorists of late-capitalist consumer culture have noted, familiarity with mass-mediated cultural scripts is precisely what enables people to identify "the authentic" when they encounter it in their own experiential worlds.[75] This criteria for establishing authenticity may lead people to overlook the ways in which mass-mediated narratives are actually contradicted by the testimony of those who recount other life stories.

For most of the participants, fulfillment of the fantasy of discovering the "truth" of rampant sexual slavery, even in the face of empirical evidence to the contrary, was the point of the tour in the first place (just as specific fantasies of sexual "openness," or erotic submissiveness, or virtuous third-world poverty may be projected onto local populations when people travel to "exotic" settings to participate in other forms of sex tourism). In the case of the reality tourists we traveled with, their own fantasies of sexual slavery and humanitarian intervention were premised upon a particular sexual morality (one which posits prostitution as unfree by definition) as well as a latent ethnocentric heteronormativity. For reality tourists, the importation of a particular set of normative convictions around gender and sexuality precluded the possibility that sexual labor could be an effective means of providing for the assertion of subjectively desired and in fact culturally meaningful forms of gender expression and sexual identity.[76]

Tourism as Advocacy

Upon return, Global Exchange will integrate the insights of the trip directly into an understanding of the nature of human trafficking in the United States and the meaning of working globally on . . . abolitionist activities. GLOBAL EXCHANGE 2013

The ambitious claim made on the Global Exchange website regarding the knowledge to be gleaned from reality tourism assures participants that their experiences in Thailand will enable them to become effective anti-trafficking advocates once they return home. It also expresses Global Exchange's conviction that the reality-tourist experience is not meant to stop at the site of consumption, but to be brought back to the United States through activism opportunities bred from the expertise that tourists have acquired firsthand. As such, we see that in the travels of trafficking, crisscrossing global circuits are as important as the hegemony of official UN and TVPA doctrine in shaping the political contours of the issue—in Thailand as well as in other regions.[77] Indeed, after the culmination of our trip, many group members joined together to create a website of reflections, notes, and photos, while several others announced that they would be attending the Freedom Forum (paying the sum of $200 for the privilege) hosted by Not for Sale in the coming fall.

Some reality tour participants crafted blog entries to raise awareness about the issue, and still others organized fund-raisers. For example, a group of social work students from a Southern California university attended the same reality tour we did one month prior to our own trip. In October 2012, they held a wine-tasting fund-raiser in Los Angeles for Urban Light, where they raised $1,200 to cover the organization's operating costs. In addition to funding Urban Light, proceeds from this fund-raiser also went to a campaign in support of the Californians against Sexual Exploitation Act, also known as Proposition 35, a highly contentious law that stipulated increased criminal sentencing for sex traffickers and sex-trafficking-related crimes.[78] The founder of Urban Light, the same woman who had led our reality tour through the commercial sex district in Chiang Mai, was able to attend the event, having allocated about half of her year to speaking and fund-raising tours around the United States. Addressing the group of just over fifty people who had gathered at this upscale wine bar, most of whom had never traveled to Thailand, she retold the stories of sexual victimization that she had narrated to our group in Chiang Mai. The reality tour participants who organized the event affirmed the director's narrative and chimed in with their own corroborating observations from their trip to Loi Kroh Road earlier that year.

These examples of subsequent activist engagement in the United States illustrate how the sex-trafficking narratives crafted by particular individuals and organizations in Thailand are reinscribed as truth once reality tour participants return home. Through fund-raisers such as the one described here, tourists translate their travel experiences into expertise that can be leveraged into new forms of consumer-based advocacy. They do so because, as Vrasti points out, their continued participation in anti-trafficking networks serves to augment forms of social capital and of "civility, social responsibility and cosmopolitan citizenship" that have become essential ingredients of success in the global economy.[79] To enact this global citizenship, tourists-turned-advocates must participate in the anti-trafficking discourse that reaffirms the hegemonic moral and political agendas of the NGOs that are supported by dominant funding streams.

Conclusion

"Human trafficking" may seem an unlikely candidate for a reality tour because the term is not only definitionally contested but also describes a multifaceted process lacking a discrete, physical site for visible witnessing and analysis. Enigmatically, it is the alleged invisibility of human trafficking that makes it an alluring object of consumption for tourists seeking to experience a meaningful alternative to conventional travel experiences. The Global Exchange and Not for Sale reality tour compensates for the invisibility of human trafficking by offering participants a glimpse into a world of deviance and more visible social problems, such as poverty, migration, and, most importantly, commercial sex. The focus on commercial sex, we suggest, is important not just for "selling" the tour to potential participants, but also for providing an affective substratum of desire, disgust, and moral outrage which serves to occlude other political contradictions.

In this way, "reality tours" also serve to confirm what participants have already learned to feel and to believe prior to traveling, perhaps because commercially packaged tours, by their very nature, must resist political complexity to appeal to a dedicated market niche of consumers. Fascination with sex and poverty drives Westerners to Thailand; however, once they arrive there, they avoid sustained interactions with sex workers—and in particular, with sex workers' rights organizations—so as to not challenge the already-cemented imaginaries of what sexual commerce in Thailand consists of. Critical of commercial sex for its purported ties to human trafficking, reality tourists are drawn to Thailand for the very same reasons as other sex tourists—for sun, sex, and life-altering adventures, to paraphrase the title of a well-known academic volume.[80] Anti-trafficking reality tours occur squarely at this intersection while also appealing to the yearnings for sexual and moral authenticity that have come to characterize neoliberal capitalism—a set of political and libidinal longings that chapter 5 unpacks in more detail. Although reality tourists attempt to distance themselves from the pervasive networks of sex and capital that have driven Thailand's global reputation and popularity as a destination of leisure, their motivations for travel are intertwined in the same erotic and economic circuits that have made Thailand a desirable touristic destination for decades.

FIVE

Redemptive Capitalism and Sexual Investability

Equal parts social movement, revival meeting, infotainment, and product launch, the annual Global Forum on Human Trafficking is held on Inspiration Way in the heart of Silicon Valley. This terrain is notable, given that its high-tech sector helped give rise to the growth and normalization of sexual commerce that those in attendance purportedly oppose.[1] At the same time, it marks the crucial relocation of political debates that a mere ten years prior would have been conducted at the State Department in Washington, DC, or at the UN headquarters in New York, with public officials convening alongside global anti-trafficking activists and newly prominent corporate-sector social actors under sunny California skies.

The precise location for the 2011 gathering of several thousand was the Aspiration Dome of Juniper Networks, which specializes in the production of routers. Mere blocks away from the gleaming facades of the marquis companies of the "Googleopolis" (Yahoo, Nokia, Lockheed Martin, and Google itself), the glossy and colorful banner for the event read "Where Freedom Meets Innovation." If the sex-technology nexus first became known through the emergence of online pornography and prostitution in the mid-1990s, it had become relevant once again in reshaping the contours of the sex industry—this time, through the creation of a growing assortment of anti-trafficking apps, online games, mapping devices, and movement-building activities such as this conference.

Present at the Global Forum were some of the most important new constituencies in contemporary campaigns to combat human trafficking, socially entrepreneurial business ventures such as Juniper Networks (whose role as host of the 2011 forum facilitated the promotion of its Free2Work anti-trafficking mobile phone app), a new crop of celebrity activists such as Mira Sorvino and Demi Moore, and multinational corporations such as the Gap, the Body Shop, and Manpower Incorporated.[2] By the final years of President Obama's first term, with the influence of the religious right no longer in ascendance, these social actors would increasingly come to displace the "strange bedfellows" coalition of secular feminists and evangelical Christians who had initially pioneered the issue of trafficking as their cause, in the process, extending its discursive range, circulation, and empirical focus. Exemplifying this shift in tenor, President Obama would highlight the important role to be played by business leaders in fighting trafficking during a landmark speech on the issue delivered at the Clinton Global Initiative just prior to the 2012 elections.[3] Broadening the implications of this position while also clarifying his core message, he went on to declare in his first State of the Union address following reelection that "progress in the most impoverished parts of our world enriches us all. Not only because it creates new markets . . . but also because it's the right thing to do . . . by connecting more people to the global economy, by empowering women, by giving our young and brightest minds new opportunities to serve."[4]

Consistent with the market-driven, multisectoral approach to combatting trafficking that Obama articulated in his speeches, at the Juniper Networks Global Forum there was also ample discussion of slavery in industries beyond the sex sector, from bonded labor in Afghanistan to domestic work in Nepal, from the production of chocolate in West Africa to the manufacture of pig iron in Brazil. These were interwoven seamlessly with references to child marriage in India and to brothel-based prostitution in Amsterdam's red-light district (a series of otherwise abrupt transitions that was helped along by audiovisual materials provided by CNN's Freedom Project, an anti-trafficking corporate media initiative).[5] As commentators such as Pardis Mahdavi have also observed, the United States' annual *Trafficking in Persons Report* (*TIP Report*) was almost exclusively focused on sex trafficking until 2009. The 2009 *TIP Report* was also the first to feature a special subheading on "public-private sector partnerships." This section singled out LexisNexis, Wyndham Hotels, Microsoft, and Carlson Hotels for their role as politically crucial "leaders" in the global movement to combat trafficking.[6]

The Juniper Networks Global Forum, together with Obama's remarks, thus signaled the beginning of a shift in the discourse of trafficking that would become increasingly ascendant during the post-Bush years—via philanthropic foundations like Humanity United (whose website pledges to "engage markets and businesses as a force for change" and to "encourage the exploration of promising ideas and innovations to build peace and advance human freedom"), a series of new technology-driven initiatives, and robust and developing public-private partnerships with a variety of corporate-sector actors. In all of these efforts, a variety of nonsexual forms of labor were newly highlighted, seemingly eliminating the problem of the overly sexual focus that had enveloped the issue of trafficking during the George W. Bush years. "Come for the sex, stay for the labor," quipped Ambassador Luis deBaca, the Obama administration official charged with directing State Department anti-trafficking efforts, during one of his routine gatherings with concerned scholars and activists.[7]

But if "human trafficking" (as popular political cause and as the signature human rights issue for a growing number of corporate as well as more conventional activist constituencies) had ceased to be simply a crude stand-in for commercial sexual exchange, of what precisely was it now understood to consist? As the name of the new Free2Work app suggests, "human trafficking" would come to designate not only all or almost all forms of sexual labor but also child labor and forced labor in a variety of other sectors. In the Free2Work app, "forced labor" refers specifically to nonsexual forms of labor that are unwaged, located in the developing markets of the Global South, and which take place outside the victims' own homes. Conversely, when sex itself is the commodity for sale, it is the *presence* of a wage that is understood to mark the difference between slavery and freedom.

The distinctions between "forced" and "free" labor that these apps posit are particularly noteworthy given Tiziana Terranova's analysis of the rise of "free labor" that is inherent in postindustrial economies (i.e., the various forms of unremunerated labor that producers and consumers perform to sustain digital commerce) as well as when considered alongside other forms of labor that are uncompensated, integral to postindustrial economic life, and yet rarely characterized as unfree—from prison labor to "workfare" to a variety of legally brokered arrangements in which workers must labor without monetary compensation to pay off debts incurred to recruiters.[8] Significantly, too, in the Free2Work app, as well as in other corporate characterizations of trafficking, sexual labor stands in contrast to a list of other forms of labor that have both "forced" and "free" variants; only prostitution is always and necessarily on "the wrong side

5.1   The Free-2-Work anti-trafficking app. Screen grab, 2012.

of the line," to use Gayle Rubin's apt and classic schema.[9] In the severing of "forced labor" from more mundane forms of labor exploitation, as well as in the suturing of the former to monetized sexual relations, the Free2Work app and the new discourse that it heralded would at last come into compliance with the curious and contradictory definitions of "trafficking" that had been encoded into the UN Protocol and the TVPA some ten years prior, mirroring their own ambiguities, political compromises, and definitional contradictions.

Such ambiguities and contradictions are illustrated even more graphically in Slavery Footprint, a competitor app whose development was funded by the State Department and Google. Like the Free2Work app, Slavery Footprint transforms users' mobile phones into scanning devices that enable individual shoppers to assess whether or not their intended purchases are "slave-free." The app thus privatizes and technologically translates the tier-ranking system of the annual US *TIP Report* (which ranks countries, not corporations) on their compliance with international trafficking protocols and, in so doing, transposes the geopolitics of censure and sanctions into morally laden instances of individual consumer choice. But the app also enables users to "find out how many slaves work for you" by responding to a fourteen-screen survey. The survey calculates the precise number of slaves by asking users a series of questions about their consumption habits, then mapping the likely supply chains for different consumable products and imputing the designations of "forced" or "free" categorically to different regions and industries. The app also asks users to specify in which city they live, what they like to eat, whether they use toiletries or wear jewelry, if they drive a car, and whether they own electronic appliances, sporting equipment, or cotton clothing. Yet crucially, the highly engaging interactive survey (it was a finalist for the 2012 Guardian Award for digital innovation) culminates with the question "How many times have you paid for sex?" on the final screen.[10] When they unzip an electronic fly, users are informed not only that the "sex industry relies on force, fraud, and coercion" but that "if you participate in these activities, you are contributing to the demand that fuels sex trafficking—making your slavery footprint inestimably bigger." Set apart from the logic of algorithmic calculability, sex trafficking serves as an unquantifiable source of moral certainty and inarticulable deep feeling.

As described in chapter 1, observers of contemporary anti-trafficking campaigns have often folded current mobilizations against "sex trafficking" into a long history of moral or "sex panics," orienting their concern toward the overly sexual focus that has taken grasp of a seemingly uncontroversial, progressive cause. Representative of this tendency, the sociologist Ron Weitzer has described feminist and conservative Christian campaigns again sex trafficking in the United States as a "moral crusade" akin to previous social mobilizations against alcohol consumption and pornography. Similarly, Carole Vance has cautioned that although the crime of trafficking no longer focuses exclusively on prostitution in ei-

5.2 (above), 5.3 (right, top), 5.4 (right, bottom)   Slavery Footprint site (www.slaveryfootprint.org). Screen grabs, March 2012.

FREE MARKET
TO
FREE PEOPLE

The Slavery Footprint Team

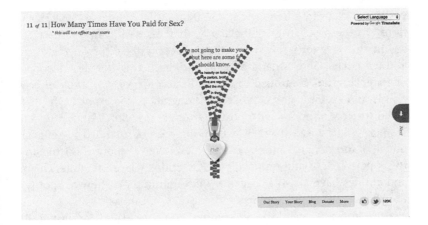

ther international or US law, "these more capacious and exploitation-based definitions compete with popular and media portrayals, which overwhelmingly favor the nineteenth-century story of sexual danger and rescue." And Gayle Rubin, perhaps the best-known theorist of the diverse social and economic transactions that have been hailed as the "traffic in women," aptly remarked in a 2011 essay: "The constant conflation of prostitution with trafficking is neither accidental nor is it new."[11]

Yet as corporations increasingly claim the issue of human trafficking as the focus of their philanthropic projects, "social responsibility" initiatives, and branding campaigns—in the process, widening the focus of "trafficking" beyond prostitution to include a host of other issues—the most salient question to ask at the current juncture may not pertain to how "sex" got entangled with human trafficking, but rather its corollary and reverse: how, why, and to what effect have these other agendas become entangled with sex?[12] In particular, what work does a more generalized concern with disparate forms of "unfree" labor do in sedimenting a particular configuration of sexual politics? Similarly, in what ways might the shift from "sex trafficking" to "human trafficking" serve to transmute other discourses of inequality and exploitation that, post-2008, have come into increasing circulation? And most generally, how have normative visions of gender and sexuality and politically and economically profitable forms of social investment become reciprocally productive?

Although the fashion and cosmetics industries, as well as the hospitality, entertainment, and even oil and pharmaceutical sectors have all recently become involved in anti-trafficking campaigns in both serious and peripheral ways by offering funding, framing, and "market-based solutions" to the problem of trafficking as they define it,[13] my primary focus in this chapter is on two particular corporate sectors—technology and temporary labor—that are useful in illuminating how the discourse of trafficking has continued to evolve in accordance with broader economic and cultural shifts. While the Body Shop, for example, has papered its store windows with posters announcing "Soft Hands Stop Sex Trafficking" (a slogan that one can presume is not intended to be taken literally) and donated money to raise "awareness" about the issue and to support various anti-trafficking NGOs, and while several hotel chains and airlines have boasted that they offer trainings on "how to spot sex trafficking" (teaching employees to critically scrutinize dyads of underage girls and adult men who appear on their premises),[14] I am specifically interested in the new array of corporate efforts that appear to broaden the terrain of "trafficking" to economic sectors beyond sex, thereby addressing what has become an important touchstone of liberal and progressive critique. My primary focus here is further confined to those corporate efforts that claim to transcend mere "cause-related marketing," humanitarian "branding," and philanthropic investment, which many corporate actors themselves admit to be of less substance than show.[15] Instead, I am most concerned with what some private-sector actors have characterized as a new paradigm of social justice "thought leadership" in a world in which the nation-state no longer reigns ascendant, or what Klaus Schwab, founder of the World Economic Forum, has provocatively termed "global corporate citizenship." In the words of Schwab, "Global corporations

5.5 (top), 5.6 (bottom), and 5.7 (following page)   A sampling of recent corporate social responsibility campaigns focused on human trafficking.

Global Business Coalition Against Human Trafficking

www.gbcat.org

Our Mission

To mobilize the power, resources and thought leadership of the business community in an effort to end human trafficking, including all forms of forced labor and sex trafficking.

- gBCAT is a global coalition of corporations committed to eradicating trafficking in supply chains, including forced labor and all sex trafficking, notably child prostitution.
- gBCAT is a thought leaders' forum to develop and share best practices for addressing the vulnerability of businesses to human trafficking in their operations.
- gBCAT companies work together across different sectors and regions, each playing their own part, suited to their sector and comparative competencies.
- gBCAT pursues collaborative initiatives such as training modules for employees, raising awareness, sharing best-practices, and informing public policy.

www.gbcat.org

have not only a license to operate in this area but also a civic duty to contribute to the world's well being. . . . [G]lobal corporate citizenship means engagement at the macro level on issues of importance to the world."[16]

The two case studies of corporate interventions that I pursue in greater detail in the pages that follow—those of Google and Manpower—are thus notable not only because they represent two different economic sectors, high technology and brokered labor, that are critical to neoliberal economic restructuring, but also because each corporation has made significant claims about its role as a "thought leader" in the social justice arena.[17] Significantly, both corporations have also made deliberate and explicit points to widen the focus of contemporary anti-trafficking campaigns to include a host of issues beyond prostitution—from domestic work to organ harvesting, from relations of debt bondage to the transparency of supply chains. As such, these campaigns are well poised to demonstrate the complex ways in which contemporary economic currents and new modes of sexual politics hinge together, whereby trafficking has become an investable—and indeed, redemptive—issue not only for feminists, evangelicals, and bipartisan state actors but also for a growing number of multinational corporate interests.

In the sections that follow, I pursue the intertwined inquiries I have outlined here through ethnographic material gleaned from the Juniper Networks Global Forum on Human Trafficking; at a variety of corporate-sponsored conferences and workshops on trafficking and corporate social responsibility that I attended between 2011 and 2012 in Silicon Valley, New York City, and Washington, DC; and via in-depth interviews with a sampling of private-sector actors (from the tech sector, the temporary help industry, and beyond) who have played a leading role in elevating and reshaping the issue.[18] I supplement this research with an analysis of recent corporate ad campaigns, products, games, apps, promotional materials, and publications, taking these as ethnographic artifacts and as politically crucial technologies of governance (in addition to serving as meaning laden "texts" or signs).[19] Finally, I draw upon background data provided by relevant press coverage and through my ongoing conversations with sex workers' rights activists who are well positioned to assess the impact of the anti-trafficking interventions described. Throughout this discussion, my central queries pertain to the broader political and cultural transformations that have guided this most recent swerve of the trafficking discourse: How did corporate investment in "trafficking" come about, and what does it materially and symbolically entail? What are the implications of this shift for broader struggles for economic justice and for prevailing debates around sex?

Capitalist Redemption

Perhaps the most straightforward approach to deciphering burgeoning corporate interest in fighting trafficking has been provided by the private sector itself, through business groups like the Global Business Coalition against Human Trafficking (gBCAT), founded by LexisNexis in 2010, and End Human Trafficking Now (EHTN), founded in 2006 by the Manpower corporation in partnership with former Egyptian first lady Suzanne Mubarak (a few short years before she was forced to relinquish her power in the region, specifically as a broker of "women's issues"[20]). Representatives from both coalitions offer a "good for the bottom line" logic of economic self-interest in arguing that corporations that do not become advocates within contemporary anti-trafficking campaigns run the risk of becoming targets themselves. As Mark Lagon, a former Bush administration official and the founder of gBCAT explained to me during a 2012 interview, "The key ingredient for getting a campaign going is finding a moral vision that works in terms of the tangible interests of the company." Citing what he referred to as the "classic example" of this in the ManpowerGroup (the world's largest labor brokerage firm, as well as the largest private-sector employer in the United States), he described the multipronged rationale of the corporation for making this issue their corporate social responsibility (CSR) focus. According to Lagon, these reasons included the reputational restoration of its labor sector, the circumvention of more thorough labor regulations, improved credit ratings, and better employee retention. In the words of William Livermore, champion of LexisNexis's CSR initiative around trafficking in persons, "We think it's good for business to do good in communities . . . by advancing the rule of law around the world, we're developing markets for ourselves."[21]

Echoing Lagon's and Livermore's chief claims, EHTN promotes the issue to the eleven corporate partners that make up the coalition as well as to prospective members through the bold declaration, "Ending human trafficking is smart business." The coalition has even circulated a compelling video (featuring stark black-and-white imagery, a strikingly energetic and upbeat soundtrack, and the rapid accent of a skyscraper leaving dollar signs in its wake) to succinctly convey to potential corporate partners "what's in it for you." While the video leaves aside questions of sexual politics in all but the most Freudian and phallic senses (see fig. 5.8), it makes explicit that advocacy on behalf of social causes can go hand in hand with risk aversion, enhanced brand value and shareholder trust, and the cultivation of new business opportunities. In the video, what World Economic Forum founder Klaus Schwab celebrates as the rise of "global corporate citizenship" can be seen as spearheading a new paradigm of social justice advocacy in which corporations not only invest in philanthropic projects but themselves become active stakeholders in advocacy campaigns, working to ensure that "social responsibility" and economic profitability coincide.[22]

Of course, diverse theoretical articulations of the so-called new capitalism (to borrow Richard Sennett's capacious term), including Nigel Thrift's "soft capitalism," Slavoj Žižek's "cultural capitalism," Jodi Dean's "communicative capitalism," and Eva Illouz's "emotional capitalism," have also pointed to such convergences, at the same time cautioning us to look beyond overly reductive attributions of corporations' material self-interest. In his well-known book *The Corrosion of Character*, Sennett deployed the term "new capitalism" to refer to the psychic counterpart of post-welfare-state economic flexibilization, which, as the title of his book suggests, he regards as individually and socially destabilizing.[23] Thrift's "soft capitalism," less singularly critical, highlights late capitalism's "adaptive characteristics and its supposedly caring, sharing ethos." For Žižek, "cultural capitalism" names the recent shift in consumptive as well as productive practices, in which commodities inspire us to remake our lives as "pleasurable and meaningful." Dean's "communicative capitalism" designates the "strange merging of democracy and capitalism" in which contemporary subjects are simultaneously "produced and trapped," while Illouz's "emotional capitalism" describes the infusing of economic relationships with emotionality as the public sphere counterpart to the incursion of economic logics into intimate terrain. And certainly, one of the key features of Deleuze's early articulation of the character of capitalism within contemporary "societies of control" was the terrifying lesson that "corporations have a soul."[24]

Within the critical social sciences, disparate empirical instances of the melding of progressive political sentiment with the profit imperative have also been traced in spheres of economic activity as diverse as the organic food and fair-trade movements,[25] ecotourism and "responsible travel" (discussed in the prior chapter), as well as in the intertwined economic, gendered, and sexual interests that coalesce in corporate campaigns around LGBT rights, women's empowerment, breast cancer, and reproductive health.[26] In a more celebratory tone, the popular press has provided an increasing stream of coverage of the melding of social justice goals with for-profit ventures, hailing these endeavors with clever monikers such as "philanthrocapitalism," "venture philanthropy," and

5.8 (top) and 5.9 (bottom)   EHTN video stills.

"spreadsheet humanitarianism."[27] At the same time, a growing number of multinational corporations—from Whole Foods to the Container
Store to TOMS—have celebrated the rise of so-called ethical, creative,
or conscious capitalism, publishing texts and sponsoring workshops on
"doing well by doing good" and "leveraging entrepreneurship for social
change."[28]

In sum, from accounts of the "soul at work" to the "conquest of cool"
to the late-capitalist appropriation of its own opponents and critique, we
have been advised to attend to the new economies of affect, meaning and
immaterial labor that circulate through and alongside relations of capitalist exchange.[29] As Boltanski and Chiapello argue, the "new spirit of
capitalism" is not solely predicated upon the capacity for accumulation,
because capitalism now "needs its enemies . . . people who provide it with
the moral foundations that it lacks, and who enable it to incorporate
justice-enhancing mechanisms whose relevancy it would not otherwise
have to acknowledge." Similarly, as Christine Harold has written in her
recent discussion of what she terms "aesthetic capitalism," "capital can no
longer rely simply on an explosion of surface-level sign value"; it must instead "go deep," operating "through the manufacture of depth rather than
the expansion of surfaces." And within Wanda Vrasti's explication of what
she describes as the new "caring capitalism" is an insistence that economic
conduct has been not only "emotionalized" but also made pleasurable in
new ways.[30] But if the theorists of the new capitalism are right and indeed
"meaning is the new money" (as the CEO from the Gap announced to the
audience during the Juniper Networks Global Forum), how can we better
understand the meanings and pleasures that are at stake here?[31]

One answer is suggested by the comments of Douglas Alexander, at the
time the shadow foreign minister of the British Labour Party, who figured
among the handful of political officials invited to speak at the Global Forum alongside an array of more prominent corporate leaders and celebrities (including representatives from Facebook, Twitter, and the Body
Shop, as well as Mira Sorvino and the Duchess of York). Telling those
in attendance that "the era of social entitlements is over," he went on
to note that "movements like these are the way to fight for a more just
capitalism. . . . [T]his is where people's passions for justice need to go."
An ideological descendent of "compassionate conservatism," Alexander
situated the morality of market exchange not in the supplementary spheres
of family, church, and charity but within capitalist enterprise itself as
a key site of feeling and belonging. Locating morality in both the consumptive and the productive moments of capitalist exchange (and in the

co-temporality of both with humanitarian endeavor), his model was notably distinct from classical liberal and free-market paradigms that situate sentiment and morality outside of it.[32] Deeply resonant with both secular and Christian, and with socially liberal and conservative worldviews, we might best term this new configuration *redemptive capitalism*—a capitalism that is understood by its proponents to be not only transforming of self but of world, and indeed, of markets themselves in a moment when "the era of social entitlements is over."

Yet this suturing of prior divides between public and private, between paid and unpaid labor, and between markets and moral sentiment also suggests some new configurations of sexual politics that need to be further explored. For example, what meanings should we attribute to the shadowy and disarticulated female torso that lurks in the background of the logo for the Slavery Footprint app described above (see fig. 5.3), hovering behind the bold declaration that free markets are the fundament of free people? And how are we to best understand Obama's assertion that empowering women is crucial to the alchemy of creating new markets while doing good? If redemptive capitalism imagines women as neither residing outside the sphere of market exchange nor as directly exchangeable commodities within it, how, precisely, is gender deployed and (re)configured? These are the questions that I turn to next, by way of a brief ethnographic foray into Google's INFO-Summit on Illicit Networks.[33]

"Illicit Networks" as Sexual Technologies and Moral Fields

If the Juniper Networks' Aspiration Dome seemed an unlikely place to hold a conference on human trafficking, the setting for the summit on Illicit Networks hosted by Google Ideas (in partnership with the Tribeca Film Festival and the Council on Foreign Relations) seems even more improbable. Held in the Four Seasons Hotel with the Hollywood hills, artificial waterfalls, and lavish spreads of food and drink as our backdrop, the officially stated aims of the event are three: "to enhance the world's understanding of illicit networks," "to explore the relationship between illicit networks and technology," and "to develop technology-based approaches to expose and disrupt illicit networks." Panel topics ranged widely, from cyber money laundering to Somali pirates, from "the human face" of illicit networks to "free expression in the face of fear." As expressed in the somber tones of an unidentified African man appearing in the summit's promotional video, "People think that there's no link, but there's a definite link between child soldiers, the drug trade, the illegal arms trade, and sex slavery." His remarks seem to point to an additional if less explicitly articulated objective as well: the creation of a "counter-network" to rival the imagined network of illicit actors that the Summit claims to oppose. This counternetwork will be drawn from the unlikely array of attendees that Google has assembled here, including cybersecurity experts and movie stars, Defense Department officials and sex workers, labor organizers, investigative journalists, hackers, and

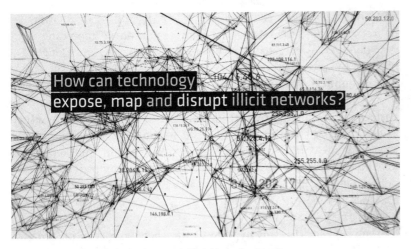

How can technology expose, map and disrupt illicit networks?

5.10 Background image from the Google Illicit Networks summit.

academics. As the official invitation for the event made clear, "Too often illicit networks, from drug smugglers and arms dealers to human traffickers and organ harvesters, are seen only in the silos of those who study them."[34] FROM MY FIELD NOTES, MALIBU, CALIFORNIA, JUNE 2012

"It's not new for Google to think beyond its borders," gushed the front page of the *Los Angeles Times* on the first morning of the Illicit Networks summit, "but its foray into some of the most troubling issues in world affairs has heated up debate over whether Google Ideas is daring to reshape the role of multinational corporations as global citizens or whether it's just another expression of Silicon Valley hubris."[35] The article went on to suggest that some combination of "both" was most likely, noting that the two-day summit was part of Google Ideas' ongoing efforts to explore "how technology can be used to address humanity's most intractable problems" (a claim that would in fact be the focus of a boastful text to be released a mere two months later by Google executives Eric Schmidt and Jared Cohen, titled *The New Digital Age*[36]). Despite the repetition of this homily during the summit itself, some uncertainties lingered about Google's true motives and intentions. In the words of one perplexed labor lawyer I encountered from Washington, DC, some "cognitive dissonance" would be required to reconcile such a peculiar constellation of topics, participants, and technological remedies.

Despite this diversity, the issue of sex trafficking remained a consistent, and seemingly requisite event feature. "Sex panic!" was thus one hypothesis that was proposed early and often by some of the more critical activists in attendance. They postulated that the summit was really a

CYA effort (the preferred acronym for "cover your ass" maneuvers, or material self-interest) in the face of vigorous anti-prostitution campaigns that had already targeted websites such as Backpage and Craigslist—branded by anti-prostitution activists as sex traffickers, the sites faced intense political pressure to remove their "adult services" sections.[37] And indeed, some of these same anti-prostitution campaigners, heady with past success, were training their eyes upon internet search engines such as Google. In a coauthored 2012 letter to the tech giant, two US representatives, Democrat Carolyn Maloney of New York and Republican Marsha Blackburn of Tennessee, challenged the company's AdWords department to eliminate the use of search terms that could allow "international and local human trafficking rings to sexually exploit and sell women and girls online."[38]

The problem with this hypothesis was that the specter of "sex trafficking," while certainly present at the forum, accounted for a relatively delimited proportion of the event overall—in fact many panels did not even address the topic, and for those that did, it was often relegated to a small, albeit emotionally powerful, segment. On the panel "North Korea: Mafia State?" for example, speakers included a former money launderer, two former opium smugglers, and a tearful sex-trafficking victim whose story of forced webcam prostitution in China brought the crowd to their feet. Another panel, "Free Expression in the Face of Fear," consisted of a whistle-blower on a Colombian drug cartel, the founder of Citivox (a crowdsourcing platform), an investigative journalist from ABC News, and a former streetwalker from Los Angeles.

But even more curious was the fact that the network coherence that Google claimed, the mapability that they promised, was simply not relevant in any of the sex-trafficking cases with which I was familiar. In a preamble to the official summit, I had been invited to Silicon Valley to participate in a roundtable with several other academic "experts" on human trafficking. At the time, we tried our best to explain that "sex trafficking" does not actually work the way it appears to in the movies: beyond the numbers being wildly exaggerated, there is not much involvement by organized crime, for example, and people's movements and labor are generally brokered informally, by family members or friends. Still determined to find a critical role for technology to fill, the Googlers also made clear that not just any mapping project would suffice. Perhaps not surprisingly, they expressed little interest in an idea suggested by Sine Plambech, then one of my doctoral students, who at the time of the workshop was engaged in fieldwork in Europe with migrant sex workers from Nigeria.[39]

After asking the women directly what type of technology they thought might be of most help, they suggested that Google create a crowdsourcing app revealing the easiest (i.e., least policed) points of entry into Europe. This could help prevent trafficking, they explained, because fewer border control agents would mean that they would require fewer third parties to help them to migrate; this would ultimately imply fewer payoffs and shorter periods of debt bondage.[40]

In fact, by the time of the official INFO-Summit, it was apparent that law enforcement and cybersecurity would constitute the most critical components of any imagined network to counter "the illicit."[41] On the second day of the summit, I was assigned to something called the LookingGlass Lab, one of ten breakout sessions focused on familiarizing ourselves with emerging cybersurveillance technologies. "This is a tool for identifying evil and for fighting the bad guys," explained the program's cofounder, after briefly recounting his background in military intelligence. Describing the twin gendered threats of terrorism and sex trafficking, he went on to explain how his platform could track criminal networks by tagging IP addresses and "neighborhoods" for different forms of bad activity. Although the majority of those present hailed from the military, defense, and security industries, perhaps the most intriguing person in the room was a young man from the Tor project, who boldly introduced himself as "an enemy of the military industrial complex" and described Tor's anonymizing software as an analogue to WikiLeaks.[42] After asking the cybersecurity men a series of flummoxing questions ("What do you do about companies like Tor that create proxy addresses?" "How do you know you're not entrapping yourselves?"), he offered to lend them his efforts on behalf of the apparently uncontroversial agenda of fighting underage sex trafficking—"this is something we can all agree on," he offered.

In the LookingGlass lab, the nodal points connecting the issues, participants, and proposed remedies of Google's Illicit Networks Summit were finally revealed. The prerequisite to creating a technological solution to the problem of "illicit networks" resided first in casting any particular social cause—be it exploited labor, child soldiers, organ harvesting, or sex trafficking—not as deriving from manifold forms of social injustice, but rather as individualized, idiosyncratic, and policeable offenses, in defining them, in short, as *crimes*. Through technologies such as LookingGlass, "criminals" and their associates, it was assumed, could then be mapped, surveilled, and intercepted. To make this project broadly palatable however, surveillance would need to be moralized first—ideally through the imagined victimization, rescue, and ultimately "empowerment" of the sexually trafficked woman or girl child. As the Tor developer remarked, this was an agenda on which "everyone could agree." In this way, sex was linked to (but did not supplant) broader agendas of criminalization, militarized humanitarianism, and capitalist redemption, serving in fact as the very technology through which these other forms of politics could occur. At the same time, the insistent connection between monetized sexual relations, terrorism, and violence served to constitute such relations as "illicit" and inherently dangerous—as opposed to, say, spheres of marginalized economic activity that might necessitate the pursuit of a vision of justice beyond criminal justice, or other kinds of social remedies.

As the 2013 scandal concerning National Security Agency surveillance made visible, Silicon Valley's earlier transition from "the smut highway to the policing of pedophilia" (to quote from media theorist Wendy Chun) has increasingly been superseded by its pivotal role in the public-private partnerships that comprise the postindustrial security state, in which practices of surveillance, marketing, and humanitarian intervention become impossible to distinguish.[43] In April 2013, just months before the massive scale of the NSA's surveillance activities became the subject of international headlines, Google would publicly launch its Global Human Trafficking Hotline Network at the White House, in partnership with the CIA-funded data analytics firm Palantir, as well as tech-friendly anti-trafficking "start-up" NGOs such as Polaris Project and Liberty Asia.[44] According to Google, the idea behind the hotline network would be "to collect data from local hotline efforts, share promising practices and create anti-trafficking strategies that build on common patterns and focus on eradication, prevention and victim protection."[45]

Although many established anti-trafficking NGOs have questioned the utility of this endeavor given the miniscule volume of calls that they currently handle,[46] its true purpose may be more symbolic than material, albeit no less politically potent. As Jennifer Musto has argued, in the Google human trafficking hotline as well as in other new technologically based anti-trafficking initiatives, "data and specifically 'big data' are seen as offering an ameliorative answer to an issue long beset by inadequate quantitative and qualitative data," potentially providing "long overdue causative and correlative evidence of the weight and magnitude of the problem."[47] Through its collaboration with Polaris Project, for example, Google can claim to have already collected data from seventy-two thousand hotline calls, even if the precise content of such calls is never specified (are these calls from victims seeking assistance, from others who simply seek information, or from college undergraduates hoping to volunteer? We are never told). Notably, California's landmark Proposition 35, financed and cosponsored by former Facebook executive Chris Kelly, featured as its key provision "the requirement that traffickers-cum-sex offenders provide law enforcement with 'information regarding Internet access and identities they use in online activities.'" As we saw in the prior chapter on sex-trafficking "reality tours," here it is the generation and manipulation of data points (rather than the specters of poverty and commercial sex) that are made to stand in for more conventional forms of evidence, thus bypassing the potential embarrassment of meager case numbers.[48]

Given the growing role of new surveillance technologies in bolstering the existence of "sex trafficking" as a political discourse, it is important to recognize how the two phenomena—sex trafficking and surveillance—have in fact become co-constitutive, with sex trafficking reciprocally serving to moralize the extension of new modes of surveillance. As they do in the fight against terror, sex and gender can play a crucial role in imbuing campaigns against trafficking—a definitionally ambiguous and shifting concept, as we have seen—with moral clarity and political conviction.[49] As distinct from campaigns against terrorism however, or from the raced and gendered agendas behind the "war on crime" more generally, in the new corporate-led fight against sex trafficking the operations of power do not reside solely in the domains of the punitive and the prohibitive. As we shall see in more detail below by way of our second case study, the discourse of trafficking has also proved flexible enough to morally recast certain (non-sexual) forms of economic exchange, including temporary labor, bonded labor, and brokered labor—all key features of capitalist production under conditions of neoliberal globalization—as progressive, good, and free.

Sex, Slavery, and Supply Chains

When there are alternatives, girls don't sell themselves into the supply network.
JEAN BADERSCHNEIDER, VICE PRESIDENT OF GLOBAL PROCUREMENT, EXXON MOBIL

In Mexico City . . . we had a simple mission . . . take women off the streets where they can't be prostituted. We saved 700,000 women a year, protecting them, getting them off the streets, letting them have children, and handing their life back to them. . . . That's how you get a return on your investment. DAVID ARKLESS, PRESIDENT OF GLOBAL AND CORPORATE AFFAIRS, MANPOWERGROUP[50]

Ending slavery is not just some charity exercise. When people are free, they create a "freedom dividend." **KEVIN BALES, FREE THE SLAVES, 2010 TED TALK**

If the high-tech sector's engagement with "sex trafficking" has worked in the interest of moralizing crime-fighting and new surveillance technologies, a bevy of new corporate efforts focused on the dynamics of labor procurement and the provision of "clean supply chains" are similarly notable for nesting the issue of sex trafficking within a broader range of social and economic issues. Indeed, some corporate spokespersons, such as Jean Baderschneider of the Exxon Mobil Corporation, David Arkless of the ManpowerGroup, and Kevin Bales of the NGO Free the Slaves (who has promoted "fighting slavery" via public-private partnerships with the corporate giants of the cocoa industry[51]), have gone so far as to identify a lack of economic opportunity as one of the most crucial risk factors in human trafficking. Providing an odd if distorted echo to a frequent progressive mantra, their focus upon slavery's economic underpinnings has enabled them to argue that multinational corporations have a vital role to play in promoting social justice, gender equality, and women's freedom, with each job created framed as a humanitarian initiative against slavery.

Corporations, they insist, can serve these ends through compliance with voluntary codes of conduct like the Athens Ethical Principles and California's Transparency in Supply Chains law, and by providing economic alternatives to enslaved, or potentially enslaved, peoples.[52] As a recent Manpower CSR report proudly declares, "In addition to raising awareness of the issue, ManpowerGroup is also focused on prevention and has entered into numerous joint ventures to provide trafficked and at-risk persons with access to education and training to help them transition to decent, honorable work."[53] And indeed, it has been not only corporations but also prominent cultural commentators who, in a rehearsal of the classical liberal idea of wage labor-as-economic freedom, have come to regard the proliferation of sweatshops in the Global South as important preventative interventions against modern forms of slavery. As Nicholas Kristof has written across his numerous columns and blogs on the topic, "My time living in Asia, seeing people prosper because of sweatshops, had made me a believer in that economic strategy. . . . The result has been to begin to give girls and women some status and power, some hint of social equality, some alternative to the sex industry."[54]

Of course in practice, as the sociologist Julia O'Connell Davidson has aptly shown, the exercise of distinguishing experiences of "slavery" from those of "freedom" is anything but straightforward. "In a world where slavery is nowhere legally recognized, so that nobody is actually formally assigned the legal status of slave," she queries, "what is slavery and who is a slave?"[55] Drawing on her own empirical research on the hardships endured by migrant domestic workers in Bangkok, in which workers were not assigned fixed hours but were rather perpetually "on call," often not paid for their work, and in which their employers explicitly prized their state of dependency, she observes the sharp resonances between many situations of live-in domestic work and conventional definitions of modern slavery. She further notes that the employers of domestic workers that she interviewed "were structurally positioned to beat, starve, sexually harass and cheat their workers with impunity, in addition to exploiting their labor." Despite these exploitative realities, these workers were nowhere addressed as "slaves" and eluded entirely the attention and interventions of local NGOs.[56]

The definitional problems with "trafficking" that O'Connell Davidson observes become particularly acute when sex trafficking is compared not just with domestic work (a clear analogue as a potentially exploitative form of gendered care provision) but with the late-capitalist organization of labor migration more generally. Although Kevin Bales's oft-quoted definition of slavery as "a social and economic relationship in which a person is controlled through violence or its threat . . . , and economically exploited,"[57] could conceivably be applied to myriad forms of oppression—from the dynamics of migrant domestic work that O'Connell Davidson describes to US prison labor to sexual abuse within families—it bears an especially close relationship to the new and proliferating forms of labor brokerage that scholars have identified as critical to the operations of twenty-first-century transnational capital. Foremost among these, as Biao Xiang has argued, have been the rapid rise in outsourcing, subcontracting, vertical (dis)integration, and ever more complex supply chains.[58] "The rhetoric of slavery, sex, crime and ignorance that shapes trafficking knowledge diverts our attention away from the basic similarities in recruitment and conditions that produce both trafficking and guest labor," writes the labor historian Adam McKeown.[59] If O'Connell Davidson is right in her assertion that the discourse of "new slavery" in fact hinges upon the persistence of "old binaries," it is also true that emergent features of capitalist production have made the already fraught division between "slavery" and "freedom" even more tenuous.

As the world's largest broker of temporary, outsourced, and other "contingent" forms of labor (with operations in eighty countries, and more than six hundred thousand workers on assignment each day) and one of the founding partners of the EHTN business coalition, the ManpowerGroup sits at an interesting intersection vis-à-vis these tensions.[60] While the rise of temporary labor in the United States has been amply critiqued by labor scholars for its role in fomenting economic precarity for a growing segment of workers, as well as for the new forms of exploitation and uncompensated labor that the worker, rather than the employer, must bear,[61] the transnational labor brokerage industry which accounts for a rapidly expanding share of Manpower's core business has come under remarkably little scrutiny.[62] With the rise in attention to nonsexual forms of labor trafficking, there have been an increasing number of accounts of "aberrant" cases of "unscrupulous" labor brokers and petty criminals who engage in spectacular acts of physical violence (abusing and torturing domestic workers in Lebanon or shrimpers on Thai fishing boats; compelling children to serve as child soldiers in Uganda or to labor in Indian brick kilns), but scant scholarly analysis of the practices engaged in by their legitimate, law-abiding counterparts.[63] This, despite the fact that the "flexibilization" of labor markets, "labor recruitment outsourcing," and transnational "labor transplant" represent rapidly expanding global paradigms of labor organization (in one of Manpower's own industry reports titled *Leading in the Human Age: Why an Era of Certain Uncertainty Requires New Approaches to the World of Work*, companies are encouraged to "reinvent themselves as flexible and adaptable Human Age Corporations" in response to post-economic-crisis chronic unpredictability).[64]

Among the few ethnographers to have studied "legitimate" labor brokerage firms in East Asia and the process of "global bodyshopping" that they engage in is Biao Xiang, who has researched unskilled workers traveling from China to Singapore. Through extraordinary participant-observational research accompanying the workers during each step of their migration, Xiang is able to describe their experiences of brokered labor migration in detail and at length. Among the most striking elements of his account are the payment of hefty agents' fees to labor recruitment companies, minimal control over the timing or trajectory of one's own movements, confiscation of passports and all other identification papers, compulsory medical exams, and the withholding of wages to prevent employees from running away ("it is standard practice for employers to pay migrant workers a monthly living allowance of between 10 and 50 percent of their wages, and then remit the balance owed immediately before their actual departure"[65]). In fact, in his depiction of the force, fraud, and coercion that Chinese migrant workers experience, many of the elements in Xiang's account are strikingly similar to those contained in the prototypical "sex slavery" scenario that I described in chapter 2.

Given these resonances, it may be hard not to conclude that Manpower's investment in the issue of human trafficking is a matter of straightforwardly decipherable material self-interest, a way of branding Manpower's own exploitative practices as "clean" while casting aspersions on similar practices engaged in by less formally organized competitors. Referencing the case of the ManpowerGroup, a lawyer who advises large corporations on their CSR campaigns posed a rhetorical question to me after the culmination of our formal interview: "When you're the world's largest recruiting company . . . what other choice do you have?" And as gBCAT's Mark Lagon repeatedly insisted, no CSR campaign can go forward if there are no tangible benefits for the company, when such efforts are not ultimately "in their interest." Building on his own arguments during his former tenure as US ambassador on trafficking in persons, he insisted that self-certification and promises of "clean supply chains" not only encouraged companies like Manpower to participate in such campaigns; they were in fact business-friendly remedies that, in a variety of ways, would serve corporate stakeholders by ultimately benefiting the company's "bottom line." "Given the nature of their industry," Lagon explained, "Manpower was of course worried about a black eye being given to their sector. This way, they could appear to be emerging on the forefront of regulation, something which, as a large corporation, they could afford. Smaller corporations, by contrast, cannot take on these costs."[66]

Yet as we have seen, the "interests" of corporations like Manpower may also reside in domains that extend beyond the realm of the purely economic, at least as the latter has been conventionally understood. In Manpower's documents, as in the anti-trafficking apps that I opened this chapter with, notions of "clean supply chains" and of "free" or "untrafficked" labor are split off from a host of other, potentially coercive, and often similarly exploitative labor relations. The small handful of instances of exploitative labor which are said to constitute "trafficking" are then sutured to the black box of prostitution (the exemplar of presumably self-evident relations of unfreedom), while the sets of labor relations that remain beyond the legal purview of trafficking, despite their empirical similarities to it, are morally redeemed through categorical contrast. "Clean" supply chains and (presumably dirty) forms of sexual labor are implicitly counterposed.

This suturing proves to be particularly crucial when the line between licit and illicit forms of labor brokerage, and thus between "slavery" and "freedom," may be a fine one indeed. This intrinsic blurriness of the categories reflects not only their empirical similarities and structural interdependence,[67] but also the minutiae of legal and thus moral distinctions (in the Philippines, brokers can legally charge employees a fee equivalent to thirty days of their salary to work, while a fee equivalent to thirty-one days' labor is "excessive" and tantamount to slavery, according to the Athens Ethical Principles[68]). With mounting political attention to labor exploitation in a growing number of sectors—from Foxconn's "i-slaves" to Bangladeshi garment workers, from construction workers at Abu Dhabi's Guggenheim museum to those laboring in Iowa food-processing plants—efforts to divide purportedly "forced" from "free" forms of labor become tenuous at best.[69] The trafficking frame serves to artificially fortify such divisions by obscuring the commonalities that exist among diverse

5.11   Attributions of slavery in other labor sectors. Image from Students & Scholars Against Corporate Misbehavior (SACOM), highlighting labor exploitation at Foxconn.

5.12   Charges of slavery at a delivery workers' protest in New York City. Photo by author, 2013.

forms of brokered labor, restricting social sanction to only the most exceptional forms of migrant worker abuse and violent crime.

At the same time, sex notably remains a necessary—even if increasingly insufficient—link in the chains of illicit practices that are understood to constitute slavery or unfreedom in the new corporate anti-
trafficking discourse. As was seen with the streetwalkers and webcam
girls who joined the panels of drug smugglers and money launderers at
the Google Ideas conference, its evocation serves to powerfully recast
the activities and personae that are situated alongside of it. As we have
seen, part of this power resides in the dense bundle of affect that "sex
trafficking" implies, imbuing what might otherwise seem to be analytically incoherent designations with both moral urgency and viscerally
felt authenticity. Significantly, in my interview with David Arkless, President of Global and Corporate Affairs for the ManpowerGroup, he was
boastful of the company's efforts to curb sex trafficking, but surprisingly
ill equipped to define it.[70] When I asked Arkless how the company understood the definition of "sex trafficking" given its notoriously contested status in contemporary feminist circles, he paused before launching into the following explanation: "Well, I know there's a huge debate

about definitions and what about when—when people put themselves willingly into a situation and being trafficked and, I just wipe all of that out, I just ignore it all. You can tell when a person is in an abusive situation, full stop. You can tell . . . you can tell when somebody, a woman or a child or a man, has been abused, so I tend to not get involved even with playing around the edges of definitions, but we know when it's happening and, um, so does everybody else." Curiously evocative of Justice Potter Stewart's infamous "I know it when I see it" definition of pornography, "sex trafficking" importantly remains fuzzy and ill defined here, its main purpose being to emotionally demarcate the illicit from the good.[71] Indeed, the definition Arkless offered me suggests that sex trafficking is not defined by any particular set of exploitative labor conditions within sex work, but is best understood in relation to its ability to evoke these viscerally dense moral sentiments.

As this example also highlights, even if trafficking is no longer "only" about sex for Manpower and other corporations, issues of sexual commerce (or of sexual violence, for that matter) are never pursued under any rubric outside of slavery—such as sex workers' rights or labor organizing. Similarly, for Manpower and other corporations, there is no moral or political urgency to attend to those forms of nonsexual labor that fall outside the narrow purview of cases that are considered to be clearly condemnable instances of human trafficking. With "labor trafficking" now severed from more widespread and mundane forms of labor exploitation, and "sex trafficking" disarticulated from other sex workers' issues, these discursive formations can be joined together in a powerful political amalgam, one that facilitates carceral agendas around sex work, and a moralization—rather than a politicization—of brokered and contingent forms of migrant labor. In this way, Manpower effectively launders its own exploitative practices by placing them on the "clean" side of the divide, one that had previously been established through the convergence of feminist, evangelical, and carceral mobilizations.

Global Corporate Citizenship and the "Girl Effect"

In the context of the current global economic recession, The Girl as human capital has become the darling of philanthrocapitalism. Prominent here is a campaign on "The Girl Effect" by the Nike Foundation . . . that promotes "The Girl" as the solution to the "world's mess." Following the investment into a girl's education . . . is a cascade of purported effects leading to the increased value of her life to her village, to women's rights, to national production, and finally, to world salvation: "invest in a girl and she will do the rest." MICHELLE MURPHY, "THE GIRL: MERGERS OF FEMINISM AND FINANCE IN NEOLIBERAL TIMES" (2013)

Women aren't the problem but the solution. The plight of girls is no more a tragedy than an opportunity. NICHOLAS KRISTOF AND SHERYL WUDUNN, *HALF THE SKY: TURNING OPPRESSION INTO OPPORTUNITY FOR WOMEN WORLDWIDE* (2010)

In her essay "War by Other Means," the sociologist Patricia Clough notes the ways in which stories of child soldiers, prisoners, prepubescent sex workers, and AIDS orphans are used in the branding of war as interested in the "protection and/or the liberation of victims, women and children especially."[72] With Craig Willse, she has also described the deployment of gender via a "political branding" that arouses and affectively activates interest in the protection and liberation of women as "modern, progressive, and civil."[73] New corporate branding strategies, as Clough and Willse explain, hinge upon not only the appeal to but also the cultivation of gendered moral demand and political interest.

Michelle Murphy has similarly demonstrated how agendas of population control, Western feminist calls for reproductive rights, and legacies of neocolonial development have congealed in capital-intensive campaigns that posit women and girls as ideal receptacles for investment. In her discussion of the Nike Foundation's popular video *The Girl Effect* (which screened to great acclaim at the 2009 World Economic Forum), girls are figured as the optimal site for economic investment, tethering "girl power" to "freedom from fertility" to greater economic prosperity.[74] Murphy devises the term "economization of life" to describe the historical emergence of "forms of governmentality that seek to govern living being, particularly sexed-living being" for the sake of fostering economic development. According to Murphy, "the 'girl effect,' in the name of feminism and as a more humanist form of neoliberalism concerned with 'human development' is congealing as the *liberal* neoliberal alternative to more brutal forms of neoliberalism associated with structural adjustment and disinvested infrastructures in the name of free markets."[75]

Following Clough, Murphy, and other feminist thinkers, I am suggesting that we ought to think about the multidirectional circulations of sex and capital that are at work in Google's campaign against illicit networks, in Manpower's campaign for clean supply chains, and beyond. To understand burgeoning corporate investment in human trafficking, we need to attend to the ways in which punitive and productive forms of power have been co-constitutive of redemptive capitalism, and why the so-called "girl effect" (a term deployed by the Nike campaign that Murphy discusses and by Nicholas Kristof) has been crucial to both projects.[76] As one corporate official remarked at a conference that I attended on business and human rights, herself noting the parallels between the gendered logics of investability that undergird traditional "women and development" agendas, microcredit campaigns, as well as contemporary attention to human trafficking, "We need to be inserting the slavery lens into international development work. Slavery is the emotional edge of what happens if development agendas are not implemented."[77]

By way of conclusion, I'd like to turn to a final illustration of contemporary corporate investment in "fighting trafficking," so as to better elucidate the multidirectional flows of sex and capital, and the disparately gendered, productive and prohibitive forms of power that accompany them. As one additional and revealing instance of this complex intertwining, we can consider a 2013 MTV anti-trafficking web campaign called The Backstory, in which certain forms of sexual relations are figured as both the emblematic problem and the vehicle for repair of contemporary social ills. In the opening sequence of MTV's pedagogically designed campaign, the viewer is instructed that there is more to seemingly innocuous online prostitution ads than initially meets the eye. Clicking on any of the apparent sex ads in fact transports the viewer to the same animated video sequence, which opens with the silhouetted figure of a young teen, one who is coded as African American by virtue of her clothes, physical features, and dance moves (which she performs to the accompaniment of a hip-hop soundtrack). While she moves to the music, an apparently African American male narrator provides a spoken-word description of the purportedly real "backstory" behind the ad:

She was fifteen years old, your average American teen . . . thinking about boys, listening to hip-hop, doing homework in between . . . Everything was fine, until her father split . . . and a man moved in, taking away the attention she used to get . . . Her mom's new boyfriend brought drugs into the mix. They couldn't survive without a fix . . . Then the fighting began, blow by blow, and when she was alone with her mom's boyfriend, you don't even want to know . . . All she had were dreams of Prince Charming, but little did she know.

As he speaks, the animated figures of the teen, her clearly irresponsible mother and father, and her mother's sexually predatory, drug-dealing boyfriend take to the screen. The video culminates with the clichéd image of the teen's new pimp-boyfriend ("Prince Charming") with his hand outstretched to receive the money that she has presumably begun to earn through prostitution.

In an eerie throwback to some of the familiar tropes of the "culture of poverty," illicit sexual relations are figured here as both the cause and the outcome of poverty, domestic violence, and other forms of social suf-

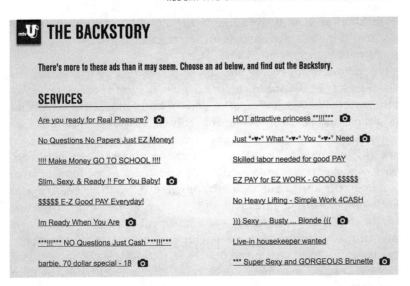

fering. Particularly striking are the familiar tropes of absent fathers, sexually promiscuous mothers, and the pathologized tangles of gender and race that are presumed to lurk behind the official "whiteface" story of online prostitution.[78] Also significant are the invocation of intertwined sexual and racial pathologies (rather than the structural transformations of neoliberalism, and its decimated public spheres), and how these prove

5.13 (top) and 5.14 (bottom)   Stills from MTV's "The Backstory."

crucial both to crafting the solution-that-proceeds-the problem (finding and punishing bad men, saving girls and women) and to reimagining the problem of trafficking in the first place.

In summary, this chapter has argued that trafficking has become the "hot" social justice issue in corporate circles not just because "sex sells," but also because sex is a capacious and broadly productive vehicle for economic and political investment. This capacity goes beyond sex-as-commodity, or the libidinal charge of the putatively prohibited, or even sex-as-stand-in for self-actualization. Rather, what emerges from this discursive exploration is sex-as-social-redemption; sex as the fundament of not only "the illicit," but also of the progressive and the good. As apparently one element among many in the networks of "bad activity" that multinational corporations are working to combat, its place is absolutely pivotal when agendas of humanitarian intervention, women's empowerment, and beneficent protection have technologies of surveillance, carceral control, and market-based exploitation as their actual illicit underside.

SIX

Imagining Freedom

The invention of the trafficking framework hasn't helped anyone. It is an umbrella frame, and if the issues were disaggregated, much more could be done for each of them. Becoming a "victim of crime" is not actually a benefit.   ASIA PACIFIC NETWORK OF SEX WORKERS, BANGKOK[1]

Instead of respect for our basic human rights under the United Nations Human Rights Council we are given "protection" under the United Nations Office on Drugs and Crime. We are forced to live with the modern lie that border controls and anti-trafficking policies are for our protection. None of us believe that lie or want that kind of protection.   EMPOWER FOUNDATION, CHIANG MAI, THAILAND[2]

Save us from our saviors. We're tired of being saved.
SLOGAN OF VAMP (VESHYA ANYAY MUKTI PARISHAD), A SEX WORKERS' COLLECTIVE IN SANGLI, INDIA[3]

Since the reemergence of "trafficking" at the turn of the twenty-first century, sex workers' rights organizations around the globe have been united in their rejection of this purportedly benevolent framework. As the Empower Foundation has documented in their research on migration and sex work, "We have been spied on, arrested, cut off from our families, had our savings confiscated, interrogated, imprisoned and placed into the hands of the men with guns, in order for them to send us home."[4] In important volumes of essays compiled by Kamala Kempadoo and her colleagues in 1998 and 2005, sex worker rights advocates like Jo Doezema protested that "international actors and agreements are rarely as vocal about promoting prostitutes' rights as they are in condemning forced prostitution. No international agreement condemns the abuse of human rights of sex workers who were not 'forced.'"[5] At Jagori, a women's center in New Delhi that is dedicated to issues of trafficking and migration, participatory action research with sex workers similarly found that while "the state looks at women who must be protected from trafficking . . . such protection often becomes a tool for the violation of women's rights by restricting their right to move."[6]

During a remarkable visit to speak with US congressional staff members that I made with sex worker activists from Mali, India, Cambodia, and Brazil, the activists, hopeful of impending policy shifts under the newly elected Obama administration, implored congressional staffers to acknowledge sex workers' experiences and to effect a change of course.[7] Sara Bradford, from the Asia Pacific Network of Sex Workers, described the impact of the US-led anti-trafficking campaign on sex workers in Cambodia, where, since 2008, the selling of sex has been criminalized in the name of "fighting trafficking." She explained that those arrested for prostitution in Cambodia were sent not to jail but to so-called "rehabilitation centers," without due process, and detailed the many human rights abuses that occur in these facilities, including verbal, physical, and sexual assault by guards; contaminated food and water; detainment of children who were with their mothers at the time of arrest; extortion and theft by guards; and death while in custody due to lack of medical care or by suicide.

As in Cambodia, activists from India reported that anti-trafficking raids failed to hold traffickers accountable and punished women in the sex trade whether they were working voluntarily or not, subjecting them to mental, physical, and sexual abuse. As reported by Shilpa Merchant of the Mumbai-based Sanghamitra Project, all the brothels in one local area were raided "thanks to the TIP report in the US, and to USAID funding." That many of the women returned to the trade after two or three months of their rescue suggested to Merchant that "rescue is really not the answer," and that more comprehensive help, along with the recognition of the rights of sex workers, including access to health care and HIV prevention, were still needed.

Although the activists' interventions did not immediately succeed in ushering in the policy swerve away from "trafficking" that participants had hoped for, in recent years sex workers' rights groups have nonetheless scored some important victories, including the issuing of statements in support of the full decriminalization of sex work by mainstream human rights entities such as UNAIDS, Human Rights Watch, the World Health Organization, and, perhaps most notably, Amnesty International.[8] Despite significant opposition on the part of mainstream feminist organizations and a slew of celebrity anti-trafficking campaigners, on August 11, 2015, Amnesty International passed an official policy advocating for the decriminalization of all aspects of sex work, one which received widespread if ambivalent coverage in the international press.[9] The new policy recognized sex workers as one of the "most marginalized groups in the world" and cited this shift as imperative for the protection of sex workers' rights.[10] Catherine Murphy, the policy adviser at Amnesty who authored the organization's original proposal, explained in a press release that the decision was based on two years of research and consultations with "sex workers, survivor and abolitionist groups, HIV agencies, women's and LGBTI rights activists, Indigenous women's groups, anti-trafficking groups and leading academics."[11] As the legal scholar and human rights advocate Chi Adanna Mgbako proudly observed at a 2015 session of the UN Commission on the Status of Women meetings, "These positive developments are really a reflection of the grass roots activism of sex workers throughout the world who for decades have been organizing for their rights."[12]

Despite these important victories, it should be noted that none of the organizations referred to have critiqued the trafficking frame directly or the carceral feminist, militarized humanitarian, and redemptive capitalist orientations that underpin it. A mere week after its initial announcement, Amnesty emphasized that it continued to support anti-trafficking measures and recognized all forms of trafficking and exploitation as "abhorrent." "What we want is a refocusing of laws to tackle acts of exploitation, abuse and trafficking—rather than catch-all offences that only criminalize and endanger sex workers," an Amnesty spokesperson declared.[13] Rather, Amnesty, like many progressive critics of contemporary anti-trafficking campaigns, sought to distinguish "sex work" from "sex trafficking," to emphasize that the two phenomena should not be regarded as self-identical, and to remind critics of their new policy that trafficking occurs in a multitude of other labor sectors beyond sex. While Amnesty's declaration was indeed a positive one for sex workers, it did not in fact displace the protean yet durable nature of the trafficking discourse or the slippage between "sex trafficking" and "human trafficking" that this discourse has relied upon from its inception, still allowing, in a gloss of Kempadoo's words, "the anti-trafficking juggernaut to roll on."[14]

Since the time that I completed the bulk of my primary research for this book, the trafficking discourse has indeed solidified its hold in the United States, Southeast Asia, and Europe, while also spreading to new territories around the globe, including Latin America, North Africa, and the Middle East.[15] It has been redeployed to befit a number of new geopolitical contexts, including the perceived threats posed by ISIS aggressions and Syrian refugees.[16] While it is possible to argue that in some regions, including the United States, popular interest in the issue has peaked as compared to a decade ago, the reemergence of "trafficking" has undeniably left a huge and durable infrastructure in its wake, including a legacy of laws, policies, institutions, practices, and symbols.[17] Viewed globally, this infrastructure has included the anti-trafficking movement's own contribution to the feminist "NGO boom" that theorists such as Sonia Alvarez have critically assessed, as well as annual *TIP* report rankings and the proliferation of UN policy and funding from its diverse branches.[18]

Meanwhile, in major US airports and transportation hubs, travelers are greeted by public service announcements created by the Department of Homeland Security which warn new arrivals to be alert for instances of trafficking that they might expect to witness, as depicted in figures 6.1–6.2. The ads and their content are presented by the department's Blue Campaign to End Human Trafficking, described on its website as the "unified voice" of the DHS: "Working in collaboration with law enforcement, government, non-governmental and private organizations," the site explains, "the Blue Campaign strives to protect the basic right of freedom and to bring those who exploit human lives to justice."[19] Evidence of this increasing institutionalization also exists in the growing numbers of anti-trafficking divisions of police departments and law enforcement-led "anti-trafficking taskforces" that have sprung up around the nation, an institutional arrangement which, like the founding of the Federal Bureau of Investigation during early twentieth-century campaigns against white slavery, is likely to prove lasting in its effects.[20] During a 2010 encounter with Luis deBaca, the former federal prosecutor who at the time served as the US Ambassador in the Office to Monitor Trafficking in Persons, he explained to me that his goal for the issue was for the anti-trafficking framework to become permanent, prosecutable, and politically uncontroversial. "We want it to be like domestic violence," he remarked proudly, unaware of the reluctance of at least some feminist activists to enthusiastically embrace this precedent.[21] This book has provided an account of how deBaca's preferred scenario has come to pass, explaining how securitized approaches to gender justice have been able to ascend to the highest platforms of US and global politics. In the 2016 US elections, Hillary Clinton became the Democratic Party's first female nominee for president—the very figure who proved pivotal in placing "the traffic in women" on the international agenda and who was also, by some accounts, one of the world's leading carceral feminists.[22] Not

6.1 "Human trafficking" public service announcement at the international terminal of the St. Louis Lambert International Airport. Photo: Ariane Rinehart.

6.2 Another public service announcement, this one at the Port Authority Bus Terminal, New York City, 2016. Photo: Ariane Rinehart.

surprisingly, her presidential campaign sought to answer the calls for law and order, immigration control, and muscular foreign policy that were also advanced by the Republican presidential nominee, Donald Trump—but with the velvet glove of feminist concern and humanitarian commitment.

The Evolution of a Discourse

Writing about the white slavery panic of a century ago, the historical sociologist Stephanie Limoncelli describes a temporal arc in which the initial contours of the anti-trafficking discourse stretched and expanded to accommodate a shifting array of geopolitical concerns. Tracing the movement from its 1875 origins in Great Britain as "a global humanitarian effort to protect women from sexual exploitation" to its development in other European countries and internationally, Limoncelli argues that nation and empire building provided the impulse for the national regulation of prostitution across Europe, displacing the original ambition of the movement to universally protect women from sexual exploitation.[23] Her discussion of the movement also includes countries outside of Europe that adhered to the succession of international anti-trafficking agreements produced by the League of Nations, including Brazil, China, Japan, Russia, Siam (now Thailand), the United States, and Uruguay. "Even a cursory glance at the list shows that trafficking proved to be of particular interest to those states that were attempting to affirm their territorial boundaries—states seeking to bolster their rule over colonial holdings, new nation-states, and established states with shifting boundaries engendered by World War I," she writes, revealing the wide spectrum of countries that eventually adopted international anti-trafficking accords. "Post-colonial states had their turn as well," Limoncelli notes, detailing the participation of countries such as Algeria, India, Pakistan, Morocco, and Myanmar who also got involved once anti-trafficking efforts resumed for the 1949 convention of the United Nations.[24]

As occurred during the predecessor panic of the past century, the contemporary anti-trafficking discourse has also proved malleable enough to accomplish multiple goals in different instances, from the expulsion of migrants from disadvantaged areas in Taiwan to the incarceration of racialized Others in the United States, from the moral redemption of corporate multinationals to the securitization of the border between Guatemala and Mexico.[25] Describing the case of Taiwan, for example, Josephine Ho reveals a dual trend in which, on the one hand, the expulsion of migrants from economically marginalized areas serves as a "gesture to the rest of the world that something is being done." On the other hand, she observes, anti-trafficking Christian groups have mobilized the discourse to push for new legislation in which "all social space may be patrolled and purified" for the sake of protecting children.[26] In Mexico, notes René Leyva, who studies the policing of sex work on the Mexico-Guatemala border, the emergence of the trafficking discourse has served to replace previous public health interventions with the expulsion of migrant populations.[27] Speaking about recent legislation in Morocco, the political scientist Myriem Aboutaher calls attention to links between new forms of illegal immigration and the rise of "trafficking," as well as the fears that both inspire in the Moroccan government. Writes Aboutaher, "Fear dominates much of today's politics in Morocco: fear of new immigration from Syria (Syrian refugees) and fear from new immigration from Africa (Senegal, Mali, etc.). Anti-trafficking policy is above all an immigration policy. While the issue is presented as one that aims to protect women, women's associations didn't even participate in drafting the most recent Moroccan legislation."[28]

Despite this geopolitical malleability, the trafficking discourse has also been notable for its more durable attributes, which have persisted unaltered during its various twists and turns. As described in chapter 5, the discursive shift from "sex trafficking" to "human trafficking" that has occurred in recent years (largely in response to the protests of secular progressives) has served to facilitate the discourse's temporal longevity and political extensions, while at the same time failing to displace sex trafficking as the moral and affective core of the issue. In a study of the news media's portrayal of human trafficking and its role in perpetuating a misinformed dominant discourse on the subject, Rachealle Sanford, Daniel Martínez, and Ronald Weitzer examined articles published from 2012 to 2013 by the *New York Times* and the *Washington Post*. They found that the number of articles on trafficking published per year in 2012 and 2013 was considerably higher than the annual tally from 1980 to 2006, averaging 232 articles per year in 2012–2013, versus only 20 articles per year in the years prior. Deploying a similar methodology to that of the authors, my own calculations for these newspapers during the period between 2014 and 2017 revealed an average of 278 articles per year. In their study, Sanford, Martínez, and Weitzer also found that the majority of articles discussing "human trafficking" in fact referred to sex trafficking, with 64 percent considering sex trafficking alone and a mere 13 percent considering trafficking into other labor sectors. Finally, the authors observed that the "victims are most often portrayed as *minors and females*"—39 percent of articles referenced children as victims, 26 percent referenced both children and adults, 19 percent referenced only adults, and 16 percent mentioned no specific age. At the same time, 55 percent referred exclusively to women, 20 percent referred to both genders, and 23 percent mentioned no gender at all—"reflecting prevailing assumptions about ideal victimhood."[29]

Critics of contemporary anti-trafficking policies usually conclude their discussions by emphasizing the need for more social services for trafficking victims, more attention to forms of trafficking that occur outside the sex sector, and—as I have highlighted earlier and elsewhere in this book—more integration of the kinds of interventions that sex workers' rights organizations and their supporters are themselves putting forward to improve the lives of women, men, and transgender people who participate in sexual economies, including enhanced labor protections for sex workers.[30] These are all excellent suggestions which I, too, endorse, and they have been made even more compelling by some activists' recent calls to abandon carceral frameworks entirely, to question the paternalistic postures of humanitarian helping interventions, and to challenge the interests of the multinational corporations and charitable foundations which fund the majority of anti-trafficking activities.

For example, the 2016 issue of the *Anti-Trafficking Review*, a publication produced by the Global Alliance against Traffic in Women in Thailand, considers the role of prosecutions in anti-trafficking efforts from a range of critical activist perspectives. In the issue, Kate D'Adamo, a policy advocate for the Sex Workers Project at the Urban Justice Center in New York City, points to the multiple social factors and forms of adversity—"poverty, housing and food instability, lack of education, labor exploitation, discrimination and/or domestic violence"—that make people vulnerable to exploitation. She argues that "we must see where we are manufacturing these vulnerabilities through our policies, and address these before someone is trafficked or exploited." Ways of addressing the "root causes" of trafficking she proposes include supporting "the work of unions which put in place labor protections, community organizations which support members in times of crisis, and gender justice organizations which address the marginalization of women and transgender individuals, all of whom are doing invaluable work to stem and prevent trafficking and exploitation."[31] Likewise, Legal Aid attorneys Abigail Swenstein and Kate Mogulescu, who represent individuals charged with prostitution offences in New York City's criminal courts, have argued that the best remedies for trafficking are "a safe and living wage, opportunities for education, and affordable housing." Swenstein and Mogulescu assert that "when trafficking is framed as an individual act of violence into which the state must intervene, criminal prosecution becomes indispensable. . . . If, instead, the state were required to take responsibility for the conditions that give rise to abuse, we would see steps taken to eradicate poverty, provide safe and affordable housing, educate more widely, and dismantle oppressive systems across the board."[32]

Similarly bold attempts to reconstrue the meanings of and policies for addressing trafficking have been offered by the Chicago-based organization the Young Women's Empowerment Project (YWEP). Created in 2002, YWEP is a member-based social justice organization run by and for young people of color with current or former experience in the sex trade (who, legally speaking, are "victims of trafficking" by definition). "We discovered early on that young people in the sex trade are natural fund-raisers," explained the organization's former director Shira Hassan at a Columbia University conference on the challenges of nonprofitization: "We call the anti-trafficking movement the 'ATM' because it's a freaking cash cow!"[33] Deftly and critically maneuvering within the bounds of the anti-trafficking framework, this group has created community spaces, a needle exchange, a community health collective, and national grassroots organizing alliances for young women involved in sex work and other informal trades. Perhaps most remarkably, they have created "bad encounter" hotlines to document abuses that sex workers suffer not only at clients' hands, but also at the hands of health-care workers and the police.[34]

As impressive and crucial as such measures are, the analysis I have presented in this book suggests that such interventions on behalf of sex workers, even in their most creative and ambitious forms, may not be in and of themselves sufficient. Nor are they likely to be adequate for addressing the egregious and daily abuses which occur in labor sectors outside the sex industry, which perhaps accounts for the reluctance of many labor rights and immigrant rights groups to readily embrace this frame.[35] Rather, if the anti-trafficking discourse has emerged and proliferated as a result of specific historical, structural, and cultural conditions, then it is these enabling conditions that must also be identified, deciphered, and challenged, as this book has aimed to do. Such an endeavor, I have argued, will ultimately have more to contribute to social justice than do dismissive attributions of some actors' puritanical sexual commitments or gestures of bad faith. Indeed, my interviews with many different parties in the anti-trafficking movement attest to the fact that large numbers of people who have pursued this cause are themselves quite well intentioned. To paraphrase Ivan Illich, it is the relative privilege and power of the "helping" classes, not the moral purity of their intentions, that is at issue here.[36]

While the discussion that I have presented in these pages suggests that the most pernicious and direct effects of the trafficking discourse have been experienced by sex workers, this issue does not stand alone in emblematizing the broader social trends that this book has deemed central to deciphering it. What Jasbir Puar has famously termed "homonationalism," for example, also melds together the putatively progressive with the geopolitically regressive, joining the pursuit of LGBTQ equality to neo-imperialist, racist, and nationalist claims. As described by Puar and other theorists, homonationalism has been on display across a range of different issues, from US-led incursions in the Middle East to domestic "wars" against terrorism and hate crimes. Homonationalism, like the carceral feminism, militarized humanitarianism, and redemptive capitalism which have enabled campaigns against sex trafficking to flourish, has proved attractive to a broad and diverse range of political constituencies.[37]

In a similar vein, the Italian social theorist Sara Farris has written astutely about the gendered bifurcation of rising anti-immigrant sentiment in Europe, where appeals for the deportation and criminalization of male migrants are matched with an assimilationist rhetoric of compassion toward migrant women (whose continued presence in Europe as domestic workers—unlike their male counterparts in other labor sectors—is understood to be crucial).[38] While the presence of a reserve labor army of male migrants fuels campaigns for criminalization and deportation, the burkha-clad migrant woman is imagined as a target to be rescued and saved. Homonationalism and what Farris terms "femmonationalism" are the products of the same amalgam of sex, political economy, and governance that has spurred us to imagine the distinction between "slavery" and "freedom" in simultaneously old and new ways, whereby sexual and gender freedoms for some are achieved at the cost of the carceral control of others and are presumed to be compatible with broader capitalist interests. If I am right in that it is this amalgam of conservative and progressive elements that has enabled the emergence and persistence of the trafficking discourse—despite its empirical and ameliorative failings—then it is worth reviewing its component parts and how these parts congeal. Only then will we be in a position to fully consider alternative ways of framing social problems and of formulating constructive interventions (what Yvonne Zimmerman has usefully termed "other dreams of freedom") that would help spur meaningful and lasting justice for sex workers, and for communities beyond.[39]

Sex and Redemption in Neoliberal Times

The final day of Shared Hope International's annual anti-trafficking conference features video clips about Shared Hope's work in South Africa, India, and Fiji, where former sex workers are put to work making toilet paper, baking bread, or assembling handicrafts and jewelry. Many of these items are, not surprisingly, for sale at this event. Founded by Linda Smith, the former Washington State Congresswoman who has become a prominent conservative Christian voice in the anti-trafficking field, we're told that the organization's "Homes of Hope" are designed to offer a family life to trafficking victims, that the women who are in residence there learn that the discipline of work pays off, and that they get a portion of what they earn making crafts. The videos also showcase a series of before/after photos of current residents, haggard, bruised, and unhappy at the time that they were "rescued," then smiling, pretty, and conventionally feminine-looking after they have been "restored."

In the Fiji segment, we learn about girls like Valerie, a former sex worker who is now herself a missionary, sharing the value of abstinence with other young women, as well as the corollary messages of discipline and hard work. "If you're lazy, you won't get anything," she confidently declares. Collete is another compelling young woman we are introduced to in the film; because she was abandoned by her father, she explains, she would eventually come to be sexually abused by others. Now she is pleased to say that she lives a life of purity and dignity.

The culminating event of the weekend—and a clear highlight of the conference for attendees—is a prayer circle and public pledge ritual led by a group of men who call themselves "The Defenders."[40] The racially mixed group of men in their 30s, 40s, and 50s takes to the center of the room to join arms and encircle one another's shoulders, each pledging earnestly to take a stand to fight "pornography, prostitution or any form of the commercial sex industry," to "hold my friends accountable for their actions toward women and children," and to "take immediate action to protect those I love from this destructive market." An especially poignant moment comes when the tallest and burliest of the men extricates himself from the circle to address the audience directly: "I always wanted to be a hero," he proudly declares. For the Defenders, as for other conference goers, there are frequent allusions to what they deem to be the moral consequences of poverty, but no account of how people come to be poor in the first place; economy is not understood to meaningfully contribute to social structures. Rather, the main meta-structure that matters is the structure of male sexual demand. FIELD NOTES, ARLINGTON, VIRGINIA, NOVEMBER 2006

As this book has argued, and as the trafficking issue demonstrates, the sexual politics of neoliberalism have served as a source of affective melding, moral investment, and perceived domain of progress that have sutured "left" and "right" together around questions of security, carcerality, and the beneficence of capitalism. Bringing sex and gender into focus thus yields fresh insights into both the dynamics of neoliberal governance and the appeal of secular and Christian ambitions to help. At the same time, foregrounding these latter issues enables a better understanding of the shape and tenor of contemporary sexual politics, which are rather more nuanced than the frequently imagined poles of "progressive" versus "conservative," "pro-sex" versus "anti-sex," or "liberatory" versus "repressive" suggest. Throughout my discussion, I have been critical of accounts of the trafficking discourse that rely solely on a notion of sex panics, and which take the politics of sex to be both historically static and exclusively prohibitive. Rather, as can be seen from the extract from my field notes as well as the analysis that I have presented in the preceding pages, the sexual politics of neoliberalism have important constitutive as well as prohibitive roles to play—in molding particular sexual subjectivities, but also in legitimizing the trademark economic policies of neoliberalism, in contributing to the burgeoning NGO sector (both secular and faith-based), and in fostering carcerally oriented commitments to a law-and-order agenda.

Why sex? On the one hand, it is, as Foucault famously argued in the first volume of *The History of Sexuality*, "an especially dense transfer point for relations of power."[41] Through the complex, affective melding that chapters 4 and 5 have described, it can draw people in while simultaneously repelling them, at once attracting the observer's gaze to the surface of an issue while discouraging deeper and more critical investigation. Following Foucault, we can also recognize how easily sex becomes the stand-in not only for the bad, the illicit, and the deviant but also for the moral, the just, and the good. When, for example, the specter of children's participation in the global sexual economy is raised (with children serving as symbols of the ever-shrinking domain of social life that is understood to reside "outside" the scope of capitalist exchange), sex readily becomes the emblem for moral transgressions of the worst sort.[42] When properly channeled, however, sex can also serve as a potent symbol of gender freedoms and liberation. This dual function is apparent in the majority of anti-trafficking rescue stories that are currently in circulation, in which two disparately gendered outcomes inevitably prevail: for women, annihilation via "sex trafficking" is transformed by rescue into a "liberated" future of deferred sexual expression that culminates in marriage and participation in the nonsexual sectors of the labor force; for men, the moral degradation of sexual patronage becomes instead a positive tale of monogamy, sexual domesticity, and heroic recognition, with or without the conventional markers of economic success.

The simultaneous moral and immoral valences of sex have served to legitimize many feminists' carceral commitments to arresting sex workers and to reforming the sexuality of heterosexual male clients, as chapter 2 described. These dual meanings of sex have also infused the militarized "rescue" operations of evangelical Christians that were presented in chapter 3, the consumer humanitarianism of both secular and faith-based reality tourists that Elena Shih and I analyzed in chapter 4, and, as recounted in chapter 5, the moral redemption that capitalist labor markets are presumed to be capable of enacting, even as specifically sexual economic exchanges are condemned. In each of these instances, it is clear that sex has been an integral ingredient in the social and cultural transitions that are the hallmark of our era, even if it has often evaded consideration by mainstream analysts of neoliberal economics and governance.

If theorists of sex panics tend to err in positing "sex negativity" as an unwavering historical constant, most scholarly and popular expositions of neoliberalism thus make the opposite mistake in regarding both sex and gender as extrinsic factors, or at best epiphenomenal to more salient social trends. This is true of the theorists of neoliberalism and carcerality surveyed in chapter 2, as well as the classic and sweeping accounts of neoliberalism's ascendance, such as those authored by David Harvey, Marcus Taylor, and Naomi Klein.[43] As these commentators have emphasized, the past several decades have marked a significant shift from industrial to finance capitalism, a shift that has been accompanied by a move toward increasingly unstable employment trajectories and decreasingly generous social safety nets, both of which create a sense of precarity for the majority of people. Yet precarity, as many scholars have noted, extends beyond conditions of employment to include intimate attachments and relations of care. The concrete, material linkages between forms of productive, reproductive, and affective labor ought to bring gender and sexuality into the center of any analysis of neoliberalism, but these connections are rarely made.[44]

Too often, prominent feminist critics of neoliberalism have remained complicit with these very same omissions. Writers like Hester Eisenstein and Nancy Fraser, for example, have asserted that the chief problem with contemporary versions of feminism is their tendency to get distracted by "postmodern," transnational, and intersectional sexual politics, as opposed to sticking to the serious work of critiquing political economy. Remaining attentive to many conventional, Marxist-feminist concerns, Eisenstein cautions that feminist ideas have been exploited by corporate actors and that processes of economic globalization have had devastating consequences for the majority of the world's women. Yet her implicit model of sexuality is still tied to a normative version of heterosexual family life, leaving her unable to see the rise of global sex work as representing anything other than a "free market in women's bodies" that feminists must oppose (a critique she reserves for the sex sector, but not for other forms of highly gendered labor, such as domestic or assembly-line work).[45] Fraser, similar to Eisenstein, argues forcefully for reasserting the attention to economics displayed by an earlier generation of socialist feminists, critiquing what she refers to as the dangerous shift from "redistribution to recognition" in contemporary feminist scholarship and activism.[46]

While I am sympathetic to Eisenstein's and Fraser's calls to reintegrate a robust critique of political economy in the mainstream of feminist politics, as other commentators have pointed out, there are indeed many existing feminisms outside the mainstream that have never relinquished this mantle, including Global South feminisms, recent scholarly and activist work in feminist economics, and the strands of sex worker activism that I have deliberately positioned as a counterpoint throughout much of this text.[47] Furthermore, recent years have brought with them a variety of intersectionally oriented social movements that have called unprecedented attention to overlapping questions of economic, racial, and sexual injustice, even within the hegemonic West. Indeed, it is possible that the remarkable rise of anti-austerity movements across the globe and the emergence of campaigns such as Occupy Wall Street and Black Lives Matter in the United States may lay the groundwork for the eventual unraveling of the trafficking discourse, ultimately proving more significant than the liberal-legal reforms that have thus far been attempted.

New Activisms

As a sex worker, I joined Occupy Wall Street because the issues that impact both myself and my community are issues that are affecting other workers: lack of affordable housing, healthcare, education, and childcare. I come to stand in solidarity with communities of color, immigrants, Indigenous folks, and LGBTQ folks who remain disproportionately impacted by a system that has failed to provide justice, decriminalization, destigmatization, and the practice of fundamental rights. HANNAH, SEX WORKER ACTIVIST[48]

Our grievances and solutions extend beyond the police killing of our people; state violence includes failing schools that criminalize our children, dwindling earning opportunities, wars on our trans and queer family that deny them of their humanity, and so much more. . . . That's why we united, with a renewed energy and purpose, to put forth a shared vision of the world we want to live in. MONTAGUE SIMMONS, ORGANIZATION FOR BLACK STRUGGLE AND MOVEMENT FOR BLACK LIVES POLICY TABLE[49]

Only an interconnected, analytically diverse, cross-fertilizing and expansive left can seize this moment to lead us elsewhere. LISA DUGGAN[50]

We may recall from the genealogy provided in chapter 1 that contemporary mobilizations against sex trafficking initially emerged on the heels of a burgeoning sex workers' rights movement, as well as the largest set of anti-globalization movements in recorded history. As the scholar-activist Kari Lerum has observed, in the early 2000s, stories of sex slaves provided a compelling counternarrative to both movements, enabling Western political leaders to recast labor exploitation in ways that took attention "away from policies that privilege the profits of transnational corporations over the rights and livelihood of local people." Lerum goes on to quote journalists Nicholas Kristof and Sheryl WuDunn's celebratory, if distorted, account of this transition, highlighting their claim that "this is not a case where we in the West have a responsibility to lead because we're the source of the problem. Rather, we single out the West because, even though we're peripheral to the slavery, our action is necessary to overcome a horrific evil."[51]

Since completing my ethnographic research, there has been some compelling evidence that social movement actors—if not yet the majority of elected officials—have begun to implement important correctives to this trend. From the anti-austerity and Occupy movements that swept the globe following the financial crisis of 2008 to the Black Lives Matter protests originating in Ferguson, Missouri, critiques of economic inequality and mass incarceration have proliferated on both the left and right ends of the political spectrum.[52] Together, these movements suggest that new possibilities for the pursuit of social justice may indeed be emerging, supplanting the postures of paternalistic liberalism that anti-trafficking campaigns have heralded ("Like you, we all have won the lottery of life, and so the question becomes, how will we discharge that responsibility?" was Sheryl Wu Dunn's presumptive introduction to her 2010 TED talk "Our Century's Greatest Injustice").[53] Increasingly, the spur towards identification upward with the charitable helping classes has been met by political identification with those situated laterally or below. "Justice for the bottom billion," a Not for Sale slogan, has been countered by the Occupy rallying cry, "We are the 99%!"

Indeed, Occupy Wall Street was not only the result of efforts to call public attention to the devastation wrought by the 2008 financial crisis, but also sought to challenge relations of social inequality more broadly. Those involved in planning the actions were inspired by the 2011 protests in Egypt and the Arab Spring; the anti-austerity movements in Greece, Spain, and Portugal; and the 2011 campaign in defense of collective bargaining rights in Madison, Wisconsin. Initiated on September 17, 2011, the Occupy movement would eventually spread to more than five hundred cities and eighty countries, demonstrating its potential for inclusivity and global reach. Although critics frequently bemoaned the movement's lack of concrete demands, many scholars and participants have argued that it was in fact the expressive amorphousness of Occupy that gave it its greatest and lasting success. In the words of Ruth Milkman, a labor sociologist who studies contemporary social movements, "the occupations created the figurative and literal spaces for systemic critique."[54] According to independent journalist and movement participant Sarah Jaffe, Occupy erased "the widespread sense that not only is capitalism the only viable political and economic system, but also that it is now impossible even to *imagine* a coherent alternative to it."[55]

The anthropologist Manissa Maharawal also observes that issues of gender—if not explicitly sexuality—were present in the movement from the outset. "Throughout Occupy encampments there was often the use of everyday tactics to address privilege, oppression, and gender inequity," she writes. "This included the use of 'progressive stack' in which 'traditionally marginalized' voices, such as those of women and people of color, were privileged when speaking. Occupy subgroups such as Women Occupying Wall Street (WOW), Women Occupy, the Safer Spaces Group, Trans Women Occupiers, and the Fem Direct Action Group also proliferated to address a variety of gendered and sexual concerns."[56]

Other Occupy affiliates—such as the Sex Workers Organizing Project in New York City, the Best Practices Policy Project, and Sex Workers' Action New York—also saw a place for articulating their concerns within the capacious contours of the movement. As representatives of these organizations, Penelope Saunders and Melissa Sontag Broudo even authored a sex workers' manifesto entitled "Why Are Sex Workers Occupying Wall Street?" explaining the importance of the movement for sex workers' struggles. As explained by Saunders and Sontag Broudo:

Sex workers, people in the sex trade and people affected by anti-prostitution policies (such as trans communities, youth) are deeply oppressed by the economic inequities that exist within our society . . . These disparities are highlighted and magnified across racial, gender, ethnic, geographic, and other lines. Many sex workers and people in the sex trade are from economically marginalized and oppressed groups and seek to address their economic needs through a wide range of sexual commerce. The criminalization and stigmatization of many forms of this work only compounds the economic and social disempowerment that many already have faced and is a deep form of injustice (that is punishing people for their desire to provide for themselves, their communities and families).

Declaring that "sex work is work," and arguing that the police must be held accountable for their abusive practices, they deftly addressed the connections between political economy, police abuse, and the intertwined entities of race, class, sex, and gender in a concise, powerfully written document.[57]

Just as the Occupy movement has brought questions of economic inequality to the fore, Black Lives Matter (BLM) has created the possibility for a broad-based critique of mass incarceration and criminal (in)justice. Initiated by three queer women of color in 2013, questions of sex and gender have been integrated with a critique of racism and police brutality since the movement's inception. BLM's multiple affiliated organizations and networks of activists have together addressed issues ranging from poverty in urban areas to racist housing markets and food systems, to the lived dynamics of sexual and gender-based violence.[58] In the words of Alicia Garza, a BLM cofounder and the special projects director for the National Domestic Workers Alliance, "When we are able to end hyper-criminalization and sexualization of Black people and end the poverty, control, and surveillance of Black people, every single person in this world has a better shot at getting and staying free."[59]

Political scientist Cathy J. Cohen, the principal investigator for one such organization, the Black Youth Project, has discussed the crucial role for feminist theory in racial justice movements and the ways in which race and gender intersect in state violence. Among campaigns that call attention to police violence, she highlights the Say Her Name campaign and the work of her own organization as facets of the BLM movement that spotlight the lesser-known instances of police violence that affect women and girls. Cohen has also praised the BLM movement for thinking "broadly and radically" about the conditions and struggles of marginalized communities. Citing the work of allied feminist organizations such as INCITE!, a national activist network with affiliates working across the United States to end violence against women of color (identifying "'violence against women of color' as a combination of 'violence *directed at* communities,' such as police violence, war, and colonialism, and 'violence *within* communities' such as sexual and domestic violence"[60]), Cohen argues that working against the prison-industrial complex "must be focused on improving and transforming the conditions under which incarcerated folks exist." Additionally, and perhaps most crucially, it must also provoke us to question the existence of prisons and to contemplate their abolition.[61]

In 2016, BLM created and released a much-heralded platform calling for the changes in policy required to secure the movement's broad-based "Vision for Black Lives." The platform consisted of six key demands: an end to "the war on black people" (criminalization, incarceration, and police violence); reparations; invest-divest, or "investments in the education, health, and safety of Black people" and divestment from "the criminalizing, caging, and harming of Black people"; economic justice; community control (over policing); and political power ("Black self determination in all areas of society"). To achieve these demands, the group proposed a set of policy solutions including the demilitarization of police forces and an end to systemic attacks on black youth, including black members of the LGBTQ community. The new platform also included a call to "end to the war on Black immigrants," drawing attention to the underrecognized impact of deportation and immigrant detention on black immigrants in the United States and linking BLM with the broader movement for immigrants' rights.[62] Another of the chief policy recommendations called for the "retroactive decriminalization and immediate release of all people convicted of drug offenses, sex work-related offenses and youth offenses."[63]

Despite the setbacks that have arisen via the presidency of Donald Trump and his attorney general Jeff Sessions, the movement for BLM, like Occupy, has been far-reaching in its effects.[64] In sharp contrast to the nearly ubiquitous "tough on crime" sensibility that has prevailed over the past three decades, many conservative and liberal politicians alike have come to embrace the idea of criminal justice reform, a political rallying cry that has been significantly advanced by BLM. As observed by political scientists David Dagan and Steven Teles, even some conservatives are "rethinking the carceral state" and "aggressively critiquing the US prison system as oversized, inefficient, and unjust."[65] This shift has been evidenced through the ascendancy of advocacy groups like Right on Crime, an organization intended to "mobilize prominent conservatives for [criminal justice] reform," and in the 2016 presidential campaigns, when even Republican presidential candidates such as Chris Christie, Rand Paul, and Rick Perry all included criminal justice reform as a pillar of their proposed policies.[66] The need for criminal justice reform was also an important component of the campaigns of the two major candidates for the Democratic nomination, Bernie Sanders and Hillary Clinton, despite the latter's prominent role in championing the law-and-order agenda of her husband in the 1990s.

These examples illustrate how movements that are not typically framed in terms of sex and gender—such as anti-austerity, anti-carceral, and anti-racist politics—have the ability, when integrating these issues, to meaningfully shift the conversation. At the same time, they reveal how sex and gender politics may be at their most effective when incorporated into a nuanced critique of contemporary forms of governance and political economy. If the "sex trafficking" framework is ultimately to be dismantled, it will also be necessary to challenge the broader trends toward carceral feminism, militarized humanitarianism, and redemptive capitalism upon which it has been predicated. This will likely necessitate a global extension and proliferation of movements such as Occupy and BLM that are ambitious in their political and analytic reach, as well as further challenges to the neoliberal paradigms of sexual freedom and gender justice that have long been taken for granted.[67]

Questions of Freedom

Writing in the journal *New Politics*, the journalist Francis Shor has summarized the obstacles facing the Black Lives Matter movement by observing the structural parameters by which current social justice activists are constrained. Such a context, according to Shor, presents barriers that extend beyond the racially dismissive taunt that "all lives," and not only black lives matter in US politics.[68] "Whereas the 1960s civil rights movement achieved its political victories in a era of an expanding welfare state and democratic rights," Shor notes "that state and those rights have been massively eroded by neoliberalism and its penchant for privatization and corporate, rather than government, solutions." Other left-leaning commentators on neoliberalism have admitted to facing similar challenges regarding plans of action after issuing otherwise trenchant critiques. For example, Wendy Brown, in her book *Undoing the Demos*, presents a stark account of the implications of neoliberal reason, marketization, and the ubiquitous presence of *Homo economicus* for social and political life. Yet she concludes her discussion flatly and bleakly, noting, "Tasked with the already difficult project of puncturing common neoliberal sense and with developing a viable and compelling alternative to capitalist globalization, the Left must also counter . . . civilizational despair."[69]

Following the shocking election of Donald Trump in 2016, this sense of political despair indeed seemed rampant. But the election also stimulated a surprising resurgence of left activism, including the markedly progressive feminist agenda that was on display at the 2017 Women's March.[70] I have argued here that some of the despair that has been wrought by the lack of perceived alternatives to neoliberal reason might be countered by the synthetic and intertwined approaches to social justice demonstrated by the Occupy and BLM movements, as well as by activist groups such as INCITE!, YWEP, and Empower. These groups, in addition to many of the other activists cited previously, provide critical examples of how neoliberalism in its various facets can be contested, models that at once propel additional political and intellectual reflection and serve as practical models to build upon. INCITE!, alongside the BLM movement, has challenged the carceral state via a combination of "direct action, critical dialogue and grassroots organizing," hosting radio shows, convening rallies against street harassment, providing self-defense trainings for women of color, and devising community accountability strategies as an alternative to state-sponsored criminal justice. YWEP has sought to empower the very same girls and young women who would otherwise qualify as de facto trafficking victims to maneuver through the funding imperatives of NGOs while serving as leaders of their own lives. ("We don't tell girls what to do, we don't give advice, and adults don't take control of youth-led projects."[71]) Meanwhile, activists from the Empower Foundation have challenged the gendered and sexual underpinnings of militarized humanitarian interventions by unfailingly insisting on the purpose and direction of their own struggle. "After raid or rescue," they have written, "we will walk the same path again, facing the same dangers at the same border crossings. Just like the women fighting to be educated, fighting to vote, fighting to participate in politics, fighting to be independent, fighting to work, to love, to live safely . . . we will not stay in the cage society has made for us, we will dare to keep crossing the lines."[72]

But what is perhaps most helpful about these efforts is not so much that they offer singular solutions to the neoliberal embrace of criminal justice, capitalist markets, or humanitarian rescue, but the inspiration that they provide to reimagine these commitments in the first place. Given sex worker rights activists' frequent assertion that trafficking-as-discourse does nothing to alleviate the lived experience of inequality and violence, what might be better ways to talk about the disparate social problems that have been grouped together under this banner, and better ways to imagine gender justice and freedom? Over the course of my research, I have often been asked what my preferred solution to the problem of "trafficking" might be. In addition to the excellent, multifaceted suggestions offered by commentators such as Mogulescu and D'Adamo, I think it is also crucial to remember that disaggregating the component parts of "trafficking"—as proposed in the APNSW epigraph that opens this chapter—would dissolve the entire framework of trafficking as it has commonly been configured. Furthermore, and as I have suggested in earlier chapters of this book, (re)considerations of trafficking as "modern-day slavery" simultaneously compel us to reimagine what we mean by freedom, its opposite. In a moment when neoliberalism as governing philosophy is being called into question in unprecedented ways, this dual reimagining, in fact, may be the most pressing task at hand.[73]

In addition to the material harms that have been wrought by the trafficking discourse—including increased border control and police intervention in sex workers' lives—perhaps its greatest perniciousness has been the tendency to provoke the wrong sets of social and political questions ("Who is trafficked?" "What causes trafficking?" "How can we free sex slaves and help trafficking victims?"). I thus end my investigation of this topic not by providing easily digestible and implementable answers to such queries but by suggesting that we redirect inquiries of this sort elsewhere. The most urgent and important questions right now concern the broad structural inequalities that undergird the various forms of violence—economic, racial, gendered, and sexual—that have come to be known as "trafficking," as well as the proliferation of labor exploitation more generally, in sectors that include but also extend well beyond sex. In addressing these issues, the most daunting challenge for us, at the moment, is to try to conjure solutions to these problems that exist outside the dominant frameworks and institutions that neoliberalism has fostered: the criminal justice system, public-private partnerships, and depoliticized versions of humanitarianism and human rights. At the same time, we must do so without resorting to nostalgic yearnings for an idealized era of welfare-state abundance, one that, at least in its prior incarnations (which were themselves premised upon a particular and problematic gendered, sexual, and racial ordering) may not be coming back.[74]

Questions such as these have received scant attention in the scholarly and activist literatures, and it is clearly beyond the scope of my investigation to resolve them here. But this is undoubtedly the political challenge that my analysis of "sex trafficking" in the preceding pages has implied, and one which must ultimately be taken up, not only by sex worker activists, but by all those who are interested in lessening global inequalities. In a world that is characterized by radically transformed contours of state, society, and governance—and the changing relations of sex and gender that have helped facilitate these shifts—these are the questions of freedom that should feature most prominently on any meaningful agenda for social change.

Afterword

For many commentators, the final months of 2016 represented nothing less than a sea change in US and global politics, with the Brexit vote in the United Kingdom, the surprise election of Donald Trump as US president, the rise of the populist right across much of Europe, and the ascension of a new form of global, masculinist politics that the political theorist Paul Amar has termed "thug love."[1] While some social critics were no doubt premature in declaring that the election of Trump, in particular, signaled not only "the end of globalism" but also "the end of neoliberalism,"[2] it is perhaps more plausible to say that it marked the temporary eclipse of "progressive" or "multicultural" neoliberalism from the highest tiers of electoral politics (even if these same political formations would survive via other institutions or in the guise of the main opposition parties, and find themselves again surging in countries like Canada and France).[3] Because the three cornerstones of the preceding analysis (carceral feminism, militarized humanitarianism, and redemptive capitalism) were closely associated with the proponents of progressive neoliberalism during the Bush and Obama years, it is fair to question what the fate of "trafficking" under the populist-right Trump administration has become.

Had Hillary Clinton triumphed in the election, as was widely anticipated, there is little doubt that the dynamics I have detailed in this book would have continued with few alterations—both because of her pivotal role in shaping the anti-trafficking agenda from the outset and because of her longstanding commitments to neoliberal versions of sexual politics. Yet for those who anticipated that Trump might choose to disregard the issue entirely based on his early critiques of globalization and his avowed hostility to women, people of color, and immigrants, the significance of these inclinations would soon prove deceptive, so much so that even some of the more progressive anti-trafficking activists would come to posit that Trump could potentially serve as an unexpected ally in the cause.[4] It is true that in the early months of the Trump administration, the issue of trafficking would recede from prominence amid the daily chaos of travel bans and attempts to overturn the Affordable Care Act, the resurgence of mass protests, and the allegations of Russian meddling in the election that still fill the pages of newspapers at the time of this writing. At the same time, the fate of "trafficking" in the Trump era also provides some important lessons about both the durability and the malleability of the trafficking discourse, as well as the cultural formations that underpin it, under otherwise divergent political regimes.

In terms of durability, what is perhaps most striking is that Trump, despite overturning so many other rules, regulations, and precedents (including stark rejections of the "globalist" Trans-Pacific Partnership, the Paris climate accords, and commitments to human rights) would choose to keep this issue alive.[5] He has done so through his endorsement of the notable FOSTA/SESTA online sex trafficking law as well as a series of bipartisan anti-trafficking roundtables, a high-profile rollout of the 2017 *TIP Report*, and by designating it as a priority concern of the Office of the Attorney General and an otherwise aimless and depleted Department of State.[6] This continuity is particularly striking given his quick reversals of other dimensions of sex and gender policy. For example, just two days after millions of women around the world marched in defiance of his presidential inauguration, Trump abruptly moved to restrict abortion rights by reinstating a federal ban on the use of US funding of international health organizations that so much as counsel women on safe abortions. His version of the policy expanded its reach as compared with prior Republican administrations by stipulating that international family planning organizations must agree not to "perform or actively promote abortion" and that every global health organization that accepts US funding must accept the same terms. Domestically, Trump has continued to whittle away at abortion rights by signing legislation to discontinue federal funding of Planned Parenthood and other organizations that provide abortions. And he has expressed his strong support for H.R. 36, the Pain-Capable Unborn Child Protection Act, an act that would make abortions after twenty weeks illegal, promising to sign it into law in an invitation he sent to anti-abortion leaders asking them to join his campaign's "Pro-Life Coalition."[7]

During his initial months in office, Trump also sought to overturn a wide array of policies pertaining to sexual and gender-based violence. On March 9, 2017—the day after International Women's Day—Trump proposed a federal budget that would implement major reductions in funding for services related to domestic violence. Several weeks later, he declared his intention to reduce US funding to the UN Population Fund from approximately $75 million to $42.5 million (more than a 40 percent reduction) for the 2017 budget, and just before Equal Pay Day, on April 10, 2017, Trump signed an executive order revoking the Fair Pay and Safe Workplaces Executive Order created by President Obama to ensure businesses that receive federal contracts adhere to labor and civil rights laws. The revocation of this rule rescinded two provisions specifically affecting women in the workplace—a ban on forced arbitration clauses that helped to keep allegations of sexual harassment, sexual assault, and discrimination out of the public record, and the requirement that employers provide information about pay scale and salaries in an effort to ensure that companies pay female employees at the same rate as male employees. Trump notably rescinded Obama-era protections on transgender students, which had required that they have access to bathrooms and locker rooms in conformity with their chosen gender identity, and also sought to bar the participation of transgender people from the US military. In September 2017, the Office of Civil Rights, under the direction of Trump-appointed secretary of education Betsy DeVos, revoked Title IX guidance documents pertaining to the adjudication of sexual assault on college campuses.[8]

Despite these bold revisions and reversals, the Trump administration's continued commitment to "fighting trafficking" has been resolute, revealing the extent to which the carceral politics and border securitization that he supports have been intrinsic to this issue from the outset. In his rollout of archconservative Jeffrey Sessions as his choice for attorney general, Trump signed three executive orders pertaining to stepped-up immigration control and law enforcement, which focused on "enforcing federal law with respect to the transnational criminal organizations," "preventing international trafficking," and "reducing violent crime" (particularly against the police).[9] In braiding these issues together, he was not incorrect in situating the US commitment to fighting trafficking as a key component of broader assaults on immigrants, crime, and the movement for black lives.

President Trump has been aided in his anti-trafficking efforts by his daughter Ivanka, a celebrated neoliberal feminist in her own right, who, very early into the Trump presidency embraced the issue as one of her signature causes.[10] With her *Women Who Work* best-selling book and website as well as her high-profile position as an adviser in her father's White House, there is arguably no bright line distinguishing Ivanka Trump's feminist commitments from those of Hillary Clinton, Sheryl Sandberg, or other neoliberal figures who understand feminism as the freedom to pursue power and success in their culturally dominant forms.[11] Within the first four months of 2017, she had already convened two well-publicized roundtables on the issue, lauding it as "a major priority for the Administration." Although members of the press were not invited to observe the meetings, the roster of invited participants suggested their likely points of consensus. Present at the roundtables were both Democratic and Republican congress members, an array of old and new evangelical Christian NGOs, representatives from law enforcement, and lobbyists from Google.[12] Recent additions to the previous anti-trafficking coalition included the nonprofit Human Trafficking Institute, whose stated goal is to "empower police and prosecutors to stop traffickers," and the McCain Institute, which since 2014 has partnered with high-tech firms like Microsoft, Palantir, Facebook, and Google on various anti-trafficking initiatives.[13]

Meanwhile, from the coalition that had dominated during the Bush and Obama years, only the feminist groups (who overwhelmingly supported Hillary Clinton in the election, and who have been vocal in opposing Trump's most misogynistic statements and actions) were cut out, revealing a new formation that could perhaps be described as carceral feminism without feminists. A survey of recent social media activity reveals the extent to which many prominent feminist anti-trafficking organizations, including the Coalition against Trafficking in Women, Equality Now, and Sanctuary for Families, have explicitly rejected Trump, both before and after he assumed his position as United States president.[14] The only feminist figure who was included at the Trump anti-trafficking roundtables was the evangelical Christian (and former secular feminist icon) Laura Lederer, who, since leaving her State Department post in 2009, has directed the anti-trafficking NGO Global Centurion, which currently holds anti-trafficking training contracts with the Department of Defense.[15] These developments reveal not only the stable features but also the fungibility of the trafficking discourse, as well as the extent to which it has been seen as remarkably compatible with everything else the Trump administration has sought to accomplish.

Like carceral feminism, militarized humanitarianism has persisted in the Trump administration while also appearing in some new guises—despite Trump's repeated allegiance to an "America First" policy in global affairs.[16] As the April 2017 air strikes against Syria made clear, the specter of suffering children could still serve as a potent motive for justifying military intervention. Trump's critics were quick to point out the irony of his actions, given that he had earlier displayed little sympathy for the women and children who were affected by his dual executive orders curtailing the US resettlement of Syrian refugees.[17] Yet the logic which guided Trump's air strikes was not terribly distinct from that of the UN Security Council, which at the end of 2016 passed a resolution on human trafficking in the context of armed conflict in Syria, linking trafficking to terrorism and to the Syrian Civil War. A supporting statement by the European Union further identified reduction of demand for trafficking as an urgent priority in addressing the Syrian crisis. As the GAATW then commented, "In the post-truth politics of anti-trafficking, the UN Security Council, unable to resolve the Syrian conflict or even ensure the delivery of humanitarian aid, resolves unanimously to address trafficking—not the conflict, and the EU tells us that the 'demand for trafficking' in the context of conflict needs to be reduced—not the conflict itself—as if a 'demand for trafficking' created or sustains the Syrian conflict." GAATW activists further observed that the EU's claim that it was honoring its responsibilities to refugees "is woefully undermined by [their] treatment," citing nearly five thousand deaths at sea in 2016 and a general fomentation of "the very vulnerability to trafficking that the EU is claiming to want to address."[18]

Significant in these examples is not only the continued melding of militaristic intervention with purportedly humanitarian concern, but also the ways this admixture relies on particular kinds of sexed and gendered victims (and perpetrators) to generate support. The most scandalous element of the travel bans that Trump implemented upon assuming office was clearly his denial of entry to citizens from Muslim-majority countries, including Syrian refugees. But importantly, both the first and the second travel bans also contained less-commented-upon—and less contested—provisions prohibiting entry into the United States of anyone who had committed acts of violence against women or sexual minorities.[19] Trump's first executive order stated explicitly that the United States would not admit people "who engage in acts of bigotry or hatred (including 'honor' killings, other forms of violence against women, or the persecution of those who practice religions different from their own) or those who would oppress Americans of any race, gender, or sexual orientation."[20] As part of the "Transparency and Data Collection" section of the original travel ban and its subsequent revision, Trump called for the collection of "information regarding the number and types of acts of gender-based violence against women . . . in the United States by foreign nationals."[21]

Trump's broader anti-immigration agenda has also been spurred by his invocations of the purported dangers of "Mexican rapists," and he has defended the construction of a wall on the Mexican border as a means to combat trafficking. He notably began his campaign for president by disparaging Mexican immigrants, remarking in the speech which announced his candidacy that "they're bringing drugs. They're bringing crime. They're rapists." Once in office, he pursued this line of attack when he referred to illegal immigrants as "animals" who "slice and dice" beautiful young girls.[22] Over the course of the following months, he frequently brought up his plan to have a wall built along the US-Mexican border that Mexico would pay for, tweeting that the wall would "help stop drugs, human trafficking etc." During an April 2017 roundtable meeting, he went further, declaring: "The wall is . . . going to stop a lot of people from coming in that shouldn't be here, and it's going to have a huge effect on human trafficking, which is a tremendous problem in this world."[23]

While carceral feminism and militarized humanitarianism have certainly persisted in the Trump administration, it is plausible to argue that redemptive capitalism may now be a more important force than ever, and not just because there is a former real estate developer and television personality in the White House who presides over a cabinet of corporate (and military) leaders.[24] Rather, this administration has extended the idea that markets must pick up the slack in an era when "social entitlements are over," reimagining state commitments to criminal justice, education, health care, transportation, and infrastructure in these terms.[25] Despite Trump's apparent critique of global capitalism during his presidential campaign, the heavy involvement of the corporate sector in these efforts (as in his administration generally) illustrates the extent to which capitalism is positioned as the solution to both domestic and global inequalities, rather than the institution that is most responsible for establishing conditions of precarity, economic hardship, and social suffering.

In terms of trafficking specifically, the trends in US legislation since Trump's election have worked to further foreground the role of the private sector in promoting its particular version of social justice. For example, the Republican-sponsored End Modern Slavery Initiative of 2017 seeks to prevent slavery and to punish perpetrators through a program whose primary source of funding comes from private corporations. Spearheaded by the Republican senator and Foreign Relations Committee chair Bob Corker, the initiative is premised on the idea that the United States has a responsibility as the world's "beacon of freedom" to lead global efforts to end modern slavery. According to Corker, his interest in modern slavery was spurred after visiting Southeast Asia and then connecting with various nongovernmental organizations and faith-based institutions, particularly the International Justice Mission. With IJM, he concluded that the solution was for the United States to respond with stronger law enforcement, because "slavery is a crime of opportunity, flourishing where enforcement is lax or nonexistent."[26] Tellingly, this bill was folded into the National Defense Authorization Act—which authorizes spending for military construction and for the military activities of the Departments of Defense and Energy—and passed with the overwhelming support of both parties.[27]

Despite these ominous trends, there have also been signs of encouragement in the waves of activism that have expanded exponentially since the time of Trump's ascension. Under circumstances of extreme duress, movements for immigrants' rights, indigenous rights, and economic justice have gathered unprecedented support. From protests against the Dakota Access Pipeline to pro-immigrant mobilizations at US airports to the movement for sanctuary cities, as well as both US and global uprisings for housing, health care, and greater economic equality, the current moment can be described as one not only of populism but also of a resurgent left.[28] The 2017 Women's March and subsequent Women's Strike were able to harness the energy of these movements—as well as of Occupy and Black Lives Matter—to articulate a remarkably intersectional feminist agenda, issuing a final platform that explicitly embraced the intertwined issues of racial justice and economic justice, as well as sex workers' rights.[29] Whether it is this vision of feminism that ultimately triumphs, or a version of carceral or "national security" feminism akin to that which I have described in these pages, the outcome will shape the fate of "trafficking" as well as of a host of other issues, including those pertaining to sex, to carcerality, and to neoliberal governance more generally.[30]

December 2017

Notes

1. The Can Do Bar is a bar owned and operated by sex workers that was founded by Empower Chiang Mai in 2006. A fuller discussion of Empower and the two organizations that sponsored our tour of sex trafficking in Thailand (Not for Sale and Global Exchange) is provided in chapter 4.

2. The seventeen tour participants were charged $1,200 each (not including airfare) for a one-week excursion. Our local tour guide told us that he was paid $200 for accompanying the group for seven days and for arranging all logistics.

3. Elena Shih is currently assistant professor of American studies at Brown University.

4. During a subsequent conversation, Liz clarified that Empower began working in the mid-1980s when forced labor in the sex industry was a more common occurrence: "This is why we are confident that the situation is not how it is portrayed and the responses are inappropriate and harmful" (email correspondence, July 28, 2017).

5. Generously calculating the likely travel costs incurred by the group (in terms of hotel fees, transportation, and labor costs for our subcontracted guides) and subtracting them from the fees charged by the two NGOs that cohosted the excursion, they estimated a net profit for the trip's organizers of US$12,600.

6. In 2013, there were nearly fifty different domestic and international NGOs engaged in anti-trafficking work in Thailand. These numbers are striking given that in 2012, there were only 305 reported trafficking cases and only ten convictions. By 2015, there were 61 registered anti-trafficking organizations in Thailand, according to data provided by the

Royal Thai Government (personal communication with Liz Hilton, July 28, 2017); see also US Department of State (2013, 2015), UN Inter-Agency Project on Human Trafficking (2013), and Humantrafficking.org (2013).

7. Shih (2015).
8. The Sex Worker Freedom Festival was held from July 21–July 26, 2012, in Kolkata, India, and was organized as an alternative to the Nineteenth International AIDS Conference held in Washington, DC. The event was conceived of by the Darbur Mahila Samanwaya Committee, a collective of sixty-five thousand sex workers in the Indian state of West Bengal and by the Bangkok-based Global Network of Sex Work Projects. The festival was organized because US travel restrictions bar anyone who has practiced prostitution in the previous ten years from entering the country, thereby prohibiting all sex worker activists from participating in discussions on AIDS in the US (see NSWP 2012).
9. For example, many had fled situations of violent armed conflict and extreme poverty in Laos and Burma at young ages and had relied on sexual labor since that time to support multiple generations of family members. On sex workers' experiences in the Mekong region more generally, see Hoefinger (2013), Molland (2012), Empower (2011a, 2011b), Roux (2011), Wilson (2004), Jeffrey (2002), and Montgomery (2001).
10. See Marks (2013, 2012a, 2012b), Marks and Sovuthy (2012), Marks and Naren (2013), Marks and Bopha (2012, 2013), and Marks and Soenthrith (2012).
11. See Mam (2007).
12. See, e.g., Kristof (2014), Grove (2014).
13. Cheng (2010: 5).
14. Shah (2014: 8). The term "abolitionism" has been used since the late nineteenth century to describe transnational feminist efforts to eliminate (rather than regulate or reform) prostitution. It has been reclaimed by those sectors of the contemporary feminist movement that share the conviction that prostitution constitutes a harm tantamount to slavery that nation-states should work to extinguish. See also Soderlund (2005).
15. Jacobsen and Skilbrei (2010). Other key works within the sociological, anthropological, and activist literatures include Bernstein and Shih (2014), Brennan (2014), Molland (2012), Lindquist (2009), Mahdavi (2011), Kotiswaran (2011), Andrijasevic (2010), Kempadoo (2012a), Parreñas (2011), Agustín (2007), and Kempadoo and Doezema (1998).
16. On the presumptive femininity of the trafficking victim, see Mai (2012) and Kaye (forthcoming).
17. See, e.g., Abu-Lughod (2013), Scott (2012), Doyle (2015), Codrea-Rado (2017), Iniko Newton (2017).
18. "Rescue industry" is a phrase coined by the cultural critic Laura Agustín (2007) to refer to the burgeoning class of helpers and saviors that has emerged in Europe over the past two decades.

19. Ivan Illich's (1968) classic essay "To Hell with Good Intentions" provides an early but still relevant critique of transnational helping gestures. The phrase "brokers and translators" is indebted to the title of Lewis and Mosse's (2006) edited collection *Development Brokers and Translators: The Ethnography and Aid and Agencies*.

20. As such, this project has obvious resonances with that of Mahmood's (2005) *Politics of Piety* and other critical works that challenge mainstream feminist presumptions regarding women's empowerment and freedom (see, e.g., Farris 2017, Abu-Lughod 2013, Ticktin 2011, Scott 2007, Haney 2010a, Cruikshank 1999).

21. See Bernstein (2007a, 2007b, 2010, 2012). In Bernstein (2007b), I focused in particular on the similarly situated postindustrial cities of San Francisco, Stockholm, and Amsterdam to demonstrate how three quite disparate versions of policy reform in the late 1990s—decriminalization in San Francisco, criminalization in Stockholm, and legalization in Amsterdam—resulted in a common series of alterations to the social geography of sexual commerce. These included the removal of economically disenfranchised and racially marginalized streetwalkers from gentrifying city centers, the de facto tolerance of a small tier of predominantly white and relatively privileged indoor sex workers, and the increased policing of illegal migrant workers, thus pushing them further underground.

22. See, for example, the US State Department (2013: 7) *Trafficking in Persons Report*, in which President Obama declared that "the injustice, the outrage, of human trafficking . . . must be called by its true name—modern slavery."

23. At the federal level, see most recently the Allow States and Victims to Fight Online Sex Trafficking Act of 2017 and the End Modern Slavery Initiative, which was included in the National Defense Authorization Act of 2017 (US Congress 2018, US Congress 2017). See also the Trafficking Victims Protection Act (US Congress 2000) and its successive reauthorizations. At the transnational level, see the *United Nations Protocol to Prevent, Suppress, and Punish Trafficking in Persons, Especially Women and Children, Supplementing the Convention Against Transnational Organized Crime* (UN General Assembly 2000).

24. See, e.g., Agustín (2007), Berman (2006), Saunders (2005), and Soderlund (2005).

25. Rosen (1982). For well-known social histories of turn-of-the-century discourses of white slavery, see also Walkowitz (1980), Hobson (1990), and Langum (1994); Doezema (2010), Limoncelli (2010), and Donovan (2006) have provided more recent accounts.

26. The 1910 Mann Act prohibited the interstate traffic in women for "immoral purposes." It later became notorious for its use in prosecuting instances of interracial sex (Langum 1994). Despite a spate of more recent legislation, it continues to be used in the prosecution of contemporary sex-trafficking cases.

27. Limoncelli (2010: 2). The first League of Nations accord was created in 1904 and established central bureaus for information exchange on trafficking,

assistance for victims in ports and railway stations, and the repatriation of women working in prostitution in foreign countries. In 1910, a second convention made all underage prostitution and the forced prostitution of women illegal. In 1921, the League of Nations expanded on these accords, making underage prostitution illegal for both sexes, raising the age of consent to twenty-one, and stipulating the extradition of traffickers. Limoncelli (2010: 9–11).

28. See, e.g., Kempadoo and Doezema (1998), Agustín (2007), Chapkis (2005).
29. Miller (2004).
30. Clinton (1995). For a critical analysis of the geopolitical interests undergirding Clinton's remarks in Beijing, see Grewal (2005: 150).
31. The feminist "sex wars" of the 1980s and 1990s were characterized by heightened debates and activism surrounding issues of sexual politics. Featured prominently in these debates was a rift between feminists surrounding the subject of pornography, with activists divided among those who were against pornography and those were opposed to sexual censorship. As Lisa Duggan points out, those feminists who rallied behind the anti-porn campaigns, who regarded pornography as violence against women and something that must be censored, allied themselves with antifeminist, moral conservatives, the result of a "convergence of binary gender categories and melodramatic narratives of female innocence and male villainy" (Duggan and Hunter 2006: 7). See also Snitow et al. (1983) and Vance (1992).
32. Buss and Herman (2003).
33. See also Hertzke (2004).
34. Bush (2003).
35. Mink (2001), Butler (2006), Stockman et al. (2006).
36. Miller (2006).
37. In 2003, President Bush's "President's Emergency Plan for AIDS Relief" was passed as the United States Leadership against HIV/AIDS, Tuberculosis, and Malaria Act of 2003. The act was part of a US initiative to address the global HIV/AIDS epidemic and included a controversial "anti-prostitution pledge" that refused funding to organizations that did not have an explicit anti-prostitution policy. The same pledge was added to the Trafficking Victims Protection Reauthorization Act of 2003, which stipulated, "No funds made available to carry out this division, or any amendment made by this division, may be used to promote, support, or advocate the legalization or practice of prostitution." It further specified that "no funds made available to carry out this division, or any amendment made by this division, may be used to implement any program . . . through any organization that has not stated in either a grant application, a grant agreement, or both, that it does not promote, support, or advocate the legalization or practice of prostitution" (US Congress 2003: section 7). In 2013, the Supreme Court ruled the anti-prostitution pledge unconstitutional for violating the First Amendment. This ruling, however, applied to only US-based organizations; the

pledge is still applicable to international organizations receiving US aid (Pieklo 2013).

38. USAID (2012). Between 2001 and 2012, expenditures averaged $16.3 million annually. In 2015, USAID spent more than $25 million on new and existing anti-trafficking programs in Africa (Democratic Republic of Congo, Mauritania, Mozambique, Ghana), Asia (Burma, Cambodia, Philippines, Thailand, Bangladesh, Nepal, Kyrgyz Republic, Kazakhstan, Azerbaijan, Albania, Moldova), Latin America (Guatemala), and the Middle East (Egypt). In 2016, USAID announced that it would contribute $10 million to the International Organization on Migration "to end the exploitation of men, women, and children subjected to forced labor and sex trafficking in Afghanistan." (USAID 2012, 2015, 2016).

39. *The Whistleblower* (Kondracki, 2010) was a dramatic reenactment of events based on the experiences of Kathryn Bolkovac, a Bosnia-based human rights investigator for the United Nations. *Taken* (2008), an action thriller, followed a former CIA agent as he worked to rescue his daughter who was kidnapped by traffickers while in Paris. The film's gross of $224 million was sufficient to warrant the production of two sequels, *Taken 2* and *Taken 3*. Lifetime's 2005 *Human Trafficking* miniseries starred Mira Sorvino as a US immigration agent who goes undercover to stop an organization of Eastern European sex traffickers. Since 1996, there have been at least 65 major fictional and documentary films made on the subject of human trafficking ("Films on Human Trafficking 2013"; Human Trafficking 2013). While other representations of sex work have continued to circulate in the media (see e.g. television series such as the Starz Network's *The Girlfriend Experience* and the Lifetime Network's *The Client List*), proliferating narratives of sex trafficking have played a key role in disseminating this framework as an apparatus of governance.

40. *Half the Sky* (2010) was cowritten by Nicholas Kristof and his wife Sheryl WuDunn (an entrepreneur and former journalist for the *New York Times*). The *Half the Sky* online game is available at www.halftheskymovement.org /pages/mobile-games.

41. See, e.g., the Tumblr http://restavekfreedom.tumblr.com/post/148354874768 /5–more-celebrities-fighting-human-trafficking. Demi Moore and Ashton Kutcher cofounded the Demi and Ashton Foundation in 2009 (following the couple's divorce, the organization has since been renamed Thorn: Digital Defenders of Children). In addition to releasing their own series of public service announcements, both Moore and Kutcher appeared in a human-trafficking public service announcement for the US Department of Homeland Security. In 2017, Kutcher testified before the Foreign Relations Committee of the US Senate about his organization's efforts to combat sex trafficking. Mira Sorvino was appointed UN goodwill ambassador for human trafficking in 2009 after starring in the Lifetime television miniseries *Human Trafficking* four years prior. Jada Pinkett Smith is the founder of the

Don't Sell Bodies public information campaign and costarred with Salma Hayek in a music video of the same title (see Klein 2017, Gonzalez 2012, Parnes 2010, UN Office on Drugs and Crime 2009).

42. Molland (2012: 33); my most recent search for the term on the *New York Times* website (www.nytimes.com) was conducted on December 8, 2017.

43. See also Jordan (2002), Miller (2004), Doezema (2010).

44. The law was reauthorized in 2003, 2005, 2008, 2013, and 2015. The complex issue of how to define sex trafficking was even raised by the US Government Accountability Office (GAO 2006). The report does not take a position on how "trafficking" should be defined but calls for better research in order to understand the problem of trafficking in the United States and credits "questionable" estimates of trafficking cases in part to a lack of "agreed-upon criteria for identification of human trafficking victims" (GAO 2006: 21).

45. Chapkis (2003: 925); see also Feingold (2005, 2010).

46. GAO (2006), Donovan (2004). Some estimates have been even higher. During the first administration of George W. Bush, Secretary of State Colin Powell stated that seven hundred thousand—and possibly up to four million people—were trafficked into the United States every year (McDonald 2004). Brennan (2008) has speculated that the subsequent shift from an international to a domestic focus in US anti-trafficking policy occurred because the US government has consistently failed to identify the overwhelming numbers of transborder victims that it previously claimed existed.

47. US Department of State (2015, 2016), US Department of Justice (2011a, 2012). Established in 2000 with the passing of the Trafficking Victims Protection Act (TVPA), T visas grant "T" (trafficking) nonimmigrant status and allow victims to stay in the country if they comply with federal investigations aimed at prosecuting those who were responsible for their trafficking (US Citizenship and Immigration Services, n.d.).

48. New York State Department of Criminal Justice services, personal communication, March 9, 2017. The discrepancies between official estimates and actual cases of sex trafficking have been so vast that they have periodically been reported by even mainstream news outlets. In 2007, an article by the journalist Jerry Markon in the *Washington Post* noted the discrepancy between the 1,362 identified victims of human trafficking in the United States and the previously estimated 50,000 a year (Markon 2007). In 2009, Nick Davies similarly debunked the numbers of sex trafficking cases in the UK with two of his articles in *The Guardian*. In an article tellingly titled "Inquiry Fails to Find Single Trafficker Who Forced Anybody into Prostitution" (Davies 2009a), he makes it known that "the UK's biggest ever investigation of sex trafficking failed to find a single person who had forced anybody into prostitution." In a subsequent article, he showed how the estimated number of 4,000 trafficking victims that was qualified by researchers as speculative came to be accepted as fact by the 2006 Home Office Minister (Davies 2009b). It was subsequently recirculated and even exaggerated by groups

such as the Christian charity CARE, the Salvation Army, and Anti-Slavery International.

49. Blanchette and da Silva (2012: 118). The study, undertaken under the auspices of an initiative called PESTRAF, was conducted by a coalition of non-profit organizations and researchers in collaboration with the International Human Rights Law Institute of DePaul University and the Brazilian Ministry of Justice. According to Blanchette and da Silva, PESTRAF's two organizers on the Brazilian side had no previous experience researching trafficking and "little experience with social scientific research of any kind" (109).

50. Steinfatt (2011: 458).

51. Ham (2011); see also Jordan (2011).

52. The initial estimates were produced by the Association of German Cities (which later renounced them), CARE for Europe, the Salvation Army, the German Women's Council, and the Nordic Council. The estimate for the 2010 World Cup in South Africa came from the South African Central Drug Authority and was repeated on numerous occasions in the international media (Ham 2011).

53. Ham (2011: 8).

54. McDonald (2004: 169).

55. Different versions of this perspective are presented in Rubin (2011), Lancaster (2011), Vance (2011), Doezema (2010), and Irvine (2008).

56. See, e.g., Weitzer (2007), Saunders (2005), Berman (2006), and Soderlund (2005).

57. See, e.g., Zimmerman (2013), Hertzke (2004), Ho (2012), and Shih (2009).

58. See, e.g., Butler (2006), Buss and Herman (2003), Wuthnow (2009), and McAlister (2008b).

59. See Bernstein and Jakobsen (2010).

60. For a discussion of the Protestant assumptions that undergird secular politics in the United States, particularly around questions of sex, see Jakobsen and Pellegrini (2004) and Bernstein and Jakobsen (2010).

61. See, e.g., Shih (2015), Jewell (2007), Baue (2006), Vital Voices Global Partnership (2007).

62. Kristof (2004c). See also Kristof (2009).

63. Mam had been critiqued by many activists for her tendency to embellish her stories, in addition to being accused of fabricating cases of sex trafficking. See, e.g., Marks and Sovuthy (2012), Penh Pal (2012), and De Launey (2005).

64. Harvey (2007) provides the classic neo-Marxist account. For Foucaultian versions, see Foucault (2008), Brown (2005: 37–60), and Rose (1999). Social science perspectives focused on state transformations include Wacquant (2009b), Lewis and Mosse (2006), and Fehrer (2007). Gowan (2013), Springer (2012), and Wacquant (2012) provide helpful summaries of the above distinctions.

65. Duggan (2003).

66. Bedford (2009a).
67. Karim (2011).
68. On corporate-driven "equality" politics in the LGBT movement, see Duggan (2003), Joseph (2002), and Chasin (2000). On the corporate "pinking" of the breast cancer movement, see Sulik (2011), Ehrenreich (2009), Klawiter (2008), and King (2006). The literature on the imbrication of seemingly progressive sexual agendas in nationalist projects is ample, but see Ticktin (2011), Clough and Willse (2011), Dudink (2011), Fassin (2011), Farris (2012), Puar (2007), Eisenstein (2009), and Scott (2007) for a sampling of perspectives on these intersections in United States and Western European contexts. The mutual reinforcements between contemporary sexual and carceral politics have been less elaborated upon, but see Lancaster (2011), Bernstein (2012), Haritaworn (2011), Wacquant (2009b), Bumiller (2008), Halley (2006), and Gottschalk (2006) for some articulations of the connections.
69. Although as commentators such as Saletan (2003) have argued, even here a formerly ample political agenda around reproductive freedoms has shifted right by being scaled back and privatized. Similarly, scholars who employ a reproductive justice frame—and in particular feminists of color—have been critical of the collapsing of a broad range of intersectional issues into the narrow, race- and class-specific lens of "reproductive rights." See, e.g., Roberts (1997) and Jordan-Young, Trainor, and Jakobsen (2010).
70. See also Halley (2006: 21).
71. Grewal (2005: 132).
72. On "global corporate citizenship," see Schwab (2008).
73. See, e.g., DeStefano (2007), Hertzke (2004), Skinner (2008).
74. See, e.g., Merry (2006), Wilson (2009), Grewal (2005), and Spivak (1996).
75. See Humanity United (n.d.) and Clinton Foundation (n.d.). In philanthropic circles, the Clinton Global Initiative (CGI) was widely credited with creating a new framework for giving and action, "convening powerful figures from government, business and charities to address global problems. Members would pay for the privilege to meet and brainstorm solutions, then make financial commitments, often multi-year plans costing tens of millions of dollars" (Clinton Foundation n.d.). Founded in 2005 by former president Bill Clinton, the CGI announced its closure in September 2016, due to criticisms that the initiative represented a conflict of interest for Hillary Rodham Clinton's campaign for the US presidency. In 2017, Bill Clinton clarified that the initiative was being downsized rather than eliminated (Talev and Allison 2016).
76. See, e.g., Brennan (2014), Chuang (2010) and Parreñas (2011).
77. For a sampling of popular journalistic accounts, see Kara (2009, 2012), Bales (2010b, 2012), Bales and Trodd (2008), and Skinner (2009). For important critiques of the anti-trafficking discourse by scholars working within the tradition of cultural studies, see Doezema (2010), Hua (2011), and Agustín (2007).

78. Doezema's (2010) account perhaps comes closest to my ambition here, although her approach is historical rather than ethnographic, and her theoretical template is more heavily indebted to notions of myth and ideology than it is to discourse.

79. See Bernstein (2007b) for a fuller discussion of my approach to theoretically driven ethnography.

80. On the United States as "imperial homeland" of global humanitarian interventions, see Maskovsky and Susser (2009), Bumiller (2008), and Grewal (2005).

81. See also Mol (2006: 9).

82. Valverde (1991: 10). Although any invocation of "discourse" is evidently indebted to Foucault, the discussion I present here deliberately sidesteps debates about the precise archaeology of his use of the term (see, e.g., Sawyer 2002).

83. Butler (1993: 94). "Discourse," however, is understood by most scholars to be less volatile than the Deleuzian notion of assemblage, its currently fashionable theoretical counterpart with which it shares certain features. See, e.g., Colebrook (2002), Wise (2005), and Puar (2007).

84. See, e.g., Moore (1999: 63); On the "productive incoherence" of contemporary cultural formations around gender and sexuality, see Sedgwick (1993: xii) and Duggan (2003: 14).

85. See, e.g., Cheng (2004), Doezema (2005), Kempadoo (2005), Kempadoo and Doezema (1998).

86. I use the term "subjectify" in Foucault's sense of the creation of subjects through power and disciplines (see, e.g., Foucault 2005: 237).

87. Butler (1993: 95).

88. Here, I follow Butler's (1993: 9) definition of social construction as "a process of materialization that stabilizes over time to produce the effect of boundary, fixity, and surface we call matter." She distinguishes this from theoretical approaches in which "culture" is imagined to act on "nature," a perspective that could be said to encompass sociological traditions ranging from the "constructivist" social problems school to frame analysis to labeling theory (see, e.g., Best 1990, Goffman 1974, Becker 1963).

89. Burawoy et al. (1991, 2000) and Scheper-Hughes (2002, 2011) are oft-cited exemplars of the multisited approach. Yet the extended case method that Burawoy and colleagues advocate, as they proudly insist, remains deeply rooted in a "realist" (i.e., objectivist) perspective. In her study of the global commerce in organs from Israel to Brazil, Scheper-Hughes (2011) uncritically adheres to the definitions contained in the UN Protocol on Trafficking in Persons (2000) and deploys the term "trafficking" as a neutral descriptor.

90. McDonald (2005: 456–457) describes "shadowing" as a classical ethnographic technique that involves a researcher closely following a particular subject over an extended period of time: "During the shadowing the researcher will write an almost continuous set of field notes. They will record participants in, and

times and contents of, conversations. . . . They will note the body language and moods of the person they are shadowing. At the end of the shadowing period the researcher will have a rich, dense and comprehensive data set which gives a detailed, first-hand and multidimensional picture of the role, approach, philosophy and tasks of the person being studied."

91. Murphy and Jerolmack (2016). For example, when Elena Shih and I circulated an earlier version of chapter 4 among Empower members, many were dismayed to discover that we had altered their personal names and the names of organizations but had chosen to precisely document their ages. In light of their expressed concerns, we decided to revise our text.

92. Shore and Wright (1997: 3, 14).

93. Riles (2000: xvi).

94. Roy (2010: xi).

95. Ferguson (1994: 17).

96. On the gendered specificity of the trafficking discourse, see Kaye (forthcoming) and Mai (2012).

97. On structural violence as an explanation for the burgeoning of sexual commerce under neoliberal globalization, see Padilla (2007), Parker (2001), and Bernstein (2007b: 3).

98. Valentine (2007: 6).

99. Ibid., 14.

100. Chew (2012).

101. Interview with Andrew Hunter, Asia Pacific Network of Sex Workers, August 3, 2012; interview with Liz Hilton, Empower Foundation, August 12, 2012.

102. On the rise of corporate social responsibility initiatives, see Anner (2012), Sulik (2011), and Richey and Ponte (2011).

103. But see Bedford (2009b), Hayhurst (2011) and Murphy (2013) for some preliminary assessments of corporate-feminist intersections.

104. See, e.g., Ticktin (2011), Puar (2007), Scott (2007), Grewal (2005), Bedford (2009a, 2009b), and Berik, van der Meulen Rodgers, and Zammit (2009).

105. See, e.g., Newman (2013), Pecheny (2013).

106. See, e.g., Brandt (1985), Luker (1998), Hobson (1990).

CHAPTER TWO

1. Donna Hughes in *National Review Online* interview with Lopez (2006); Dorchen Leidholdt, speech to the UN Commission on the Status of Women, New York, March 2, 2007; NOW rally, New York City, February 1, 2007.

2. The Profits of Pimping panel took place on 10 July 2008.

3. Formed in 1988 during the neoconservative Reagan era and the initial phase of the so-called sex wars, the Coalition against Trafficking in Women (CATW) subscribes to the version of feminism that views all forms of monetary exchange for sexual intimacy as inherently violating (see also

Doezema 2000). The Coalition to End Sexual Exploitation (CESE) is an umbrella organization that comprises 143 separate groups, which work together to "stop pornography and sexual exploitation from harming individuals and families." The coalition's website asserts that "pornography is inherently dehumanizing" and that its' eradication, along with the eradication of other forms of sexual exploitation, will both "defend dignity" and "protect innocence."

4. Halley (2006).

5. See, e.g., Walkowitz (1983), Brown (1995).

6. Lederer served in this capacity from 2001 to 2009. A figure previously associated with the secular feminist mainstream, Laura Lederer's career has taken her from grassroots anti-pornography activism to the shaping of governmental agendas around sex trafficking. *Take Back the Night*, the classic second-wave feminist text that Lederer compiled in the late 1970s, stands in notable contrast to her later advocacy work in several ways. Although the authors of the volume call for the suppression of pornography through legal means, they do not posit this as their primary strategy; instead, they emphasize public protests and other consciousness-raising measures. This mode of response stands in sharp contrast to the criminal-legal orientation of much of the feminist antiviolence movement today.

7. Chesler and Hughes (2004). In addition to serving as the Elinor M. Carlson endowed Chair of Women's Studies at the University of Rhode Island, Hughes has been a regular contributor to the right-wing journal the *National Review*. Both Hughes and Chesler were participants in the 2007 right-wing, anti-Islam campaign on US college campuses called "Islamofacism Awareness Week."

8. The conservative talk-show host and former Republican vice-presidential candidate Sarah Palin highlighted her participation in feminist organizations such as Feminists for Life and the Susan B. Anthony List during the 2008 US presidential elections. Ayaan Hirsi Ali, a feminist activist of Somali origin and a prominent critic of Islam, has served as a fellow at the right-wing American Enterprise Institute since 2006 (Schafer and Koth 2007).

9. See, e.g., Baker (2013), Ditmore and Wijers (2003), "Odd Coalition" (2004).

10. See, e.g., Chapkis (2005), Kempadoo (2005b), and Ticktin (2008). On the contemporary feminist embrace of the security state, see also Abu-Lughod (2013) and Grewal (2017).

11. Bernstein (2007b). See, e.g., Davis (2016), Nair (2016), O'Brien (2015), Wypijewski (2014), Law (2014) and Segura (2014). The term has also made its way onto social media platforms such as Twitter (a quick search of the term yields nearly three thousand results) and Tumblr. For example, there is a "carceral feminist cat" Tumblr, which includes pictures of a cat wearing a pearl necklace, accompanied by various sayings such as "Kidnapped and assaulted and now don't feel safe? Come with us. Oh, don't mind the cuffs . . ." and "Demands fresh toy mice for new Women's Prison" (see carceralfeministcat 2014).

12. Pollitt (2014). See, e.g., Lancaster (2011: 211), Spade (2011) and Haritaworn (2011).
13. Foucault (1979).
14. See, e.g., Conner (2016), Musto (2013), Leon and Shdaimah (2012), Hassan (2013).
15. Garland (2001a, 2001b) excepted, most theorists begin from the premise that the incarceration rate has augmented dramatically while crime and victimization rates have declined. For a powerful articulation of these disparate trends, see Zimring (2007).
16. Feeley and Simon (1992).
17. Foucault (1979).
18. Garland (2001a: xiii).
19. Wacquant (2009b).
20. Simon (2007).
21. Jim Crow laws in the United States were enacted during the Reconstruction Era, after the Civil War ended and slavery was formally abolished. A tactic of Southern conservatives to maintain the racial status quo (alongside bombings, lynchings, and mob violence), these laws established a system of racial segregation that kept blacks separate from whites in schools, restaurants, hotels, public restrooms, and many other public establishments. The Supreme Court ruling *Brown v. Board of Education* found the segregation of public schools unconstitutional in 1954, and the Civil Rights Act of 1964 officially dismantled the Jim Crow system of discrimination in public accommodations, employment, voting, education, and federally financed activities (Alexander 2010).
22. Alexander (2010: 16).
23. Sudbury (2005: xiv); see also Madriz (1997), Davis (2003), Haney (2004), Bohrman and Murakawa (2005), and Wood (2005).
24. See Gruber (2007), Kapur (2005), and Simon (2007).
25. See, e.g., Bumiller (2008) and Richie (2012). The Violent Crime Control and Law Enforcement Act greatly expanded the state's carceral capabilities, including via the creation of sixty new death penalty offenses, the overturning of a law that permitted inmates to receive funding for education while incarcerated, an added mandate for life imprisonment after three federal violent offenses, and the financing of enormous boosts in law enforcement and prison construction budgets.
26. Richie (2012).
27. The bill, New York S.B. 5902, passed with broad support from New York feminist organizations on June 6, 2007.
28. Spitzer was ironically a strong ally of the New York feminist movement before resigning from office on March 13, 2008, for patronizing a prostitute (Powell and Confessore 2008).
29. Such claims disregard a body of social scientific evidence that has found that women and girls often enter into prostitution at their families' behest,

so as to better provide for their parents and children; see, e.g., Montgomery (2001), Agustín (2007), Bernstein (2007b).

30. Miller (2004: 32).

31. Jordan (2002: 2).

32. See Kaye (2007), Gallagher (2001), Jordan (2002), and Coomaraswamy (2000).

33. US Congress (2000), sec. 107. As Kaye (2007) points out, the right to stay in the United States during a criminal investigation had already been granted to illegal immigrants in 1994 through the Violent Crime Control and Law Enforcement Act. Furthermore, before 1994 illegal immigrants assisting with criminal cases were often "paroled in" or granted a status of "deferred action," thereby allowing them to stay in the United States via bureaucratic procedure rather than statutory grant (see also Pearson 2002: 121, Chapkis 2005).

34. Chuang (2006). In its annual *Trafficking in Persons* reports, the US Department of State tasks itself with ranking other national governments on their efforts to combat trafficking. Critics contend that the political interests that guide the *TIP* rankings have been manifest from the outset, as Venezuela became an early example of how the *TIP Report* could be molded to reflect current US diplomatic relations and used as a tool to justify the denial or granting of international aid (tier 3 countries face certain trade-related sanctions and restrictions on various forms of US aid). Venezuela, for example, received a tier 3 ranking in the 2004 *TIP Report*, after it was shown in 2002 that the United States supported a coup against Venezuela's leader, Hugo Chávez, and it preceded the United States' pulling of $250 million in loans requested by Venezuela from international financing institutions. Venezuela's trafficking conditions were cited as the reason for the revoked aid (Soderlund 2005). Several observers have also suggested that other tier 3 countries that are also defined as sanctionable by the US State Department have been those "who oppose US imperialism, such as Iran, and countries made up of Arab and Muslim populations, such as Indonesia, United Arab Emirates, Afghanistan, Bahrain, Lebanon, Sudan, Qatar, Turkey, and Saudi Arabia" (Capous Desyllas 2007: 67).

Concerns that the United States would use the TVPA and the UN Protocol to advance unrelated political interests were again ignited following the release of the 2015 *TIP Report* (US Department of State 2015). The US State Department was criticized by various human rights groups for moving Cuba and Malaysia up to a tier 2 watch list from tier 3 despite little or no tangible change in the countries' policies toward human trafficking. Cuba's promotion came not long after the United States reopened its embassy in Havana and the bettering of US-Cuban relations, while Malaysia's promotion occurred just in time for the Trans-Pacific Partnership, a US-led trade deal between Malaysia and eleven other Southeast Asian countries (Kelly 2015). In the 2017 *TIP Report*, China was downgraded to tier 3 status, prompting some observers to argue that the downgrade was "part of a cascade of signals from Washington" that relations between the United States and China were rapidly deteriorating. See US Department of State (2017), Harris (2017).

35. In 2012, researchers at the Young Women's Empowerment Project (YWEP) found that sex workers experienced seven times as many incidents of violence by police officers and care workers as they experienced from pimps (Moore 2015).

36. As of 2015, thirty-four states had passed safe-harbor laws providing some level of service provision for sexually exploited minors. See Schweig, Malangone, and Goodman (2015), Polaris Project (2015).

37. Hassan (2013), Conner (2016), Leon and Shdaimah (2012).

38. Schwartz (2008: 268).

39. Musto (2013: 270). Musto's research shows that law enforcement agents and social service providers are not unaware of the harm that detention of youth may cause—many represent the detainment of youth in the juvenile justice system as a less-than-ideal but necessary response, given a lack of other options. As one police officer she interviewed remarked: "I don't necessarily like putting victims in jail. I recognize that's what we're doing. I'm incarcerating a victim. But I'm doing it for their best interest. Give me another option and we'll do it!" (Musto 2013: 267).

40. See, e.g., Stillman (2011). In chapter 5, I provide a fuller discussion of the Obama administration's greater attention to trafficking into labor sectors beyond sex.

41. The term "radical feminist" may be largely a misnomer given a political trajectory that has carried many of the original activists associated with this point of view to prominent positions in national and international governance (see Bernstein 2010b, Halley 2008a).

42. Saunders (2005), Weitzer (2007), and Soderlund (2005).

43. A fuller discussion of Tanya and the dynamics of her work is provided in Bernstein (2007a). In one of the first trafficking cases in the United States, on September 25, 2001, Russian national Victor Nikolayevich Virchenko was found guilty by the US District Court for the District of Alaska for immigration fraud and transporting minors for illegal sexual activity. According to court documents, Virchenko was "a dance instructor of some renown in his native country," who obtained visas for six women (two of whom were minors) by claiming they "were coming to Alaska to perform Russian folk dances in cultural festivals." Virchenko initially told the women that in addition to performing folk dances, they might also dance in "exhibitions" that could include partial nudity. When some of the women objected to these conditions, Virchenko informed them that they could not return home until they earned enough money dancing to pay for their tickets and other expenses. Most eventually acquiesced and began to dance topless and then fully nude. See US Department of Justice (2001b),

United States v. Kennard (2001). See also *United States v. Sabil Mumin Mujahid* (2010).

44. Marcus et al. (2011).
45. His lawyers contacted me by telephone after hearing me speak on a national radio show about my research on trafficking and prostitution.
46. Prison-abolitionist feminists such as Angela Davis have argued, nonetheless, that there are alternatives to incarceration for even the most violent offenders. In her book *Are Prisons Obsolete?*, the alternatives she considers range from conflict resolution to restorative or reparative justice, modes of justice which are enforced by the local community instead of the criminal justice system. These forms of justice seek to rehabilitate offenders through conflict resolution and reconciliation with their victims and the broader community. Restorative or reparative justice in particular focuses on the accountability of offenders instead of their punishment, and resonates with Herman Bianchi's proposal to reimagine crime "in terms of tort" such that "[the lawbreaker] is thus no longer an evil-minded man or woman, but simply a debtor, a liable person whose human duty is to take responsibility for his or her acts, and to assume the duty of repair" (Davis 2003: 113–114, Deflem 2006).
47. Ben-Moshe (90–92), Davis (2003).
48. Gottschalk (2015).
49. Prejean (2001).
50. In this regard, sex trafficking follows the precedents established through federal legislation around domestic violence, in which prosecutors can also proceed with arrests in the absence of victim testimony, and mandate victim participation in criminal trials. Mandatory arrests were explicitly encouraged by the Violence against Women Act of 1994, which provided federal funding to state and local police departments that certified their adoption of either pro- or mandatory arrest policies (Goodmark 2011). "No-drop" policies that prevent women from discontinuing prosecution when they are no longer interested in or even adamantly opposed to it take this element even further. Such policies limit the prosecutor's discretion to drop a case solely because the victim is unwilling to cooperate and were endorsed at the federal level by the Child Abuse, Domestic Violence, Adoption, and Family Services Act of 1992 (Corsilles 1994: 864).
51. *United States v. Davis* (2008).
52. The federally recorded incidents of intimate partner violence (IPV) in the United States far exceed the numbers of recorded incidents of sex trafficking. For example, the Bureau of Justice Statistics cited 620,850 incidents of IPV in 2011, while investigations into human trafficking cases (for both sex and labor) during the same year came to only 1,254 (US Department of Justice 2013).
53. Indictment number 1923/2012 (courtesy of John Temple, New York County District Attorney's Office, Human Trafficking Response Unit, personal communication, December 1, 2015).

54. CBS New York (2013).
55. The Georges were ultimately acquitted of the sex-trafficking charges, which would have been accompanied by prison sentences of up to twenty-five years. They were convicted of the lesser charges of money laundering and promoting prostitution and sentenced to three to nine years in prison (Buettner 2013a, 2013b, Associated Press 2013).
56. Doezema (2001: 16); see also Brown (1995).
57. Sun (2007: 245), Anderberg (2004).
58. See, e.g., Gordon (1982), Walkowitz (1980).
59. Barry (1995).
60. For a discussion of the distinction, see Bernstein (2007a).
61. See, e.g., Bunch (1972), Morgan (1973), and Echols (1989).
62. Horowitz, who is employed by the neoconservative think tank, the Hudson Institute, was a pivotal figure in cementing the anti-trafficking coalition during the Bush presidency (see Hertzke 2004).
63. May (2006).
64. See Clarke (2004).
65. In her classic essay the "Traffic in Women," the feminist anthropologist Gayle Rubin (1975) drew on the works of Marx and Engels, Claude Lévi-Strauss, and Jacques Lacan (in addition to a wealth of cross-cultural data) to argue that the linchpin of women's oppression resides in the social conventions of marriage and kinship.
66. See, e.g., Morgan (1973), Barry (1995), MacKinnon (1989).
67. Grewal (2006). See also Grewal (2017): chap. 4.
68. See, e.g., Ho (2012), Jeffrey (2002), Eisenstein (2009), Desai (2009).
69. Demographic research has shown that whereas high educational attainment and the capacity for economic independence were once marital deterrents for women, highly educated white women are now the most likely group to be married (see, e.g., Martin 2006, Goldstein and Kenney 2001).
70. Other events at which strikingly similar stories were told include the CATW's "End Demand" conference at the United Nations' Commission on the Status of Women meetings on March 2, 2007; the CATW "Abolishing Sexual Slavery from Stockholm to Hunts Point" conference held at the New York City Bar Association on November 6, 2008; and the conference on "Sex Trafficking and the New Abolitionists," held at the Brooklyn Museum on December 13, 2008.
71. Although by some estimates trafficking for domestic work has been found to be more prevalent than trafficking into the sex sector (see, e.g., Feingold 2005), the former is more compatible with professional-class women's gendered interests in the home.
72. There is an abundance of critical feminist scholarship that demonstrates the contrary; see, e.g., Bernstein (2007b), Agustín (2007), Brennan (2004), Chapkis (1997).
73. US Department of Justice (2004, 2005, 2006, 2007, 2008, 2009).

74. The perceived efficacy of contemporary anti-trafficking campaigns for restructuring contemporary masculinities can also be found in the quasi-feminist Real Men Don't Buy Sex campaign, launched in 2011 by celebrity-activists Ashton Kutcher and Demi Moore. The campaign centered on a number of videos featuring high-profile celebrities, which curiously provided no information about the phenomenon of trafficking or its victims. Playful and ironic in tone, each fifty-second clip featured a celebrity doing some mundane task "like a man" narrator. In interviews, Kutcher has claimed that the goal of the campaign was to hold men "a bit more accountable" and "to make something akin to a pledge." Notably, the campaign received a digital rekindling in 2014 after three hundred Nigerian girls were kidnapped by Boko Haram militants (Kavner 2011, Hebblethwaite 2014).

75. Agustín (2007) has described the anxieties that circulate around trafficking in terms of displaced concerns about women "leaving home" for sex. Here, I highlight feminists' concerns about men's, and specifically husbands', extradomestic sexual pursuits.

76. See Bernstein (2007b) and Hobson (1999). Components of the Swedish criminalization model have since been adopted in countries ranging from Norway and Iceland to South Korea, the Philippines, and Chile. Although the Swedish law specifically criminalizes only the customers of prostitutes (but not sex workers themselves), transnational feminist activists and nation-states that claim the Swedish mantle have used it to widen the sphere of criminalization to encompass both sex workers and their clients.

77. Duggan (2003: 14).

78. Bumiller (2008).

79. Sharma (2005). See also my discussion of Operation Gilded Cage in California in 2005 (Bernstein 2007a). In this instance, the anti-trafficking raids resulted in the arrest of nearly 150 women, less than a dozen of whom were ultimately declared to be legitimate victims. When police determined that more than half of the women in police custody were not coerced, they were immediately deported and threatened with arrest for prostitution in Korea. The federal government forcibly kept another forty-six women as material witnesses (Bernstein 2007a).

80. Cheng (2010), Shah (2008: 27).

81. Maher et al. (2015), Bradford (2009).

82. Gallagher and Pearson (2019: 76–77). See also Lee (2014: 209).

83. See, e.g., the case of Anthony Curry, who received a life sentence for compelling a teenage girl to work as a stripper (Weisberg 2015). See also the anti-trafficking statute of the State of Massachusetts, held constitutional in 2015, which stipulates sentences of life in prison for convicted traffickers and which does not require prosecutors to demonstrate fraud, coercion, or force (*Commonwealth of Massachusetts v. Tyshaun McGhee* 2015).

84. With the aim of shifting enforcement priorities toward street prostitution in urban areas, the 2005 TVPRA established $5 million in federal grants to

local law enforcement agencies to investigate and prosecute sex trafficking in the United States (US Congress 2005).

85. US Department of Justice (2011b). These statistics are the result of a 2011 US Department of Justice report on *Characteristics of Suspected Human Trafficking Incidents* specific to the years 2008–2010. As an isolated report that was never updated, this report provides the only DOJ data on trafficking that breaks down trafficking cases as they pertain to race.

86. Chen (2007).

87. See also Day (2010).

88. Jakobsen (2008).

89. King's College is an evangelical Christian institution housed in the basement of the Empire State building in New York City. Prominent Christian-right figures associated with the institution include former provost Marvin Olasky (2000), founder of the movement for "compassionate conservatism," and former president Dinesh D'Souza, a prominent author and political commentator who in 2014 was found guilty of making illegal campaign contributions (Ax 2014).

90. The poster also spuriously claims that the average age of entry into the sex industry is thirteen years old, a figure that has come into wide circulation among abolitionist feminists. The scholar-activist Emi Koyama (www.emi nism.org) has pointed out the logical fallacies inherent in this assertion by systematically tracking the FBI's anti-prostitution raids. Observing that most of the young people detained in raids are sixteen or seventeen, she notes that "for the average age to be around 13, there needs to be many more 5–12 years olds that are forced into prostitution than are empirically plausible" (cited in Moore 2015: 10).

91. On the spread of harsh criminal laws against sex offenders in Europe, see "Unjust and Ineffective" (2009). On the heteronormative underpinnings of World Bank development policy, see Bedford (2009a).

92. See also Halley (2008a, 2008b), Grewal (2006), and Miller (2004).

93. Halley (2006: 21).

CHAPTER THREE

1. Quoted in Landesman (2004).

2. Quoted in Jewell (2007).

3. Virgil (2007). In 2015, *Amazing Grace* also opened as a Broadway musical and ran for a brief stint at the Nederlander Theater. Similar to the film, the live production told the story of the Englishman John Newton, who wrote the lyrics to the famous hymn that gives the show its title, culminating with a swelling rendition of the song (Isherwood 2015, Stasio 2015).

4. Haugen (2005: 21).

5. O'Connell Davidson (2015: 28, 36).

6. Bales (2012: 29). Free the Slaves was founded in 2000 as the sister organization of Anti-Slavery International, a British organization that first emerged
   in 1839 to oppose chattel slavery. Although no longer affiliated with Anti-
   Slavery International, Bales credits his organization with "reinstat[ing] slavery as a key human rights issue on the research agenda for the twenty-first
   century" (Griffiths 2010).
7. Mink (2001), Butler (2006), Stockman et al. (2006).
8. Jakobsen and Pellegrini (2009).
9. Roe (n.d.) quoted in Soderlund (2013).
10. Soderlund (2013: 7). Clifford Roe wrote several books on the topic of white
    slavery and dedicated his life's work in law to campaigning against it. In
    his capacity as an assistant state's attorney, he started a campaign against
    pimping that spread across the country. His obituary in the *United States
    Law Review* (1934) credits him with breaking up the "larger 'white slavery'
    rings of the time" by producing the Illinois Pandering Act, "which imposed
    severe penalties and which is said to have been the first statue of the kind
    adopted in any state." Roe later helped to write the Mann Act but later
    denounced it as having become a means of extortion. Roe continued his
    campaign as special prosecutor in Chicago and later in New York as the at-
    torney of a committee headed by John D. Rockefeller Jr.
11. Hobson (1990), Walkowitz (1980), Rosen (1982).
12. See, e.g., Agustín (2007), Saunders (2005), Berman (2006), Soderlund
    (2005).
13. Saunders (2005).
14. Berman (2006: 272, 276).
15. Soderlund (2005: 79).
16. Hertzke (2004: 6).
17. See, e.g., Balmer (2006) and Beisel and Krimmel (2006).
18. See, e.g., Earll (2007), Janney (2006), Jewell (2007), and Davis (2007). Be-
    tween 2007 and 2017, the organization Focus on the Family published
    57 pieces on sex trafficking through its print magazine and website. The
    magazine *Today's Christian Woman* published 30 pieces, and the conserva-
    tive Christian *World* magazine published 109.
19. Griffith (1997), Kintz (1997), Smith (2000).
20. Berman (2006: 287).
21. See Luker (1984), Stein (2001), Frank (2005).
22. Luker (1984: 7).
23. Stein (2001: 6).
24. Richard Cizik (2006), the former president of the National Association of
    Evangelicals has described evangelical "moderates" and "progressives" as
    accounting for approximately 55 percent of the US evangelical popula-
    tion, with the other 45 percent constituted by evangelical "traditionalists."
    According to recent data compiled by the Pew Research Center, 29 percent

of Democrats and 45 percent of Republicans are self-identified evangelicals (a total 36 percent of registered voters). Among evangelical Democrats, 34 percent identify as conservative, 38 percent as moderate, and 23 percent as liberal. Among evangelical Republicans, 78 percent identify as conservative, 17 percent as moderate, and 4 percent as liberal (Pew Research Center 2014). It is worth noting that 60 percent of evangelical Democrats are nonwhite, compared with the 13 percent of nonwhite Republican evangelicals (Smith and Masci 2016).

In the wake of the 2016 US presidential elections, there has been much writing and speculation over the fact that some 80 percent of white evangelicals voted for Republican candidate Donald Trump, with explanations ranging from concerns about abortion and Supreme Court vacancies to personal dislike of Democratic candidate Hillary Clinton to racial backlash (Smith and Martínez 2016, Bailey 2016, Zylstra and Weber 2016). At the same time, it is important to recognize that while the Christian Right electorate provided surprisingly strong support for Trump, many evangelicals took vocal stands against him, particularly evangelical leaders and the most urban and educated (Goodstein 2016, Bruinius 2017, Claiborne 2016). Others who may have voted for him have nonetheless been critical of the Trump administration's stance on immigrants, refugees, and violence-against-women issues (see, e.g., Burke 2017, Bruinius 2017, Goodstein 2016).

25. For discussions of the spread of evangelicalism amongst the affluent and educated professional middle classes, see Wuthnow (1988), Smith (2000), and Balmer and Winner (2002).

26. See also Butler (2006), Luker (2006).

27. See, e.g., Campolo (2006), Wallis (2005).

28. This concern has also circulated more broadly in liberal and progressive evangelical circles. Following the 2016 election of Donald Trump to the presidency, Tony Campolo and Shane Claiborne penned an op-ed in the *New York Times* arguing that "Jesus-centered faith needs a new name." The two progressive faith leaders urged other dissident evangelicals to join them in identifying as "Red Letter Christians" (Campolo and Claiborne 2016). See also the website https://www.redletterchristians.org.

29. Many of my secular academic colleagues have been surprised to learn that large metropolitan centers such as New York City and Washington, DC, where much of my research was situated, contain significant populations of evangelical Christians. In fact, the island of Manhattan alone supports multiple evangelical megachurches (conventionally defined as churches whose weekly attendance exceeds two thousand people) as well as a growing number of faith-based anti-trafficking organizations. The newfound prominence of evangelicals in postindustrial urban centers can be attributed both to burgeoning immigrant populations and to the spread of evangelical Christianity into the professional middle classes (see, e.g., Lindsay 2007, Balmer and Winner 2002).

30. While not necessarily identifying themselves as feminists, most of the new evangelical anti-trafficking activists that I interviewed rejected the evangelical ideal of male "headship" in the family, while supporting women's leadership roles both professionally and in the church.

31. Shane Claiborne (2006, 2016) and Brian McLaren (2007, 2016), popular figures on the progressive evangelical speaker circuit, constitute important exceptions to this trend in highlighting the political-economic underpinnings of injustice. Their sexual politics do not range far beyond heteronormative liberal feminism, however.

32. Haugen (2008: 111).

33. Ibid., 107.

34. See Power (2009), Soderlund (2005), Jones (2003).

35. Bertone (2008).

36. Aita (2007), Ellerman (2004). More recently, the organization Operation Underground Railroad has received favorable press coverage for its ambition to send the organization's members to infiltrate child-trafficking rings. Tim Ballard, the organization's founder and a former official at the US Department of Homeland Security, has cited his Mormon faith as a key motivator in breaking away from government work (Stackpole 2015).

37. Kazmin (2004), Power (2009). From 2013 to 2017, Samantha Power was the US Permanent Representative to the United Nations, the youngest person to ever hold this position. Power previously served as the president and senior director for multicultural affairs and human rights on the National Security Council at the White House. Before serving in the Obama administration, Power was a war correspondent, journalist, and Anna Lindh Professor of Global Leadership and Public Policy at Harvard's John F. Kennedy School of Government. Her book *A Problem from Hell: America and the Age of Genocide* won the 2003 Pulitzer Prize ("Samantha Power" n.d.: 216; US Mission to the United Nations 2016).

38. Power (2009: 52).

39. See, e.g., Kintz (1997), Bartkowski (2004).

40. Johnson (2017). Johnson conducted ethnographic fieldwork from 2006 to 2008 at the Mars Hill Church of Seattle, a growing evangelical enterprise at the time that comprised fifteen facilities and thirteen thousand attendees across the United States. Johnson examined the "militarized and sexualized lexicon" and visual culture that made up the "rebranding" of masculinity within the church, including the church's use of male volunteers to enforce security during services.

41. Kristof (2004a, 2004b, 2004d). Although Kristof has discussed his attempted rescue of the girls by explaining that he breaks journalistic "code" by inserting himself into the story, emotionally and physically, as media historian Gretchen Soderlund (2011: 196) points out, he is not the first to do this for journalistic and sensationalistic benefit. She puts William Stead's 1885 serialized account of purchasing a virginal girl for a brothel in

the same "revelatory discourse" category as today's Kristof. She also notes that Stead helped establish the format for this "stunt journalism" that has played out time and time again since its publishing many years ago.

42. Kara (2009: 180–182).

43. Such ventriloquizing ambitions mimic the shifting racial politics of abortion, in which white pro-life activists increasingly claim to speak on behalf of the black and brown unborn. See, e.g., Beisel and Krimmel (2006), Scott (2015). On the recurrent theme of "giving voice to the voiceless" in evangelical and secular anti-trafficking campaigns, see also Cheng (2008) and Kempadoo (2015).

44. Grewal (2005: 142). See also Mohanty (2003).

45. Mohanty (1991: 56).

46. Abu-Lughod (2013: 84).

47. A similar dynamic may also account for the popularity of best-selling pornographic texts like *Fifty Shades of Grey* among young evangelical women (see, e.g., Banks 2012).

48. In fact, *Nightline* has done multiple specials on abortion, including a 1998 special on the anti-abortion group Army of God, a three-part series in 2009 on ethical debates surrounding abortion, a 2013 special on Mississippi's only abortion clinic, and a 2015 feature on young activists in the contemporary anti-abortion movement (ABC 1980).

49. See, e.g., Wilkins (2008).

50. As Shih (2015) describes, many of the women who participate in the "rehabilitation" projects are non-Christians who regard their daily prayer sessions as part of their new jobs.

51. Wuthnow (2009: 32). Many evangelicals make reference to the "10/40 window" in their discussions of the global focus of their social interventions. The 10/40 window refers to the area of the world between ten and forty degrees north of the equator that holds the most "unreached" people in the world (or Muslims, Hindus, and Buddhists who are ripe for conversion to Christianity). Groups such as the Joshua Project have also emphasized that a large percentage of the world's poor lives in this area: "There is a remarkable overlap between the poorest countries of the world and those that are least evangelized" (Joshua Project 2017). In addition to the poverty and lack of the Gospel in this area, evangelical organizations also profess that "horrific abuse of women and children remains unchecked, including an epidemic of pedophilia," as well as "rampant" child prostitution and slavery (Window International Network 2017).

52. McAlister (2008b: 871).

53. McAlister (2014: 91), McAlister (2008b: 879). The construction of a global Christianity via the trope of suffering, McAlister argues, began amid the anti-communist sentiment of the Cold War. More recently, US evangelicals have defined themselves against the specter of a new common enemy: Islam. McAlister regards the civil war in Sudan as a particularly apt representation

of this, as US evangelicals shaped the image of "African Arabs" (North Sudan) versus "Black Christians" (South Sudan) so as to racialize the conflict in a way that US evangelicals could implicitly understand. This formulation has served to bond both white and black US evangelicals around a shared notion of suffering (what McAlister [2014: 104] terms "Christians without borders"), displacing the racial divisions implied by the American history of slavery.

54. McAlister (2008a: 27). Castelli explains this "critical theory of suffering" as a paradoxical component of religion. She argues that the role of suffering in religion and religious texts is to show practitioners how to respond to suffering and how to interpret it, but by making one of religion's callings a response to human suffering, religion teaches its subjects to both desire to alleviate it and to maintain its existence. Religion accomplishes this by simultaneously illuminating suffering and also rationalizing it as part of a divine sanction, which works to "blunt the impulse to alleviate it" (Castelli 2004: 203).

55. Buss and Herman (2003: xxiv), Butler (2006).

56. Evangelical missionaries have had particular success in exporting the values of conservative Christian churches in the United States to Uganda, as documented by Roger Ross Williams's (2013) Academy Award–winning documentary *God Loves Uganda*. Instances of the traction of evangelical teachings on sexual morality in Uganda include the Ugandan parliament's initial consideration in 2009 of the Anti-Homosexuality Bill, which ordered the death penalty as punishment for homosexuality; a Ugandan paper publishing pictures and addresses of homosexuals, calling for their hanging; the murder of gay rights activist David Kato; and the signing of the Anti-Homosexuality Bill into law in 2014, which penalizes homosexual acts with life imprisonment as a substitute for the death penalty. See also Cheney (2012) and Boyd (2013).

57. Berman (2006), Zimmerman (2010).

58. From the perspective of contemporary evangelicals, the recruitment and use of children as soldiers is also considered a form of trafficking. For this reason, several evangelical organizations that had focused their work on trafficking (like the Salvation Army) praised the Kony 2012 campaign for calling attention to the plight of children who had been abducted to serve in the Lord's Resistance Army (LRA). This understanding is shared by the United Nations and World Health Organization, both of which consider child soldiers to be one of many potential types of human trafficking victims (UN Office on Drugs and Crime 2016, World Health Organization 2012).

59. See Invisible Children (2014).

60. Von Engelhardt and Jansz (2014). To date, more than one hundred million people worldwide have viewed the video on YouTube.

61. Flock (2012).

62. Several critics understood these problems as not unique to Kony 2012 but as part of a long-standing tradition that was "once used to justify colonial

exploitation" (see, e.g., Mackey 2012). Kagumire (2012), for example, objected to the campaign's representation of the victims' helplessness, asking that Kony 2012 supporters not speak in the place of the people the issue affects. Other critics remarked that the amount of screen time cofounder Jason Russell and his family received in the short film seemed bizarre and inappropriate to Ugandans, who were expecting to see their own perspectives represented (Al Jazeera English 2012).

63. Keating (2012), Deibert (2012).

64. By contrast, Al Jazeera has typically covered issues of human trafficking through a far less critical framework. In 2012, Al Jazeera launched a human trafficking documentary series titled *Slavery: A 21st Century Evil*. The series consisted of seven twenty-five-minute episodes, narrated by British journalist Rageh Omaar, covering many facets of modern slavery: food-chain slaves, bridal slaves, charcoal slaves, child slaves, bonded slaves, sex slaves, and prison slaves. The series also hosted a panel on why modern slavery persists today and what can be done to address it, featuring the head of the US State Department's Office to Monitor and Combat Trafficking in Persons, Luis C. deBaca; the president of Free the Slaves, Kevin Bales; the president of Not for Sale, David Batstone; and the UN special rapporteur on trafficking in persons, Joy Ezeilo. While Bales argued that it is inherent in human nature for some people to seek to exert dominance over others, Ezeilo insisted that criminalization was therefore essential to contain the threats posed by trafficking and prostitution ("Slavery: Alive and Well in the 21st Century").

65. Teju Cole teaches literature and art history at Bard College. In addition to serving as writer in residence at Bard, Cole contributes regularly to leading publications such as the *New York Times*, *New Yorker*, and *Atlantic*.

66. Cole (2012).

67. Garfield and Gladstone (2012).

68. Titeca and Sebastian (2014). In the days following the negative media coverage of his film, Jason Russell was picked up by San Diego police officers after he stripped off his clothes, pounded cars with his fists, and threw himself against the pavement while yelling obscenities (captured on video, Russell's breakdown itself became a viral sensation). Although Russell was detained by the police, no formal charges were filed, and he was taken to a hospital for a medical evaluation. According to a report of the incident published in *Business Insider*, "His doctors never agreed on a definitive diagnosis but he was sectioned in a psychiatric hospital suffering from what may have been a schizophrenic manic episode brought on by post-traumatic stress." In the article, Russell is quoted as saying that he was unable to reconcile the "polar opposite" responses to his campaign from the public, identifying the negative attention he received as the cause of his manic state (Cadwalladr 2013; see also Harris 2012).

　　Although Invisible Children announced in 2014 that all of its work would be transferred to partner groups, the organization instead restructured its operations so that its US work was reduced by 67 percent and most of its programs in Central Africa remained (see Invisible Children n.d.).

69. Clough (2012), Shah (2009).

70. A German Protestant theologian, Dietrich Bonhoeffer was executed in the Flossenbürg concentration camp on April 9, 1945 for his resistance to the Nazis and for conspiring to assassinate Hitler. Since his death, Bonhoeffer has become widely known as one of the few dissenting Christians in the face of Nazism, and his letters and theological works have been influential for Christians around the world. Bonhoeffer's theological approach has resonated with many evangelical Christians in combining spiritual devotion with a demand for the responsibility of Christians to exercise justice in the secular world (Nullens 2011, Gauer 2005, Westmoreland-White 1997). Bonhoeffer and his work have also been claimed as an inspiration for varied communities of Christians worldwide, including those persecuted in North Korea, people fighting apartheid in South Africa, and practitioners of liberation theology in Latin America (Moe 2014, De Santa Ana 1976).

71. Also frequently mentioned were Kate Bushnell, a prominent anti-prostitution activist at the turn of the nineteenth century and a member of the Women's Christian's Temperance Union, and Jessie Daniel Ames, a white evangelical woman who in the 1930s founded the Association of Southern Women for the Prevention of Lynching. Both are featured prominently in Gary Haugen's (1999) first book, *Good News about Injustice: A Witness of Courage in a Hurting World.*

72. "Project Lantern" was funded by a $5 million grant from the Bill and Melinda Gates foundation in 2005, given to IJM for the purpose of a five-year anti-trafficking program (IJM 2010). The funds allowed IJM to open a new office in Cebu, Philippines, to boost local law enforcement efforts against traffickers, to "reduce the availability of trafficked women and children for sexual exploitation in commercial sex establishments and street-based prostitution in Metro Cebu," and to show that a law enforcement-based anti-trafficking strategy was effective (IJM 2010). IJM has cited a 79 percent reduction in the "availability of minors for sex" as a direct result of Project Lantern's increased anti-trafficking law enforcement, but it has also reported issues with "non-IJM trained police" arresting freelance sex workers and charging them with vagrancy.

73. See Banet-Weiser (2012), Mukherjee and Banet-Weiser (2012).

74. Weber (2000).

75. Moreton (2009: 87). Akin to Moreton's notion of "free enterprise as Christian service" is Tim Gloege's (2015) discussion of "corporate evangelicalism," which he links to earlier cultural trends. In his book *Guaranteed Pure: The Moody Bible Institute, Business and the Making of Modern Evangelicalism*, Gloege tells of a network of businessmen, ministers, and evangelists during the Gilded Age and Progressive Era who developed this particular brand of evangelicalism and a new connection between evangelicalism

and economic identity. In particular, he identifies the "salesman-turned-revivalist" Dwight L. Moody and Quaker Oats president and "promotional genius" Henry Crowell as key figures in modifying the message of Christian theology to include the religious identity of the "Christian worker" and eventual consumer. Gloege argues that "the Bible became analogous to a work contract—filled with promises and requirements for God's employees. Under Cromwell, MBI [the Moody Bible Institute] shifted the primary identity from Christian worker to savvy consumer. What God required of faithful believers, they taught, was to choose and consume 'pure religion'" (Carter 2015). Darren E. Grem's (2016) book *The Blessings of Business: How Corporations Shaped Conservative Christianity* adds to the growing body of scholarship on the business of American evangelicalism, examining how "in and through corporate America, conservative evangelicals defined and redefined themselves and attempted to stake their claim on American society" (9).

76. See www.bamglobal.org and Business as Mission Think Tank (2013: 3).
77. See Agustín (2007), Smith-Rosenberg (1986), Hobson (1990).
78. Kristof (2009). In this regard, Kristof hews closely to the perspective of prominent liberal economists such as Jeffrey Sachs (2005: 11), renowned for his argument that "sweatshops are the first rung on the ladder out of extreme poverty."
79. See Brown (1995).
80. In this regard, policy trends on trafficking resembled those pertaining to a number of other issues, including escalated deportations and drone attacks. See, e.g., Jackson (2013), Corones (2015), Serle (2015).
81. See, e.g., Skinner (2009). I witnessed this enthusiasm first-hand, as deBaca soon became a frequently sought out speaker at the anti-trafficking conferences sponsored by secular liberal constituencies.
82. See, e.g., Jordan (2002).
83. See, e.g., Wacquant (2009a, 2009b), Ticktin (2008), Kulick (2003), Sudbury (2005).
84. Amar (2013), Romero, Montejo, and Madrid (2014), Lamas (2014).
85. See, e.g., Kempadoo (2012b).
86. See, e.g., Lamas (2014), Varela (2013), Sharma (2005).

CHAPTER FOUR

1. Global Exchange and Everette (2011).
2. I had traveled to Thailand for the first time while conducting research for my book *Temporarily Yours* (Bernstein 2007b). Elena had been involved in research in the region for several years while pursuing research for her PhD (Shih 2015). Key ethnographic works on sex work and sex trafficking in Thailand include Molland (2012, 2013), Roux (2011), Wilson (2004), Bishop and Robinson (1998), and Hamilton (1997).

3. On anti-trafficking activism in the 1980s and 1990s, see Bertone (2008) and Chew (2012). On Thai sex workers in Europe, see Ruenkaew (2002), Spanger (2002), and Vanaspong (2002).
4. GAATW (2007: 174).
5. Interview with Matt Friedman, UN Inter-Agency Project on Human Trafficking, Bangkok, August 6, 2012.
6. Arnold and Bertone (2002).
7. Molland (2012: 309), Molland (2013: 301).
8. See, e.g., Clough (1992), Marcus and Fischer (1986), Clifford and Marcus (1986).
9. In his book *Culture on Tour*, Edward Bruner (2005) compiles his research on cultural tourism spanning twenty years and six countries. In the introduction, Bruner recounts his experience as both an anthropologist and tour guide in Indonesia—expected to give tours as "a 1930s realist ethnographer," he was fired for his reflexive and "interventional" approach (e.g., photographing tourists without their permission as they do to local people, explaining that the Balinese frog dance they would see and others were invented to appeal to tourists but that "change is inherent in all cultures, and that the dances were still quintessentially 'Balinese'"; Bruner 2005: 4, 3). Such anecdotes illustrate the theoretical approach guiding the different sites of tourism that Bruner investigates, which posits cultural tourism as worthy of ethnographic investigation and requiring reflexivity. With this approach, he considers the role of place, affect, stories, and narrative in structuring the experience of tourism; the contestation of site and narrative between official production (the state and historians) and folk or popular culture; localized interactions between natives and tourists as they express global politics, the relationship between ethnography and tourism, and the blurred line between the two.
10. On tourism and authenticity, see, e.g., MacCannell (1973), Cohen (1988, 2008), West and Carrier (2004), and Vrasti (2012). On sex tourism and sex trafficking, see Brennan (2004, 2005), Padilla (2007), Kempadoo (1999), Bernstein (2007, 2010, 2012), Hoang (2013), and Vance (2012).
11. See, e.g., Empower Foundation (2012a), Kempadoo, Sanghera, and Pattanaik (2012), Kempadoo and Doezema (1998).
12. See, e.g., http://www.bryan.edu/human-trafficking-study-trip-set-to -cambodia/, and http://classic.marshall.usc.edu/ciber/projects/study -abroad.htm.
13. See also Shih (2016).
14. Global Exchange (2016).
15. Not for Sale (2016). Initially made famous by Muhammad Yunus's Nobel Prize–winning Grameen Bank, social entrepreneurship has gained popularity with a diverse range of actors ranging from large corporations to small evangelical missionary groups. Karim (2011) provides a powerful critique of this model.

16. Shih (2015).
17. Humanitarian reason is Didier Fassin's (2011) term for describing an ascendant form of moral and political discourse that disavows the relations of inequality and violence that underpin both social suffering and contemporary helping interventions.
18. Cohen (1988), Peleggi (1996), Kontogeorgopoulos (1999).
19. See Mastercard (2015), "Best Cities in Asia" (2016).
20. See ThaiWebsites.com and Department of Tourism, Thailand (2017).
21. Lacher and Nepal (2010). See also Rojek and Urry (1997), Smith (1989), Sturken (2007), Coleman and Crang (2002).
22. Wearing (2001), Higgins-Desbiolles (2008), Stronza (2001), McGehee and Santos (2005).
23. Often these experiences cost tourists more than their predecessor forms of mass tourism, and some commentators have voiced concerns over the inaccurate designation of these experiences as "volunteerism" (Wearing 2001, McGehee and Santos 2005, Vrasti 2012).
24. Steinbrink (2012), Linke (2012), Bloul (2012).
25. Parreñas (2012: 673).
26. Heron (2007: 46–47). See also Mathers (2010), Mowforth and Munt (2009), West and Carrier (2004), Urry and Larsen (2011).
27. Vrasti (2012: 28, 52).
28. See, e.g., Weber (2000), Boltanski and Chiapello (2005).
29. Morris (1994, 15). See also Manderson and Jolly (1997).
30. Interview with Global Exchange staff person, April 9, 2012.
31. We use the term "sex tourist" advisedly, aware of Laura Agustín's (2007) caution that the distinctions between those who travel for work, sex, and other forms of leisure are never absolute.
32. Cohen (1996), Wilson (2004).
33. Dassé (1978), Meyer (1988), Askew (2002), Askew (1999: 133).
34. Wilson (2004, 75), Truong (2000), Phongpaichit and Baker (2002), Skrobanek, Boonpakdi, and Janthakeero (1997).
35. See Feingold (2003), Huguet and Punpuing (2005).
36. Empower Foundation (2012a), Wilson (2004), Jeffrey (2002), Molland (2012).
37. See, e.g., Rojanapithayakorn (2006).
38. Jeffrey (2002), Roux (2009), Liz Hilton, Empower Foundation coordinator (personal correspondence, August 15, 2013).
39. Montgomery (2001, 198). See also Cohen (1986), Hamilton (1997), Jeffrey (2002), Wilson (2004), Visrutaratna et al. (2010), Cohen and Neal (2012).
40. Hoang (2013, 2015: 5).
41. Chacón (2006).
42. Empower's overview of the history of sex work in Chiang Mai further cautions that "red-light districts" are an inaccurate moniker to describe commercial sex establishments in Thailand, which originally used green lights and other modes of advertisement (Empower Foundation 2011a).

43. *Taken* was the first major American motion film about trafficking, starring Liam Neeson as a father trying to save his daughter from becoming a victim of sex trafficking during a vacation to Paris. *Born into Brothels*, which won the 2004 Academy Award for best documentary film, focuses not on trafficking per se but on the children of Calcutta's sex workers.
44. Heron (2007: 3).
45. Vrasti (2012: 28).
46. As described in chapter 1, the Global Alliance against Traffic in Women (GAATW) is a network of organizations concerned with the human rights of trafficked persons, while the Empower Foundation and the Asia Pacific Network of Sex Workers (APNSW) promote sex worker rights, organizing, and advocacy in the Asia Pacific region. See their websites at www.gaatw.org, www.empowerfoundation.org, and www.apnsw.org.
47. See, e.g., Shimizu (2007).
48. Interview with Andrew Hunter, Asian Pacific Network of Sex Workers, August 3, 2012.
49. See, e.g., O'Connell Davidson and Sánchez Taylor (2005), Padilla (2007).
50. Brennan (2005: 41).
51. West (2006: 8).
52. MacCannell (1973).
53. Hill-tribe trekking in Thailand is a prevalent type of ecotourist offering that dates back to the early 1970s, attracting tourists to hike through diverse geographical and cultural landscapes, often including overnight stays in hill-tribe villages. As Erik Cohen (1989, 1996) points out, tour companies offering hill tribe trekking have been known to engage in the staging of villages to appear remote and untouched.
54. Mirror Foundation (2014).
55. See Toyota (2005), Kammerer (1989).
56. See also McKinnon (2005), Gillogly (2004), and Toyota (2006).
57. Vrasti (2012: 52).
58. See, e.g., Olivie (2008), UN Inter-Agency Project on Human Trafficking (2009). See also Environmental Justice Foundation (2013) and Urbina (2015).
59. Under the Thailand Anti-Trafficking in Persons Act B.E. 2551, all commercial sex workers younger than age eighteen are considered victims of trafficking, while all those older than age eighteen are criminals—either arrested and placed in prison (if Thai nationals) or deported (if not Thai). Those older than eighteen can also be considered trafficking victims if they can prove they were victims of "force, fraud or coercion" and are willing to testify against their traffickers in court.
60. Vance (2012: 208).
61. Empower Foundation (2012a); see also Lee (2014).
62. Empower Foundation (2012a: x–xi).
63. Gallagher and Pearson (2010: 96).
64. Empower Foundation (2012a: 61), Lee (2014: 210).

65. Gallagher and Pearson (2010: 112).
66. Empower Foundation (2012b).
67. Roux (2007) has argued that the HIV epidemic, which began in the mid-1980s, led Empower to import certain Western scripts about sex worker agency to survive amid competitive international funding requirements. He further contends that by advocating for labor rights on the basis of sex worker identity, Empower's approach may obscure the needs of the majority of sex workers who do not work in legal commercial establishments, including streetwalkers, brothel-based sex workers, and other workers employed in unregistered venues.

    Although we take Roux's cautions seriously, Shih's ongoing research with the organization makes both of us more inclined to agree with Jeffrey (2002: 121), who documents the ways the organization, since its inception, has strived to distinguish itself from prevailing versions of the Western "sex workers' rights position" through its emphasis on economic issues rather than sexual freedoms. Roux's (2007) argument, furthermore, is based primarily on fieldwork in the Bangkok Patpong location of Empower, whereas our interactions are based on participatory observation research with Empower, Chiang Mai. During a supplementary four-month stint of ethnographic fieldwork with Empower, Chiang Mai, Shih became well acquainted with the sex workers affiliated with the organization and directly witnessed the myriad forms of advocacy and service provision the organization offered to sex workers on a daily basis—including outreach to the small handful of brothels with undocumented workers—which requires long-standing relationships to access.
68. See also Empower Foundation (2011b: 21, 53, 105).
69. Doezema (1998: 45).
70. On the Western fantasy of the Orient as the antithesis of potent, adult masculinity, see, e.g., Eng (2001) and Fung (1991). On Western tourists' infantilization of Thai persons more generally, see Montgomery (2001).
71. See Urban Light (n.d.).
72. According to some commentators, this is related to the specter of homosexuality that overlaps with the issue, as in evangelical Christian advocacy against prison rape. Interview with Andrew Hunter, Asia Pacific Network of Sex Workers, August 2, 2012.
73. Locally referred to as "beer bars," these are common workplaces for male, female, and third-gender sex workers, where clients purchase drinks for sex workers in exchange for time and companionship.
74. Significant throughout the trip was the erasure of our own reliance on multiple forms of exploited labor, including the many levels of subcontracting that facilitated our tour. Ethnic handicraft industries have been critiqued by scholars and activists for inducting communities into exploitative labor markets, while promoting uneven distribution of profits (Novelli et al. 2012). Additionally, the Thai silk found in night markets in Chiang Mai

has been shown to be part of capitalist commodity chains rife with exploitation of human and natural resources (Graham 2011).

75. See, e.g., Illouz (1997).

76. Classic works on Thai genders and sexualities include Morris (1994), Jackson and Sullivan (1999), and Jackson (1989).

77. See, e.g., Mahdavi (2011), Plambech (2014), Shah (2014), Amar (2013), Lamas (2014).

78. The bill passed in November of 2012 and was soon challenged by the American Civil Liberties Union and the Electronic Frontier Foundation, who argued that the legislation imposed unacceptable limits to free speech (Almendrala 2012). Opponents of the law also argued that the definitions of sex trafficking contained in the law were so broad that many sex workers and their families would be criminally liable (Musto and boyd 2014). In January 2013, the US District Court for the Northern District of California granted a preliminary injunction blocking enforcement of the law on the grounds that Proposition 35 might be unconstitutional (Fakhoury 2013). On November 18, 2014, the Ninth Circuit Court of Appeals upheld the lower court's ruling (ACLU 2014). The court ruled that in requiring registered sex offenders to disclose their email addresses, usernames, and other online identifiers with local law enforcement, Proposition 35 violated free speech rights, and it gave legislators until the end of 2016 to correct for this. In 2016, Senator Ben Hueso (D–San Diego) introduced legislation (S.B. 448) that limited these requirements, applying only when offenders "used the internet to collect private information on the victim of the crime, to traffic the victim, or collect or distribute obscene material or child pornography" and identifying only that information used "to investigate sex-related crimes, kidnappings, or human trafficking" and kept private except under court order (Thompson 2016). The bill passed 7–0 in June 2016 and has been in effect since 1 January 2017.

79. Vrasti (2012: 96).

80. See Kempadoo (1999).

CHAPTER FIVE

1. For discussions of the role of digital technologies in transforming the social dynamics of sexual commerce, see e.g., Bernstein (2007b), Chun (2007), and Lane (2000).

2. On the rise of celebrity-activism around trafficking and other issues, see Haynes (2014), Richey and Ponte (2011), Kapoor (2013), Colapinto (2012), and Molina-Guzmán (2012).

3. As a venue dedicated to using "market-based solutions to empower girls and women," the Clinton Global Initiative provided a fitting venue for Obama's remarks. The Clinton Initiative focused its advocacy efforts upon issues of women and entrepreneurship, women in corporate supply

chains, and the trafficking and slavery of women and girls (see www.clinton foundation.org).

4. See Obama (2012, 2013). Obama's September 2012 speech at the Clinton Initiative received ample praise from evangelical, feminist, and even progressive human rights constituencies (see, e.g., Buzard 2012, Futures without Violence 2013, Freedom Network 2012).

5. Founded in 2011, the CNN Freedom Project consists of a website and a series of television broadcasts oriented toward "shining a spotlight on the horrors of modern-day slavery, amplifying the voices of the victims, highlighting success stories and helping unravel the complicated tangle of criminal enterprises trading in human life" (CNN 2011).

6. Mahdavi (2014).

7. DeBaca (2012). I am grateful to Jennifer Musto for bringing these remarks to my attention.

8. See, e.g., Terranova (2000), Collins (2008), Guevarra (2010), and Haney (2010b).

9. See Rubin (1993).

10. See The Guardian (2012). The app employs an algorithm to calculate precise numbers; my own completion of the survey turned up the number 43. According to Adrian MacKenzie (2013: 392), the rise of predictive analytics and other algorithmic forms of "machine learning" demonstrate the extent to which new technologies increasingly target "individual actions, sentiments and desires" rather than stratified population aggregates.

11. Weitzer (2007), Vance (2011: 138), Rubin (1975), Rubin (2011: 67).

12. "Corporate social responsibility" is a broad rubric for an array of self-regulating practices in which businesses seek to address the social and environmental impact of their organizations and products. Notably, these commitments usually take the form of adherence to a set of voluntary principles, as opposed to compliance with local, national, or supranational laws and policies (see, e.g., Carroll 1999). Significantly, the period of burgeoning corporate social responsibility efforts (roughly the past three decades) maps closely onto the period of corporate-sector deregulation, particularly in the United States, as well as corporate-sector opposition to unions, the growth of outsourcing, and cuts to workers' health and pension benefits (see, e.g., Stiglitz 2003, Klein 2000).

13. In 2014, the American Bar Association reported that a majority of Fortune 100 companies had enacted official policies on human trafficking and forced labor. In 2015, the European Bankers' Alliance, comprised of the continent's leading financial institutions, launched a campaign to fight trafficking by using data to identify irregular banking transactions (Mis 2015).

14. Interview with Brenda Schultz, head of responsible business for the Carlson Group, May 31, 2012. Besides publishing sex trafficking "progress cards" on various countries, the Body Shop promoted the sale of a $10 tube of "Soft Hands Kind Heart" hand cream, $6 of which was donated to the NGO End

Child Prostitution, Child Pornography and Trafficking of Children for Sexual Purposes (Howard 2009).

15. Interview with Mark Lagon, founder of the Global Business Coalition against Human Trafficking, June 15, 2012, Washington, DC; Berglind and Nakata (2005); L'Etang (2006). As Naomi Klein (2000) has written in *No Logo*, her well-known text on corporate branding, the practice of branding has transformed over the past few decades from a simple representation of a product (visual representations that mediated people's concerns regarding the anonymity of packaged goods), to the packaging of feelings and ideas. As Klein describes, effective branding makes the consumer associate their goals and sense of self with a brand, such that consumers ultimately purchase the brand rather than the product; for further discussion of branding, see also Conroy (2007), Lury (2004), and Banet Weiser (2012). In the 1980s, a new form of brand marketing was born called cause-related marketing (CRM), a hybrid of brand advertising and the packaging of CSR initiatives for public consumption, in which corporate identities were linked to nonprofit organizations and laudable causes. American Express first used the phrase "cause-related marketing" in 1983 to describe its campaign to raise money for the Statue of Liberty's restoration. The success of this venture in terms of the company's own profit margins was not lost on other businesses. In the 1990s, cause-related marketing, along with its affiliated mantra of "doing well while doing good," undergirded McDonald's ongoing contributions to the Ronald McDonald House and the Avon Corporation's contributions to the fight against breast cancer (see, e.g., Smith and Higgens 2000, Tannen et al. 1999, Pringle and Thompson 1999).

16. Schwab (2008: 114).

17. As the communications historian Robert McChesney (2013: 28) points out, "With the advent of the internet economy, many of the successful giants—Apple and Google come to mind—were begun by idealists who may have been uncertain whether they really wanted to be old-fashioned capitalists" (see also Vaidhyanathan 2011). Google's corporate image has admittedly undergone profound transformations in recent years, in particular in the wake of the accusations of Russian meddling in the 2016 US elections by way of its platforms as well as the 2013 revelations that the National Security Agency had tapped into Google's user data and the ensuing intimations of the corporation's complicity in this infiltration (see, e.g., Nedig 2017, Leonard 2013, Sanger and Miller 2014, Leopold 2014). Despite this tarnish, as well as revelations of the corporation's associations with a host of right-wing causes and operatives (Sengupta and Lipton 2013, Eilperin 2013, Surgey 2013), remnants of Google's carefully cultivated image as "outsiders" to the most pernicious aspects of capitalism and political power, as well as residues of its early "don't be evil" motto, linger.

In 2011, Manpower Inc. changed its name to the ManpowerGroup in order to "reflect the new challenges and complexity brought by the Human

Age." ManpowerGroup announced that it would provide a "suite of solutions" through its various brands and subdivisions, including Manpower (its contingent and permanent staffing business), Experis (a talent organization for positions in IT, finance, and engineering), Right Management (a career transition and organizational consulting firm), and Manpower Group Solutions (a firm providing outsourced recruitment and workforce management) (ManpowerGroup 2016). Because my research occurred both before and following this organizational shift, in my discussion I use "Manpower Incorporated" and "ManpowerGroup" interchangeably. The corporation has boasted of its pioneering efforts not only around human trafficking but also around issues such as youth unemployment and the environment (interview with Branca Minic, Director of Global Corporate and Government Affairs, July 11, 2012; see also www.manpower.com).

18. In addition to interviews with multiple representatives of Google and Manpower, interviews were also conducted with representatives of Microsoft, LexisNexis, and Carlson Hotels, as well as pertinent actors from the state and NGO sectors who have partnered with a variety of different corporations on this issue.

19. With this, I mean to point to the fact that such media not only serve to shape the broader terms of political debate in general ways, as cultural theorists from the Frankfurt School onward have argued, or simply that mass-mediated consumption has become a bastion of contemporary politics (see, e.g., Dávila 2001, Ginsburg, Abu-Lughod, and Larkin 2002). Rather, I am focusing here on the variety of games, apps, ad campaigns, and technologies that have been explicitly formulated by private corporations (often in partnership with state actors) as handmaidens to more conventional public policy regimes. My methodological approach thus also has affinities with that articulated by Shore and Wright (1997: 3), who, in taking policy as their ethnographic object, seek to discern "mobilizing metaphors and linguistic devices" that grant political legitimacy, as well as the ways in which normative claims "are used to present a particular way of defining a problem and its solution."

20. In 2010, Mubarak hosted an event at the Temple of Luxor, featuring celebrities, corporate officials, and many heavily armed guards, in addition to one cultural critic who later blogged about the event. For her critical and humorous first-person reports on the gathering, see Agustín (2010, 2011). On Mubarak's role as an anti-trafficking advocate and as a spokesperson for women's issues more generally, see the Protection Project (2010) and Hansen (2012).

21. Interview with Mark Lagon, June 15, 2012, Washington, DC; interview with William Livermore, December 18, 2008, New York City. The Lexis-Nexis Group offers the world's largest electronic database for legal and public records. During our interview, Livermore went on to further explain that the company's business is precisely "to provide transparency in the legal

system. So that makes it an even more compelling reason to be involved in trafficking, which we see as a 'rule of law' issue. As the legal anthropologist Kamari Clarke (2009: 25) has noted, "The contemporary expansion of the rule of law movement . . . reflects various powerful phenomena working in tension. One involves the way that particular neoliberal moral values are gaining global traction through the efforts of governmental and nongovernmental institutions and organizations to provide those who have been socially marginalized with spaces from which to make justice claims . . . [a]nother . . . is the economic force of neoliberal capitalism."

22. Schwab (2008). Schwab explicitly acknowledges Muhammad Yunus, the Nobel Price–winning inventor of microcredit, as an inspiration.

23. Sennet (1998). See also Sennet (2006).

24. Deleuze (1992: 6); see also Thrift (2005: 11), Žižek (2009: 52), Dean (2009: 22), Illouz (2007).

25. See, e.g., Jaffee (2007), Lyon and Moberg (2010), Mukherjee and Banet-Weiser (2012).

26. On corporate-driven equality politics in the LGBT movement, see Duggan (2003), Joseph (2002), and Chasin (2000). On the corporate "pinking" of the breast cancer movement, see Sulik (2011), Ehrenreich (2009), and King (2006). On women's reproductive health more generally, see Murphy (2012).

27. See, e.g., Barry (2004), "How Good Should Your Business Be" (2008), "The Birth of Philanthrocapitalism" (2006), Frank (2008), Seligson (2011), Gates and Kiviat (2008), and Strong (2009).

28. In the case of Whole Foods, the pursuit of "conscious capitalism" has been explicitly opposed to traditional left-wing causes, such as support for universal health care, workers' rights to organize in unions, and concerns about climate change (see, e.g., Harkinson 2013). With the rise of explicitly for-profit models of activism, progressive critiques of the funding imperatives implied by the "non-profit industrial complex" (e.g., INCITE! Women of Color against Violence 2007, Sharma 2006) and of burgeoning cultures of social enterprise (see, e.g., Karim 2011, Roy 2010) may very well be superseded by what LexisNexis executive William Livermore declared to be the next twist in social justice interventions: the supplanting of "public-private" partnerships by "private-private" partnerships, in which two or more corporations join forces to address a pressing social cause (William Livermore, personal interview, December 18, 2008).

29. Berardi (2009), Frank (1997). See also Boltanski and Chiapello (2005), Duggan (2003), Ferguson and Hong (2012), Ferguson (2012), and Reddy (2011).

30. Boltanski and Chiapello (2005: 163), Harold (2009: 611), Vrasti (2011).

31. The presence of a Gap spokesperson at this event was noteworthy, given the company's long-standing association among labor activists with sweatshops and child labor (see, e.g., Krupat 1997, Brooks 2007), as well as its

persistent refusal, even in the wake of recent factory fires and infrastructural collapses that have proved deadly to thousands of workers, to sign the Bangladesh Fire and Building Safety Agreement. Along with Walmart, Target, and other corporations, the company has instead created its own fire safety plan with no transparency, no role for workers or their trade unions, no commitment to pay prices to suppliers that make it feasible for them to operate responsibly, and no binding commitments of any kind (International Labor Rights Forum et al. 2016, Kamat and Kaplan 2016, Roshe 2016).

32. See, e.g., Smith (1986), Friedman (1960), Olasky (2000), and Berlant (2004).

33. Fraser (2013) also takes up some of these questions in her recent work. I consider Fraser's contributions in more detail in chapter 6.

34. As Thakor and boyd (2013: 284) have written: "Through language and normative judgment, anti-trafficking actors produce their own network—a matrix of actors who are simultaneously enrolled and mobilized through their commitment to producing and distributing information about the issues of anti-trafficking and at philosophical odds with one another based on moral, strategic, and tactical differences. Anti-trafficking—in its moral, activist, legal and data-driven constitutions, can be seen as an emergent network parallel to the trafficking that it seeks to address." Currently, boyd serves as a senior researcher for the anti-trafficking efforts being coordinated by Microsoft.

35. Guynn (2012).

36. Schmidt and Cohen (2013). Google Ideas has also explicitly dedicated itself to addressing problems such as fragile states, violent extremism, and organized crime, issues for which the company is poised to profit at multiple levels from the advent of a technological "solution."

37. See Musto and boyd (2014), Thakor and boyd (2013), Musto (2016). After repeated attempts to avoid criminal prosecution, on April 6, 2018 Backpage was shut down by federal authorities, who alleged that the site facilitated trafficking in women and children (Jackman and O'Donnell 2017, Savage and Williams 2018). Following the passage of the Allow States and Victims to Fight Online Sex Trafficking Act (colloquially known as FOSTA/SESTA) on April 11, 2018, portions of Craigslist and other sex trade advertising forums were also taken down (Cole 2018).

38. Anzia (2012). In response to the letter, a Google spokeswoman insisted that the company already banned ads for sex trafficking, child pornography and prostitution, while adding that "it's a constant battle against these bad actors so we are always looking at ways to improve our systems and practices—including by working with leading anti-trafficking organizations" (Sasso 2012). In response to a second letter from Maloney, Google also removed an app that highlighted paid sex opportunities in users' geographic vicinities from its digital media store (Hamsher 2012).

39. See Plambech (2014). Plambech is currently a researcher at the Danish Institute for International Studies in Copenhagen.

40. Clearly, the barriers to the creation of such an app are ones of governance priorities rather than technological incapacity. In 2009, Ricardo Dominguez, a professor in the University of California, San Diego, Visual Arts Department, made headlines by designing his own "transborder immigrant tool" to help guide illegal immigrants across the desert by pinpointing where food, water, and shelter were available (Schilling 2009).

41. For a critical, insider's look into the background planning behind the Illicit Networks conference, see Mahdavi (2014).

42. Tor Project (n.d.). Originally developed by the US Naval Research Academy for the purpose of protecting government communications, Tor continues to receive funding from the US Departments of Defense and of State, as well as major corporations such as Google. But the project has attracted sharp critique from these same quarters for its role as a haven for terrorists, child pornographers, and other criminals who can use the software to operate anonymously. It has also recently come under critical scrutiny from the National Security Agency (NSA) in the wake of its role of facilitating the release of documents via WikiLeaks, as well as disclosures of NSA documents by Edward Snowden (see, e.g., Moyer 2013, Lee 2013, Harris and Hudson 2013).

43. Chun (2007: chap. 2). There are, nonetheless, important precedents. In the United States, the alliance between government surveillance projects and anti-trafficking politics dates back to turn-of-the-century concerns with "white slavery," as Gretchen Soderlund has shown in her analysis of the historical origins of the FBI (Soderlund 2013: 99). See also Pliley (2014).

44. In June 2013, Palantir (whose principle clients reside in the governmental, security, and financial sectors) publicly denied that their Prism software was the basis for the NSA surveillance system of the same name (Greenberg 2013). Liberty Asia, which describes itself as a "Hong Kong based student network for Asia," is not known to have previously worked with any of the established anti-trafficking scholars or activists in the region (Elena Shih, personal communication, September 25, 2013; Sealing Cheng, personal communication, 6 January 2014). Started by two undergraduate students from Brown University in 2002 who admitted that they knew little about the issue before embarking on their activist engagement, the Polaris Project initially made its name in the field of anti-trafficking work by participating directly with the police to facilitate raids and rescues of brothels (Batstone 2007b, Polaris Project 2004). Since that time, the organization has become a favorite of corporate funders, state agents, and the media, regularly shape-shifting and adapting in accordance with new corporate initiatives (Haynes 2014).

45. See Google (2013).
46. Kate Sheill, Global Alliance against Trafficking in Women (GAATW), personal communication, October 3, 2013.
47. Musto (2016).
48. To date, the US Department of Justice has reported just 896 convictions in human trafficking cases, for sex and labor combined (US Department of State 2016, 2017; US Department of Justice 2011, 2012). See also my discussion in chapter 1 of the pressures that the US government has faced to downgrade its estimates of the prevalence of trafficking in the United States, given these comparatively low figures.
49. See also Mahdavi (2014: 38).
50. Badeschier's and Arkless's comments were made at the Conference on the Role of Corporations in Human Rights and Human Trafficking, George Washington University, Washington DC, December 11, 2011. Both have since retired from their positions.
51. See Parenti (2009).
52. The Athens Ethical Principles were initially adopted by a consortium of businesses in Athens, Greece, in 2006. As part of a public-private initiative to help combat the spread of human trafficking, signees pledge to create a corporate strategy against trafficking, to create public "awareness" programs, and to encourage their business partners to also adopt such principles (Athens Ethical Principles 2006).

     California's much vaunted Transparency in Supply Chains Act was signed into law in 2010, and requires businesses in the state of California that have more than $100 million in global receipts to "disclose their efforts to eradicate slavery and human trafficking from their direct supply chains for tangible goods offered for sale." It has been described by Manpower's own David Arkless, one of the law's chief architects and proponents, as "not having teeth" (personal interview, August 22, 2012). Other corporate interviewees that I spoke with also noted that they supported the law precisely because the regulations contained within the legislation were not onerous: "There is no mandate for what companies must do—all that is required is that companies *report* what they are doing to monitor their supply chains. It is lowest common denominator legislation, which sets some standards, and principles of transparency, and backing this might abate more severe regulations later on."
53. ManpowerGroup (2011: 27).
54. See Kristof (2004a, 2004b) and Sachs (2005). On slavery and freedom in classical liberal thought, see Dru Stanley (1998), O'Connell Davidson (2010, 2015), and McKeowan (2012).
55. O'Connell Davidson (2010: 250).
56. O'Connell Davidson (2010: 252). On the often arbitrary circumstances that enable domestic worker abuse to legally qualify as "trafficking" or "slavery," see Brennan (2014).

57. Bales and Trodd (2009).
58. Xiang (2012). See also Rodriguez (2010) and Guevarra (2010).
59. McKeown (2012: 43). On the social organization of transnational labor migration, see Xiang (2012), Rodriguez (2010), and Guevarra (2010).
60. ManpowerGroup (2013a).
61. As David van Arsdale (2008: 76) has noted, "Flexible employment practices have made temporary help the most popular form of work in the United States," an industry within which Manpower is the largest employer. In addition to having no claim to social benefits or entitlements, in temporary labor the worker must invest their own, unremunerated time into transportation between multiple jobs and regular, lengthy periods of waiting for reassignment. Contingent labor thus moves away from Fordist production models to something much closer to the wage slavery of classical Marxist accounts (see, e.g., Arsdale 2008, Purser 2012, Parker 1994).
62. Manpower notably boasts exclusive "recruitment process outsourcing" arrangements with the Chinese state, as well as across many of the developing markets of East and Southeast Asia and Latin America (see ManpowerGroup 2017). Nevertheless, no academic studies of Manpower's current non-US operations have thus far been carried out.
63. See, e.g., Bales and Trodd (2008), Skinner (2008), Kara (2012), Brysk and Choi-Fitzpatrick (2011).
64. Manpower (2013b). See also Peck, Theodore, and Ward (2005).
65. Xiang (2012: 722).
66. Mark Lagon, personal interview, Washington DC, June 15, 2012.
67. Marx himself pointed out "free" labor's frequent underpinning by slave labor. In *Capital*, for example, he noted the fact that "the veiled slavery of the wage earners in Europe needed the unqualified slavery of the New World as its pedestal" (1976: 925). See also Cohen (1987).
68. Verité (2012: 31).
69. See, e.g., Students and Scholars against Corporate Misbehavior (2012), Harris (2013), Ouroussoff (2011), Associated Press (2010).
70. Manpower's efforts to combat sex trafficking include anti-prostitution awareness campaigns (oriented both towards the public and to their own employees) and partnership with anti-prostitution NGOs domestically and globally (interview with David Arkless, August 22, 2012).
71. See *Jacobellis v. Ohio* (1964).
72. Clough (2012: 155).
73. Clough and Willse (2011: 48).
74. Murphy (2011).
75. Ibid., 30–31.
76. "The Girl Effect" is the title of the first chapter of Nicholas Kristof and Sheryl WuDunn's book *Half the Sky* (2009). The "*Half the Sky* movement" also consists of a film, Facebook game, and several prominent celebrity and NGO partnerships and was partially funded by Nike (see www.halftheskymovement.org).

77. "Getting Rights . . . Right: How Companies Are Implementing the Guiding Principles in Business and Human Rights," George Washington University Elliott School of International Affairs, December 8, 2011.
78. See, e.g., Cocca (2004), Ferguson (2003).

CHAPTER SIX

1. Interview with members of Asia Pacific Network of Sex Workers, August 3, 2012.
2. Empower Foundation (2012a).
3. Seshu and Bandhopadhyay (2009: 14).
4. Empower Foundation (2012a).
5. Kempadoo and Doezema (1998), Kempadoo, Sanghera, and Pattanaik (2012), Doezema (1998: 41).
6. Jagori (2012: 172).
7. I am grateful to Ann Jordan for facilitating this meeting, which took place on February 20, 2009. For additional testimony from the activists, see Center for Health and Gender Equity and Center for Human Rights and Humanitarian Law (2010).
8. UNAIDS announced its position on decriminalization with the publication of the UN Development Programme's report "The Global Commission on HIV and the Law: Risks, Rights and Health." The 2012 report laid out a rationale for the decriminalization of sex work, stating that criminalization only worked to increase the stigma and risk of HIV as well as abuse toward sex workers from law enforcement. It explicitly supports the decriminalization of clients as well as sex workers, as well as removing laws that criminalize activities such as soliciting, pimping, and brothel running (UN Development Programme 2012). In January 2014, Human Rights Watch (2014: 47) released its *World Report: 2014*. In the report, HRW explains how the criminalization of voluntary sex work and drug use "can cause or exacerbate a host of ancillary human rights violations, including exposure to violence from private actors, police abuse, discriminatory law enforcement, and vulnerability to blackmail, control, and abuse by criminals," and that these consequences of criminalization "mean it is unreasonable and disproportionate for the state to use criminal punishment to discourage either practice." The World Health Organization first advocated for the decriminalization of sex work in 2014, as part of a list of guidelines to reducing the global spread of HIV/AIDS. In "Consolidated Guidelines on HIV Prevention, Diagnosis, Treatment and Care for Key Populations," WHO (2014: 90) lists "decriminalizing sexual behaviors and drug use" as "critical enablers that can change a hostile environment for key populations into a supportive environment." Without such policy changes, the WHO argues, there will be significant barriers to health care for these populations (as a result of fear, stigma, or complete lack of access) that will result in harm to their health and the continued spread of HIV/AIDS.

The Amnesty decision, in particular, led some commentators to question whether the politics surrounding the issue of sex trafficking had in fact reversed course (in May 2016, the *New York Times* went so far as to declare the emergence of a "new approach" to prostitution, even though sex workers' rights activists have campaigned for decriminalization since the 1970s; see Bazelon (2016).

9. The announcement of Amnesty's official position was met with a great deal of criticism. The Coalition against Trafficking in Women (CATW) drafted an open letter to Amnesty in July 2015 in response to the decriminalization proposal that Amnesty was going to bring to a vote, which had been leaked in January 2014 (Doyle 2014). CATW argued that by proposing the decriminalization of all aspects of sex work, Amnesty was essentially supporting legalizing "pimping, brothel owning, and sex buying" and would actually further endanger the lives of women in the industry. They also criticized Amnesty's heavy reliance on HIV/AIDS organizations for consultation on the proposal, particularly UNAIDS (CATW 2015b: 1).

After the new policy passed in August, CATW drafted a "Global Declaration" to Amnesty, urging followers to sign it. The declaration rejected Amnesty's decision to decriminalize all aspects of sex work, arguing that all prostitution is steeped in a history of violence against women, particularly marginalized women of color. They also rejected Amnesty's deeming of prostitution as "sex work," instead referring to it as "gender-based violence and discrimination perpetuated by the multi-billion dollar commercial sex trade and fueled by buyers" (CATW 2015a: 2). Included on the list of more than three thousand signees of CATW's original petition were actors Anne Hathaway, Meryl Streep, Lena Dunham, Angela Bassett, Kevin Kline, Marcia Gay Harden, Kate Winslet, Lisa Kudrow, Chris Cooper, Allison Williams, Emily Blunt, and Emma Thompson (E. Brown 2015).

10. Amnesty International (2015).

11. Murphy (2015).

12. Mgbako (2016).

13. Murphy (2015), Amnesty International (2015).

14. Kempadoo (2012a: 249).

15. See, e.g., Lamas (2014), Romero, Montejo, and Madrid (2014), Rodriguez (2014), Mahdavi (2011), UN Women (2015), Ganesan (2016).

16. See, e.g., Hesford (2017), Callimachi (2015, 2016), Al Jazeera (2015), Schmidt and Chan (2016), Malm (2015).

17. Recall that in the early 2000s, the "traffic in women" was featured in major speeches by both Bush and Obama. Notably, in the lead-up to the 2016 presidential elections, neither of the two leading presidential contenders raised the issue directly, despite Hillary Clinton's early and crucial role in putting the issue on the international agenda and her experience in directing the US Office of Trafficking in Persons while serving as Obama's secretary of state.

18. Alvarez (1999); see also Bernal and Grewal (2014), INCITE! Women of Color against Violence (2007).

19. See US Department of Homeland Security (2016). The posters themselves were created by the National Council of Jewish Women (NCJW), which launched its anti-trafficking initiative, EXODUS, in the fall of 2014, although NCJW had publicly campaigned for anti-trafficking reform as early as 2005 (National Council of Jewish Women 2014, 2005). EXODUS focuses on trafficking in the United States and looks to disseminate information about trafficking and resources for victims. The campaign also specifically calls upon the Jewish people's history of slavery in Egypt and even has specialized anti-trafficking literature for Passover (National Council of Jewish Women 2016).

20. Pliley (2014). A 2016, state-by-state tally revealed sixteen new police department anti-trafficking units, and fifty-three state-level anti-trafficking taskforces, comprised of political officials, NGOs, and the police.

21. Informal interview, Conference on Rethinking Human Trafficking, Woodrow Wilson International Center for Scholars, Washington DC, March 2010.

22. See, e.g., Nair (2016), Daniels (2016), Wypijewski (2014).

23. Limoncelli (2010: 2).

24. Ibid., 11.

25. Kempadoo (2012a: 249–261), Leyva (2015).

26. Ho (2012: 251).

27. Leyva (2015).

28. Myriem Aboutaher, personal communication, May 28, 2016.

29. Italics in original. Sanford, Martínez, and Weitzer (2016: 153).

30. See, e.g., Brennan (2014), Kempadoo (2012b), Romero, Montejo, and Madrid (2014), McCarthy (2016), Thiemann (2016), Thukral (2016).

31. D'Adamo (2016: 113).

32. Swenstein and Mogulescu (2016: 121).

33. Center for Gender and Sexuality Law, Columbia University (2013).

34. According to former and current members, the organization was "compelled to close their non-profit 501c3 status in 2013 due to capacity, funding, and political pressures." The work of the project currently continues as a grassroots entity (Intermodal 2016, YWEP n.d.).

35. The Coalition of Immokalee Workers, which has done excellent advocacy on behalf of migrant farmworkers in Florida under the rubric of "fighting slavery" (organizing boycotts against popular restaurants like Chipotle and other major fast-food chains), constitutes an important exception. During a conversation with a staffer at the organization, he explained to me the difference in approach between his organization and that of California's United Farmworkers by noting, "Florida is much more conservative than California, and a labor rights, legislative approach would never work there. So we had to do the boycott. There was no other option. No one supports labor rights for illegal immigrants."

36. Illich (1968).

37. Puar (2007). On homonationalism and LGBT agendas, see also *The Economist* (n.d.), Duggan (2003), and Currah (2016). Thanks to Louisa Schein for bringing the *Economist*'s Pride and Prejudice campaign to my attention.
38. Farris (2012, 2017).
39. Zimmerman (2013).
40. See also Shared Hope International (2017).
41. Foucault (1978: 93).
42. See also O'Connell Davidson (2005).
43. Harvey (2007), Taylor (2006), Klein (2008).
44. For an extension of this argument, see Bernstein and Jakobsen (2013).
45. Eisenstein (2009: 159).
46. Fraser (2013).
47. For a cogent critique of Fraser's work, see Aslan and Gambetti (2011). See also Duggan (2003) and Butler (1997).
48. Quoted in Saunders and Sontag Broudo (2011).
49. Lee (2016).
50. Duggan 2003 (xxii).
51. Kristof and WuDunn (2010: 25; quoted in Lerum 2017: 10).
52. On the right end of the political spectrum, the ascent of anti-immigrant parties across Europe, the 2016 Brexit vote, and Donald Trump's successful campaign for US president all represented the melding of economic critique with anti-globalist isolationism. The Brexit decision, in particular, has been described as the rejection—even the end—of globalization and its model of open trade and immigration (Chandran 2016, Tankersley 2016). Numerous commentators have also applied this explanation to the remarkable presidential campaign of Donald Trump, who in his acceptance speech for the Republican nomination explicitly contrasted his socioeconomic vision against that of Democratic nominee Hillary Clinton in a move toward the populist right. Throughout his campaign, Trump emphasized his economic vision or "credo" of "Americanism not globalism," while promising to lower tax rates for American companies, renegotiate the North American Free Trade Agreement (NAFTA), and reject the Trans-Pacific Partnership (TPP) (see, e.g., Bump, Phillips, and Borchers 2016, Stoller 2017, Fraser 2017).
53. WuDunn (2010).
54. Milkman, Lewis, and Luce (2013b: 195).
55. Jaffe (2013); see also Milkman, Lewis, and Luce (2013a). Additional evidence of Occupy's legacy includes Occupy offshoot groups fighting student debt like Strike Debt, Rolling Jubilee, and Debt Collective, President Obama's introduction of a plan to create two years of free community college, and the political careers of New York Mayor Bill de Blasio and Massachusetts Senator Elizabeth Warren ("Since entering the Senate, Warren has drafted numerous bills to address income inequality. . . . Warren is the closest thing to an Occupy candidate the movement ever got"; Levitin 2015). Others have cited the campaigns of US 2016 presidential primary candidates—from

both left and right—as evidence of Occupy's lasting social and cultural imprint. Several candidates provided vocal recognition of Occupy's key issues, including income inequality, the nationwide worker-led campaign for a $15–an-hour minimum wage and better working conditions, university and institutional divestment from the fossil-fuel industry, grassroots anti-fracking activism, and resolutions to reform campaign finance. Particular attention has been devoted to the ample support for democratic socialist Bernie Sanders's presidential campaign and the role played by Occupy Wall Street in powering it (Krieg 2016, McCreesh 2016).

56. Maharawal (2016, 3–4).
57. Saunders and Broudo (2011).
58. Chatelain (2015), Marcos (2016).
59. Shor (2015).
60. INCITE! describes the framework guiding its work as one of "dangerous intersections," meaning that it recognizes that "women, gender non-conforming and trans people live in the dangerous intersections of sexism and racism, as well as other oppressions," and thus it places these people at the center of its activism, working to end not only sexual and domestic violence in communities of color but also the state and institutional violence inflicted on these communities (http://www.incite-national.org).
61. Cohen and Jackson (2015).
62. Specifically, the platform called for the "repeal of the Illegal Immigration Reform and Immigrant Responsibility Act that President Bill Clinton signed into law in 1996, which expanded the grounds for deportation to include criminal and non-criminal offenses" (Rivas 2016).
63. Lee (2016), Movement for Black Lives (2016).
64. Since taking office, the Trump administration has rolled back many Obama-era recommendations on sentencing and policing. In response to mounting opioid overdoses, President Trump and Attorney General Jeff Sessions have expressed their intention to reignite the war on drugs, including its reliance on heavily armed police and mandatory sentencing (see, e.g., Sands 2017, Patterson 2017).
65. Dagan and Teles (2015: 127).
66. Keller (2015), Easley (2015).
67. For other recent examples from different regional contexts, see, e.g., Daring, Rogue, Shannon, and Volcano (2012), Windpassinger (2010), Bacchetta, El-Tayeb, and Haritaworn (2015).
68. As George Yancy and Judith Butler (2015) pointed out in a *New York Times* op-ed, those with this response "misunderstand the problem, but not because their message is untrue. It is true that all lives matter, but it is equally true that not all lives are understood to matter, which is precisely why it is important to name the lives that have not mattered and are struggling to matter in a way they deserve."
69. Brown (2015: 222).

70. See, e.g., Bellafante (2017), Cauterucci (2017), L'Heureux (2017).
71. YWEP (2009). As such, their version of community empowerment is notably distinct from the neoliberal, responsibilizing implications of this term that have been discussed by Cruikshank (1999) and others.
72. Empower Foundation (2012a).
73. See, e.g., Monbiot (2016), Harvey (2016), Shivani (2016).
74. See, e.g., Bernstein and Jakobsen (2013).

AFTERWORD

1. Amar (2016). On sexual nationalisms and the rise of the populist right in Europe, see Fassin (2017).
2. See, e.g., C. West (2016), Jacques (2016), KPFA (2016).
3. On progressive neoliberalism and its demise, see Fraser (2017). On multicultural neoliberalism, see Ferguson (2012), Melamed (2011), and Reddy (2011). On Canada's Trudeau and France's Macron as progressive neoliberal figures, see Salutin (2017), Tonneau (2017), and Žižek (2017).
4. See, e.g., Gallagher (2017).
5. See Rich (2017), Shear (2017), Gearan and Morello (2017).
6. US Congress (2018), Shuham (2017), Gearan and Morello (2017).
7. See, e.g., Bassett (2017), Hirschfield Davis (2017), Boseley (2017), Sampathkumar (2017), Tatum (2017).
8. Women in the World Staff (2017), Haberman (2017), Smith and Redden (2017), Bumiller (2017).
9. Shuham (2017).
10. This, despite the fact that both Ivanka Trump and her father have been accused of relying on labor exploitation in their private businesses that may be severe enough to constitute trafficking. See, e.g., Varagur (2017), Denyer (2017), Grant (2017), Gold et al. (2017), Garcia (2016), J. West (2016).
11. See Trump (2017), Ferguson (2017: s57).
12. In the summer of 2017, Google, Facebook, and other tech giants briefly came under critical scrutiny by anti-trafficking activists for their objections to the Allow States and Victims to Fight Online Sex Trafficking Act of 2017, before reversing their position. The legislation allows victims to sue websites "that knowingly support sex trafficking on their site," and empowers state attorneys general to pursue websites with sex trafficking content (Kang 2017). It has been opposed by both First Amendment defenders and sex worker activists, who argue that it endangers their working conditions and livelihoods because of their inability to advertise online: "SESTA is putting people on the streets, where we face more violence and harassment and arrest and brutality by the police" (Cole 2018, Simon 2017). It was speculated that the tech companies reversed their position on FOSTA/SESTA following heightened scrutiny regarding their role in disseminating Russian propaganda during the 2016 presidential election (Nedig 2017).

13. Grant (2017). The Human Trafficking Institute (www.traffickinginstitute .org) was founded by Victor Boutros, a former federal prosecutor who is coauthor (with the International Justice Mission's Gary Haugen) of *The Locust Effect: Why the End of Poverty Requires the End of Violence*. The book argues that vulnerability to violence is an essential feature of poverty, the best response to which is heightened law enforcement (see Haugen and Boutros 2015). On the McCain Institute, see McCain (2017). The Human Trafficking Advisory Council of the McCain Institute is chaired by Cindy McCain, senator John McCain's wife, who was honored for her work in this capacity by the FBI Director's 2015 Community Leadership Award "for her work helping to combat crime" (FBI Phoenix 2016).

14. For example, Sanctuary for Families participated in the worldwide Women's March against his presidency and Equality Now expressed support for the march via Twitter. CATW denounced Trump for dismissing his boasts of sexual assault, while Equality Now recirculated a tweet that described Trump as a sexual offender. Additionally, Equality Now criticized the Administration for ending the Obama-led Let Girls Learn initiative and posted a link to an article on how Trump's presidency had inspired eleven thousand women to run for office (CATW and Raymond 2017, c_stewart_esq 2017, NARAL 2017). Some mainstream feminist organizations have also been critical of Trump's nativist rhetoric and discriminatory travel ban, with Sanctuary for Families retweeting multiple links, articles, and videos affirming the rights of immigrants in the face of Trump's anti-immigrant statements, Immigration and Customs Enforcement raids, and travel prohibitions (see, e.g., ssffny 2017b, madiatoure 2017, Choi 2017).

15. See Global Centurion (n.d.). Lederer's organization drew controversy when, a few days before the White House meeting, the Center for Family and Human Rights reported that Global Centurion demanded the government exclude groups that fail to condemn abortion and sex work from future anti-trafficking efforts (including the International Justice Mission) and deem them ineligible for federal funding (Grant 2017).

16. See, e.g., Wertheim (2017), Adams (2017), Wilkinson (2017).

17. See, e.g., Abramson (2017), Baker-Jordan (2017), Chen (2017).

18. The Global Alliance against Traffic in Women (2017).

19. On January 27, 2017, President Trump signed an executive order on immigration that "indefinitely barred Syrian refugees from entering the United States, suspended all refugee admissions for 120 days and blocked citizens of seven Muslim-majority countries, refugees or otherwise, from entering the United States for 90 days: Iran, Iraq, Libya, Somalia, Sudan, Syria and Yemen." This included people from those countries with active US visas, green cards, and approved refugee status from entering or reentering the country after leaving. The order immediately faced a bevy of legal challenges (Stack 2017, Shear 2017, Sherman 2017).

On March 6, 2017, President Trump released a revised executive order on immigration that included minor changes. The new order removed Iraq from its list of blocked countries and applied only to people seeking new visas (those with current visas and green cards were permitted reentry). The revised order received its first legal challenge on March 8, filed by the attorney general of Hawaii, Doug Chin. Chin called the new executive order the same policy "dressed up differently" and claimed that it remained unconstitutional (Burns 2017). In June 2017, the US Supreme Court revealed that it would rule on the legality of the ban in October and would temporarily allow Trump to prohibit entry of citizens from the specified countries, while exempting close family members of current US citizens (Shear and Liptak 2017).

Two weeks before the ban was scheduled to be argued at the Supreme Court, on September 24, the Trump administration filed a third version of the ban. Like previous versions, it kept people from six Muslim-majority countries from traveling to the United States but also prohibited travel for North Koreans and certain Venezuelan government officials (ACLU 2017). Unlike the prior versions of the ban, this version did not contain specific language about gender-based violence. At the time of this writing, the third ban was under review by the US Supreme Court and was awaiting a verdict.

20. Trump (2017a).
21. Trump (2017b).
22. See Reilly (2016), Oppenheim (2017).
23. Baker and Steinhauer (2017), Rosenblatt (2017).
24. See Democracy Now (2017), *New York Times* (2017a).
25. *New York Times* Editorial Board (2017), Nussbaum (2017), Hirschfeld Davis and Kelly (2017), Smith (2017).
26. Corker (2015).
27. US Congress (2017), Corker (2016).
28. See also Brown (2016), citing a "fifth wave of feminism" that is inflected by robust queer and trans movements, as well as by the surging popularity of Bernie Sanders in the United States, Jeremy Corbyn in the United Kingdom, and the political parties Syriza in Greece and Podemos in Spain.
29. Women's March (2017), Alcoff et al. (2017). The controversies pertaining to race, abortion, and sex work that preceded the final platform of the Women's March, and the roster of invited speakers, are well documented. See, e.g., Tolentino (2017), Maloney (2017), Best Practices Policy Project (2017).
30. See Levine (2017) and Tran (2017) on the carceral feminist tendencies of the gathering "#MeToo" movement. See also Hudson and Cohen's (2016) manifesto for women's rights as a "national security issue," published just after Trump's election.

References

Abramson, Alana. 2017. "Hillary Clinton: We Can't Protect Syrian Babies While Banning Refugees." *Time*, 7 April. http://time.com /4731485/hillary-clinton-syria-airstrikes-refugees-travel-ban -donald-trump/.

Abu-Lughod, Lila. 2013. *Do Muslim Women Need Saving?* Cambridge, MA: Harvard University Press.

Adams, Paul. 2017. "Is Trump Abandoning US Global Leadership?" *BBC News*, 1 June. http://www.bbc.com/news/world-us -canada-40127896.

Agustín, Laura María. 2011. "Mrs. Mubarak's Anti-Trafficking Project Endangered: Imelda Marcos, Anyone?" *Naked Anthropologist*, 12 February. http://www.lauraagustin.com/mrs-mubaraks-anti -trafficking-project-endangered-imelda-marcos-anyone.

———. 2010. "The Naked Anthropologist Attends a UN Event to End Human Trafficking." *Naked Anthropologist*, 10 December. http:// www.lauraagustin.com/the-naked-anthropologist-attends-a -un-event-to-end-human-trafficking.

———. 2007. *Sex at the Margins: Migration, Labour Markets and the Rescue Industry*. London: Zed Books.

Aita, Judy. 2007. "Private Groups Spearhead Anti-trafficking Efforts." US Diplomatic Mission to Italy, US Department of State, 14 February. http://www.usembassy.it/viewer/article.asp?articlep /file2007_02/alia/a7021407.htm.

Alcoff, Linda Martín, Cinzia Arruzza, Tithi Bhattacharya, Nancy Fraser, Barbara Ransby, Keeanga-Yamahtta Taylor, Rasmea Yousef Odeh, and Angela Davis. 2017. "Women of America: We're Going on Strike. Join Us So Trump Will See Our Power." *The Guardian*, 6 February. https://www.theguardian.com /commentisfree/2017/feb/06/women-strike-trump-resistance -power.

Alexander, Michelle. 2010. *The New Jim Crow: Mass Incarceration in the Age of Colorblindness*. New York: New Press.

Al Jazeera English. 2012. "Kony Screening Provokes Anger in Uganda." http://www.aljazeera.com/news/africa/2012/03/201231432421227462.html.

Almendrala, Anna. 2012. "Prop 35 Passes: California Voters Approve Harsher Sentencing for Human Traffickers." *Huffington Post*, 7 November. https://www.huffingtonpost.com/2012/11/07/prop-35-passes-california_n_2089305.html.

Alvarez, Sonia. 1999. "Advocating Feminism: The Latin American Feminist NGO 'Boom.'" *International Feminist Journal of Politics* 1(2): 181–209.

Amar, Paul. 2016. "Thug Love: Sexuality and New Authoritarian Populism in Megarabia." Workshop on Global Attachments: Sexuality and the Changing State, Williams College, Williamstown, MA, 15 October.

———. 2013. *The Security Archipelago: Human-Security States, Sexuality Politics, and the End of Neoliberalism*. Durham, NC: Duke University Press.

American Bar Association. 2014. "Majority of Fortune 100 Companies Have Policies on Human Trafficking and Forced Labor." *ABA News*, 2 June. http://www.americanbar.org/news/abanews/aba-news-archives/2014/05/majority_of_fortune.html.

American Civil Liberties Union. 2017. "Timeline of the Muslim Ban." https://www.aclu-wa.org/pages/timeline-muslim-ban.

———. 2014. "Appeals Court Rules in Favor of Anonymous Speech in California Prop 35," 18 November. https://www.aclunc.org/news/appeals-court-rules-favor-anonymous-speech-california-prop-35-case.

Amnesty International. 2015. "Global Movement Votes to Adopt Policy to Protect Human Rights of Sex Workers," 11 August. https://www.amnesty.org/en/latest/news/2015/08/global-movement-votes-to-adopt-policy-to-protect-human-rights-of-sex-workers/.

Anderberg, Kirsten. 2004. "No More 'Porn Nights.'" In *Not for Sale: Feminists Resisting Prostitution and Pornography*, ed. Christine Sark and Rebecca Whisnant, 275–277. North Melbourne, Australia: Spiniflex.

Andrijasevic, Rutvica. 2010. *Migration, Agency, and Citizenship in Sex Trafficking*. London: Palgrave Macmillan.

Anner, Mark. 2012. "Corporate Social Responsibility and Freedom of Association Rights: The Precarious Quest for Legitimacy and Control in Global Supply Chains." *Politics and Society* 40(4): 609–644.

Anzia, Lys. 2012. "US Congress Puts Global Microscope on Google about Sex-Trafficking." *Women News Network*, 19 April. http://womennewsnetwork.net/2012/04/19/us-congress-microscope-google/.

Arnold, Christina, and Andrea M. Bertone. 2002. "Addressing the Sex Trade in Thailand: Some Lessons Learned from NGOS, Part 1." *Gender Issues* 20(1): 26–52.

Arsdale, D. Van. 2008. "The Recasualization of Blue-Collar Workers: Industrial Temporary Help Work's Impact on the Working Class." *Labor: Studies in Working-Class History of the Americas* 5(1): 75–99.

Askew, Marc. 2002. *Bangkok: Place, Practice and Representation*. New York: Routledge.

———. 1999. "Strangers and Lovers: Thai Women, Sex Workers and Western Men in the 'Pleasure Space' of Bangkok." In *Converging Interests: Traders, Travelers and Tourists in Southeast Asia*, ed. Jill Forshee, Christina Fink, and Sandra Cate, 109–148. Berkeley: University of California Press.

Aslan, Özlem, and Zeynep Gambetti. 2011. "Provincializing Fraser's History: Feminism and Neoliberalism Revisited." *History of the Present* 1(1): 130–147.

Associated Press. 2013. "Father and Son Pimps Are Sentenced to 3 to 9 Years in Prison." *New York Times*, 8 July. http://www.nytimes.com/2013/07/09/nyre gion/father-and-son-pimps-are-sentenced-to-3-to-9-years-in-prison.html.

———. 2010. "Kosher Slaughterhouse Owner on Trial in Iowa for Child Labor." *Newsday*, 10 May. http://www.newsday.com/classifieds/jobs/kosher-slaughter house-owner-on-trial-in-iowa-for-child-labor-1.1904556.

"Athens Ethical Principles." 2006. *UN.GIFT.HUB: Global Initiative to Fight Human Trafficking*. Office on Drugs and Crime, 23 January. http://www.ungift.org /docs/ungift/pdf/Athens_principles.pdf.

Ax, Joseph. 2014. "Anti-Obama Author D'Souza Pleads Guilty to Campaign Finance Violation." *Reuters*, 20 May. http://www.reuters.com/article/2014/05/20/us -usa-politics-dsouza-idUSBREA4J0H520140520.

Bacchetta, Paola, Fatima El-TaYeb, and Jin Haritaworn. 2015. "Queer of Color Formations and Translocal Spaces in Europe." *Environment and Planning D: Society and Space* 33(5): 769–778.

Bailey, Sarah Pulliam. 2016. "White Evangelicals Voted Overwhelmingly for Donald Trump, Exit Polls Show." *Washington Post*, 9 November. https://www .washingtonpost.com/news/acts-of-faith/wp/2016/11/09/exit-polls-show -white-evangelicals-voted-overwhelmingly-for-donald-trump/?postshare=48 1478670946843&tid=ss_tw&utm_term=.72a69fa55287.

Baker, Carrie N. 2013. "Moving Beyond 'Slaves, Sinners, and Saviors': An Intersectional Feminist Analysis of US Sex-Trafficking Discourses, Law and Policy." *Journal of Feminist Scholarship* 4: 1–23.

Baker, Peter, and Jennifer Steinhauer. 2017. "Wall 'Will Get Built,' Trump Insists, as He Drops Funding Demand." *New York Times*, 25 April. https://www.nytimes .com/2017/04/25/us/politics/mexico-wall-spending-trump.html.

Baker-Jordan, Skylar. 2017. "If Trump Really Cared about Syrian Children, He Wouldn't Ban Them from Entering the US." *The Independent*, 7 April. http:// www.independent.co.uk/voices/syria-us-missile-attack-traval-ban-refugees -would-let-them-enter-a7672396.html.

Bales, Kevin. 2010a. "How to Combat Modern Slavery." *TED*. https://www.ted.com /talks/kevin_bales_how_to_combat_modern_slavery?language=en.

———. 2010b. *The Slave Next Door: Human Trafficking and Slavery in America Today*. Berkeley: University of California Press.

———. 2012. *Disposable People: New Slavery in the Global Economy*. 3rd ed. Berkeley: University of California Press.

Bales, Kevin, and Zoe Trodd. 2008. *To Plead Our Own Cause: Personal Stories by Today's Slaves*. Ithaca, NY: Cornell University Press.

Balmer, Randall. 2006. *Thy Kingdom Come: How the Religious Right Distorts Faith and Threatens America*. New York: Basic.

Balmer, Randall, and Lauren Winner. 2002. *Protestantism in America*. New York: Columbia University Press.

Banet-Weiser, Sarah. 2012. *Authentic™: The Politics of Ambivalence in a Brand Culture*. New York: New York University Press.

Banks, Adelle. 2012. "'Fifty Shades of Grey' Moves Evangelicals Beyond Black and White Sexuality." *Religion News Service*, 29 November. http://www.religion news.com/2012/11/29/fifty-shades-of-grey-moves-evangelicals-beyond-black -and-white-sexuality/.

Barry, Andrew. 2004. "Global Governmentality." In *Global Governmentality: Governing International Spaces*, ed. Wendy Larner and William Walters, 195–211. London: Routledge.

Barry, Kathleen. 1995. *The Prostitution of Sexuality: The Global Exploitation of Women*. New York: New York University Press.

Bartkowski, John. 2004. *The Promise Keepers: Servants, Soldiers, and Godly Men*. New Brunswick, NJ: Rutgers University Press.

Bassett, Laura. 2017. "Donald Trump Defunds Global Maternal Health Organization." *Huffington Post*, 3 April. http://www.huffingtonpost.com/entry/trump -defunds-un-population-fund_us_58de8cece4b0b3918c831b79.

Batstone, David. 2007a. "Cry Freedom: The Modern Slave Trade and Those Who Fight It." *Sojourners* (March): 12.

———. 2007b. *Not for Sale: The Return of the Global Slave Trade—And How We Can Fight It*. San Francisco: HarperCollins.

Baue, Bill. 2006. "Marriott Combats Child Sexual Exploitation." *Social Funds*, 11 December. http://www.socialfunds.com/news/article.cgi/2179/html.

Bazelon, Emily. 2016. "Should Prostitution Be a Crime?" *New York Times Magazine*, 5 May. http://www.nytimes.com/2016/05/08/magazine/should-prostitution -be-a-crime.html.

Becker, Howard S. 1963. *Outsiders: Studies in the Sociology of Deviance*. New York: Free Press.

Bedford, Kate. 2009a. *Developing Partnerships: Gender, Sexuality, and the Reformed WorldBank*. Minneapolis: University of Minnesota Press.

———. 2009b. "Doing Business with the Ladies: Gender, Legal Reform, and Entrepreneurship in the International Finance Corporation." *Capital and Society* 42(1–2): 168–194.

Beisel, Nicki, and Kathryn Krimmel. 2006. "Blonde Babies and Black Genocide: Advocating Equal Protection for the Unborn." Unpublished manuscript.

Bellafante, Ginia. 2017. "New Yorkers Rediscover Activism in the Trump Presidency Era." *New York Times*, 20 January. https://www.nytimes.com/2017/01/20 /nyregion/trump-presidency-new-york-city.html?hpw&rref=nyregion&ac tion=click&pgtype=Homepage&module=well-region&region=bottom-well &WT.nav=bottom-well&_r=0.

Ben-Moshe, Liat. 2013. "The Tension between Abolition and Reform." In *The End of Prisons*, ed. Mechthild E. Nagel and Anthony J. Nocella II, 83–92. Leiden: Brill/Rodopi.

Berardi, Franco "Bifo." 2009. *The Soul at Work: From Alienation to Autonomy*. Los Angeles: Semiotext(e).

Berglind, Matthew, and Cheryl Nakata. 2005. "Cause-Related Marketing: More Buck Than Bang?" *Business Horizons* 48(5): 443–453.

Berik, Günseli, Yana van der Meulen Rodgers, and Ann Zammit, eds. 2009. *Social Justice and Gender Equality: Rethinking Development Strategies and Macroeconomic Policies*. New York: Routledge.

Berlant, Lauren, ed. 2004. *Compassion: The Culture and Politics of an Emotion*. New York: Routledge.

——. 1999. "The Subject of True Feeling: Pain, Privacy, and Politics." In *Cultural Pluralism, Identity Politics, and the Law*, ed. Austin Sarat and Thomas R. Kearns, 49–84. Ann Arbor: University of Michigan Press.

Berman, Jacqueline. 2006. "The Left, the Right, and the Prostitute: The Making of US Antitrafficking in Persons Policy." *Tulane Journal of International and Comparative Law* 14(2): 269–293.

Bernal, Victoria, and Inderpal Grewal, eds. 2014. *Theorizing NGOs: States, Feminisms, and Neoliberalism*. Durham, NC: Duke University Press.

Bernstein, Elizabeth. 2012. "Carceral Politics as Gender Justice? The 'Traffic in Women' and Neoliberal Circuits of Crime, Sex, and Rights." *Theory and Society* 41: 233–259.

——. 2010. "Militarized Humanitarianism Meets Carceral Feminism: The Politics of Sex, Rights, and Freedom in Contemporary Anti-Trafficking Campaigns," *Signs: Journal of Women in Culture and Society* 36(1): 45–71.

——. 2007a. "The Sexual Politics of the 'New Abolitionism.'" *Differences* 18(3): 128–151.

——. 2007b. *Temporarily Yours: Intimacy, Authenticity, and the Commerce of Sex*. Chicago: University of Chicago Press.

Bernstein, Elizabeth, and Janet Jakobsen. 2013. "Gender, Justice, and Neoliberal Transformations: Introduction." *Scholar and Feminist Online* 11.1–11.2. http://sfonline.barnard.edu/gender-justice-and-neoliberal-transformations /introduction/.

——. 2010. "Sex, Secularism and Religious Influence in US Politics." *Third World Quarterly* 31(6): 1023–1039.

Bernstein, Elizabeth, and Elena Shih. 2014. "The Erotics of Authenticity: Sex Trafficking and 'Reality Tourism' in Thailand." *Social Politics* 22(4): 430–460.

Bertone, Andrea Marie. 2008. "Human Trafficking on the International and Domestic Agendas: Examining the Role of Transnational Advocacy Networks between Thailand and United States." PhD dissertation, University of Maryland.

Best, Joel. 1990. *Threatened Children: Rhetoric and Concern about Child-Victims*. Chicago: University of Chicago Press.

"The Best Cities in Asia." *Travel and Leisure*. http://www.travelandleisure.com /worlds-best/cities-in-asia#intro.

"The Birth of Philanthrocapitalism." 2006. *The Economist*, 25 February. http:// www.economist.com/node/5517656.

Bishop, Ryan, and Lillian S. Robinson. 1998. *Night Market: Sexual Cultures and the Thai Economic Miracle*. London: Routledge.

Blanchette, Thaddeus, and Ana Paula da Silva. 2012. "On Bullshit and the Trafficking of Women: Moral Entrepreneurs and the Invention of Trafficking of Persons in Brazil," *Dialectical Anthropology* 36(1–2): 107–125.

Bloul, Rachel. 2012. "Ain't I a Woman? Female Landmine Survivors' Beauty Pageants and the Ethics of Staring." *Social Identities* 18(1): 3–18.

Bohrman, Rebecca, and Naomi Murakawa. 2005. "Remaking Big Government: Immigration and Crime Control in the United States." In *Global Lockdown: Race, Gender and the Prison-Industrial Complex*, ed. Julia Sudbury, 109–126. London: Routledge.

Boltanski, Luc, and Eve Chiapello. 2005. *The New Spirit of Capitalism*. London: Verso.

Boseley, Sarah. 2017. "How Trump Signed a Global Death Warrant for Women." *The Guardian*, 21 July. https://www.theguardian.com/global-development /2017/jul/21/trump-global-death-warrant-women-family-planning-popula tion-reproductive-rights-mexico-city-policy?CMP=share_btn_link.

Boyd, Lydia. 2013. "The Problem with Freedom: Homosexuality and Human Rights in Uganda." *Anthropological Quarterly* 86(3): 697–724.

Bradford, Sara. 2009. "The Impact of Anti-Trafficking and Anti-Prostitution Campaigns on Sex Workers in Cambodia." Presentation at the Human Trafficking, HIV/AIDS, and the Sex Sector conference, Washington College of Law, Center for Human Rights and Humanitarian Law, American University, 3–18. http://me dia.wcl.american.edu/Mediasite/Play/5f44296a-5048-4aaf-8557-34aaf34fe814.

Brandt, Allan. 1985. *No Magic Bullet: A Social History of Venereal Disease in the United States Since 1880*. New York: Oxford University Press.

Brennan, Denise. 2014. "Migrants at Risk: How US Policies Facilitate Human Trafficking." *Dissent: A Quarterly of Politics and Culture*, 24 March. http://www .dissentmagazine.org/online_articles/migrants-at-risk-how-u-s-policies-facili tate-human-trafficking.

———. 2013. *Life Interrupted: Trafficking into Forced Labor in the United States*. Durham, NC: Duke University Press.

———. 2008. "Competing Claims of Victimhood? Foreign and Domestic Victims of Trafficking in the United States." *Sexuality Research and Social Policy* 5(4): 45–61.

———. 2005. "Methodological Challenges in Research with Trafficked Persons: Tales from the Field." *International Migration* 43(1–2): 35–54.

———. 2004. *What's Love Got to Do with It? Transnational Desires and Sex Tourism in the Dominican Republic*. Durham, NC: Duke University Press.

Brooks, Ethel C. 2007. *Unraveling the Garment Industry: Transnational Organizing and Women's Work*. Minneapolis: University of Minnesota Press.

Brown v. Board of Education of Topeka. 1954. 347 U.S. 483.

Brown, Elizabeth Nolan. 2015. "Celebs Protest Amnesty International Call to Decriminalize Prostitution." *Reason.com*, 28 July. http://reason.com/blog/2015/07/28/celebs-protest-amnesty-international.

Brown, Wendy. 2016. "The End of the World as We Know It." *Artforum International* 55(4): 244–247.

———. 2015. *Undoing the Demos: Neoliberalism's Stealth Revolution*. Cambridge, MA: MIT Press.

———. 2005. *Edgework: Critical Essays on Knowledge and Politics*. Princeton, NJ: Princeton University Press.

———. 1995. *States of Injury: Power and Freedom in Late Modernity*. Princeton, NJ: Princeton University Press.

Bruinius, Harry. 2017. "Trump's Evangelical Support Is Wide: But How Deep?" *Christian Science Monitor*, 3 February. https://www.csmonitor.com/USA/Politics/2017/0203/Trump-s-evangelical-support-is-wide.-But-how-deep.

Bruner, Edward M. 2005. *Culture on Tour: Ethnographies of Travel*. Chicago: University of Chicago Press.

Bryan College. 2014. "Human Trafficking Study Trip Set to Cambodia." Bryan College, 4 June. http://www.bryan.edu/news/2014/06/human-trafficking-study-trip-set-to-cambodia/.

Brysk, Alison, and Austin Choi-Fitzpatrick. 2011. *From Human Trafficking to Human Rights: Reframing Contemporary Slavery*. Philadelphia: University of Pennsylvania Press.

Buettner, Russ. 2013a. "Father and Son Acquitted of Sex Trafficking Charges." *New York Times*, 19 June. http://www.nytimes.com/2013/06/20/nyregion/sex-trafficking-prosecution-fails-in-case-of-pimps-defended-by-prostitutes.html.

———. 2013b. "Prostitutes Testify in Defense of Pimps at Sex Trafficking Trial." *New York Times*, 28 May. http://www.nytimes.com/2013/05/29/nyregion/prostitutes-testify-in-defense-of-pimps-at-sex-trafficking-trial.html.

Bumiller, Kristin. 2008. *In an Abusive State: How Neoliberalism Appropriated the Feminist Movement against Sexual Violence*. Durham, NC: Duke University Press.

———. 2017. "In the Name of Victims." *Boston Review*, 1 November. http://bostonreview.net/education-opportunity/kristin-bumiller-name-victims.

Bump, Phillip, Amber Phillips, and Callum Borchers. 2016. "Donald Trump's Economic Speech, Annotated." *Washington Post*, 8 August. https://www.washingtonpost.com/news/the-fix/wp/2016/08/08/donald-trumps-economic-speech-annotated/.

Bunch, Charlotte. 1972. "Lesbians in Revolt." In *We Are Everywhere: A Historical Sourcebook of Gay and Lesbian Politics*, ed. Mark Blasius and Shane Phelan, 420–424. New York: Routledge.

Burawoy, Michael, Joseph A. Blum, George Sheba, Zsuzsa Gille, and Millie Thayer, eds. 2000. *Global Ethnography: Forces, Connections, and Imaginations in a Postmodern World.* Berkeley: University of California Press.

———. 1991. *Ethnography Unbound: Power and Resistance in the Modern Metropolis.* Berkeley: University of California Press.

Burke, Daniel. 2017. "100 Evangelical Leaders Sign Ad Denouncing Trump's Refugee Ban." *CNN,* 8 February. http://edition.cnn.com/2017/02/08/politics/evangelicals-ad-trump/index.html.

Burns, Alexander. 2017. "Hawaii Sues to Block Trump Travel Ban; First Challenge to the Order." *New York Times,* 8 March. https://www.nytimes.com/2017/03/08/us/trump-travel-ban-hawaii.html?_r=0.

Bush, George W. 2003. "Address to the United Nations General Assembly." United Nations, 23 September, New York. https://georgewbush-whitehouse.archives.gov/news/releases/2003/09/20030923-4.html.

Business as Mission Think Tank. 2013. "A Business Takeover: Combating the Business of Sex Trade with Business as Mission." Edited by Jo Plummer and Mats Tunehag. http://bamglobal.org/wp-content/uploads/2015/12/BMTT-IG-BAM-and-Human-Trafficking-Final-Report-October-2013.pdf.

Buss, Doris, and Didi Herman. 2003. *Globalizing Family Values: The Christian Right in International Politics.* Minneapolis: University of Minnesota Press.

Butler, Jennifer S. 2006. *Born Again: The Christian Right Globalized.* London: Pluto.

Butler, Judith. 1997. "Merely Cultural." *Social Text* 52–53: 265–277.

———. 1993. *Bodies That Matter: On the Discursive Limits of "Sex."* New York: Routledge.

Buzard, Allison. 2012. "America's New Move against Modern-Day Slavery." *Relevant Magazine,* 1 October. http://www.relevantmagazine.com/reject-apathy/loss-of-innocents/features/26320-americas-new-move-against-modern-day-slavery.

Cadwalladr, Carole. 2013. "The Guy behind the Kony 2012 Video Finally Explains How Everything Went So Weird." *Business Insider,* 3 March. http://www.businessinsider.com/the-guy-behind-the-kony-2012-video-finally-explains-how-everything-went-so-weird-2013-3?page=3.

Callimachi, Rukmini. 2016. "To Maintain Supply of Sex Slaves, ISIS Pushes Birth Control." *New York Times,* 12 March. http://www.nytimes.com/2016/03/13/world/middleeast/to-maintain-supply-of-sex-slaves-isis-pushes-birth-control.html?_r=0.

———. 2015. "Isis Enshrines a Theology of Rape." *New York Times,* 13 August. http://www.nytimes.com/2015/08/14/world/middleeast/isis-enshrines-a-theology-of-rape.html.

Campbell, Jacquelyn. 2015. "Campus Sexual Assault Perpetration: What Else We Need to Know." *JAMA Pediatrics,* 13 July. http://archpedi.jamanetwork.com/article.aspx?articleID=2375126.

Campolo, Tony. 2006. *Letters to a Young Evangelical.* New York: Basic Books.

Campolo, Tony, and Shane Claiborne. 2016. "The Evangelicalism of Old White Men Is Dead." *New York Times*, 29 November. https://www.nytimes.com/2016/11/29 /opinion/the-evangelicalism-of-old-white-men-is-dead.html?_r=0.

Capous Desyllas, Moshoula. 2007. "A Critique of the Global Trafficking Discourse and US Policy." *Journal of Sociology and Social Welfare* 34(4): 57–80.

carceralfeministcat. 2014. *Carceral Feminist Cat.* Tumblr. http://carceralfeminist cat.tumblr.com.

Carroll, Archie B. 1999. "Corporate Social Responsibility: Evolution of a Definitional Construction." *Business & Society* 38(3): 268–295.

Carter, Heath. 2015. "Guaranteed Pure: A Conversation with Tim Gloege." *Religion in American History*, April 17. http://usreligion.blogspot.com/2015/04 /guaranteed-pure-conversation-with-tim.html.

Castelli, Elizabeth. 2004. *Martyrdom and Memory: Early Christian Culture Making.* New York: Columbia University Press.

Cauterucci, Christina. 2017. "The Women's March on Washington Has Released an Unapologetically Progressive Platform." *Slate*, 12 January. http://www .slate.com/blogs/xx_factor/2017/01/12/the_women_s_march_on_washing ton_has_released_its_platform_and_it_is_unapologetically.html.

CBS New York. 2013. "Closing Arguments Under Way In NYC Sex Trafficking Case." *CBS New York*, 6 June. http://newyork.cbslocal.com/2013/06/06 /closing-arguments-underway-in-nyc-sex-trafficking-case/.

Center for Health and Gender Equity and Center for Human Rights and Humanitarian Law. 2010. *Human Trafficking, HIV/AIDS, and the Sex Sector: Human Rights for All.* Washington, DC: Center for Gender Health and Equity and Center for Human Rights and Humanitarian Law at American University, Washington College of Law.

Chacón, Jennifer M. 2006. "Misery and Myopia: Understanding the Failures of US Efforts to Stop Human Trafficking." *Fordham Law Review* 74(6): 2977– 3040.

Chandran, Nyshka. 2016. "How Brexit Impacts Globalization." *CNBC*, 28 June. http://www.cnbc.com/2016/06/28/how-brexit-impacts-globalization.html.

Chapkis, Wendy. 2005. "Soft Glove, Punishing Fist: The Trafficking Victims Protection Act of 2000." In *Regulating Sex: The Politics of Intimacy and Identity*, ed. Elizabeth Bernstein and Laurie Schaffner, 51–66. New York: Routledge.

———. 2003. "Trafficking, Migration, and the Law Protecting Innocents, Punishing Immigrants." *Gender & Society* 17(6): 923–937.

———. 1997. *Live Sex Acts: Women Performing Erotic Labor.* New York: Routledge.

Chasin, Alexandra. 2000. *Selling Out: The Gay and Lesbian Movement Goes to Market.* New York: St. Martin's.

Chatelain, Marcia. 2015. "Black Lives Matter: An Online Roundtable with Alicia Garza, Dante Barry, and Darsheel Kaur." *Dissent*, 19 January. https://www.dis sentmagazine.org/blog/blacklivesmatter-an-online-roundtable-with-alicia -garza-dante-barry-and-darsheel-kaur.

Chen, Michelle. 2017. "Why Trump's Travel Ban Hits Women the Hardest." *The Guardian*, 16 July. https://www.theguardian.com/commentisfree/2017/jul/16/why-trumps-travel-ban-hits-women-the-hardest?CMP=share_btn_link.

Chen, Pamela. 2007. Presentation at the 3rd Korean Americans against Trafficking (KAAT) Conference, New York Asian Women's Center, Flushing, NY, 29 August.

Cheney, Kristen. 2012. "Locating Neocolonialism, 'Tradition,' and Human Rights in Uganda's 'Gay Death Penalty.'" *African Studies Review* 55(2): 77–95.

Cheng, Sealing. 2010. *On the Move for Love: Migrant Entertainers and the US Military in South Korea*. Philadelphia: University of Pennsylvania Press.

———. 2008. "The Traffic in 'Trafficked Filipinas': Sexual Harm, Violence, and Victims' Voices." In *Violence and Gender in a Globalized World*, ed. Sanja Bahun-Radunovic and Julie Rajan, 141–156. London: Ashgate.

———. 2004. "Good Intentions Can Do Harm." *Korea Times*, 13 December.

Chesler, Phyllis, and Donna M. Hughes. 2004. "Feminism in the 21st Century." *Washington Post*, 22 February, B07.

Chew, Lin Lap. 2012. "Reflections by an Anti-Trafficking Activist." In *Trafficking and Prostitution Reconsidered: New Perspectives on Migration, Sex Work, and Human Rights*, 2nd ed., ed. Kamala Kempadoo, 65–82. London: Routledge.

Choi, Steven (SteveChoiNYIC). 2017. "Here's the #ICE memo on their NY operations. We won't be silent while they terrorize #immigrants http://bit.ly/ICEinNY #nobannowallnoraids." Twitter, 12 February. https://twitter.com/SteveChoiNYIC/status/830758641510862848.

Chuang, Janie A. 2010. "Rescuing Trafficking from Ideological Capture: Anti-Prostitution Reform and Anti-Trafficking Law and Policy." *University of Pennsylvania Law Review* 158: 1655–1728.

———. 2006. "The United States as Global Sheriff: Using Unilateral Sanctions to Combat Human Trafficking." *Michigan Journal of International Law* 27(2): 437–494.

Chun, Wendy Hui Kyong. 2007. *Control and Freedom: Power and Paranoia in the Age of Fiber Optics*. Cambridge, MA: MIT Press.

Cizik, Richard. 2006. "Do Evangelicals Play Too Great a Role in American Foreign Policy?" Lecture, Bard College Globalization and International Affairs Program, New York, 11 May.

Claiborne, Shane. 2016. *Executing Grace: How the Death Penalty Killed Jesus and Why It's Killing Us*. New York: HarperOne.

———. 2006. *The Irresistible Revolution*. Grand Rapids, MI: Zondervan.

Clarke, D. A. 2004. "Prostitution for Everyone: Feminism, Globalisation, and the 'Sex' Industry." In *Not for Sale: Feminists Resisting Prostitution and Pornography*, ed. Christine Stark and Rebecca Whisnant, 149–206. North Melbourne, Australia: Spiniflex.

Clarke, Kamari Maxine. 2009. *Fictions of Justice: The International Criminal Court and the Challenge of Legal Pluralism in Sub-Saharan Africa*. Cambridge: Cambridge University Press.

Clifford, James, and George E. Marcus, eds. 1986. *Writing Culture: The Poetics and Politics of Ethnography*. Berkeley: University of California Press.

Clinton, Hillary Rodham. 1995. "Women's Rights are Human Rights." Speech at the UN Fourth World Conference on Women: Action for Equality, Development and Peace, Beijing, 5 September.

Clinton Foundation. n.d. "Clinton Global Iniatiative." Clinton Foundation. https://www.clintonfoundation.org/clinton-global-initiative.

Clough, Patricia Ticineto. 2012. "War by Other Means: What Differences Do(es) the Graphic(s) Make?" In *Digital Cultures and the Politics of Emotion: Feelings, Affect and Technological Change*, ed. Athina Karatzogianni and Adi Kuntsman, 21–32. New York: Palgrave Macmillan.

———. 1992. *The End(s) of Ethnography*. New York: Sage Publications.

Clough, Patricia, and Craig Willse. 2011. "Human Security/National Security: Gender Branding and Population Racism." In *Beyond Biopolitics: Essays on the Governance of Life and Death*, ed. Patricia Ticineto Clough and Craig Willse, 46–64. Durham, NC: Duke University Press.

CNN. 2011. *The CNN Freedom Project: Ending Modern-Day Slavery*. http://thecnn freedomproject.blogs.cnn.com.

Coalition against Trafficking in Women. 2015a. *Global Declaration: Calling on Amnesty International to Uphold Human Rights*. August. http://catwinternational .org/Content/Images/Article/630/attachment.pdf.

———. 2015b. "Open Letter to Amnesty International." 17 July. http://catwinter national.org/Content/Images/Article/623/attachment.pdf.

Coalition against Trafficking in Women and Janice G. Raymond. 2017. "Highlighting CATW-AP's Tireless Efforts in the Filipino Woman-Led Resistance against Duterte," 5 May. http://www.catwinternational.org/Home/Article/706-high lighting-catwaps-tireless-efforts-in-the-filipino-womanled-resistence-against -duterte.

Cocca, Carolyn. 2004. *Jailbait: The Politics of Statutory Rape Laws in the United States*. Albany: State University of New York Press.

Codrea-Rado. 2017. "#MeToo Floods Social Media With Stories of Harassment and Assault." *New York Times*, 16 October. https://www.nytimes.com/2017/10/16 /technology/metoo-twitter-facebook.html.

Cohen, Cathy, and Sarah Jackson. 2015. "Ask a Feminist: A Conversation with Cathy Cohen on Black Lives Matter, Feminism, and Contemporary Activism." *Signs*. http://signsjournal.org/ask-a-feminist-cohen-jackson/.

Cohen, Erik. 2008. *Explorations in Thai Tourism: Collected Case Studies*. Vol. 11. London: Emerald Group.

———. 1996. *Thai Tourism: Hill Tribes, Islands and Open-Ended Prostitution, Collected Papers*. Vol. 4. Bangkok: White Lotus.

———. 1989. "Primitive and Remote: Hill Tribe Trekking in Thailand." *Annals of Tourism Research* 16(1): 30–61.

———. 1988. "Authenticity and Commoditization in Tourism." *Annals of Tourism Research* 15(3): 371–386.

———. 1986. "Lovelorn Farangs: The Correspondence between Foreign Men and Thai Girls," *Anthropological Quarterly* 59(3): 155–178.

Cohen, Erik, and Mark Neal. 2012. "A Middle Eastern Muslim Tourist Enclave in Bangkok." *Tourism Geographies* 14(4): 570–598.

Cohen, Robin. 1987. *The New Helots: Migrants in the International Division of Labour.* Aldershot, UK: Avebury.

Colapinto, John. 2012. "Looking Good: The New Boom in Celebrity Philanthropy." *New Yorker*, 26 March, 56–64.

Cole, Samantha. 2018. "Trump Just Signed SESTA/FOSTA, a Law Sex Workers Say Will Literally Kill Them." *Motherboard.* 11 April. https://motherboard .vice.com/amp/en_us/article/qvxeyq/trump-signed-fosta-sesta-into-law-sex -work?_twitter_impression=true.

Cole, Teju. 2012. "The White-Savior Industrial Complex." *The Atlantic*, 21 March. http://www.theatlantic.com/international/archive/2012/03/the-white-savior -industrial-complex/254843/.

Colebrook, Claire. 2002. *Gilles Deleuze.* New York: Routledge.

Coleman, Simon, and Mike Crang. 2002. *Tourism: Between Place and Performance.* New York: Berghahn Books.

Collins, Janet. 2008. "The Specter of Slavery." In *New Landscapes of Inequality: Neoliberalism and the Erosion of Democracy in America*, ed. Jane Collins, Micaela di Leonardo, and Brett Williams, 131–152. Santa Fe: School for Advanced Research.

Commonwealth of Massachusetts v. Tyshaun McGhee. 2015. 472 Mass. 405 (Sup. Ct.).

Conner, Brendan M. 2016. "*In loco aequitatis*: The Dangers of 'Safe Harbor' Laws for Youth in the Sex Trades." *Stanford Journal of Civil Rights and Civil Liberties* 12(1): 43–119.

Conroy, Michael E. 2007. *Branded! How the "Certification Revolution" Is Transforming Global Corporations.* Gabriola Island, BC: New Society.

Coomaraswamy, Radhika. *Report of the Special Rapporteur on Violence against Women, Its Causes and Consequences, Ms. Radhika Coomaraswamy, on Trafficking in Women, Women's Migration and Violence against Women, Submitted in Accordance with Commission on Human Rights Resolution 1997/44.* United Nations, 2000.

Corker, Bob. 2016. "What They're Saying: End Modern Slavery Initiative Awaits President's Signature." 21 December. https://www.corker.senate.gov/public/index .cfm/2016/12/end-modern-slavery-initiative-awaits-president-s-signature.

———. 2015. "We Can End Human Slavery Once and for All." *Tennessean*, 26 February. http://www.tennessean.com/story/opinion/contributors/2015/02/26 /can-end-human-slavery/24060515/.

Corones, Mike. 2015. "Tracking Obama's Deportation Numbers." *Reuters Blogs* (blog), http://blogs.reuters.com/data-dive/2015/02/25/tracking-obamas-deportation -numbers/.

Corsilles, Angela. 1994. "No-Drop Policies in the Prosecution of Domestic Violence Cases: Guarantee to Action or Dangerous Solution." *Fordham Law Review* 63: 853.

Cruikshank, Barbara. 1999. *The Will to Empower: Democratic Citizens and Other Subjects.* Ithaca, NY: Cornell University Press.

Currah, Paisley. 2013. "Homonationalism, State Rationalities, and Sex Contradictions." *Theory & Event* 16(1).

D'Adamo, Kate. 2016. "Prioritising Prosecutions Is the Wrong Approach." *Anti-Trafficking Review* 6: 111–113. http://www.antitraffickingreview.org/index.php/atrjournal/article/view/173/176.

Dagan, David, and Steven M. Teles. 2015. "The Social Construction of Policy Feedback: Incarceration, Conservatism, and Ideological Change." *Studies in American Political Development* 29(2): 127–153.

Daniels, Jessie. 2016. "Hillary Clinton's Nomination: A Victory for White Feminism." *Racism Review*, 8 June. http://www.racismreview.com/blog/tag/white-feminism/.

Daring, C. B., J. Rogue, Deric Shannon, and Abbey Volcano, eds. 2012. *Queering Anarchism: Addressing and Undressing Power and Desire*. Oakland, CA: AK Press.

Dassé, Martial. 1978. *La face politique cachée de la Thaïlande*. Bangkok: Duang Kamol.

Dávila, Arlene M. 2001. *Latinos, Inc.: The Marketing and Making of a People*. Berkeley: University of California Press.

Davies, Nick. 2009a. "Inquiry Fails to Find Single Trafficker Who Forced Anybody into Prostitution." *The Guardian*, 19 October. www.theguardian.com/uk/2009/oct/20/government-trafficking-enquiry-fails.

———. 2009b. "Prostitution and Trafficking—The Anatomy of a Moral Panic." *The Guardian*, 19 October. http://www.theguardian.com/uk/2009/oct/20/trafficking-numbers-women-exaggerated.

Davis, Angela Y. 2016. *Freedom Is a Constant Struggle: Ferguson, Palestine, and the Foundations of a Movement*. Edited by Frank Barat. Chicago: Haymarket Books.

———. 2003. *Are Prisons Obsolete?* New York: Seven Stories.

Davis, Cara. 2007. "Call to Justice: Gary Haugen and International Justice Mission." *Relevant* (March–April): 51.

Day, Sophie. 2010. "The Re-Emergence of 'Trafficking': Sex Work between Slavery and Freedom." *Journal of the Royal Anthropological Institute* 16: 816–834.

De Launey, Guy. 2005. "Cambodian Women 'Not Abducted.'" *BBC News*, 18 February. http://news.bbc.co.uk/2/hi/asia-pacific/4275943.stm.

De Santa Ana, Julio. 1976. "The Influence of Bonhoeffer on the Theology of Liberation." *Ecumenical Review* 28(2): 188–197.

Dean, Jodi. 2009. *Democracy and Other Neoliberal Fantasies: Communicative Capitalism and Left Politics*. Durham, NC: Duke University Press.

"Death of Clifford G. Roe." 1934. *United States Law Review* 68: 448.

DeBaca, Luis. 2012. "Human Trafficking: Past and Present: Crossing Disciplines, Crossing Borders." Rice University, Houston, TX, 23 October.

Deflem, Mathieu. 2006. *Sociological Theory and Criminological Research: Views from Europe and the United States*. Bradford, UK: Emerald Group.

Deibert, Michael. 2012. "The Problem with Invisible Children's 'Kony 2012.'" *Huffington Post*, 7 March. http://www.huffingtonpost.com/michael-deibert/joseph-kony-2012-children_b_1327417.html.

Deleuze, Gilles. 1992. "Postscript on the Societies of Control." *October* 59: 3–7.

Democracy Now! 2017. "Full Interview: Naomi Klein on 'No Is Not Enough: Resisting Trump's Shock Politics,'" 13 June. https://www.democracynow.org/2017/6/13/full_interview_naomi_klein_on_no.

Denyer, Simon. 2017. "Activists Investigating Ivanka Trump Brands in China Arrested, Missing." *Washington Post*, 31 May. https://www.washingtonpost.com/world/activists-investigating-ivanka-trump-brands-in-china-arrested-missing/2017/05/30/a6cb90f8-459e-11e7-b08b-1818ab401a7f_story.html?tid=ss_mail&utm_term=.98fa3cde4bf0.

Desai, Manisha. 2009. *Gender and the Politics of Possibilities: Rethinking Globalization*. Lanham, MD: Rowman & Littlefield.

DeStefano, Anthony. 2007. *The War on Human Trafficking: US Policy Assessed*. New Brunswick, NJ: Rutgers University Press.

Dillon, Justin, dir. *Call and Response*. 2008. Oakland, CA: Fair Trade Pictures.

Ditmore, Melissa, and Marjan Wijers. 2003. *Sex, Money, Migration and Crime: The Negotiations on the United Nations Protocol on Trafficking in Persons*. Utrecht, Netherlands: Nemesis.

Doezema, Jo. 2010. *Sex Slaves and Discourse Masters: The Construction of Trafficking*. London: Zed Books.

———. 2005. "Now You See Her, Now You Don't: Sex Workers at the UN Trafficking Protocol Negotiation." *Social and Legal Studies* 14(61): 61–89.

———. 2001. "Ouch! Western Feminists' 'Wounded Attachment' to the 'Third World Prostitute.'" *Feminist Review* 67: 16–38.

———. 2000. "Loose Women or Lost Women? The Re-Emergence of the Myth of White Slavery in Contemporary Discourses of Trafficking of Women." *Gender Issues* 18(1): 23–50.

———. 1998. "Forced to Choose: Beyond the Voluntary vs. Forced Prostitution Dichotomy." In *Global Sex Workers: Rights, Resistance, and Redefinition*, ed. Kamala Kempadoo and Jo Doezema, 34–51. London: Routledge.

"Donald Trump's Cabinet Is Complete. Here's the Full List." 2017. *New York Times*, 11 May. https://www.nytimes.com/interactive/2016/us/politics/donald-trump-administration.html?_r=0.

Donovan, Brian. 2006. *White Slave Crusades: Race, Gender, and Anti-Vice Activism, 1887–1917*. Urbana: University of Illinois Press.

Donovan, Pamela. 2004. *No Way of Knowing: Crime, Urban Legends and the Internet*. New York: Routledge.

Doyle, Jack. 2014. "Amnesty Calls for Legal Prostitution: Charity Says Laws That Ban People Buying or Selling Sex Breach 'Human Rights.'" *Daily Mail*, 23 January. http://www.dailymail.co.uk/news/article-2545003/Amnesty-calls-legal-prostitution-Charity-says-laws-ban-people-buying-selling-sex-breach-human-rights.html.

Doyle, Jennifer. 2015. *Campus Sex, Campus Security*. South Pasadena, CA: Semiotext(e).

Dudink, Stefan P. 2011. "Homosexuality, Race, and the Rhetoric of Nationalism." *History of the Present* 1(2): 259–264.

Duguay, Christian, dir. *Human Trafficking*. 2005. Lifetime Television.

Duggan, Lisa. 2003. *The Twilight of Equality? Neoliberalism, Cultural Politics and the Attack on Democracy*. Boston: Beacon.

Duggan, Lisa, and Nan D. Hunter. 2006. *Sex Wars: Sexual Dissent and Political Culture*. 10th anniversary ed. New York: Routledge.

Earll, Carrie Gordon. 2007. "Women in the Bull's-Eye." *Focus on the Family* (January): 20.

Easley, Jonathan. 2015. "GOP Contenders Embrace Criminal Justice Reform." *The Hill*, 15 July. http://thehill.com/campaign-issues/248069-gop-contenders-embrace-criminal-justice-reform.

Echols, Alice. 1989. *Daring to Be Bad: Radical Feminism in America, 1967–1975*. Minneapolis: University of Minnesota Press.

The Economist. 2009. "Unjust and Ineffective," 6 August. http://www.economist.com/node/14164614.

———. n.d. "The Economist Events: Pride and Prejudice." http://prideandprejudice.economist.com/.

Ehrenreich, Barbara. 2009. *Bright-Sided: How Positive Thinking Is Undermining America*. New York: Picador.

Eilperin, Juliet. 2013. "Anatomy of a Washington Dinner: Who Funds the Competitive Enterprise Institute?" *Washington Post*, 20 June. https://www.washingtonpost.com/news/the-fix/wp/2013/06/20/anatomy-of-a-washington-dinner-who-funds-the-competitive-enterprise-institute/?utm_term=.c907aeeea6f0.

Eisenstein, Hester. 2009. *Feminism Seduced: How Global Elites Use Women's Labor and Ideas to Exploit the World*. Boulder, CO: Paradigm.

Ellerman, Derek. 2004. "My Work: Building a Citizen Movement to Put an End to Human Trafficking." Ashoka.org. https://www.ashoka.org/en/fellow/derek-ellerman.

Empower Foundation. 2012a. *Hit and Run: The Impact of Anti-Human Trafficking Policy and Practice on Sex Workers' Human Rights in Thailand*. Bangkok: Empower University Press.

———. 2012b. *I Came on My Own*. Bangkok: Empower University Press.

———. 2011a. *Bad Girls of Lanna: Our Story of Sex Work in Chiang Mai, Thailand*. Bangkok: Empower University Press.

———. 2011b. *Bad Girls Tales*. Bangkok: Empower University Press.

Eng, David L. 2001. *Racial Castration: Managing Masculinity in Asian America*. Durham, NC: Duke University Press.

Environmental Justice Foundation. 2013. "Sold to the Sea—Human Trafficking in Thailand's Fishing Industry." https://ejfoundation.org/films/sold-to-the-sea.

"EU Anti-Trafficking Mission Launched in Mediterranean." 2015. *Al Jazeera*, 7 October. http://www.aljazeera.com/news/2015/10/eu-anti-trafficking-mission-launched-mediterranean-151007052123233.html.

Fakhoury, Hanni. 2013. "Court to Hear Arguments on Right to Anonymous Speech in Prop. 35 Case," 9 September. https://www.eff.org/deeplinks/2013/09/court-hear-arguments-right-anonymous-speech-today-prop-35-case.

Farris, Sara R. 2017. *In the Name of Women's Rights: The Rise of Femonationalism.* Durham, NC: Duke University Press.

———. 2012. "Femonationalism and the 'Regular' Army of Labor Called Migrant Women." *History of the Present* 2(2): 184–199.

Fassin, Didier. 2011. *Humanitarian Reason: A Moral History of the Present.* Berkeley: University of California Press.

Fassin, Eric. 2017. *Populisme: Le grand ressentiment.* Paris: Textuel.

———. 2011. "From Criticism to Critique." *History of the Present* 1(2): 265–274.

FBI Phoenix. 2016. "Cindy H. McCain Honored by FBI Director for Helping Combat Crime," 15 April. https://www.fbi.gov/contact-us/field-offices/phoenix/news/press-releases/cindy-h.-mccain-honored-by-fbi-director-for-helping-combat-crime/layout_view.

Feeley, Malcolm, and Jonathan Simon. 1992. "The New Penology: Notes on the Emerging Strategy of Corrections and Its Implications." *Criminology* 30(4): 449–474.

Feher, Michel. 2007. "Self-Appreciation, or the Aspirations of Human Capital. *Raisons politiques* 28(4): 11–31.

Feingold, David. 2010. "Trafficking in Numbers: The Social Construction of Human Trafficking Data." In *Sex, Drugs, and Body Counts: The Politics of Numbers in Global Crime and Conflict,* ed. Peter Andraes and Kelly M. Greenhill, 46–75. Ithaca, NY: Cornell University Press.

———. 2005. "Human Trafficking." *Foreign Policy* 150: 26–32.

———. 2003. *Trading Women.* Bangkok: Ophidian Film Institute.

Ferguson, James. 1994. *The Anti-Politics Machine: "Development," Depoliticization, and Bureaucratic Power in Lesotho.* Cambridge: Cambridge University Press.

Ferguson, Michaele L. 2017. "Trump Is a Feminist, and Other Cautionary Tales for Our Neoliberal Age." *Theory & Event* 20(1): 53–67.

Ferguson, Roderick A. 2012. *The Reorder of Things: The University and Its Pedagogies of Minority Difference.* Minneapolis: University of Minnesota Press.

———. 2003. *Aberrations in Black: Toward a Queer of Color Critique.* Minneapolis: University of Minnesota.

Ferguson, Roderick A., and Grace Kyungwon Hong. 2012. "The Sexual and Racial Contradictions of Neoliberalism." *Journal of Homosexuality* 59(7): 1057–1064.

"Films on Human Trafficking." 2013. UN.Gift.Hub: Global Initiative to Fight Human Trafficking. http://www.ungift.org/knowledgehub/media/films.html.

Finnegan, Conor. 2017. "A Timeline of Trump's Battle with the Courts to Keep His Travel Ban Alive." ABC News, 19 October. http://abcnews.go.com/Politics/timeline-trumps-battle-courts-travel-ban-alive/story?id=50559798.

Flock, Elizabeth. 2012. "Kony 2012 Campaign Gets Support of Obama, Others." *Washington Post,* 8 March. https://www.washingtonpost.com/blogs/blogpost/post/kony-2012-campaign-gets-support-of-obama-others/2012/03/08/gIQArnHkzR_blog.html.

Foucault, Michel. 2008. *The Birth of Biopolitics: Lectures at the Collège de France, 1978–1979.* Basingstoke, UK: Palgrave Macmillan.

———. 2005. *The Hermeneutics of the Subject: Lectures at the Collège de France, 1981–1982*. Basingstoke, UK: Palgrave Macmillan.

———. 1979. *Discipline and Punish: The Birth of the Prison*. New York: Vintage Books.

———. 1978. *The History of Sexuality*. New York: Random House.

Frank, Robert. 2008. "The Perils of Philanthrocapitalism." *Wealth Report* (blog), 13 May. http://blogs.wsj.com/wealth/2008/05/13/the-perils-of-philanthro capitalism/.

Frank, Thomas. 2005. *What's the Matter with Kansas? How Conservatives Won the Heart of America*. New York: Holt.

———. 1997. *The Conquest of Cool: Business Culture, Counterculture, and the Rise of Hip Consumerism*. Chicago: University of Chicago Press.

Fraser, Nancy. 2017. "The End of Progressive Neoliberalism." *Dissent*, 2 January. https://www.dissentmagazine.org/online_articles/progressive-neoliberalism -reactionary-populism-nancy-fraser.

———. 2013. *Fortunes of Feminism: From State-Managed Capitalism to Neoliberal Crisis*. London: Verso.

Freedom Network. "Clinton Global Initiative." 2012. *Freedom Network USA*, 26 September. http://freedomnetworkusa.org/tag/clinton-global-initiative/.

Friedman, Milton. 1960. *Capitalism and Freedom*. Chicago: University of Chicago Press.

Fung, Richard. 1991. "Looking for My Penis: The Eroticized Asian in Gay Video Porn." In *How Do I Look? Queer Film and Video*, ed. Bad Object-Choices, 145–168. Seattle: Bay Press.

Gallagher, Anne. 2017. "Could Trump Be an Ally in the Fight Against Human Trafficking?" *Open Democracy*, 4 July. https://www.opendemocracy.net/5050 /anne-t-gallagher/could-trump-be-ally-fight-human-trafficking.

———. 2001. "Trafficking, Smuggling, and Human Rights: Tricks and Treaties." *Forced Migration Review* 12: 25–28.

Gallagher, Anne, and Elaine Pearson. 2010. "The High Cost of Freedom: A Legal and Policy Analysis of Shelter Detention for Victims of Trafficking." *Human Rights Quarterly* 32(1): 73–114.

Ganesan, Sharmilla. 2016. "The Anti-Human Trafficking Crusader." *The Atlantic*, 4 August. http://www.theatlantic.com/business/archive/2016/08/agnes -igoye-human-trafficking/492239/.

Garcia, Feliks. 2017. "Donald Trump Modeling Agency 'Encouraged' Models to Work in US Illegally." *The Independent*, 30 August. http://www.independent .co.uk/news/world/americas/donald-trump-modeling-agency-illegal-work -visas-immigration-a7217246.html.

Garfield, Bob, and Brooke Gladstone. 2012. "What to Make of Kony 2012." *WNYC*, 16 March. http://www.onthemedia.org/story/192713-what-make-kony-2012 /transcript/.

Garland, David. 2001a. *The Culture of Control: Crimes and Social Order in Contemporary Society*. Chicago: University of Chicago Press.

———, ed. 2001b. *Mass Imprisonment: Social Causes and Consequences*. London: Sage.

Gates, Bill, and Barbara Kiviat. 2008. "Making Capitalism More Creative." *Time Magazine*, 31 July. http://content.time.com/time/subscriber/article/0,33009,1828417-3,00.html.

Gauer, Laura. 2005. "Point of View: A Christian Perspective on Poverty and Social Justice: Sin Is More Than Just Flawed Character." *Social Work and Christianity* 32: 354–365.

Gearan, Anne, and Carol Morello. 2017. "Tillerson Stays Close to Trump, but the State Department Seems to Be Benched." *Washington Post*, 19 July. https://www.washingtonpost.com/world/national-security/tillerson-stays-close-to-trump-but-the-state-department-seems-to-be-benched/2017/07/19/90e64b1e-6341-11e7-8adc-fea80e32bf47_story.html?tid=ss_mail&utm_term=.50a9f12f7e11.

"Getting Rights . . . Right: How Companies are Implementing the UN Guiding Principles on Business and Human Rights." 2011. George Washington University, Marvin Center, Washington, DC, 8 December.

Gillogly, Kathleen. 2004. "Developing the Hill Tribes of Northern Thailand." In *Civilizing the Margins: Southeast Asian Government Policies for the Development of Minorities*, ed. Christopher Duncan, 116–149. Ithaca, NY: Cornell University Press.

Ginsburg, Faye D., Lila Abu-Lughod, and Brian Larkin. 2002. *Media Worlds: Anthropology on New Terrain*. Berkeley: University of California Press.

Global Alliance against Traffic in Women (GAATW). 2017. *GAATW e-Bulletin January 2017* (Bangkok), 27 January.

———. 2007. *Collateral Damage: The Impact of Anti-Trafficking Measures on Human Rights around the World*. Bangkok.

Global Centurion. n.d. "Global Centurion Foundation: Fighting Modern Slavery by Focusing on Demand." http://www.globalcenturion.org.

Global Exchange. n.d. "About Us." https://globalexchange.org/about-us/.

Global Exchange and Malia Everette. 2011. "Just Announced: Your Chance to Win a Trip of a Lifetime!" *Global Exchange* (blog), 10 August. https://globalexchange.org/2011/08/10/just-announced-your-chance-to-win-a-trip-of-a-lifetime/.

Global Network of Sex Work Projects (NSWP). 2012. "IAC 2012—Kolkata." http://www.nswp.org/page/iac-2012-kolkata.

Gloege, Timothy E. W. 2015. *Guaranteed Pure: The Moody Bible Institute, Business, and the Making of Modern Evangelicalism*. Chapel Hill: University of North Carolina Press.

Goffman, Erving. 1974. *Frame Analysis: An Essay on the Organization of Experience*. Cambridge, MA: Harvard University Press.

Gold, Matea, Drew Harwell, Maher Satter, and Simone Denyer. 2017. "Ivanka Inc." *Washington Post*, 14 July. https://www.washingtonpost.com/graphics/2017/politics/ivanka-trump-overseas/?utm_term=.ofb73a7ebb5e.

Goldstein, Joshua R., and Catherine T. Kenney. 2001. "Marriage Delayed or Marriage Forgone: New Cohort Forecasts of First Marriage for US Women." *American Sociological Review* 66(4): 506–519.

Gonzalez, Andres. 2012. "Jada Pinkett Smith Urges Action against Human Trafficking, Testifies before Senate." *Huffington Post*, 17 July. http://www.huffing tonpost.com/2012/07/17/jada-pinkett-smith-urges-_n_1680260.html.

Goodmark, Leigh. 2011. *A Troubled Marriage: Domestic Violence and the Legal System.* New York: New York University Press.

Goodstein, Laurie. 2016. "Donald Trump Reveals Evangelical Rifts That Could Shape Politics for Years." *New York Times*, 17 October. https://www.nytimes .com/2016/10/17/us/donald-trump-evangelicals-republican-vote.html ?emc=eta1.

Google. "Fighting Human Trafficking." 2013. *Official Google Blog*, 9 April. http:// googleblog.blogspot.com/2013/04/fighting-human-trafficking.html.

Gordon, Linda. 1982. "Why Nineteenth-Century Feminists Did Not Support Birth Control and Twentieth-Century Feminists Do: Feminism, Reproduction and the Family." In *Rethinking the Family: Some Feminist Questions*, ed. Barrie Thorne and Marilyn Yalom, 140–154. New York: Longman.

Gottschalk, Marie. 2015. *Caught: The Prison State and the Lockdown of American Politics.* Princeton, NJ: Princeton University Press.

———. 2006. *The Prison and the Gallows: The Politics of Mass Incarceration in America.* Cambridge: Cambridge University Press.

Gowan, Teresa. 2013. "Thinking Neoliberalism, Gender, Justice." *Scholar and Feminist Online* 11(1–2): http://sfonline.barnard.edu/gender-justice-and-neo liberal-transformations/thinking-neoliberalism-gender-justice/.

Graham, Mark. 2011. "Perish or Globalize: Network Integration and the Reproduction and Replacement of Weaving Traditions in the Thai Silk Industry." *ACME: An International e-Journal for Critical Geographies* 10(3): 458–482.

Grant, Melissa Gira. 2017. "Ivanka Trump's Trafficking Troubles." *Pacific Standard*, 23 May. https://psmag.com/social-justice/ivanka-trumps-trafficking-troubles.

Greenberg, Andy. 2013. "Startup Palantir Denies Its 'Prism' Software Is the NSA's 'PRISM' Surveillance System." *Forbes*, 6 July. http://www.forbes.com/sites /andygreenberg/2013/06/07/startup-palantir-denies-its-prism-software-is -the-nsas-prism-surveillance-system/.

Grem, Darren. 2016. *The Blessings of Business: How Corporations Shaped Conservative Christianity.* Oxford: Oxford University Press.

Grewal, Inderpal. 2017. *Saving the Security State: Exceptional Citizens in Twenty-First-Century America.* Durham, NC: Duke University Press.

———. 2006. " 'Security Moms' in the Early Twenty-First Century United States: The Gender of Security in Neoliberalism." *Women's Studies Quarterly* 34(1–2): 25–39.

———. 2005. *Transnational America: Feminisms, Diasporas, Neoliberalisms.* Durham, NC: Duke University Press.

Griffith, R. Marie. 1997. *God's Daughters: Evangelical Women and the Power of Submission.* Berkeley: University of California Press.

Griffiths, Claire. 2010. "Behind Closed Doors: Exposing Modern Slavery on a Global Scale: An Interview with Kevin Bales, Professor Emeritus at Roehampton

University, London, and President of Free the Slaves." *Equality, Diversity and Inclusion: An International Journal* 29(7): 716–721.

Grove, Lloyd. 2014. "Who's Telling the Truth about Somaly Mam?" *Daily Beast,* 19 September. http://www.thedailybeast.com/articles/2014/09/19/who-s-telling-the-truth-about-somaly-mam-a-smashed-icon-a-media-brawl-and-a-comeback.html.

Gruber, Aya. 2007. "The Feminist War on Crime." *Iowa Law Review* 92: 741–833.

"Guardian Awards for Digital Innovation: Winners 2012." 2012. *The Guardian,* 23 March. http://www.theguardian.com/megas/winners-2012.

Guevarra, Anna Romina. 2010. *Marketing Dreams, Manufacturing Heroes: The Transnational Labor Brokering of Filipino Workers*. New Brunswick, NJ: Rutgers University Press.

Guynn, Jessica. 2012. "Google Ideas Exploring How Technology Can Address Global Troubles." *Los Angeles Times*, 17 July. http://articles.latimes.com/2012/jul/17/business/la-fi-google-ideas-20120717.

Haag, Pamela. 1999. *Consent: Sexual Rights and the Transformation of American Liberalism*. Ithaca, NY: Cornell University Press.

Haberman, Maggie. 2017. "Furious Gay Rights Advocates See Trump's 'True Colors.'" *New York Times*, 26 July. https://www.nytimes.com/2017/07/26/us/politics/furious-gay-rights-advocates-see-trumps-true-colors.html?emc=eta1.

Halley, Janet. 2008a. "Rape at Rome: Feminist Interventions in the Criminalization of Sex-Related Violence in Positive International Criminal Law." *Michigan Journal of International Law* 30(1): 1–123.

———. 2008b. "Rape in Berlin: Reconsidering the Criminalization of Rape in the International Law of Armed Conflict." *Melbourne Journal of International Law* 9(1): 78–124.

———. 2006. *Split Decisions: How and Why to Take a Break from Feminism*. Princeton, NJ: Princeton University Press.

Ham, Julie. 2011. *What's the Cost of a Rumour? A Guide to Sorting Out the Myths and the Facts about Sporting Events and Trafficking*. Bangkok: Global Alliance against Traffic in Women.

Hamilton, Annette. 1997. "Primal Dream: Masculinism, Sin and Salvation in Thailand's Sex Trade." In *Sites of Desire, Economies of Pleasure: Sexualities in Asia and the Pacific*, ed. Lenore Manderson and Margaret Jolly, 145–165. Chicago: University of Chicago Press.

Hamsher, Jane. 2012. "Bytegeist Exclusive: Rep. Maloney Letter Blasting Google's Larry Page over Android Sex App Marketed to Students." *Bytegeist*, 18 September. http://bytegeist.firedoglake.com/2012/09/18/bytegeist-exclusive-rep-maloney-letter-blasting-googles-larry-page-over-android-sex-app-marketed-to-students/.

Haney, Lynne A. 2010a. *Offending Women: Power, Punishment and the Regulation of Desire*. Oakland: University of California Press.

———. 2010b. "Working through Mass Incarceration: Gender and the Politics of Prison Labor from East to West." *Signs* 36(1): 73–97.

———. 2004. "Introduction: Gender, Welfare, and States of Punishment." *Social Politics* 11(3): 333–362.

Haritaworn, Jinthana K. 2011. "Queer Injuries: The Cultural Politics of 'Hate Crimes' in Germany." *Social Justice* 37(1): 69–91.

Harkinson, Josh. 2013. "Whole Foods CEO Welcomes Climate Change, Warns of Fascism." *Mother Jones*, 18 January. http://www.motherjones.com/environment/2013/01/whole-foods-market-john-mackey-interview-conscious-capitalism.

Harold, Christine. 2009. "On Target: Aura, Affect, and the Rhetoric of 'Design Democracy.'" *Public Culture* 21(3): 599–618.

Harris, Gardiner. 2017. "China Is among Worst Human Trafficking Offenders, State Dept. Says." *New York Times*, 27 June. https://www.nytimes.com/2017/06/27/world/asia/china-human-trafficking.html?emc=eta1.

———. 2013. "Bangladeshi Factory Owners Charged in Fire That Killed 112." *New York Times*, 22 December. http://www.nytimes.com/2013/12/23/world/asia/bangladeshi-factory-owners-charged-in-fatal-fire.html?_r=0.

Harris, Paul. 2012. "Kony 2012 Campaigner Jason Russell Detained for Public Rampage." *The Guardian*, 16 March. http://www.theguardian.com/world/2012/mar/16/kony-2012-campaigner-detained.

Harris, Shane, and John Hudson. 2013. "Not Even the NSA Can Crack the State Dept's Favorite Anonymous Network." *Foreign Policy* (blog), 4 October. https://foreignpolicy.com/2013/10/04/not-even-the-nsa-can-crack-the-state-depts-favorite-anonymous-network/.

Harvey, David. 2016. "Neoliberalism Is a Political Project: David Harvey on What Neoliberalism Actually Is—and Why the Concept Matters." *Jacobin*, 23 July. https://www.jacobinmag.com/2016/07/david-harvey-neoliberalism-capitalism-labor-crisis-resistance/.

———. 2007. *A Brief History of Neoliberalism*. New York: Oxford University Press.

Hassan, Shira. 2013. "Queer Dreams and Nonprofit Blues Conference: Funding the Unpopular." Presentation at Barnard College, New York, 5 October.

Haugen, Gary A. 2008. *Just Courage: God's Great Expedition for the Restless Christian*. Downers Grove, IL: InterVarsity Press.

———. 2005. *Terrify No More: Young Girls Held Captive and the Daring Undercover Operation to Win Their Freedom*. Nashville, TN: W Publishing.

———. 1999. *Good News about Injustice: A Witness of Courage in a Hurting World*. Downers Grove, IL: InterVarsity Press.

Haugen, Gary A., and Victor Boutros. 2015. *The Locust Effect: Why the End of Poverty Requires the End of Violence*. Oxford: Oxford University Press.

Hayhurst, Lyndsay. 2011. "Corporatising Sport, Gender and Development: Postcolonial IR Feminisms, Transnational Private Governance and Global Corporate Social Engagement." *Third World Quarterly* 32(3): 531–549.

Haynes, Dina. 2014. "The Celebration of Human Trafficking." *Annals of the American Academy of Political and Social Science* 653: 25–45.

Hebblethwaite, Cordelia. 2014. "#BBCtrending: #RealMenDontBuyGirls and the #BringBackOurGirls Campaign." *BBC Trending* (blog), 8 May. http://www.bbc .com/news/blogs-trending-27328414.

Heron, Barbara. 2007. *Desire for Development: Whiteness, Gender, and the Helping Imperative.* Waterloo, ON: Wilfrid Laurier University Press.

Hertzke, Allen D. 2004. *Freeing God's Children: The Unlikely Alliance for Global Human Rights.* Lanham, MD: Rowman & Littlefield.

Hesford, Wendy S. 2017. "Enslaved Girlhoods: Gendering Terror, Human Trafficking, and Human Security." Lecture at Watson Institute for International Studies, Brown University, Providence, RI, 7 April.

Higgins-Desbiolles, Freya. 2008. "Justice Tourism and Alternative Globalisation." *Journal of Sustainable Tourism* 16(3): 345–364.

Hirschfeld Davis, Julie. 2017. "Trump Signs Law Taking Aim at Planned Parenthood Funding." *New York Times,* 13 April. https://www.nytimes.com/2017/04/13 /us/politics/planned-parenthood-trump.html?_r=0.

Hirschfeld Davis, Julie, and Kate Kelly. 2017. "Trump Plans to Shift Infrastructure Funding to Cities, States and Business." *New York Times,* 3 June. https://www .nytimes.com/2017/06/03/us/politics/trump-plans-to-shift-infrastructure -funding-to-cities-states-and-business.html.

Ho, Josephine. 2012. "From Anti-Trafficking to Social Discipline; or, The Changing Role of Women's NGOs in Taiwan." In *Trafficking and Prostitution Reconsidered: New Perspectives on Migration, Sex Work, and Human Rights,* 2nd ed., ed. Kamala Kempadoo, 83–105. Boulder, CO: Paradigm.

Hoang, Kimberly Kay. 2015. *Dealing in Desire: Asian Ascendancy, Western Decline, and the Hidden Currencies of Global Sex Work.* Oakland: University of California Press.

———. 2013. "Performing Third World Poverty: Racialized Femininities in Sex Work." In *The Kaleidoscope of Gender: Prisms, Patterns, and Possibilities,* 4th ed., ed. Joan Z. Spade and Catherine G. Valentine, 225–232. New York: Sage Publications.

Hobson, Barbara. 1999. "Women's Collective Agency, Power Resources and the Framing of Citizenship Rights." In *Extending Citizenship, Reconfiguring States,* ed. Michael Hanagan and Charles Tilly, 149–178. Lanham, MD: Rowman and Littlefield.

———. 1990. *Uneasy Virtue: The Politics of Prostitution and the American Reform Tradition.* Chicago: University of Chicago Press.

Hoefinger, Heidi. 2013. *Sex, Love and Money in Cambodia: Professional Girlfriends and Transactional Relationships.* London: Routledge.

Howard, Hilary. 2009. "Doing Good, with Soft Hands." *New York Times,* 30 September. http://www.nytimes.com/2009/10/01/fashion/01Skin-2.html?_r=1&ref =fashion.

"How Good Should Your Business Be?" 2008. *The Economist,* 17 January. http:// www.economist.com/node/10533974.

Hua, Julietta. 2011. *Trafficking Women's Human Rights.* Minneapolis: University of Minnesota Press.

Hudson, Valerie M., and Dara Kay Cohen. 2016. "Women's Rights Are a National Security Issue." *New York Times*, 26 December. https://www.nytimes.com/2016 /12/26/opinion/womens-rights-are-a-national-security-issue.html?action=click &pgtype=Homepage&clickSource=story-heading&module=opinion-c-col -left-region&region=opinion-c-col-left-region&WT.nav=opinion-c-col-left -region&_r=1.

Huguet, Jerrold, and Sureeporn Punpuing. 2005. *International Migration in Thailand*. Bangkok: International Organization for Migration, Regional Office for Asia and the Pacific. https://www.iom.int/asia-and-pacific.

Humanity United. n.d. "Humanity United." https://humanityunited.org.

"A Human Rights Report on Trafficking in Persons, Especially Women and Children: Egypt." 2010. *Protection Project*. http://www.protectionproject.org/wp -content/uploads/2010/09/Egypt.pdf.

Human Rights Watch. 2014. *World Report: 2014*. https://www.hrw.org/sites/default /files/wr2014_web_0.pdf.

HumanTrafficking.org. 2013. *HumanTrafficking.org: A Web Resource for Combating Human Trafficking in the East Asia Pacific Region*. http://domainsdata.org /images/humantrafficking.org.jpg.

Illich, Ivan. 1968. "To Hell with Good Intentions." Address to the Conference on InterAmerican Student Projects, Cuernavaca, Mexico, 20 April. http://www .swaraj.org/illich_hell.htm.

Illouz, Eva. 2007. *Cold Intimacies: The Making of Emotional Capitalism*. Cambridge, UK: Polity Press.

———. 1997. *Consuming the Romantic Utopia: Love and the Cultural Contradictions of Capitalism*. Berkeley: University of California Press.

INCITE! Women of Color against Violence, ed. 2007. *The Revolution Will Not Be Funded: Beyond the Non-Profit Industrial Complex*. Cambridge, UK: South End.

Iniko Newton, Arielle. 2017. "What I Learned from #MeToo." *Colorlines*, 19 October. https://www.colorlines.com/articles/what-i-learned-metoo-stop-instant -harsh-critiquing-opinion.

Intermodal. 2016. *YWEP Still Works*. https://soundcloud.com/intermodal-1/ywep -wasnt-she-as-501c3.

International Justice Mission. 2010. *Project Lantern Results Summary*. https://www .ijm.org/sites/all/modules/paragonn/pagemod/files/project-lantern/Project -Lantern-Results-Summary.pdf?v=1.1.

International Labor Rights Forum, Worker Rights Consortium, Clean Clothes Campaign, and Maquila Solidarity Network. 2016. "Dangerous Delays on Worker Safety Walmart, Gap, VF, Target & Hudson's Bay Have Failed to Address Deadly Hazards in Many Factories, but Bangladesh Alliance Downplays the Problem with Rosy Status Reports." http://www.laborrights.org/sites /default/files/publications/Dangerous_Delays_Nov2016.pdf.

Invisible Children. 2014. "Kony 2012." https://invisiblechildren.com/kony-2012/.

———. n.d. "FAQ: Questions about Invisible Children." Invisible Children. https:// invisiblechildren.com.

Irvine, Janice. 2008. "Transient Feelings: Sex Panics and the Politics of Emotions." *GLQ: A Journal of Lesbian and Gay Studies* 14(1): 1–40.

Isherwood, Charles. 2015. "Review: 'Amazing Grace,' the Story of a Slave Trader's Moral Awakening." *New York Times*, 16 July. http://www.nytimes.com/2015/07/17/theater/review-amazing-grace-the-story-of-a-slave-traders-moral-awakening.html.

Jackman, Tom, and Jonathan O'Connell. 2017. "Backpage Has Always Claimed It Doesn't Control Sex-Related Ads: New Documents Show Otherwise." *Washington Post*, 11 July. https://www.washingtonpost.com/local/public-safety/backpage-has-always-claimed-it-doesnt-control-sex-related-ads-new-documents-show-otherwise/2017/07/10/b3158ef6-553c-11e7-b38e-35fd8e0c288f_story.html?tid=ss_mail&utm_term=.e66c691f9921.

Jackson, Brooks. 2013. "Obama's Numbers (Quarterly Update)," 16 April. http://www.factcheck.org/2013/04/obamas-numbers-quarterly-update/.

Jackson, Peter A. 1989. *Male Homosexuality in Thailand: An Interpretation of Contemporary Thai Sources*. London: Global Academic.

Jackson, Peter A., and Gerard Sullivan. 1999. *Lady Boys, Tom Boys, Rent Boys: Male and Female Homosexualities in Contemporary Thailand*. London: Routledge.

Jacobellis v. Ohio. 1964. 378 U.S. 184.

Jacobsen, Christine M., and May-Len Skilbrei. 2010. "'Reproachable Victims'? Representations and Self-Representations of Russian Women Involved in Transnational Prostitution." *Ethnos* 75(2): 190–212.

Jacques, Martin. 2016. "The Death of Neoliberalism and the Crisis in Western Politics." *The Guardian*, 21 August. https://www.theguardian.com/commentisfree/2016/aug/21/death-of-neoliberalism-crisis-in-western-politics?CMP=share_btn_link.

Jaffe, Sarah. 2013. "Occupy Wall Street Was Humbling to Many of Us." *Sociological Quarterly* 54(2): 198–202.

Jaffee, Daniel. 2007. *Brewing Justice: Fair Trade Coffee, Sustainability, and Survival*. Berkeley: University of California Press.

Jagori. 2012. "Migration, Trafficking, and Sites of Work." In *Trafficking and Prostitution Reconsidered: New Perspectives on Migration, Sex Work, and Human Rights*, 2nd ed., ed. Kamala Kempadoo, 159–175. Boulder, CO: Paradigm.

Jakobsen, Janet. 2008. "Gender, Culture, and Politics." Plenary session at the annual meeting of the Cultural Studies Association, New York University, 22 May.

Jakobsen, Janet, and Ann Pellegrini. 2009. "Obama's Neo-New Deal." *Social Research* 76(4): 1227–1254.

———. 2004. *Love the Sin: Sexual Regulation and the Limits of Religious Tolerance*. New York: New York University Press.

Janney, Rebecca Price. 2006. "Daughters in Darkness." *Today's Christian Woman* (November–December): 58.

Jeffrey, Leslie Ann. 2002. *Sex and Borders: Gender, National Identity, and Prostitution Policy in Thailand*. Honolulu: University of Hawai'i Press.

Jewell, Dawn Herzog. 2007. "Red-Light Rescue: The Business of Helping the Sexually Exploited Help Themselves." *Christianity Today* (January): 28–37.

Johnson, Jessica. 2017. "Under Conviction: 'Real Men' Reborn on Spiritual and Cinematic Battlefields." *Feminist Studies* 43(1): 42–67.

Jones, Maggie. "Thailand's Brothel Busters." *Mother Jones*. http://www.mother jones.com/politics/2003/11/thailands-brothel-busters/.

Jordan, Ann. 2011. "Fact or Fiction: What Do We Really Know about Human Trafficking?" Issue Paper No. 3. Washington, DC: Program on Human Trafficking and Forced Labor, and Center for Human Rights and Humanitarian Law.

———. 2002. *Annotated Guide to The Complete UN Trafficking Protocol*. Washington, DC: Initiative against Trafficking in Persons.

Jordan-Young, Rebecca, Lucy Trainor, and Janet Jakobsen. 2010. *New Feminist Solutions: Reproductive Justice in Action*. Vol. 6. New York: Barnard Center for Research on Women.

Joseph, Miranda. 2002. *Against the Romance of Community*. Minneapolis: University of Minnesota.

Joshua Project. 2017. "10/40 Window." https://joshuaproject.net/resources/arti cles/10_40_window.

Kagumire, Rosebell. 2012. "Kony 2012: My Response to Invisible Children's Campaign." *Rosebell's Blog* (blog), 8 March. http://rosebellkagumire.com/2012 /03/08/kony2012-my-response-to-invisible-childrens-campaign/.

Kamat, Anjali, and Fred Kaplan. 2016. "'We Are Nothing but Machines to Them.'" *Slate*, 15 December. http://www.slate.com/articles/business/the_grind/2016/12 /bangladesh_s_apparel_factories_still_have_appalling_worker_conditions .html.

Kammerer, Cornelia Ann. 1989. "Territorial Imperatives: Akha Ethnic Identity and Thailand's National Integration." In *Hill Tribes Today: Problems in Change*, ed. John McKinnon and Bernard Vienne, 259–230. Bangkok: White Lotus.

Kang, Cecilia. 2017. "In Reversal, Tech Companies Back Sex Trafficking Bill." *New York Times*, 3 November. https://www.nytimes.com/2017/11/03/technology /sex-trafficking-bill.html?emc=edit_tnt_20171104&nlid=10901466&tntema il0=y&_r=0.

Kapoor, Ilan. 2013. *Celebrity Humanitarianism: The Ideology of Global Charity*. New York: Routledge.

Kapur, Ratna. 2005. *Erotic Justice: Law and the New Politics of Postcolonialism*. London: Glass House Press.

Kara, Siddharth. 2012. *Bonded Labor: Tackling the System of Slavery in South Asia*. New York: Columbia University Press.

———. 2009. *Sex Trafficking: Inside the Business of Modern Slavery*. New York: Columbia University Press.

Karim, Lamia. 2011. *Microfinance and Its Discontents: Women in Debt in Bangladesh*. Minneapolis: University of Minnesota Press.

Kavner, Lucas. 2011. "Ashton Kutcher and Demi Moore Launch 'Real Men Don't Buy Girls' Campaign." *Huffington Post*, 11 April. http://www.huffington post.com/2011/04/11/ashton-kutcher-demi-moore-trafficking_n_847291 .html.

Kaye, Kerwin. Forthcoming. "The Gender of Trafficking; or, Why Can't Men Be Sex Slaves?" In *Not Just in the Alleys: New Perspectives on Sex Work*, ed. May Len Skilbrei and Marlene Spanger. London: Routledge.

———. 2007. "Anti-Trafficking Discourses and National Identity in the United States: A Historical Perspective." Conference presentation at Chinese University of Hong Kong, Hong Kong, 10 July.

Kazmin, Amy. 2004. "Deliver Them from Evil." *Financial Times*, 10 July. http://www.ft.com/cms/s/0/b135415a-d20d-11d8-85fc-00000e2511c8.html?ft_site =falcon&desktop=true#axzz4JysXGT4q.

Keating, Joshua. 2012. "Guest Post: Joseph Kony Is Not in Uganda (and Other Complicated Things)." *Foreign Policy*, 7 March. http://foreignpolicy.com /2012/03/07/guest-post-joseph-kony-is-not-in-uganda-and-other-com plicated-things/?wp_login_redirect=0.

Keller, Bill. 2015. "Prison Revolt." *New Yorker*, 29 June. http://www.newyorker .com/magazine/2015/06/29/prison-revolt.

Kelly, Annie. 2015. "US Human Trafficking Report under Fire as Cuba and Malaysia Are Upgraded." *The Guardian*, 27 July. http://www.theguardian.com/global -development/2015/jul/27/us-human-trafficking-in-persons-report-under -fire-cuba-malaysia-upgraded.

Kempadoo, Kamala. 2015. "The Modern-Day White (Wo)man's Burden: Trends in Anti-Trafficking and Anti-Slavery Campaigns." *Journal of Human Trafficking* 1(1): 8–20.

———, ed. 2012a. *Trafficking and Prostitution Reconsidered: New Perspectives on Migration, Sex Work, and Human Rights*. 2nd ed. Boulder, CO: Paradigm.

———. 2012b. "The Anti-Trafficking Juggernaut Rolls On." In *Trafficking and Prostitution Reconsidered: New Perspectives on Migration, Sex Work, and Human Rights*, 2nd ed., ed. Kamala Kempadoo, 249–261. Boulder, CO: Paradigm.

———. 2005. "Victims and Agents of Crime: The New Crusade Against Trafficking." In *Global Lockdown: Race, Gender, and the Prison-Industrial Complex*, ed. Julia Sudbury, 35–55. London: Routledge.

———. 1999. *Sun, Sex, and Gold: Tourism and Sex Work in the Caribbean*. Lanham, MD: Rowman & Littlefield.

Kempadoo, Kamala, and Jo Doezema, eds. 1998. *Global Sex Workers: Rights, Resistance, and Redefinition*. New York: Routledge.

King, Samantha. 2006. *Pink Ribbons, Inc.: Breast Cancer and the Politics of Philanthropy*. Minneapolis: University of Minnesota Press.

Kintz, Linda. 1997. *Between Jesus and the Market: The Emotions That Matter in Right-Wing America*. Durham, NC: Duke University Press.

Klawiter, Maren. 2008. *The Biopolitics of Breast Cancer: Changing Cultures of Disease and Activism*. Minneapolis: University of Minnesota Press.

Klein, Betsy. 2017. "Ashton Kutcher Passionately Testifies on His Anti-Sex Trafficking Efforts." *CNN*, 15 February. http://www.cnn.com/2017/02/15 /politics/ashton-kutcher-testifies-before-the-senate-on-sex-trafficking/index .html.

Klein, Naomi. 2008. *The Shock Doctrine: The Rise of Disaster Capitalism*. New York: Picador.

———. 2000. *No Logo: Taking Aim at the Brand Bullies*. New York: Picador.

Kondracki, Larysa, dir. 2010. *The Whistleblower*. New York: Samuel Goldwyn Films.

Kontogeorgopoulos, Nick. 1999. "Sustainable Tourism or Sustainable Development? Financial Crisis, Ecotourism, and the 'Amazing Thailand' Campaign." *Current Issues in Tourism* 2(4): 316–332.

Kotiswaran, Prabha. 2011. *Dangerous Sex, Invisible Labor: Sex Work and the Law in India*. Princeton, NJ: Princeton University Press.

KPFA. 2016. "Trump and the End of Neoliberalism?" *Against the Grain*. Podcast.

Krieg, Gregory. 2016. "Occupy Wall Street Rises Up for Sanders." *CNN*, 13 April. http://www.cnn.com/2016/04/13/politics/occupy-wall-street-bernie -sanders-new-york-primary/.

Kristof, Nicholas. 2014. "When Sources May Have Lied." *New York Times*, 7 June. http:// kristof.blogs.nytimes.com/2014/06/07/when-sources-may-have-lied/?_r=0.

———. 2009. "Where Sweatshops Are a Dream." *New York Times*, 14 January. http://www.nytimes.com/2009/01/15/opinion/15kristof.html?_r=0.

———. 2004a. "Bargaining for Freedom." *New York Times*, 21 January. http://www .nytimes.com/2004/01/21/opinion/bargaining-for-freedom.html.

———. 2004b. "Girls for Sale." *New York Times*, 17 January. http://www.nytimes .com/2004/01/17/opinion/girls-for-sale.html.

———. 2004c. "Inviting All Democrats." *New York Times*, 14 January. http://www .nytimes.com/2004/01/14/opinion/14KRIS.html.

———. 2004d. "Stopping the Traffickers." *New York Times*, 31 January. http://www .nytimes.com/2004/01/31/opinion/stopping-the-traffickers.html?_r=0.

Kristof, Nicholas D., and Sheryl WuDunn. 2010. *Half the Sky: Turning Oppression into Opportunity for Women Worldwide*. New York: Vintage Books.

Krupat, Kitty. 1997. "From War Zone to Free Trade Zone." In *No Sweat: Fashion, Free Trade, and the Rights of Garment Workers*, ed. Andrew Ross, 51–78. New York: Verso.

Kulick, Don. 2003. "Sex in the New Europe: the Criminalization of Clients and the Swedish Fear of Penetration." *Anthropological Theory* 3(2): 199–218.

Lacher, R. Geoffrey, and Sanjay K. Nepal. 2010. "From Leakages to Linkages: Local-Level Strategies for Capturing Tourism Revenue in Northern Thailand." *Tourism Geographies* 12(1): 77–99.

Lamas, Marta. 2014. "¿Prostitución, trabajo o trata? Por un debate sin prejuicios." *Debate feminista* 25(50): 160–186.

Lancaster, Roger. 2011. *Sex Panic and the Punitive State*. Berkeley: University of California Press.

Landesman, Peter. 2004. "The Girls Next Door." *New York Times Magazine*, 25 January. http://www.nytimes.com/2004/01/25/magazine/the-girls-next-door .html?pagewantedp1.

Lane, Frederick S. 2000. *Obscene Profits: The Entrepreneurs of Pornography in the Cyber Age*. New York: Routledge.

Langum, David J. 1994. *Crossing over the Line: Legislating Morality and the Mann Act.* Chicago: University of Chicago Press.

Law, Victoria. 2014. "Against Carceral Feminism: Relying on State Violence to Curb Domestic Violence Only Ends Up Harming the Most Marginalized Women." *Jacobin,* 17 October. https://www.jacobinmag.com/2014/10/against-carceral-feminism/.

Lederer, Laura, ed. 1980. *Take Back the Night: Women on Pornography.* New York: William Morrow.

Lee, Maggie. 2014. "Gendered Discipline and Protective Custody of Trafficking Victims in Asia." *Punishment and Society* 16(2): 206–222.

Lee, Timothy B. 2013. "Everything You Need to Know about the NSA and Tor in One FAQ." *Washington Post,* 4 October. http://www.washingtonpost.com/blogs/the-switch/wp/2013/10/04/everything-you-need-to-know-about-the-nsa-and-tor-in-one-faq/.

Lee, Trymaine. 2016. "Black Lives Matter Releases Policy Agenda." *NBC News,* 1 August. http://www.nbcnews.com/news/us-news/black-lives-matter-releases-policy-agenda-n620966.

Leon, Chrysanthi S., and Corey S. Shdaimah. 2012. "JUStifying Scrutiny: State Power in Prostitution Diversion Programs." *Journal of Poverty* 16(3): 250–273.

Leonard, Andrew. 2013. "2013: The Year We Stopped Trusting Technology." *Salon,* 20 December. http://www.salon.com/2013/12/20/2013_the_year_we_stopped_trusting_technology/.

Leopold, Jason. 2014. "Exclusive: Emails Reveal Close Google Relationship with NSA." *Al Jazeera America,* 6 May. http://america.aljazeera.com/articles/2014/5/6/nsa-chief-google.html.

Lerum, Kari. 2017. "Slaves, Supermen & Serpents: How Masculinist Tropes Fuel Carceral Anti-Trafficking Policies." Unpublished manuscript.

Levine, Judith. 2017. "Will Feminism's Past Mistakes Haunt #MeToo?" *Boston Review.* 8 December. http://bostonreview.net/gender-sexuality/judith-levine-will-feminisms-past-mistakes-haunt-metoo.

L'Etang, Jacquie. 2006. "Corporate Responsibility and Public Relations Ethics." In *Public Relations: Critical Debates and Contemporary Practice,* ed. Jacquie L'Etang and Magda Pieczka, 405–421. Mahwah, NJ: Lawrence Erlbaum Associates.

Levitin, Michael. 2015. "The Triumph of Occupy Wall Street." *The Atlantic,* 10 June. http://www.theatlantic.com/politics/archive/2015/06/the-triumph-of-occupy-wall-street/395408/.

Lewis, David, and David Mosse, eds. 2006. *Development Brokers and Translators: The Ethnography of Aid and Agencies.* Bloomfield, CT: Kumarian.

Leyva, René. 2015. "Aspectos de salud pública en el trabajo sexual: Estudio de caso de la frontera sur." Presentation at the forum Sexo, poder y dinero: Perspectivas críticas sobre "la trata de mujeres," Universidad Nacional Autónoma de México, Mexico City, 19 May. https://www.youtube.com/watch?v=5OJF19LYjtY&feature=youtu.be.

L'Heureux, Catie. 2017. "Read Janet Mock's Empowering Speech on Trans Women of Color and Sex Workers." *The Cut*, 21 January. https://www.thecut.com/2017/01/read-janet-mocks-speech-at-the-womens-march-on-washington-trans-women-of-color-sex-workers.html?utm_source=eml&utm_medium=e1&utm_campaign=sharebutton-t.

Limoncelli, Stephanie. 2010. *The Politics of Trafficking: The First International Movement to Combat the Sexual Exploitation of Women*. Stanford, CA: Stanford University Press.

Lindquist, Johan. 2009. *The Anxieties of Mobility: Migration and Tourism in the Indonesian Borderlands*. Honolulu: University of Hawai'i Press.

Lindsay, Michael. 2007. *Faith in the Halls of Power: How Evangelicals Joined the American Elite*. Oxford: Oxford University Press.

Linke, Uli. 2012. "Mobile Imaginaries, Portable Signs: Global Consumption and Representations of Slum Life." *Tourism Geographies* 14(2): 294–319.

Lopez, Kathryn Jean. 2006. "The New Abolitionist Movement: Interview with Donna Hughes." *National Review Online*, 26 January. http://www.nationalreview.com/interrogatory/hughes200601260824.asp.

Luker, Kristin. 2006. *When Sex Goes to School: Warring Views on Sex—and Sex Education—Since the Sixties*. New York: Norton.

———. 1998. "Sex, Social Hygiene, and the State: The Double-Edged Sword of Social Reform." *Theory and Society* 27: 601–634.

———. 1984. *Abortion and the Politics of Motherhood*. Berkeley: University of California Press.

Lury, Celia. 2004. *Brands: The Logos of the Global Economy*. London: Routledge.

Lyon, Sarah, and Mark Moberg. 2010. *Fair Trade and Social Justice: Global Ethnographies*. New York: New York University Press.

MacCannell, Dean. 1973. "Staged Authenticity: Arrangements of Social Space in Tourist Settings." *American Journal of Sociology* 79: 589–603.

Macgregor Wise, J. 2005. "Assemblage." In *Gilles Deleuze: Key Concepts*, ed. Charles J. Stivale, 91–102. New York: Acumen.

Mackenzie, Adrian. 2013. "Programming Subjects in the Regime of Anticipation: Software Studies and Subjectivity." *Subjectivity* 6(4): 391–405.

Mackey, Robert. 2012. "African Critics of Kony Campaign See a 'White Man's Burden' for the Facebook Generation." *New York Times*, 9 March. http://thelede.blogs.nytimes.com/2012/03/09/african-critics-of-kony-campaign-hear-echoes-of-the-white-mans-burden/?_r=0.

MacKinnon, Catharine. A. 1989. *Toward a Feminist Theory of the State*. Boston: Harvard University Press.

Madriz, Esther. 1997. *Nothing Bad Happens to Good Girls: Fear of Crime in Women's Lives*. Berkeley: University of California Press.

Maharawal, Manissa M. 2016. "Occupy Movements." In *The Wiley Blackwell Encyclopedia of Gender and Sexuality Studies*, ed. Nancy A. Naples, 1–5. Hoboken, NJ: John Wiley & Sons.

Mahdavi, Pardis. 2014. *From Trafficking to Terror: Constructing a Global Social Problem*. London: Routledge.

———. 2011. *Gridlock: Labor, Migration, and Human Trafficking in Dubai*. Palo Alto, CA: Stanford University Press.

Maher, Lisa, Thomas Crewe Dixon, Pisith Phlong, Julie Mooney-Somers, Ellen S. Stein, and Kimberly Page. 2015. "Conflicting Rights: How the Prohibition of Human Trafficking and Sexual Exploitation Infringes the Right to Health of Female Sex Workers in Phnom Penh, Cambodia." *Health and Human Rights* 17(1): 2–16.

Mahmood, Saba. 2005. *Politics of Piety: The Islamic Revival and the Feminist Subject*. Princeton, NJ: Princeton University Press.

Mai, Nick. 2012. "The Fractal Queerness of Non-Heteronormative Migrants Working in the UK Sex Industry." *Sexualities* 15(5–6): 570–585.

Malm, Sara. 2015. "Human Traffickers Are Preying on Refugees across Europe and Forcing Them into Slave Labour or Child Prostitution, Warn Europol." *Daily Mail*, 2 November. http://www.dailymail.co.uk/news/article-3300016 /Human-traffickers-preying-refugees-Europe-forcing-slave-labour-child -prostitution-warn-Europol.html.

Maloney, Devon. 2017. "Some Inconvenient Truths about the Women's March on Washington." *Daily Good*, 22 January. https://www.good.is/articles/seeking -solidarity-at-the-womens-march-in-washington.

Mam, Somaly. 2007. *The Road of Lost Innocence: The True Story of a Cambodian Childhood*. London: Virago.

Manderson, Lenore, and Margaret Jolly, eds. 1997. *Sites of Desire, Economies of Pleasure: Sexualities in Asia and the Pacific*. Chicago: University of Chicago Press.

ManpowerGroup. 2017. "Recruitment Process Outsourcing." http://www.man powergroupsolutions.com/solutions/recruitment-process-outsourcing.

———. 2016. "ManpowerGroup—Company History." http://www.right.com/wps /wcm/connect/manpowergroup-en/home/about/history#.WfUB1IZrx0I.

———. 2013a. "Align Flexible Workforce Models to Thrive ManpowerGroup Says Manpower US Pressroom." *Manpower US Pressroom*, 6 September. http:// press.manpower.com/press/2013/align-flexible-workforce-models-with -business-strategy-to-thrive-in-economic-uncertainty-manpowergroup-says -as-unemployment-rate-falls-to-7-3/.

———. 2013b. "ManpowerGroup Reveals Why Leading in the Human Age Requires New Approaches to the World of Work at World Economic Forum." *PR Newswire*, 22 January. http://www.prnewswire.com/news-releases/manpowergroup -reveals-why-leading-in-the-human-age-requires-new-approaches-to-the-world -of-work-at-world-economic-forum-187850521.html.

———. 2011. *Corporate Social Responsibility Update: Teaching a Man to Fish Is Humanly Possible*. Milwaukee, WI: ManpowerGroup. http://www.manpower.us /Website-File-Pile/Articles/Corporate-Social-Responsibility-Update.pdf.

Marcos, Angie. 2016. "CSUF Expert Explains Why the Black Lives Matter Is Different from Past Black Civil Rights Movements." *Orange County Register*, 21 June. http://www.ocregister.com/articles/black-720133-lives-matter.html.

Marcus, Anthony, Robert Riggs, Amber Horning, Sarah Rivera, Ric Curtis, and Efram Thompson. 2011. "Is Child to Adult as Victim Is to Criminal? Social Policy and Street-Based Sex Work in the United States." *Sexuality Research and Social Policy* 9: 153–166.

Marcus, George E., and Michael Fischer. 1986. *Anthropology as Cultural Critique: An Experimental Moment in the Human Sciences*. Chicago: University of Chicago Press.

Markon, Jerry. 2007. "Human Trafficking Evokes Outrage, Little Evidence." *Washington Post*, 23 September. http://www.washingtonpost.com/wp-dyn/content /article/2007/09/22/AR2007092201401.html.

Marks, Simon. 2013. "The Rise of the Somaly Mam Foundation." *Cambodia Daily*, 13 October. https://www.cambodiadaily.com/archives/the-rise-of-the-somaly -mam-foundation-44976/.

———. 2012a. "Former Afesip Director Denies Claim of Killings." *Cambodia Daily*, 23 April. https://www.cambodiadaily.com/archives/former-afesip-director -denies-claim-of-killings-3648/.

———. 2012b. "Somaly Mam Admits to Inaccuracies in Speech to UN." *Cambodia Daily*, 26 April. https://www.cambodiadaily.com/archives/somaly-mam -admits-to-inaccuracies-in-speech-to-un-1590/.

Marks, Simon, and Khy Sovuthy. 2012. "Questions Raised Over Symbol's Slavery Story." *Cambodia Daily*, 26 October. http://www.cambodiadaily.com/archive /questions-raised-over-symbols-slavery-story-4809/.

Marks, Simon, and Kuch Naren. 2013. "Once Coached for TV, Now Asked to Keep Quiet." *Cambodia Daily*, 4 November. https://www.cambodiadaily.com /archives/once-coached-for-tv-now-asked-to-keep-quiet-46510/.

Marks, Simon, and Phorn Bopha. 2013. "Sex Slave Story Revealed to Be Fabricated." *Cambodia Daily*, 12 October. https://www.cambodiadaily.com/archives/secrets -and-lies-44964/.

———. 2012. "More Questions over Somaly Mam's Kidnapping Claim." *Cambodia Daily*, 25 April. https://www.cambodiadaily.com/archives/more-questions -over-somaly-mams-kidnapping-claim-1592/.

Marks, Simon, and Saing Soenthrith. 2012. "Police Deny Killings at Somaly Mam Center." *Cambodia Daily*, 21 April. https://www.cambodiadaily.com/archives /police-deny-killings-at-somaly-mam-center-3652/.

Martin, Steven P. 2006. "Trends in Marital Dissolution by Women's Education in the United States." *Demographic Research* 15–20: 537–560.

Marx, Karl. 1976. *Capital: A Critique of Political Economy, Vol. 1*. London: Penguin Books, 1990.

Maskovsky, Jeff, and Ida Susser, eds. 2009. *Rethinking America: The Imperial Homeland in the 21st Century*. Boulder, CO: Paradigm.

MasterCard. 2015. *Global Destinations City Index: 2015*. https://newsroom.mastercard .com/wp-content/uploads/2015/06/MasterCard-GDCI-2015-Final-Report1.pdf.

Mathers, Kathryn. 2010. *Travel, Humanitarianism, and Becoming American in Africa.* New York: Palgrave Macmillan.

May, Meredith. 2006. "Sex Trafficking: San Francisco Is a Major Center for International Crime Networks That Smuggle and Enslave." *San Francisco Examiner*, 6 October. http://articles.sfgate.com/2006-10-06/news/17316911_1_traf ficking-victims-human-trafficking-new-owners.

McAlister, Melani. 2014. "US Evangelicals and the Politics of Slave Redemption as Religious Freedom in Sudan." *South Atlantic Quarterly* 113(1): 87–108.

———. 2008a. "The Politics of Persecution." *Middle East Report* 249: 18–27.

———. 2008b. "What Is Your Heart For? Affect and Internationalism in the Evangelical Public Sphere." *American Literary History* 20(4): 870–895.

McCain Institute for International Leadership at Arizona State University. 2017. "Human Trafficking." https://www.mccaininstitute.org/human-trafficking -mission/.

McCarthy, Lauren A. 2016. "Transaction Costs: Prosecuting Child Trafficking for Illegal Adoption in Russia." *Anti-Trafficking Review* 6: 31–47.

McChesney, Robert Waterman. 2013. *Digital Disconnect: How Capitalism Is Turning the Internet against Democracy.* New York: New Press.

McCreesh, Shawn. 2016. "'March for Bernie' Is an Occupy Wall Street Homecoming." *Rolling Stone*, 31 January. http://www.rollingstone.com/politics/news /march-for-bernie-is-an-occupy-wall-street-homecoming-20160131.

McDonald, Seonaidh. 2005. "Studying Actions in Context: A Qualitative Shadowing Method for Organizational Research." *Qualitative Research* 5(4): 455–473.

McDonald, William. 2004. "Traffic Counts, Symbols, and Agendas: A Critique of the Campaign against Trafficking of Human Beings." *International Review of Victimology* 11(1): 143–176.

McGehee, Nancy Gard, and Carla Almeida Santos. 2005. "Social Change, Discourse and Volunteer Tourism." *Annals of Tourism Research* 32(3): 760–779.

McKeown, Adam. 2012. "How the Box Became Black: Brokers and the Creation of the Free Migrant." *Pacific Affairs* 85(1): 21–45.

McKinnon, Katharine. 2005. "(Im)mobilization and Hegemony: 'Hill Tribe' Subjects and the 'Thai' State." *Social & Cultural Geography* 6(1): 31–46.

McLaren, Brian. 2016. *The Great Spiritual Migration: How the World's Largest Religion Is Seeking a Better Way to Be Christian.* New York: Convergent Books.

———. 2007. *Everything Must Change: Jesus, Global Crisis, and a Revolution of Hope.* Nashville, TN: Thomas Nelson.

Megaton, Olivier, dir. 2012. *Taken 2.* EuropaCorp.

———, dir. 2014. *Taken 3.* EuropaCorp.

Melamed, Jodi. 2011. "Reading Tehran in Lolita: Seizing Literary Value for Neoliberal Multiculturalism." In *Strange Affinities: The Gender and Sexual Politics of Comparative Racialization*, ed. Grace Kyungwon Hong and Roderick A. Ferguson, 76–112. Durham, NC: Duke University Press.

Merry, Sally Engle. 2006. *Human Rights and Gender Violence: Translating International Law into Local Justice.* Chicago: University of Chicago Press.

Meyer, Walter. 1988. *Beyond the Mask: Toward a Transdisciplinary Approach of Selected Social Problems Related to the Evolution and Context of International Tourism in Thailand.* Saarbrücken, Germany: Verlag Breitenbach Publishers.

Mgbako, Chi Adanna. 2016. Introduction to panel discussion "Which Policies Best Respect Sex Workers' Rights? A Conversation with Sex Worker Rights Defenders." 60th session of the Commission on the Status of Women. 18 March. New York.

Milkman, Ruth, Penny Lewis, and Stephanie Luce. 2013a. *Changing the Subject: A Bottom-Up Account of Occupy Wall Street in New York City.* New York: CUNY, Joseph S. Murphy Institute for Worker Education and Labor Studies.

———. 2013b. "The Genie's out of the Bottle: Insiders' Perspectives on Occupy Wall Street." *Sociological Quarterly* 54(2): 194–198.

Miller, Alice. 2004. "Sexuality, Violence against Women, and Human Rights: Women Make Demands and Ladies Get Protection." *Health and Human Rights* 7(2): 16–48.

Miller, John. 2006. "A Statement from Ambassador John R. Miller." *HumanTrafficking.org*, 15 December. http://www.humantrafficking.org/updates/524.

Mink, Gwendolyn. 2001. "Faith in Government?" *Social Justice* 28(1): 5–10.

Mirror Foundation. 2014. "Why Do We Help?" 20 August. http://www.themir rorfoundation.org/themirrorfoundation/index.php/21-current-projects /project-to-combat-trafficking-in-women-and-children/10-working-structure.

Mis, Magdalena. 2015. "European Banks Join Drive to Combat Human Trafficking Using Data." *Reuters*, 9 June. https://www.reuters.com/article/europe-crime -trafficking/european-banks-join-drive-to-combat-human-trafficking-using -data-idUSL5N0YR1T620150609.

Moe, David Thang. 2014. "What Has Dietrich Bonhoeffer to Do with Asian Theology?" *Asia Journal of Theology* 28(2): 175–202.

Mohanty, Chandra Talpade. 2003. *Feminism without Borders: Decolonizing Theory, Practicing Solidarity.* Durham, NC: Duke University Press.

———. 1991. "Under Western Eyes: Feminist Scholarship and Colonial Discourse." In *Third World Women and the Politics of Feminism*, ed. Chandra Talpade Mohanty and Ann Russo, 51–80. Bloomington: Indiana University Press.

Mol, Annemarie. 2006. *The Logic of Care: Health and the Problem of Patient Choice.* London: Routledge.

Molina-Guzmán, Isabel. 2012. "Salma Hayek's Celebrity Activism: Constructing Race, Ethnicity, and Gender as Global Mainstream Commodities." In *Commodity Activism: Cultural Resistance in Neoliberal Times*, ed. Roopali Mukherjee and Sarah Banet-Weiser, 134–153. New York: New York University Press.

Molland, Sverre. 2013. "Tandem Ethnography: On Researching 'Trafficking' and 'Anti-Trafficking.'" *Ethnography* 14(3): 300–323.

———. 2012. *The Perfect Business? Anti-Trafficking and the Sex Trade along the Mekong.* Honolulu: University of Hawai'i Press.

Monbiot, George. 2016. "Neoliberalism—The Ideology at the Root of All Our Problems." *The Guardian*, 15 April. https://www.theguardian.com/books/2016 /apr/15/neoliberalism-ideology-problem-george-monbiot.

Montgomery, Heather. 2001. *Modern Babylon? Prostituting Children in Thailand.* New York: Berghahn.

Moore, Donald S. 1999. "The Crucible of Cultural Politics: Reworking 'Development' in Zimbabwe's Eastern Highlands." *American Ethnologist* 26: 654–689.

Moore, Elizabeth Ann. 2015. "Special Report: Money and Lies in Anti-Human Trafficking NGOs." *Truthout*, 27 January. http://www.truth-out.org/news/item /28763-special-report-money-and-lies-in-anti-human-trafficking-ngos.

Morel, Pierre, dir. 2008. *Taken.* EuropaCorp.

Moreton, Bethany. 2009. *To Serve God and Wal-Mart: The Making of Christian Free Enterprise.* Cambridge, MA: Harvard University Press.

Morgan, Robin. 1973. "Lesbianism and Feminism: Synonyms or Contradictions?" In *We Are Everywhere: A Historical Sourcebook of Gay and Lesbian Politics*, ed. Mark Blasius and Shane Phelan, 424–435. New York: Routledge.

Morris, Rosalind C. 1994. "Three Sexes and Four Sexualities: Redressing the Discourses on Gender and Sexuality in Contemporary Thailand." *Positions* 2(1): 15–43.

Movement for Black Lives. n.d. "Platform." https://policy.m4bl.org/platform/.

Mowforth, Martin, and Ian Munt. 2009. *Tourism and Sustainability: Development, Globalisation and New Tourism in the Third World.* New York: Taylor & Francis.

Moyer, Edward. 2013. "NSA Sought to Unmask Users of Net-Privacy Tool Tor, Says Report." *CNET*, 4 October. http://www.cnet.com/news/nsa-sought-to-unmask -users-of-net-privacy-tool-tor-says-report/.

Mukherjee, Roopali, and Sarah Banet-Weiser, eds. 2012. *Commodity Activism: Cultural Resistance in Neoliberal Times.* New York: New York University Press.

Murphy, Alexandra, and Colin Jerolmack. 2016. "Ethnographic Masking in an Era of Data Transparency." *Contexts* 15(2): 14–17.

Murphy, Catherine. 2015. "Sex Workers' Rights Are Human Rights." *Amnesty International*, 14 August. https://www.amnesty.org/en/latest/news/2015/08/sex -workers-rights-are-human-rights/.

Murphy, Michelle. 2013. "The Girl: Mergers of Feminism and Finance in Neoliberal Times." *Scholar and Feminist Online* 11(1–2). http://sfonline.barnard .edu/gender-justice-and-neoliberal-transformations/the-girl-mergers-of-fem inism-and-finance-in-neoliberal-times/.

———. 2012. *Seizing the Means of Reproduction: Entanglements of Feminism, Health, and Technoscience.* Durham, NC: Duke University Press.

———. 2011. "Distributed Reproduction." In *Corpu: An Interdisciplinary Reader on Bodies and Knowledge*, ed. Monica Casper and Paisley Currah, 21–38. London: Palgrave Macmillan.

Musto, Jennifer. 2016. *To Control and Protect: Anti-Trafficking Rescue Politics in the United States.* Berkeley: University of California Press.

———. 2013. "Domestic Minor Sex Trafficking and the Detention to Protection Pipeline." *Dialectical Anthropology* 37: 257–276.

Musto, Jennifer, and danah boyd. 2014. "The Trafficking-Technology Nexus." *Social Politics: International Studies in Gender, State, and Society* 21(3): 461–483.

Nair, Yasmin. 2016. "Marry the State, Jail the People: Hillary Clinton and the Rise of Carceral Feminism." In *False Choices: The Faux Feminism of Hillary Rodham Clinton*, ed. Lisa Featherstone, 101–111. London: Verso.

NARAL. 2017. "Donald Trump's presidency has inspired 11,000 women to run for office: http://huff.to/2oIq8R7 @HuffPostWomen," 25 April.

National Council of Jewish Women. 2016. "EXODUS: NCJW's Anti-Sex Trafficking Initiative." http://act.ncjw.org/trafficking/.

———. 2014. *National Council of Jewish Women and Polaris Join Forces to Raise Awareness about Human Trafficking*, 28 October. https://trafficking-monitor .blogspot.com/2014/11/national-council-of-jewish-women-and.html.

———. 2005. *NCJW Condemns Human Trafficking*, 6 December. http://www.ncjw .org/content_3137.cfm.

Nedig, Harper. 2017. "Senate Panel Approves Online Sex Trafficking Bill." *The Hill*, 8 November. http://thehill.com/policy/technology/359358-senate-panel-ap proves-online-sex-trafficking-bill.

Newman, Janet. 2013. "Spaces of Power: Feminism, Neoliberalism and Gendered Labor." *Social Politics: International Studies in Gender, State, and Society* 20(2): 200–221.

New York Times Editorial Board. 2017. "Under Mr. Trump, Private Prisons Thrive Again." *New York Times*, 24 February. https://www.nytimes.com/2017/02/24 /opinion/under-mr-trump-private-prisons-thrive-again.html.

Not for Sale. 2016. "Not For Sale: End Modern Slavery and Human Trafficking through Business and Impact Sourcing." https://www.notforsalecampaign .org.

Novelli, Marina, Anne Tisch-Rottensteiner, O. Moufakkir, and P. M. Burns. 2012. "Authenticity versus Development: Tourism to the Hill Tribes of Thailand." In *Controversies in Tourism*, ed. Omar Mouffakir and Petter Burns, 54–72. Wallingford, Oxfordshire: CABI.

Nullens, Patrick. 2011. "Dietrich Bonhoeffer: A Third Way of Christian Social Engagement." *European Journal of Theology* 20(1): 60–69.

Nussbaum, Matthew. 2017. "Trump Celebrates Senate's Step Forward on Health Care." *Politico*, 25 July. http://www.politico.com/story/2017/07/25/trump -health-care-vote-reaction-240947.

Obama, Barack. 2013. "President Barack Obama's State of the Union Address—As Prepared for Delivery," 12 February. http://www.whitehouse.gov /the-press-office/2013/02/12/president-barack-obamas-state-union-address.

———. 2012. "Remarks by the President to the Clinton Global Initiative," 25 September. http://www.whitehouse.gov/the-press-office/2012/09/25/remarks -president-clinton-global-initiative.

O'Brien, Avens. 2015. "My Feminist Outrage Stops at 'Manspreading,' but Here's My Solution." *The Nation*, 5 June. http://thelibertarianrepublic.com /my-feminist-outrage-stops-at-manspreading-but-heres-my-solution/.

O'Connell Davidson, Julia. 2015. *Modern Slavery: The Margins of Freedom*. London: Palgrave Macmillan.

―――. 2010. "New Slavery, Old Binaries: Human Trafficking and the Borders of 'Freedom.'" *Global Networks* 10: 244–261.

―――. 2005. *Children in the Global Sex Trade*. Cambridge, UK: Polity Press.

O'Connell Davidson, Julia, and Jacqueline Sánchez Taylor. 2005. "Travel and Taboo: Heterosexual Sex Tourism in the Caribbean." In *Regulating Sex: The Politics of Intimacy and Identity*, ed. Elizabeth Bernstein and Laurie Schaffner, 83–99. New York: Routledge.

Olasky, Marvin. 2000. *Compassionate Conservatism: What It Is, What It Does, and How It Can Transform America*. New York: Free Press.

Olivie, André. 2008. "Identifying Cambodian Victims of Human Trafficking among Deportees from Thailand." Bangkok: UN Inter-Agency Project on Human Trafficking.

Oppenheim, Maya. 2017. "Donald Trump Brands Illegal Immigrant Gang Members 'Animals' Who 'Slice and Dice' Young Beautiful Girls." *The Independent*, 26 July. http://www.independent.co.uk/news/world/americas/donald-trump-illegal-immigrants-animals-slice-dice-young-beautiful-girls-us-president-a7861596.html.

Ouroussoff, Nicolai. 2011. "Abu Dhabi Guggenheim Faces Protest." *New York Times*, 17 March. https://www.nytimes.com/2011/03/17/arts/design/guggenheim-threatened-with-boycott-over-abu-dhabi-project.html.

Padilla, Mark. 2007. *Caribbean Pleasure Industry: Tourism, Sexuality, and AIDS in the Dominican Republic*. Chicago: University of Chicago Press.

Parenti, Christian. 2009. "Free the Truth: A Response to Kevin Bales." *Democracy Now!*, 14 September. http://www.democracynow.org/blog/2009/9/14/free_the_truth_a_response_to_kevin_bales.

Parker, Richard. 2001. "Sexuality, Culture, and Power in HIV research," *Annual Review of Anthropology* 30: 163–179.

Parker, Robert E. 1994. *Flesh Peddlers and Warm Bodies: The Temporary Help Industry and Its Workers*. New Brunswick, NJ: Rutgers University Press.

Parnes, Amie. 2010. "Moore Talks Trafficking." *Politico*, 4 May. http://www.politico.com/click/stories/1005/moore_talks_trafficking.html.

Parreñas, Rhacel Salazar. 2011. *Illicit Flirtations: Sex Trafficking and the Moral Control of Migrant Women in Tokyo*. Stanford, CA: Stanford University Press.

Parreñas, Rheana "Juno" Salazar. 2012. "Producing Affect: Transnational Volunteerism in a Malaysian Orangutan Rehabilitation Center." *American Ethnologist* 39(4): 673–687.

Patterson, Brandon E. 2017. "The Feds Had Been Moving Away from Mass Incarceration for Years: Then Jeff Sessions Came Along." *Mother Jones*, 19 May. http://www.motherjones.com/politics/2017/05/jeff-sessions-charging-gudelines/.

Pearson, Elaine. 2002. *Human Traffic, Human Rights: Redefining Victim Protection*. London: Anti-Slavery International.

Pecheny, Mario. 2013. "Sexual Politics and Post-Neoliberalism in Latin America." *Scholar and Feminist Online* 11(1–2). http://sfonline.barnard.edu/gender-justice

-and-neoliberal-transformations/sexual-politics-and-post-neoliberalism-in
-latin-america/.

Peck, Jamie, Nik Theodore, and Kevin Ward. 2005. "Constructing Markets for Temporary Labor: Employment Liberalization and the Internationalization of the Staffing Industry." *Global Networks* 5(1): 3–26.

Peleggi, Maurizio. 1996. "National Heritage and Global Tourism in Thailand." *Annals of Tourism Research* 23(2): 432–448.

Penh Pal. 2012. "Somaly Mam Overreaches Herself." *Penh Pal*, 23 April. http://penhpal.com/2012/04/somaly-mam-overreaches-herself/.

Pew Research Center. 2014. "Detailed Tables on the Evangelical Electorate: Religious Landscape Study." http://assets.pewresearch.org/wp-content/uploads/sites/12/2016/03/FT_16.03.14.EvangelicalVote2.pdf.

Pheterson, Gail. 2008. "Tracing a Radical Feminist Vision from the 1970's to the Present: Left-Right, North-South." Talk given at Graduate Gender Program, University of Utrecht, 25 September.

Phongpaichit, Pasuk, and Christopher John Baker. 2002. *Thailand, Economy and Politics*. New York: Oxford University Press.

Pieklo, Jessica Mason. 2013. "Supreme Court Strikes Anti-Prostitution Pledge for American Organizations Fighting HIV/AIDS." *Rewire*, 20 June. https://rewire.news/article/2013/06/20/supreme-court-strikes-anti-prostitution-pledge-for-american-organizations-fighting-hivaids/.

Plambech, Sine. 2014. "Points of Departure—Migration Control and Anti-Trafficking in the Lives of Nigerian Sex Worker Migrants after Deportation from Europe." PhD dissertation, University of Copenhagen.

Pliley, Jessica R. 2014. *Policing Sexuality: The Mann Act and the Making of the FBI*. Cambridge, MA: Harvard University Press.

Plummer, Jo, and Mats Tunehag, eds. 2013. "A Business Takeover: Combating the Business of the Sex Trade with Business as Mission." http://bamthinktank.org/report-trafficking/.

Polaris Project. 2015. *Human Trafficking Issue Brief*. Washington, DC: Polaris Project. https://polarisproject.org/sites/default/files/2015%20Safe%20Harbor%20Issue%20Brief.pdf.

———. 2004. "Law Enforcement Toolkit on Trafficking in Persons." Washington, DC: Polaris Project.

Pollitt, Katha. 2014. "Why Do So Many Leftists Want Sex Work to Be the New Normal? Yes, Let's Erase Stigma. But Feminists, Please: Let's Not Forget to Talk about Male Privilege." *The Nation*, 2 April. http://www.thenation.com/article/why-do-so-many-leftists-want-sex-work-be-new-normal/.

Powell, Michael, and Nicholas Confessore. 2008. "4 Arrests, Then 6 Days to a Resignation." *New York Times*, 13 March. http://www.nytimes.com/2008/03/13/nyregion/13recon.html.

Power, Samantha. 2009. "The Enforcer: A Christian Lawyer's Global Crusade." *New Yorker*, 19 January, 52–63.

Prejean, Helen. 2001. "Moratorium 2000: Putting an End to the Death Penalty." Lecture at Barnard College, New York, 13 September. http://sfonline.barnard .edu/prison/prejean_01.htm.

"President Obama Addresses Human Trafficking." 2013. Futures without Violence. http://www.futureswithoutviolence.org/content/features/detail/2159/.

Pringle, Hamish, and Marjorie Thompson. 1999. *Brand Spirit: How Cause Related Marketing Builds Brands.* Chichester, UK: Wiley.

Puar, Jasbir K. 2007. *Terrorist Assemblages: Homonationalism in Queer Times.* Durham, NC: Duke University Press.

Purser, Gretchen. 2012. "'Still Doin' Time:' Clamoring for Work in the Day Labor Industry." *WorkingUSA: The Journal of Labor and Society* 15: 397–415.

Reddy, Chandan. 2011. *Freedom with Violence: Race, Sexuality, and the US State.* Durham, NC: Duke University Press.

Reilly, Katie. 2016. "Here Are All the Times Donald Trump Insulted Mexico." *Time,* 31 August. http://time.com/4473972/donald-trump-mexico-meeting-insult/.

Rich, Motoko. 2017. "TPP, the Trade Deal Trump Killed, Is Back in Talks without US" *New York Times,* 14 July. https://www.nytimes.com/2017/07/14/business /trans-pacific-partnership-trade-japan-china-globalization.html?_r=0.

Richey, Lisa Ann, and Stefano Ponte. 2011. *Brand Aid: Shopping Well to Save the World.* Minneapolis: University of Minnesota Press.

Richie, Beth. 2012. *Arrested Justice: Black Women, Violence, and America's Prison Nation.* New York: New York University Press.

Riles, Annelise. 2000. *The Network Inside Out.* Ann Arbor: University of Michigan Press.

Rivas, Jorge. 2016. "Black Lives Matter Is Joining the Fight against Deportations—and It Could Be a Game Changer." *Fusion,* 3 August. http://fusion.net/story /333395/black-lives-matter-fighting-deportations/.

Roberts, Dorothy E. 1997. *Killing the Black Body: Race, Reproduction, and the Meaning of Liberty.* New York: Pantheon.

Rodriguez, Robyn Magalit. 2010. *Migrants for Export: How the Philippine State Brokers Labor to the World.* Minneapolis: University of Minnesota.

Roe, Clifford. n.d. "The Dangers of a Large City, Or The System of the Underworld: Exposing the White Slave Traffic. Chicago: n.p.

Rojanapithayakorn, W. 2006. "The 100% Condom Use Programme in Asia." *Reproductive Health Matters* 14: 41–52.

Rojek, Chris, and John Urry. 1997. *Touring Cultures: Transformations of Travel and Theory.* London: Routledge.

Romero, Elvira Madrid, Jamie Montejo, and Rosa Icela Madrid. 2014. "Trabajadoras sexuales conquistan derechos laborales." *Debate feminista* 25(50): 137–159.

Rose, Nikolas S. 1999. *Powers of Freedom: Reframing Political Thought.* Cambridge: Cambridge University Press.

Rosen, Ruth. 1982. *The Lost Sisterhood: Prostitution in America, 1900–1918.* Baltimore: Johns Hopkins University Press.

Rosenblatt, Kalhan. 2017. "Will Trump's Border Wall Prevent Human Trafficking? Experts Aren't Sure." *NBC News*, 26 April. http://www.nbcnews.com/news/us-news/will-trump-s-border-wall-prevent-human-trafficking-experts-aren-n751466.

Roshe, Dominic. 2016. "Retail Group Approves Bangladesh Factories as Safety Concerns Persist, Report Finds." *The Guardian*, 21 November. https://www.theguardian.com/world/2016/nov/21/bangladesh-garment-factories-safety-alliance-rana-plaza-report.

Roux, Sébastien. 2011. "No Money, No Honey: Economies intimes du tourisme sexuel en Thaïlande." PhD dissertation, La Découverte.

———. 2009. "Le savant, le politique et le moraliste: Historiographie du 'tourisme sexuel' en Thaïlande." *A contrario* 1(11): 28–42.

———. 2007. "Importer pour exister: Empower et le travail sexuel en Thaïlande." *Lien social et politiques* 58: 145–154.

Roy, Ananya. 2010. *Poverty Capital: Microfinance and the Making of Development*. New York: Routledge.

Rubin, Gayle. 2011. "The Trouble with Trafficking." In *Deviations: A Gayle Rubin Reader*, 66–86. Durham, NC: Duke University Press.

———. 1993. "Thinking Sex: Notes for A Radical Theory of the Politics of Sexuality." In *The Lesbian and Gay Studies Reader*, ed. Henry Abelove, Michéle Aina Barala, and David M. Halperin, 3–45. New York: Routledge.

———. 1975. "The Traffic in Women: Notes on the 'Political Economy' of Sex." In *Toward an Anthropology of Women*, ed. Rayna Reiter, 157–210. New York: Monthly Review Press.

Ruenkaew, Pataya. 2002. "The Transnational Prostitution of Thai Women to Germany: A Variety of Transnational Labour Migration?" In *Transnational Prostitution: Changing Patterns in a Global Context*, ed. Susanne Thorbek and Bandana Pattanaik. London: Zed Books.

Sachs, Jeffrey. 2005. *The End of Poverty: Economic Possibilities for Our Time*. New York: Penguin.

Safe Horizon (@sffny). 2017. "What to Do If Immigration Agents (ICE) Are at Your Door https://www.aclu.org/know-your-rights/what-do-if-immigration-agents-ice-are-your-door . . . via @aclu." Twitter, 11 February.

Saletan, William. 2003. *Bearing Right: How Conservatives Won the Abortion War*. Berkeley: University of California Press.

Salutin, Rick. 2017. "Will Justin Trudeau Be the Last Neo-Liberal Standing?" *Toronto Star*, 6 January. https://www.thestar.com/opinion/commentary/2017/01/06/will-justin-trudeau-be-the-last-neo-liberal-standing-salutin.html.

"Samantha Power." n.d. *Forbes*. http://www.forbes.com/profile/samantha-power/#.

Sampathkumar, Mythili. 2017. "Donald Trump Defunding of UN's Women's Health Service Will Cause 'Millions to Suffer.'" *The Independent*, 4 April. http://www.independent.co.uk/news/world/americas/us-politics/donald-trump-abortion-defunding-global-mexico-city-rule-un-population-fund-a7666916.html.

Sands, Darren. 2017. "What Happened to Black Lives Matter?" *BuzzFeed News*, 21 June. https://www.buzzfeed.com/darrensands/what-happened-to-black -lives-matter?utm_term=.pdk5DjkzB#.bdJKOQzP7.

Sanford, Rachealle, Daniel E. Martínez, and Ronald Weitzer. 2016. "Framing Human Trafficking: A Content Analysis of Recent US Newspaper Articles." *Journal of Human Trafficking* 2(2): 139–155.

Sanger, David E., and Claire C. Miller. 2014. "In Keeping Grip on Data Pipeline, Obama Does Little to Reassure Industry." *New York Times*, 18 January. http:// www.nytimes.com/2014/01/18/technology/in-keeping-grip-on-data-pipeline -obama-does-little-to-reassure-industry.html?_r=0.

Sasso, Brendan. 2012. "Lawmakers Question Google on Efforts to Prevent Online Human Trafficking." *The Hill*, 4 April. http://thehill.com/blogs/hillicon-valley /technology/219975-lawmakers-question-google-on-human-trafficking.

Saunders, Penelope. 2005. "Traffic Violations: Determining the Meaning of Violence in Sexual Trafficking versus Sex Work." *Journal of Interpersonal Violence* 20(3): 343–360.

Saunders, Penelope, and Melissa Sontag Broudo. 2011. "Why Are Sex Workers and Their Allies Occupying Wall Street?" *Feministing*, 27 October. http://www .bestpracticespolicy.org/2011/10/27/ows20111/.

Savage, Charlie, and Timothy Williams. 2018. "U.S. Seizes Backpage.com, a Site Accused of Enabling Prostitution." *New York Times*. 7 April. https://www.nytimes .com/2018/04/07/us/politics/backpage-prostitution-classified.html.

Sawyer, R. Keith. 2002. "A Discourse on Discourse: An Archaeological History of an Intellectual Concept." *Cultural Studies* 16(3): 433–456.

Schafer, David, and Michelle Koth. 2007. "Absolute Infidel: The Evolution of Ayaan Hirsi Ali." *The Humanist*, 22 December. http://thehumanist.com/magazine /january-february-2008/features/absolute-infidel-the-evolution-of-ayaan-hirsi-ali.

Schaffner, Laurie. 2005. *Girls in Trouble with the Law*. New Brunswick, NJ: Rutgers University Press.

Scheper-Hughes, Nancy. 2011. "Mr Tati's Holiday and João's Safari—Seeing the World through Transplant Tourism." *Body and Society* 17(2–3): 55–92.

———. 2002. "Commodity Fetishism in Organs Trafficking." In *Commodifying Bodies*, ed. Nancy Scheper-Huges and Loïc Wacquant, 31–63. London: Sage Publications.

Schilling, Chelsea. 2009. "Want to Sneak into US? There's an App for That." *WND*, 12 June. http://www.wnd.com/2009/12/117865/.

Schisgall, David, Nina Alvarez, and Priya Swaminathan, dirs. 2008. *Very Young Girls*. New York: Girls Educational and Mentoring Services.

Schmidt, Eric, and Jared Cohen. 2013. *The New Digital Age: Reshaping the Future of People, Nations and Business*. London: John Murray.

Schmidt, Michael S., and Sewell Chan. 2016. "NATO Will Send Ships to Aegean Sea to Deter Human Trafficking." *New York Times*, 11 February. http://www.ny times.com/2016/02/12/world/europe/nato-aegean-migrant-crisis.html?_r=2.

Schwab, Klaus. 2008. "Global Corporate Citizenship: Working with Governments and Civil Society." *Foreign Affairs* (January): 107–118.

Schwartz, Shelby. 2008. "Harboring Concerns: The Problematic Conceptual Reorientation of Juvenile Prostitution Adjudication in New York." *Columbia Journal of Gender and Law* 18: 235.

Schweig, Sarah, Danielle Malangone, and Miriam Goodman. 2015. *Prostitution Diversion Programs*. New York: Center for Court Innovation. http://www.courtinnovation.org/sites/default/files/documents/CI_Prostitution%207.5.12%20PDF.pdf.

Scott, Joan. 2012. "The Vexed Relationship of Emancipation and Equality." *History of the Present: A Journal of Critical History* 2(2): 148–168.

———. 2007. *The Politics of the Veil*. Princeton, NJ: Princeton University Press.

Sedgwick, Eve Kosofsky. 1993. *Tendencies*. Durham, NC: Duke University Press.

Segura, Liliana. 2014. "No, We Don't Need a Law against Catcalling." *The Intercept*, 3 November. https://firstlook.org/theintercept/2014/11/03/we-dont-need-a-law-against-catcalling/.

Seligson, Hannah. 2011. "Unreasonable, Maybe, but It's on a Social Mission." *New York Times*, 22 October. https://nytimes.com/2011/10/23/business/unreasonable-institute-teaches-new-paths-to-social-missions.html.

Sengupta, Somini, and Eric Lipton. 2013. "Silicon Valley Group's Political Effort Causes Uproar." *New York Times*, 8 May. https://www.nytimes.com/2013/05/09/technology/fwus-raises-uproar-with-advocacy-tactics.html.

Sennett, Richard. 2006. *The Culture of the New Capitalism*. New Haven, CT: Yale University Press.

———. 1998. *The Corrosion of Character: The Personal Consequences of Work in the New Capitalism*. New York: W. W. Norton.

Serle, Jack. 2015. "Monthly Updates on the Covert War: Almost 2,500 Now Killed by Covert US Drone Strikes since Obama Inauguration Six Years Ago." *Bureau of Investigative Journalism*, 2 February. https://www.thebureauinvestigates.com/2015/02/02/almost-2500-killed-covert-us-drone-strikes-obama-inauguration/.

Seshu, Meena, and Nandinee Bandhopadhyay. 2009. "How the Development Industry Imagines Sex Work: Interview with Cheryl Overs." *Development* 52(1): 13–17.

Shah, Svati P. 2014. *Street Corner Secrets: Sex, Work, and Migration in the City of Mumbai*. Durham, NC: Duke University Press.

———. 2009. "Sexuality and 'The Left': Thoughts on Intersections and Visceral Others." *Scholar and Feminist Online* 7(3): http://sfonline.barnard.edu/sexecon/shah_01.htm.

———. 2008. "South Asian Border Crossings and Sex Work: Revisiting the Question of Migration in Anti-Trafficking Interventions." *Sexuality Research and Social Policy* 5(4): 19–30.

Shapiro, Rebecca. 2017. "Donald Trump's Presidency Has Inspired 11,000 Women to Run for Office." *Huffington Post*, 24 April. http://www.huffingtonpost.com/entry/donald-trumps-presidency-has-inspired-11000-women-to-run-for-office_us_58fd863ae4b06b9cb917d111?section=us_women.

Shared Hope International. 2017. "The Defenders USA: Will You Take the Pledge?" https://sharedhope.org/join-the-cause/become-a-defender/the-defenders-pledge/.

Sharma, Aradhana. 2006. "Crossbreeding Institutions, Breeding Struggle: Women's Empowerment, Neoliberal Governmentality, and State (Re)formation in India." *Cultural Anthropology* 21(1): 60–95.

Sharma, Nandita. 2005. "Anti-Trafficking Rhetoric and the Making of a Global Apartheid." *NWSA Journal* 17(3): 88–111.

Shear, Michael. 2017. "TPP, the Trade Deal Trump Killed, Is Back in Talks without US" *New York Times*, 1 June. https://www.nytimes.com/2017/06/01/climate/trump-paris-climate-agreement.html?mtrref=undefined.

Shear, Michael, and Adam Liptak. 2017. "Supreme Court Takes Up Travel Ban Case, and Allows Parts to Go Ahead." *New York Times*, 26 June. https://www.nytimes.com/2017/06/26/us/politics/supreme-court-trump-travel-ban-case.html?_r=1.

Sherman, Erik. 2017. "Appellate Court Upholds Temporary Ban on Trump Immigration Order." *Forbes*, 9 January. http://www.forbes.com/sites/eriksherman/2017/02/09/appellate-court-upholds-temporary-ban-on-trump-immigration-order/#6d09d76d1810.

Shih, Elena. 2016. "Not in My 'Backyard Abolitionism': Vigilante Rescue against American Sex Trafficking." *Sociological Perspectives* 59(1): 1–23.

———. 2015. "Freedom Markets: Moral and Political Economies of Human Trafficking in China, Thailand and the US." PhD dissertation, University of California, Los Angeles.

———. 2009. "Humanitarian Work: The Production and Consumption of Jewelry Made by Trafficked Women." MA thesis, University of California, Los Angeles.

Shimizu, Celine Parreñas. 2007. *The Hypersexuality of Race: Performing Asian/American Women on Screen and Scene*. Durham, NC: Duke University Press.

Shivani, Anis. 2016. "This Is Our Neoliberal Nightmare: Hillary Clinton, Donald Trump, and Why the Market and the Wealthy Win Every Time." *Salon*, 6 June. http://www.salon.com/2016/06/06/this_is_our_neoliberal_nightmare_hillary_clinton_donald_trump_and_why_the_market_and_the_wealthy_win_every_time/.

Shor, Francis. 2015. "'Black Lives Matter' Constructing a New Civil Rights and Black Freedom Movement." *New Politics* XV-3(59): http://newpol.org/content/%E2%80%9Cblack-lives-matter%E2%80%9D-constructing-new-civil-rights-and-black-freedom-movement.

Shore, Cris, and Susan Wright, eds. 1997. *Anthropology of Policy: Critical Perspectives on Governance and Power*. London: Routledge.

Shuham, Matt. 2017. "Trump Signs Exec Orders, Says Cartels 'Destroying the Blood of Our Youth.'" *Talking Points Memo*, 9 February. http://talkingpointsmemo.com/livewire/trump-signs-executive-orders-justice-department.

Siegal, Erin, dir. 2006. *Taking the Pledge*. Network of Sex Work Projects (NSWP). http://blip.tv/sexworkerspresent/taking-the-pledge-185356.

Simon, Caty. 2017. "What Sex Workers Need to Know About This Month's Anti-Trafficking Bills." *Tits and Sass*. September 22. http://titsandsass.com/what-sex-workers-need-to-know-about-this-months-anti-trafficking-bills/.

Simon, Jonathan. 2007. *Governing through Crime: How the War on Crime Transformed American Democracy and Created a Culture of Fear.* New York: Oxford University Press.

Skinner, E. Benjamin. 2009. "Obama's Abolitionist." *Huffington Post,* 25 March. http://www.huffingtonpost.com/ben-skinner/obamas-abolitionist_b_178781.html.

———. 2008. *A Crime so Monstrous: Face-to-Face with Modern-Day Slavery.* New York: Free Press.

Skrobanek, Siriporn, Nattaya Boonpakdi, and Chutima Janthakeero. 1997. *The Traffic in Women: Human Realities of the International Sex Trade.* London: Zed Books.

"Slavery: A 21st Century Evil." 2012. *Al Jazeera.* http://www.aljazeera.com/programmes/slaverya21stcenturyevil/slaverya21stcenturyevil.html.

Smith, Adam. 1986. *The Essential Adam Smith.* Edited by Robert L. Heilbroner. New York: W. W. Norton.

Smith, Christian. 2000. *Christian America? What Evangelicals Really Want.* Berkeley: University of California Press.

Smith, David. 2017. "Betsy DeVos: Trump's Illiberal Ally Seen as Most Dangerous Education Chief Ever." *The Guardian,* 26 July. https://www.theguardian.com/us-news/2017/jul/26/betsy-devos-education-secretary-trump.

Smith, David, and Molly Redden. 2017. "Trump Administration Rescinds Obama-Era Protections for Transgender Students." *The Guardian,* 23 February. https://www.theguardian.com/us-news/2017/feb/22/transgender-students-bathroom-trump-obama?CMP=share_btn_link.

Smith, Gregory A., and David Masci. 2016. "Exit Polls and the Evangelical Vote: A Closer Look." *Pew Research Center,* 14 March. http://www.pewresearch.org/fact-tank/2016/03/14/exit-polls-and-the-evangelical-vote-a-closer-look/.

Smith, Gregory A., and Jessica Martínez. 2016. "How the Faithful Voted: A Preliminary 2016 Analysis." *Pew Research Center,* 9 November. http://www.pewresearch.org/fact-tank/2016/11/09/how-the-faithful-voted-a-preliminary-2016-analysis/.

Smith, Valene, ed. 1989. *Hosts and Guests: The Anthropology of Tourism.* Philadelphia: University of Pennsylvania Press.

Smith-Rosenberg, Carroll. 1986. *Disorderly Conduct: Visions of Gender in Victorian America.* New York: Oxford University Press.

Snitow, Ann, Christine Stansell, and Sharon Thompson. 1983. *Powers of Desire: The Politics of Sexuality.* New York: Monthly Review Press.

Soderlund, Gretchen. 2013. *Sex Trafficking, Scandal, and the Transformation of Journalism, 1885–1917.* Chicago: University of Chicago Press.

———. 2011. "The Rhetoric of Revelation: Sex Trafficking and the Journalistic Exposé." *Humanity: An International Journal of Human Rights, Humanitarianism, and Development* 2(2): 193–211.

———. 2005. "Running from the Rescuers: New US Crusades against Sex Trafficking and the Rhetoric of Abolition." *NWSA Journal* 17(3): 64–87.

Spade, Dean. 2011. *Normal Life: Administrative Violence, Critical Trans Politics, and the Limits of Law.* Brooklyn, NY: South End.

Spanger, Marlene. 2002. "Black Prostitutes in Denmark." In *Transnational Prostitution: Changing Patterns in a Global Context*, ed. Susanne Thorbek and Bandana Pattanaik, 121–136. London: Zed Books.

Spivak, Gayatri. 1996. "'Woman' as Theatre." *Radical Philosophy* 75: 2–4.

Springer, Simon. 2012. "Neoliberalism as Discourse: Between Foucauldian Political Economy and Marxian Poststructuralism." *Critical Discourse Studies* 9(2): 133–147.

Stack, Liam. 2017. "Trump's Executive Order on Immigration: What We Know and What We Don't." *New York Times*, 29 January. https://www.nytimes .com/2017/01/29/us/trump-refugee-ban-muslim-executive-order.html.

Stackpole, Thomas. 2015. "The New Abolitionists." *Foreign Policy* 213(8): 84–93.

Stanley, Amy Dru. 1998. *From Bondage to Contract: Wage Labor, Marriage, and the Market in the Age of Slave Emancipation*. Cambridge: Cambridge University Press.

Stasio, Marilyn. 2015. "Broadway Review: 'Amazing Grace.'" *Variety*, 17 July. http:// variety.com/2015/legit/reviews/amazing-grace-review-broadway-musical -1201538916/.

Steckel, Richard. 1999. *Making Money While Making a Difference: How to Profit with a Nonprofit Partner*. Homewood, IL: High Tide.

Stein, Arlene. 2001. *The Stranger Next Door: The Story of a Small Community's Battle over Sex, Faith, and Civil Rights*. Boston: Beacon.

Steinbrink, Malte. 2012. "'We Did the Slum!'—Urban Poverty Tourism in Historical Perspective." *Tourism Geographies* 14(2): 213–234.

Steinem, Gloria. 2008. Presentation at conference Sex Trafficking and the New Abolitionists. Brooklyn Museum, Brooklyn, New York, 28 April.

Steinfatt, Thomas. 2011. "Sex Trafficking in Cambodia: Fabricated Numbers versus Empirical Evidence." *Crime, Law and Social Change* 56(5): 443–462.

Stewart, Christa (@c_stewart_esq). 2017. "Sad. 'Trump administration reportedly puts an end to Let Girls Learn' @equalitynow." Twitter, 1 May. https://twitter .com/c_stewart_esq/status/859140932968558593.

Stiglitz, Joseph E. 2003. *The Roaring Nineties: A New History of the World's Most Prosperous Decade*. New York: W. W. Norton.

Stillman, Sarah. 2011. "The Invisible Army." *New Yorker*, 6 June. http://www.new yorker.com/magazine/2011/06/06/the-invisible-army.

Stockman, Farah, Michael Kranish, Petter S. Canellows, and Kevin Baron. 2006. "Bush Brings Faith to Foreign Aid: As Funding Rises, Christian Groups Deliver Help—With a Message." *Boston Globe*, 8 October. http://www.boston.com /news/world/africa/articles/2006/10/08/bush_brings_faith_to_foreign_aid.

Stoller, Matt. 2017. "Democrats Can't Win Until They Recognize How Bad Obama's Financial Policies Were." *Washington Post*, 12 January. https://www.wash ingtonpost.com/posteverything/wp/2017/01/12/democrats-cant-win-until -they-recognize-how-bad-obamas-financial-policies-were/?tid=ss_mail&utm _term=.e32b0d38f08f.

Strong, Michael. 2009. *Be the Solution: How Entrepreneurs and Conscious Capitalists Can Solve All the World's Problems*. Hoboken, NJ: Wiley.

Stronza, Amanda. 2001. "Anthropology of Tourism: Forging New Ground for Ecotourism and Other Alternatives." *Annual Review of Anthropology*: 261–283.

Students and Scholars against Corporate Misbehavior. 2012. *Sweatshops Are Good for Apple and Foxconn, but Not for Workers*. 31 May. http://sacom.hk /sweatshops-are-good-for-apple-and-foxconn-but-not-for-workers/.

Sturken, Marita. 2007. *Tourists of History: Memory, Kitsch, and Consumerism from Oklahoma City to Ground Zero*. Durham, NC: Duke University Press.

Sudbury, Julia, ed. 2005. *Global Lockdown: Race, Gender, and the Prison-Industrial Complex*. New York: Routledge.

Sulik, Gayle A. 2011. *Pink Ribbon Blues: How Breast Cancer Culture Undermines Women's Health*. New York: Oxford University Press.

Sun, Chyng. 2007. "The Fallacies of Phantasies." In *Pornography: Driving the Demand in International Sex Trafficking*, ed. David E. Guinn, 233–251. Culver City, CA: Captive Daughters Media.

Surgey, Nick. 2013. "The Googlization of the Far Right: Why is Google Funding Grover Norquist, Heritage Action and ALEC?" *Center for Media and Democracy's PR Watch*, 27 November. https://www.prwatch.org/news/2013/11/12319 /google-funding-grover-norquist-heritage-action-alec-and-more.

Swenstein, Abigail, and Kate Mogulescu. 2016. "Resisting the Carceral: The Need to Align Anti-Trafficking Efforts with Movements for Criminal Justice Reform." *Anti-Trafficking Review* 6: 118–122.

Talev, Margaret, and Bill Allison. 2016. "Clinton Global Initiative Ends with Some of Shine Worn Off." *Bloomberg*, 19 September. https://www.bloomberg.com /news/articles/2016-09-19/clinton-global-initiative-ends-run-with-some-of -shine-worn-off.

Tankersley, Jim. 2016. "Britain Just Killed Globalization as We Know It." *Washington Post*, 25 June. https://www.washingtonpost.com/news/wonk/wp/2016/06/25 /great-britain-just-killed-globalization-as-we-know-it/.

Tannen, Norman, Richard Steckel, Robin Simons, and Jeffrey Simons. 1999. *Making Money While Making a Difference: How to Profit with a Non-Profit Partner*. Homewood, IL: High Tide Press.

Tatum, Sophie. 2017. "House Passes Ban on Abortion after 20 Weeks of Pregnancy." *CNN*, 3 October. http://www.cnn.com/2017/10/03/politics/house-vote-abor tion-after-20-week-ban/index.html.

Taylor, Marcus. 2006. *From Pinochet to the "Third Way": Neoliberalism and Social Transformation in Chile*. London: Pluto Press.

Terranova, Tiziana. 2000. "Free Labor: Producing Culture for the Digital Economy." *Social Text* 18(2): 33–58.

Thakor, Mitali, and danah boyd. 2013. "Networked Trafficking: Reflections on Technology and the Anti-Trafficking Movement." *Dialectical Anthropology* 37(2): 277–290.

ThaiWebsites.com and Department of Tourism, Thailand. 2017. "Tourism Statistics Thailand 2000–2017." http://www.thaiwebsites.com/tourism.asp.

Thiemann, Inga. 2016. "Villains and Victims, but No Workers: Why a Prosecution-Focused Approach to Human Trafficking Fails Trafficked Persons." *Anti-Trafficking Review* 6: 126–129.

Thompson, Don. 2016. "California Seeks Fix on Sex-Offender Reporting Requirement." San Diego Union Tribune, 21 June. http://www.sandiegouniontribune.com/sdut-california-seeks-fix-on-sex-offender-reporting-2016jun21-story.html.

Thrift, Nigel. 2005. *Knowing Capitalism*. London: Sage Publications.

Thukral, Juhu. 2016. "Human Rights and Economic Opportunity Will End Trafficking." *Anti-Trafficking Review* 6: 134–137.

Ticktin, Miriam. 2011. *Casualties of Care: Immigration and the Politics of Humanitarianism in France*. Berkeley: University of California.

———. 2008. "Sexual Violence as the Language of Border Control: Where French Feminist and Anti-Immigrant Rhetoric Meet." *Signs: Journal of Women in Culture and Society* 33(4): 863–889.

Titeca, Kristof, and Matthew Sebastian. 2014. "Why Did Invisible Children Dissolve?" *Washington Post*, 30 December. https://www.washingtonpost.com/blogs/monkey-cage/wp/2014/12/30/why-did-invisible-children-dissolve/.

Tolentino, Jia. 2017. "The Somehow Controversial Women's March on Washington." *New Yorker*, 18 January. http://www.newyorker.com/culture/jia-tolentino/the-somehow-controversial-womens-march-on-washington.

Tonneau, Olivier. 2017. "Macron's Tragedy Is That He Still Believes in a Discredited Economic System." *The Guardian*, 8 May. https://www.theguardian.com/commentisfree/2017/may/08/emmanuel-macron-france-economics-neoliberalism.

Tor Project. n.d. "Tor Project: Privacy Online." https://www.torproject.org/.

Toure, Madina (@madinatoure). 2017. ".@CarmenMariaRey or @sffny: Despite @realDonaldTrump rhetoric, what law is, immigrants' rights/protections to stay in US haven't changed." Twitter, 23 March. https://twitter.com/madinatoure/status/845081618981294080.

Toyota, Mika. 2006. *Securitizing Border-Crossing: The Case of Marginalized Stateless Minorities in the Thai-Burma Borderlands*. Singapore: Institute of Defence and Strategic Studies, Nanyang Technological University.

———. 2005. "Subjects of the Nation without Citizenship: The Case of 'Hill Tribes' in Thailand." In *Multiculturalism in Asia*, ed. Will Kymlicka and Baogang He, 110–135. Cambridge: Oxford University Press.

Tran, Kim. 2017. "5 Transformative Justice Experts on What We Should Do with 'Sexual Predators' in Our Communities." *Everyday Feminism*, 16 November. https://everydayfeminism.com/2017/11/me-too-transformative-justice/.

Trump, Donald J. 2017a. "Executive Order: Protecting the Nation from Foreign Terrorist Entry into the United States." Washington, DC: White House, Office of the Press Secretary, 27 January. https://www.whitehouse.gov/the-press

-office/2017/01/27/executive-order-protecting-nation-foreign-terrorist-entry
-united-states.

———. 2017b. "Executive Order: Protecting the Nation from Foreign Terrorist Entry into the United States." Washington, DC: White House, Office of the Press Secretary, 6 March. https://www.whitehouse.gov/the-press-office/2017/03/06 /executive-order-protecting-nation-foreign-terrorist-entry-united-states.

Trump, Ivanka. 2017. *Women Who Work: Rewriting the Rules for Success*. London: Portfolio.

Truong, Thanh-Dam. 2000. "A Feminist Perspective on the Asian Miracle and Crisis: Enlarging the Conceptual Map of Human Development." *Journal of Human Development* 1(1): 159–164.

UN Development Programme. 2012. *The Global Commission on HIV and the Law: Risks, Rights and Health*, July. New York: United Nations. https://hivlawcom mission.org/wp-content/uploads/2017/06/FinalReport-RisksRightsHealth -EN.pdf.

UN General Assembly. 2000. *Protocol to Prevent, Suppress and Punish Trafficking in Persons, Especially Women and Children, Supplementing the United Nations Convention against Transnational Organized Crime*, 15 November. UN Doc. A/55/383. New York: United Nations.

UN Inter-Agency Project on Human Trafficking. 2013. *Links to Key Actors in Human Trafficking in Thailand*. http://www.no-trafficking.org/thailand_links.html.

———. 2009. *Siren Report: Exploitation of Cambodian Men at Sea: Facts about the Trafficking of Cambodian Men onto Thai Fishing Boats*. 22 April, CB-03. Phnom Penh, Cambodia.

United States Leadership against HIV/AIDS, Tuberculosis, and Malaria Act of 2003. Pub. Law. No. 108-25.

United States v. Kennard. 2001. 01-30346. US Court of Appeals, Ninth Circuit. https:// www.justice.gov/sites/default/files/crt/legacy/2010/12/14/kennard.pdf.

United States v. Davis. 2008. 3: 07cr11(JCH). US District Court, District of Connecticut.

United States v. Sabil Mumin Mujahid. 2010. 11-30276, 12-30070. US Court of Appeals, Ninth Circuit.

UN Office on Drugs and Crime. 2016. *Human Trafficking: People for Sale*. https:// www.unodc.org/toc/en/crimes/human-trafficking.html.

———. 2009. "Mira Sorvino to be Appointed Goodwill Ambassador." 12 February. http://www.unodc.org/unodc/en/frontpage/mira-sorvino-to-be-appointed -goodwill-ambassador.html.

UN Women. 2015. "New Draft Law to Combat Human Trafficking Brings Hope in Morocco." 9 September. http://www.unwomen.org/en/news/stories/2015/9 /new-draft-law-to-combat-human-trafficking-brings-hope-in-morocco.

Urban Light. n.d. "Our Work—Urban Light Youth Center." https://www.urban -light.org/our-work/#eightpillars.

Urbina, Ian. 2015. "'Sea Slaves': The Human Misery That Feed Pets and Livestock." *New York Times*, 27 July. https://www.nytimes.com/2015/07/27/world/outlaw -ocean-thailand-fishing-sea-slaves-pets.html.

Urry, John, and Jonas Larsen. 2011. *The Tourist Gaze 3.0.* New York: Sage Publications.

USAID. 2016. "USAID Contributes $10 Million to Fight Human Trafficking," 7 March. https://www.usaid.gov/afghanistan/news-information/press-releases /usaid-contributes-10-million-fight-human-trafficking.

———. 2015. *USAID Countertrafficking in Persons (CTIP) Report FY 2015.* https:// www.usaid.gov/open/counter-trafficking/fy2015.

———. 2012. "Counter-Trafficking in Persons Policy," February. https://www.usaid .gov/trafficking.

US Citizenship and Immigration Services. n.d. "Victims of Human Trafficking: T Nonimmigrant Status." https://www.uscis.gov/humanitarian/victims -human-trafficking-other-crimes/victims-human-trafficking-t-nonimmigrant -status.

US Congress. 2018. *Allow States and Victims to Fight Online Sex Trafficking Act of 2017.* Pub. L. 115-164.

———. 2017. *National Defense Authorization Act for Fiscal Year 2017.* Pub. L. 114-328.

———. 2015. *Justice for Victims of Trafficking Act of 2015.* Pub. L. 114-22.

———. 2013. *Violence against Women Reauthorization Act of 2013.* Pub. L. 113-4.

———. 2008. *William Wilberforce Trafficking Victims Protection Reauthorization Act of 2008.* Pub. L. 110-457.

———. 2005. *Trafficking Victims Protection Reauthorization Act of 2005.* Pub. L. 109-164.

———. 2003. *Trafficking Victims Protection Reauthorization Act of 2003.* Pub. L. 108-193.

———. 2000. *Victims of Trafficking and Violence Protection Act of 2000.* Pub. L. 106-386.

US Department of Homeland Security. 2016. "Partnerships." DHS Blue Campaign: One Voice, One Mission, End Human Trafficking. https://www.dhs.gov/blue -campaign/partnerships.

US Department of Justice. 2013. *Intimate Partner Violence: Attributes of Victimization, 1993–2011*, by Shannon Catalano. NCJ 243300, November. Washington, DC.

———. 2012. *Attorney General's Annual Report to Congress and Assessment of US Government Activities to Combat Trafficking in Persons: Fiscal Year 2011.* Washington, DC: US Department of Justice. https://www.justice.gov/archive/ag /annualreports/agreporthumantrafficking2011.pdf.

———. 2011a. *Attorney General's Annual Report to Congress and Assessment of US Government Activities to Combat Trafficking in Persons: Fiscal Year 2010.* Washington, DC: US Department of Justice. https://www.justice.gov/archive/ag /annualreports/agreporthumantrafficking2010.pdf.

———. 2011b. *Characteristics of Suspected Human Trafficking Incidents, 2008–2010.* By Duren Banks and Tracey Kyckelhahn. NCJ 233732. April. Washington, DC: US Department of Justice.

———. 2009. *Attorney General's Annual Report to Congress on US Government Activities to Combat Trafficking in Persons: Fiscal Year 2008.* Washington, DC: US Department of Justice. https://www.justice.gov/archive/ag/annualreports /tr2008/agreporthumantrafficing2008.pdf.

———. 2008. *Attorney General's Annual Report to Congress and Assessment of the US Government Activities to Combat Trafficking in Persons Fiscal Year 2007.* Washington, DC: US Department of Justice. https://www.justice.gov/archive/ag /annualreports/tr2007/agreporthumantrafficing2007.pdf.

———. 2007. *Attorney General's Annual Report to Congress on US Government Activities to Combat Trafficking in Persons Fiscal Year 2006.* Washington, DC: US Department of Justice. https://www.justice.gov/archive/ag/annualreports /tr2006/agreporthumantrafficing2006.pdf.

———. 2006. *Attorney General's Annual Report to Congress on US Government Activities to Combat Trafficking in Persons Fiscal Year 2005.* Washington, DC: US Department of Justice. https://www.justice.gov/archive/ag/annualreports /tr2005/agreporthumantrafficing2005.pdf.

———. 2005. *Report to Congress from Attorney General Alberto R. Gonzales on US Government Efforts to Combat Trafficking in Persons in Fiscal Year 2004.* Washington, DC: US Department of Justice. https://www.justice.gov/archive/ag /annualreports/tr2004/agreporthumantrafficing.pdf.

———. 2004. *Report to Congress from Attorney General John Ashcroft on US Government Efforts to Combat Trafficking in Persons Fiscal Year 2003.* Washington, DC: US Department of Justice. https://www.justice.gov/archive/ag/annualre ports/tr2003/050104agreporttocongresstvprav10.pdf.

———. 2001a. "Alaska Man Sentenced to 30 Months for Immigration Fraud and Transporting Minors from Russia to Dance in an Anchorage Strip Club" (DOJ 01-438), 28 August. Washington, DC. http://www.justice.gov/archive/opa/pr /2001/August/438cr.htm.

US Department of State. 2017. *Trafficking in Persons Report.* June. Washington, DC: US Department of State. https://www.state.gov/documents/organization /271339.pdf.

———. 2016. *Trafficking in Persons Report.* June. Washington, DC: US Department of State. https://www.state.gov/documents/organization/258876.pdf.

———. 2015. *Trafficking in Persons Report.* July. Washington, DC: US Department of State.

———. 2013. *2013 Trafficking in Persons Report.* June. Washington, DC: US Department of State.

———. 2009. *2009 Trafficking in Persons Report.* June 2009. Washington, DC: US Department of State.

———. 2004. *2004 Trafficking in Persons Report.* June 2004. Washington, DC: US Department of State.

———. 2001. "Alaska Man Sentenced to 30 Months for Immigration Fraud and Transporting Minors from Russia to Dance in an Anchorage Strip Club" (DOJ

01-438). Washington, DC, 28 August. http://www.justice.gov/archive/opa/pr/2001/August/438cr.htm.

US Government Accountability Office. 2006. *Human Trafficking: Better Data, Strategy, and Reporting Needed to Enhance US Antitrafficking Efforts Abroad*. Report to the Chairman, Committee on the Judiciary and the Chairman, Committee on International Relations, House of Representatives, Washington, DC. http://www.gao.gov/new.items/d06825.pdf.

US Mission to the United Nations. "Ambassador Samantha Power." http://usun.state.gov/leadership/6625.

Vaidhyanathan, Siva. 2011. *The Googlization of Everything (And Why We Should Worry)*. Berkeley: University of California Press.

Valentine, David. 2007. *Imagining Transgender: An Ethnography of a Category*. Durham, NC: Duke University Press.

Valverde, Mariana. 1991. *The Age of Light, Soap, and Water: Moral Reform in English Canada, 1885–1925*. Toronto: McClelland & Stewart.

Vanaspong, Chitraporn. 2002. "A Portrait of the Lady: The Portrayal of Thailand and Its Prostitutes in the International Media." In *Transnational Prostitution: Changing Patterns in a Global Context*, ed. Susanne Thorbek and Bandana Pattanaik, 139–155. London: Zed Books.

Vance, Carole. 2012. "Innocence and Experience: Melodramatic Narratives of Sex Trafficking and Their Consequences for Law and Policy." *History of the Present* 2(2): 200–218.

———. 2011. "Thinking Trafficking, Thinking Sex." *GLQ* 17(1): 135–143.

———, ed. 1992. *Pleasure and Danger: Exploring Female Sexuality*. London: Routledge & Kegan Paul.

———. 1989. "The War on Culture." *Art in America* 77: 39–45.

Varagur, Krithika. 2017. "Revealed: Reality of a Life Working in an Ivanka Trump Clothing Factory." *The Guardian*, 13 June. https://www.theguardian.com/us-news/2017/jun/13/revealed-reality-of-a-life-working-in-an-ivanka-trump-clothing-factory?CMP=share_btn_link.

Varela, Cecilia Inés. 2013. "De la 'letra de la ley' a la labor interpretante: La 'vulnerabilidad' femenina en los procesos de judicialización de la ley de trata de personas (2008–2011)." *Cadernos Pagu* 41: 265–302.

Verité. 2012. *Human Trafficking & Global Supply Chains: A Background Paper*. Ankara: Verité.

Virgil, Delfin. 2007. "'Amazing Grace' Unites Churches in Global Anti-Slavery Sing-Along." *San Francisco Chronicle*, 19 February. https://www.sfgate.com/bayarea/article/BAY-AREA-Amazing-Grace-unites-churches-in-2616431.php.

Visrutaratna, Surasing, Wongchai Siriporn, Manoon Jaikueankaew, Eiko Kobori, Kihara Masako, and Kihara Masahiro. 2010. "Sexual Behavior of Japanese Tourists Visiting Thailand: A Key Informant Approach." *Journal of Public Health and Development* 8(1): 33–44.

Von Engelhardt, Johannes, and Jeroen Jansz. 2014. "Challenging Humanitarian Communication: An Empirical Exploration of Kony 2012." *International Communication Gazette*, 76(6): 464–484.

Vrasti, Wanda. 2012. *Volunteer Tourism in the Global South: Giving Back in Neoliberal Times*. London: Routledge.

———. 2011. "'Caring' Capitalism and the Duplicity of Critique." *Theory & Event* 14(4): 1–22.

Wacquant, Loïc. 2012. "Three Steps to a Historical Anthropology of Actually Existing Neoliberalism." *Social Anthropology* 20(1): 66–79.

———. 2009a. *Prisons of Poverty*. Minneapolis: University of Minnesota Press.

———. 2009b. *Punishing the Poor: The Neoliberal Government of Social Insecurity*. Durham, NC: Duke University Press.

Walkowitz, Judith. 1983. "Male Vice and Female Virtue: Feminism and the Politics of Prostitution in Nineteenth Century Britain." In *Powers of Desire: The Politics of Sexuality*, ed. Ann Snitow, Christine Stansell, and Sharon Thompson, 419–439. New York: Monthly Review Press.

———. 1980. *Prostitution and Victorian Society: Women, Class, and the State*. Cambridge: Cambridge University Press.

Wallis, Jim. 2005. *God's Politics: Why the Right Gets It Wrong and the Left Doesn't Get It*. San Francisco: HarperCollins.

Wearing, Stephen. 2001. *Volunteer Tourism: Experiences That Make a Difference*. Oxford, UK: Cabi Press.

Weber, Max. 2000. *The Protestant Ethic and the Spirit of Capitalism*. Translated by Talcott Parsons. New York: Routledge. Originally published 1930.

Weisberg, Brent. 2015. "Pimp Gets Life for Making Girl, 15, Be Stripper." KOIN6, 12 August. http://koin.com/2015/08/12/pimp-gets-life-for-making-girl-15-be -stripper/.

Weitzer, Ronald. 2007. "The Social Construction of Sex Trafficking: Ideology and Institutionalization of a Moral Crusade." *Politics and Society* 35(3): 447–475.

Wertheim, Stephen. 2017. "Donald Trump's Plan to Save Western Civilization." *New York Times*, 22 July. https://www.nytimes.com/2017/07/22/opinion/sunday /donald-trumps-plan-to-save-western-civilization.html?_r=0.

West, Cornel. 2016. "Goodbye, American Neoliberalism: A New Era Is Here." *The Guardian*, 17 November. https://www.theguardian.com/commentisfree /2016/nov/17/american-neoliberalism-cornel-west-2016-election?CMP =share_btn_link.

West, James. 2016. "Former Models for Donald Trump's Agency Say They Violated Immigration Rules and Worked Illegally." *Mother Jones*, 30 August. http:// www.motherjones.com/politics/2016/08/donald-trump-model-management -illegal-immigration/.

West, Paige. 2006. *Conservation Is Our Government Now: The Politics of Ecology in Papua New Guinea*. Durham, NC: Duke University Press.

West, Paige, and James G. Carrier. 2004. "Getting Away from It All? Ecotourism and Authenticity." *Current Anthropology* 45: 483–498.

Westmoreland-White, Michael. 1997. "Contributions to Human Rights in Dietrich Bonhoeffer's Ethics." *Journal of Church & State* 39(1): 67–83.

Wilkins, Amy. 2008. "'Happier Than Non-Christians': Collective Emotions and Symbolic Boundaries among Evangelical Christians." *Social Psychology Quarterly* 71(3): 281–301.

Wilkinson, Tracy. 2017. "Trump's 'America First' Policy Changes US Role on Global Stage." *Los Angeles Times*, 2 June. http://www.latimes.com/nation/la-fg-trump-assess-20170602-story.html.

Williams, Roger Ross, dir. 2013. *God Loves Uganda*. New York: Full Credit Productions.

Wilson, Ara. 2009. "Sex at the Forum: Sexual Justice and the Alter-Globalization Movement." *Scholar and Feminist Online* 7(3): http://sfonline.barnard.edu/sexecon/wilson_01.htm.

———. 2004. *The Intimate Economies of Bangkok: Tomboys, Tycoons, and Avon Ladies in the Global City*. Berkeley: University of California Press.

Window International Network. 2017. "About the 10/40 Window." 2017. http://win1040.com/about-the-1040-window.php.

Windpassinger, Gwendolyn. 2010. "Queering Anarchism in Post-2001 Buenos Aires." *Sexualities* 13(4): 495–509.

Women in the World Staff. 2017. "Trump Quietly Revoked Fair Pay Order, Leaving Women Vulnerable to Workplace Abuse." *New York Times*, 4 April. nytlive.nytimes.com/womenintheworld/2017/04/04/trumps-revocation-of-fair-pay-order-leaves-women-vulnerable-to-workplace-abuse/.

Women's March on Washington. 2017. "Guiding Vision and Definition of Principles." https://static1.squarespace.com/static/584086c7be6594762f5ec56e/t/58796773414fb52b57e20794/1484351351914/WMW+Guiding+Vision+&+Definition+of+Principles.pdf.

"Women's March 2017: As Expected, the Erasure of Sex Workers Rights." 2017. *Best Practices Policy*, 17 January. http://www.bestpracticespolicy.org/2017/01/17/womens-march-2017-as-expected-the-erasure-of-sex-workers-rights/.

Wood, Jennifer K. 2005. "In Whose Name? Crime Victim and the Punishing Power of Protection." *NWSA Journal* 17(3): 1–17.

World Health Organization. 2014. *Consolidated Guidelines on HIV Prevention, Diagnosis, Treatment and Care for Key Populations*. July. Geneva: World Health Organization. http://apps.who.int/iris/bitstream/10665/128048/1/9789241507431_eng.pdf?ua=1&ua=1.

———. 2012. "Understanding and Addressing Violence against Women: Human Trafficking." WHO/RHR/12.42. http://apps.who.int/iris/bitstream/10665/77394/1/WHO_RHR_12.42_eng.pdf.

WuDunn, Sheryl. 2010. "Our Century's Greatest Injustice." *TED Global*, July. https://www.ted.com/talks/sheryl_wudunn_our_century_s_greatest_injustice/transcript?language=en.

Wuthnow, Robert. 2009. *Boundless Faith: The Global Outreach of American Churches*. Berkeley: University of California Press.

———. 1988. *The Restructuring of American Religion*. Princeton, NJ: Princeton University Press.

Wypijewski, JoAnn. 2014. "Liberals and Feminists, Stop Enabling the Police State." *The Nation*, 10 September. http://www.thenation.com/article/how-feminists-and-liberals-enabled-modern-police-state/.

Xiang, Biao. 2012. "Labor Transplant: 'Point-to-Point' Transnational Labor Migration in East Asia." *South Atlantic Quarterly* 111(4): 721–739.

Yancy, George, and Judith Butler. 2015. "What's Wrong With 'All Lives Matter'?" *Opinionator* (blog), 12 January. http://opinionator.blogs.nytimes.com/2015/01/12/whats-wrong-with-all-lives-matter/.

Young Women's Empowerment Project. 2009. *Girls Do What They Have to Do to Survive: Illuminating Methods Used by Girls in the Sex Trade and Street Economy to Fight Back and Heal*. Chicago: Young Women's Empowerment Project.

Zimmerman, Yvonne. 2013. *Other Dreams of Freedom: Religion, Sex, and Human Trafficking*. New York: Oxford University Press.

———. 2010. "From Bush to Obama: Rethinking Sex and Religion in the United States' Initiative to Combat Human Trafficking." *Journal of Feminist Studies in Religion* 26(1): 79–99.

Zimring, Franklin. 2007. *The Great American Crime Decline*. New York: Oxford University Press.

Žižek, Slavoj. 2017. "Don't Believe the Liberals—There Is No Real Choice Between Le Pen and Macron." *The Independent*, 3 May. http://www.independent.co.uk/voices/french-elections-marine-le-pen-emmanuel-macron-no-real-choice-a7714911.html.

———. 2009. *First as Tragedy, Then as Farce*. London: Verso.

Zylstra, Sarah Eekhoff, and Jeremy Weber. 2016. "Top 10 Stats Explaining the Evangelical Vote for Trump or Clinton." *Christianity Today*, 11–16 November. http://www.christianitytoday.com/gleanings/2016/november/top-10-stats-explaining-evangelical-vote-trump-clinton-2016.html.

Index

abolitionism, 68, 69, 73, 95, 161, 190n14, 206n90; new, 9, 77–78, 92

abortion, 55, 76, 86, 88, 95, 96, 182, 210n48, 234n15, 235 n29; coerced, 73; opposition to, 80; politics of, 210n43

Abortion and the Politics of Motherhood (Luker), 73

Aboutaher, Myriem, 165

Abu-Lughod, Lila, 86

activism, 88, 92, 161, 172–77; anti-client, 54; anti-gay rights, 30, 79–80; anti-globalization, 20, 95, 172; anti-lynching, 91; anti-pornography, 30, 79, 199n6; anti-prostitution, 57, 91, 144; anti-violence, 41, 42, 199n6; breast cancer, 20, 139, 196n68, 221n15, 223n26; consumer-friendly/corporate-driven, 92; evangelical, 30, 69, 70, 84, 89, 218n72; human rights, 18; rescue/restore model of, 81; sex worker, 46, 69, 99, 101, 122, 160, 172, 190n8, 229n8; social justice, 3, 81, 92, 177. *See also* anti-trafficking activists; feminist activists

advertisements, 110, 137, 216n42, 224n37; anti-human trafficking, 135 (figs.), 136 (fig.); prostitution, 156, 224n38; sex trafficking, 224n38

Affordable Care Act (ACA), 182

African Americans, 35, 48, 62, 64, 65, 156; criminalizing/caging/harming, 176; education/health/safety of, 176; surveillance of, 175

Agustín, Laura, 190n18, 205n75, 216n31

Akha community (Chiang Rai Thailand), 116, 117, 120; photo of, 117

Alexander, Douglas, 141–42

Alexander, Michelle, 40, 48, 66

Ali, Ayaan Hirsi, 36, 199n8

Al Jazeera, 90, 212n64

Alvarez, Sonia, 162

Amar, Paul, 181

Amazing Change, 68, 93

Amazing Grace (film), 68, 94, 206n3

Amazing Thailand tourist campaign, 104

American Association of University Women (AAUW), 57

American Bar Association, 57, 220n13

American Enterprise Institute, 35, 199n8

Ames, Jessie Daniel, 213n71

Amnesty International, 160, 161, 229n8, 229n9

Anthropology of Policy (Shore and Wright), 27

anti-abortion movement, 30, 79, 182, 210n48

anti-immigration agenda, 61, 71, 168, 186